# Born To Play Loud

## The
## Vivian Campbell
## Story

Brian Ireland

# Born To Play Loud

## The Vivian Campbell Story

Brian Ireland

WP
WYMER
PUBLISHING
Bedford, England

First published in 2025 by Wymer Publishing, Bedford, England
www.wymerpublishing.co.uk Tel: 01234 326691
Wymer Publishing is a trading name of Wymer (UK) Ltd.



Print edition (fully illustrated): **ISBN: 978-1-915246-70-7**

Edited by Jerry Bloom.



Printed and bound in Great Britain by
CMP, Dorset.

A catalogue record for this book is available from the British Library.

eBook formatting by Lin White at Coinlea Services.
Typeset/Design by Andy Bishop / Tusseheia Creative
Cover design: Tusseheia Creative.
Front cover photo: WENN Rights Ltd/ Alamy Stock Photo.

# Contents


*Introduction*                                                    7

**Chapter 1**                                                     13
Born To Play Loud: Sweet Savage

**Chapter 2**                                                     25
Rainbows and Dragons: The Dio Years

**Chapter 3**                                                     97
Snakes, Dogs, and Kings

**Chapter 4**                                                     131
'All I ever wanted to do was
play guitar in a Rock band': Def Leppard

**Chapter 5**                                                     179
Clock, Two Sides Of If, Thin Lizzy, and Last In Line

*Epilogue*                                                        221

*Discography & Videography*                                       227

*Notes*                                                           230

# Introduction

On Easter Monday, April 20, 1992, Vivian Patrick Campbell and his new bandmates in Def Leppard stepped out on to the stage at Wembley Stadium in London in front of a crowd of around 70,000 people. The occasion was the Freddie Mercury Tribute Concert and Def Leppard were one of many artists invited to take part.

Campbell had joined Def Leppard only a few weeks before and had little time to learn Def Leppard's catalogue, nor to rehearse with the band. However, he adapted quickly and played his part professionally and without error. He even got to perform with Queen's Brian May when the guitarist joined Def Leppard in an energetic rendition of the Queen track 'Now I'm Here.' There really wasn't a bigger stage or event to introduce Campbell as the newest member of what was at the time perhaps the most popular British rock band of the 1980s, the multi-platinum-selling Def Leppard.

Despite his dramatic 'unveiling' at one of the biggest cultural and music events of the 1990s, and his ongoing participation with Def Leppard, Vivian Campbell remains the least recognised music superstar to emerge from Northern Ireland in recent years. In the 1980s he was mentioned in the same conversations as Gary Moore, Eddie Van Halen, Randy Rhoads, Steve Vai and Yngwie Malmsteen, who were the cream of hard rock guitarists in that era. Today those musicians remain well known, with, for example, Vai, Rhoads and Van Halen all featuring in *Rolling Stone* magazine's 2023 poll of the '250 Greatest Guitarists Of All Time'; in contrast, Campbell could probably walk through the streets of Belfast and remain unrecognised.

When he was a teenager, Campbell formed a band called Sweet Savage, which had some modest success as a support act for the likes of Thin Lizzy and Motörhead. They were part of the so-called New Wave of British Heavy Metal (NWoBHM) and later caught the ear of Metallica, who covered the band's song 'Killing Time.'

Sweet Savage couldn't attract the attention of a major label however, and when Campbell was offered the opportunity to join ex-Black Sabbath and Rainbow frontman Ronnie James Dio's new band, he accepted readily. Dio had firmly established himself as one of the great rock singers of the 1970s, so this was a huge break for the young Belfast guitarist. With Dio, Campbell released three critically acclaimed and commercially successful albums before a dispute with the singer led to Campbell being fired in the middle of a world tour.

Campbell was then recruited by David Coverdale into Whitesnake, who had just released their most commercially successful album to date, the multi-platinum *Whitesnake / 1987*. Campbell's profile raised considerably when he appeared in Whitesnake's infamous 'Still Of The Night' video, before he embarked with the band on a World Tour that lasted into 1988. However, once more Campbell fell afoul of a temperamental and controlling lead singer and was fired for the second time from a major rock band.

Campbell then hooked up with a new American band called Riverdogs and recorded one critically acclaimed album with that outfit. Despite that album selling well, Riverdogs lost the support of their record label, a victim of the profound shift in musical tastes caused by the emergence in the early 1990s of Grunge bands such as Nirvana, Pearl Jam, Soundgarden, and Alice In Chains. Campbell then joined with ex-Foreigner vocalist Lou Gramm in a new venture called Shadow King. The band released one well-received album and played one gig in London before breaking up due to poor sales of the album and Gramm's ongoing drug problems.

While Shadow King was imploding, Joe Elliott of Def Leppard, asked Campbell to audition for the band as a replacement for Steve Clark, who had tragically passed away in early 1991 as a result of drug and alcohol addictions. Campbell impressed at the audition and if rumours are to be believed, beat out the likes of John Sykes (Whitesnake and Thin Lizzy), Jake E. Lee (Ozzy Osbourne), and Adrian Smith (Iron Maiden).

It later emerged that it was Campbell's personality as well as his playing that impressed the members of Def Leppard. As he had previously been fired from two popular and successful rock bands, Campbell had garnered a reputation in some quarters as a troublemaker. However, Def Leppard — Joe Elliott, Rick Allen, Rick Savage, and Steve Collen — found him friendly, professional and personable. Campbell made his live debut at a small club gig in Dublin; a week later, he played with Def Leppard at the Freddie Mercury Tribute in London. Today, over 30 years later, Campbell is still with the band: in that time, he has contributed to seven original studio albums and toured extensively all around the world.

The musical journeys of Dio, Whitesnake, and Def Leppard have been well-documented. They have mainly taken the form of band biographies or biographies of individuals. Autobiographies are also a valuable primary source of information. Each source must be handled with caution, however: official biographies tend not to explore the more controversial aspects of a band's career, while autobiographies typically avoid painting the subject in a bad light. Neither format usually lingers on the ins and outs of touring because they assume readers don't want to hear about the quotidian minutia of those events — tours, like wars, mainly involve long periods of boredom punctuated by short periods of excitement, and people only want to read about the excitement and not the details and facts.

In contrast, these were exactly the concerns of specialist rock and music equipment magazines, who catered to serious fans and gearheads. It is in genre and equipment magazines that the most detailed information is available about, for example, the types of amplifiers, guitars, strings, racks and guitar techniques used by Campbell over the course of his musical journey.

Newspapers are a valuable source of information but also need to be treated with a degree of caution. They are most valuable as data sources for dates of concerts, venues, crowd sizes, concert and album reviews, and band news. However, when journalists go beyond this basic who, what, when, where, and how reporting, they often slip up. Most small, local newspapers did not employ dedicated music reviewers, and information was often not always available.

Research for some of my previous books on the Woodstock and Altamont festivals, on the Rolling Stones in America, and on Gary Moore, was hampered to an extent by difficulty in finding material. In the case of the Rolling Stones, for example, unearthing concert reviews from the early 1960s was a particular challenge. On occasion, even confirming correct venues and dates was difficult, and this is, don't forget, one of the most well-known and most written about group of musicians in the last 60 years.

In contrast, much of Campbell's career took place in the digital age, particularly during his period with Def Leppard. Modern technology such as mobile cameras and social media ensure that a vast amount of material is now available online. After initial reluctance, the band also embraced social media and have taken to documenting tours and releasing news updates on their own band web pages as well as on video-sharing websites. The challenge then is to choose sources selectively otherwise this book could be overloaded by information, while interesting and informative, may not necessarily progress the narrative, nor help the reader trace Campbell's musical development. I tread a fine line between providing data, statistics, and figures and providing enough context to give that information meaning.

As this is a biography of Campbell and not the bands he has been involved with, my focus is primarily on Campbell's activities. That's why I tend not to analyse full albums and instead focus mainly on Campbell's specific role. The same approach applies to live performances, where I've tried to be indicative rather than exhaustive to avoid losing focus on my primary subject. In the case of Def Leppard, their tours are so extensive, and so well-documented, that an in-depth discussion of each tour is not practical. I therefore focus only on Campbell's first tour with the band, which was his most important. He was, after all, replacing a much-loved member of the band in Steve Clark, and it was unclear if fans would accept him. It was also crucial in cementing his place in the band. While being selective, at the same time, I've provided as much context as is needed to ensure the broader picture isn't lost.

This is, primarily, a biography that focuses on Campbell's musical activities, and I only stray into his private life on rare occasions when I think that will shed some light on his music. Even on those occasions my comments are based on information that has been reported in the music press, or on information Campbell has chosen to reveal in interviews. Aside from that, I have no real interest in Campbell's private life: it doesn't affect my appreciation of his phenomenal guitar solo on 'Rainbow in the Dark' nor the catchy riffs of 'Caught In The Middle.'

At time of writing, there are no published biographies of Campbell, although he does feature in the biographies of people he has collaborated with. Ronnie James Dio comes immediately to mind. He also appears in band biographies, for example, the recent official Def Leppard band biography, *Definitely: The Official Story of Def Leppard* (2023), and in Phil Collen's 2015 memoir, *Adrenalized: Life, Def Leppard and Beyond.* Yet these books provide only snapshots of Campbell's life, whereas my my aim is to tie together various stages of Campbell's life and to trace his musical journey from a young Belfast rocker to one of the great rock guitarists of his era.

To aid clarity, the book is structured chronologically, from Campbell's early influences (Marc Bolan, Rory Gallagher and Gary Moore), his first semi-professional band, Sweet Savage, his first real musical break with Ronnie James Dio, his success with Dio and tumultuous breakup, touring with Whitesnake, and then his decades-long relationship with Def Leppard. In this instance, a chronological structure is more effective than a thematic structure, which would risk losing focus amid a slew of dates, stats and overlapping events.

While there isn't space here to explore all of Campbell's collaborations and guest appearances, there is reason behind my discussion of Campbell's work with Lou Gramm in the band Shadow King, and his time spent with Riverdogs. That occurred after Campbell had left Whitesnake but before he joined Def Leppard, and analysis of those albums and live appearances sheds some light on Campbell's evolution from heavy rock 'guitar hero' to a more nuanced player who would rather serve the song with his playing than bring down the house with a 20-minute guitar solo.

In addition, Campbell released a solo blues album (*Two Sides Of If* in 2005) and worked with other musicians while still a member of Def Leppard. From 2010 to 2011, for instance, he went on tour with that era's iteration of Thin Lizzy (Scott Gorham, Brian Downey, Darren Wharton, Marco Mendoza and Ricky Warwick). Calling himself a 'stunt guitarist' in the band, Campbell enjoyed the experience so much that he created a new outfit called Last In Line just to play live again.

Last In Line was basically a rebirth of the Dio band but without Ronnie James Dio, who had sadly passed away in 2010. In part, these projects beyond Def Leppard were a result of that band's frequent inactivity. However, they also demonstrate Campbell's desire to rediscover and explore his roots, playing the blues and blues-based rock, and returning to the 'angry' guitar style of his earlier days.

As usual, when I write I deploy the skills and techniques of the history lecturer and academic researcher that I used to be, and with that in mind, I tend to avoid burdening readers with my own opinions. Instead, I aim to present the necessary information and context to enable readers to make up their own minds.

However, I do offer analysis and draw conclusions when it's pertinent to do so. I admit though that my objectivity may, on occasion, be found wanting. When Campbell received the Oh Yeah Legend Award in 2017, he said 'I am not used to getting awards. I am not a celebrity, the only people who know me are the hard rock fans and guitar junkies.'[1]

I admit that I fall squarely into both of those categories. The 2017 award marked some belated recognition for Campbell in his hometown. This book is an attempt to build on that acknowledgement and to introduce Campbell to a wider, modern audience.

# Chapter 1

## Born To Play Loud: Sweet Savage

*'If Thin Lizzy and Motörhead had a baby, it would have been called Sweet Savage'*

Vivian Campbell[2]

By the time of his debut performance with Def Leppard, Campbell had already experienced a long musical journey from relatively humble roots. He was born August 25, 1962, to Mary (nee McCrory) and Vivian Snr, who were both from Co Tyrone, Northern Ireland. Mary was the eldest of ten children, brought up in a small two-bedroom house on the outskirts of Dungannon, Co Tyrone, a small town set in a rural location a few miles west of Lough Neagh.[3] In her adult years, Mary was a local beauty queen when she met Vivian Snr and love blossomed. They married and had four children, whom they chose to raise in Lisburn, a small town a few miles southwest of Belfast.

Vivian was too young to understand the seismic social and political changes that were occurring in Northern Ireland in the 1960s, but as the next decade progressed, he became more aware of the hard reality of the troubled land in which he lived. And like many young people during that time, he turned to music as an escape. The music that shaped his formative experiences was not that of the Irish and Northern Irish musicians that immediately preceded him: the likes of Henry McCullough, Van Morrison, Gary Moore, Eric Bell and Rory Gallagher grew up listening to post-World War Two pop, rock and blues, and the formative musical influences of these musicians was that of their teenage years. That also turned out to be the case with Vivian.

He aspired to play guitar, and he often cites a performance by Marc Bolan's T-Rex's on BBC's *Top of the Pops* as a particularly influential experience. Bolan became Vivian's first guitar hero and the one whose sound and look convinced him that this was the musical world he wanted to embrace. As his interest in the instrument grew, Vivian then discovered

Rory Gallagher, Ritchie Blackmore, Jeff Beck, and then his all-time favourite, fellow Northern Irish guitarist Gary Moore, whom Vivian called 'the ultimate rock guitarist.'[4]

Gallagher was a particularly exciting blues guitarist, who was one of only a few popular musicians from outside Northern Ireland to perform there in the early 1970s, when civil unrest was particularly disruptive and threatening. It was not just that these musicians were worried about their personal safety, it was also very difficult to obtain insurance coverage for a gig in the province. This added to the already-existing burden of having to ferry over their equipment from mainland UK, and the result was that only a handful of international musicians performed in Ulster in those years. Gallagher was one of those intrepid few. His band Taste often played the Maritime Club in Belfast city centre, where Rory met teenager Gary Moore for the first time.[5]

When Taste broke up, Rory pursued a solo career and insisted that his band perform in Belfast at least once a year. Vivian would later recall that the first concert he ever went to was one of Rory's gigs at the Ulster Hall in Belfast. Vivian joked that Rory's annual Belfast gigs were also the second and third concert he ever went to as Rory was virtually the only major artist to come to Belfast in those days. 'I remember the feeling of huge energy at that gig and being really inspired by it,' Vivian said. 'That fuelled my desire for music even more.'[6]

When asked by *Guitar & Bass* magazine in 2016 to choose the records that set him on his musical journey, Vivian chose two of Gallagher's — the 'first vinyl I ever had,' *Live! In Europe* (1972) and *Against The Grain* (1975). Vivian joked: 'I picked up a lot of my early guitar-playing habits from Rory; it's ingrained in my DNA. I blame my two greatest guitar heroes — Rory and Gary Moore — for my bad habits!'[7]

Indeed, Vivian cited two albums featuring Moore among his influences, which were Moore's second solo album, *Back On The Streets* (1978) and Thin Lizzy's *The Black Rose* (1978). 'I was so into Gary Moore at the time,' he recalled, and Moore featured heavily on this album. Vivian was particularly interested in the track 'Róisín Dubh (Black Rose): A Rock Legend,' which he referred to as 'such a challenge to learn as a guitar player, such an epic. It's not only a great song and a great, great lyric from Phil Lynott, but absolute rip-your-face-off guitar playing.'[8] Vivian also praised Thin Lizzy for being one of the few bands to play in Northern Ireland in the early 1970s.

Vivian 'totally absorbed' *Back On The Streets* upon its release. Moore shared Gallagher's forceful style of playing, although Campbell also admired the jazz-fusion elements on the album, as well as Moore's work in that genre with Jon Hiseman's Colosseum II. But mostly it was Moore's aggression that Campbell admired, saying: 'I never heard Gary Moore play anything like he didn't mean it. Gary played the guitar like he wanted to fucking kill it every time he played.'[9]

Young Vivian aspired to own a Fender Stratocaster like Rory Gallagher, but he didn't have enough money to buy one. His father surprised him on his fifteenth birthday with a Fender Telecaster Thinline, having misheard or misunderstood his son's comments about wanting a Stratocaster. Vivian hid his disappointment and played the Telecaster for about a year until he was able to put together enough cash for a Stratocaster. By the time that happened however, he had discovered Gary Moore, who at the time was playing jazz-fusion rock in Colosseum II, and to emulate Moore's sound Vivian now wanted a Gibson Les Paul. In 1977, he therefore traded the Telecaster for a Les Paul Deluxe, which he sanded and repainted black. Whenever he mentions it, he usually quotes its serial number, 72987537, which demonstrates the lasting effect the instrument had on the teenage guitarist.

By this time, Vivian had become a proficient guitarist. He learned by listening to his heroes and in those days of vinyl records and cassettes he would hit the rewind button on a cassette or reset the needle on a record player to listen over and over to a chord structure or guitar solo to try to replicate it. He never took a guitar lesson though: 'I couldn't find anyone to teach me' he recalled. 'I basically ended up teaching myself. I remember being about 11 or 12 and taking piano lessons, just so I could learn how chords were made up and how they corresponded to guitar strings. After two months I was like, "Thank you, I'm done." There was no support or resources available for young people wanting to get into music, although I was lucky to have a supportive dad who could see how passionate and deadly serious, I was. My school principal used to take me aside once a month and try and talk me into a real career, but I knew all I wanted to do was play guitar. Looking back, nobody really believed in me, other than my dad.'[10]

Vivian sacrificed almost everything to learn guitar, even the attention of girls. He told the *Irish News* he was 'thirsty for knowledge — anyone who owned a guitar or knew a chord, I'd be bugging them to show me. Back when I was 12 or 13, I had a crush on a girl from school. I went round to her house one Saturday afternoon and discovered that her mother had a guitar — so I spent the afternoon bugging the mother to show me what she knew. She showed me the lick to 'Daytripper' by The Beatles!'[11] Unsurprisingly, the girl showed no further interest in Vivian!

When Vivian was just 14 years of age, and a pupil at Rathmore

Grammar school, he formed an amateur band called Teaser. He later joked that every band back then named themselves Teaser: 'It was like calling your dog Fido.'[12]

Campbell explained how that first band came about: 'the first time I played live music with people was when I was in school. I would find out that so-and-so had a drum kit and that was it. I was like, "When can we play together?" You know, my course was set from the first time I ever did that.'[13]

When he was 15, he met Trevor Fleming, and the duo started writing together. Fleming then introduced Vivian to Ray Haller who became the bass player and singer in a new band they named Sweet Savage. Drummer David Bates completed the line-up.[14] By 1979, Sweet Savage — also the title of a 1979 American pornographic film, although it's not known if the band took any inspiration from that source — had developed into a semi-professional outfit based in Belfast. Vivian would later reveal that he and Haller were the group leaders who made all the decisions.[15]

Sweet Savage never made a full album while Vivian was with the band, and only one single was released during that period. However, Sweet Savage made a name for itself through extensive touring, which included a prime support slot for Motörhead when Lemmy's band played Maysfield Pavilion in Belfast on December 13, 1980. Sweet Savage would also support the likes of Budgie, Wishbone Ash, Ozzy Osbourne, and Wild Horses, where Vivian would meet bassist Jimmy Bain for the first time, as well as former Thin Lizzy guitarist Brian Robertson.

Although at the time they probably wouldn't have referred to themselves in this way, Sweet Savage was part of the so-called New Wave of British Heavy Metal' (NWoBHM). In 1979, *Sounds* journalist Geoff Barton coined the phrase in his review of a trio of new-ish bands playing at The Music Machine venue in London. Barton did little to distinguish this 'new wave' from other British rock music. According to his headline, it was 'flashbombs and dry ice and confetti,' but those were hardly new effects at a rock concert.[16]

The bands playing that evening were Angel Witch, Iron Maiden and Samson, 'three new British metal merchants' as Barton described them. How did they fare? Barton described Angel Witch's sound as 'the first Black Sabbath album being played through a cement mixer.' He noted that Iron Maiden singer Paul Di'Anno stalked the stage 'Geldof-style' (namechecking Bob Geldof the lead vocalist of the punk band The Boomtown Rats), and he said Samson's main attribute was 'excess.'

There was nothing new about any of this: in fact, Iron Maiden had been around since 1975 and Samson since 1977, albeit both with different and evolving line-ups. And Barton compared Angel Witch to a Black Sabbath album from almost a decade earlier. Yet Barton's reference to Geldof hinted at what made Maiden stand out. Di'Anno wore his hair short, and his stage garb was jeans and a leather biker's jacket, a look made popular in that era by American punk band, The Ramones. When Iron Maiden's 3-track EP came out later that year Di'Anno's snarling vocal delivery, together with the raw energy generated by the band's dual guitar leads, helped showcase Maiden's punk sensibilities.

What Barton was really describing then was the emergence of late 1970s rock bands that owed a debt to forerunners like Thin Lizzy, Black Sabbath, Deep Purple, and Led Zeppelin, but were also influenced to a greater or lesser extent by the back-to-basics aesthetic of the punk movement. Vivian would later reveal: 'At the time, we were inspired by the New Wave of British Heavy Metal and Thin Lizzy and Motörhead, but there was also a real punk element to the band and to the actual recording. Of course, I just wanted to play as many notes as I could possibly fit in!'[17] He concluded, 'if Thin Lizzy and Motörhead had a baby, it would have been called Sweet Savage.'[18]

While Barton didn't outline the sound of the new wave, others have since done so. Author Michael Hann described, for example, 'the palm-muted chug of guitars [that] took over from the vast open chords of Black Sabbath and Led Zeppelin' and that both the bands and their fans developed a 'uniform': the bands wore 'spandex, leather denim and studs,' while their fans wore 'battle jackets' covered with patches.[19] Soon, musicians with no obvious connections to each other, and who were from different parts of the UK and Ireland, were linked as part of the NWoBHM scene.

By giving it a name, Barton provided these bands with a marketing opportunity that soon brought to the fore the likes of Motörhead (London), Tygers of Pan Tang (Tyne and Wear), Diamond Head (West Midlands), Saxon (Barnsley), Heavy Pettin' (Glasgow), Sweet Savage (Belfast) and Def Leppard (Sheffield).

The success of these outfits also raised the profile of rock bands from the 1960s and 1970s who had struggled when disco emerged, and the likes of Budgie, Judas Priest, Scorpions, UFO, and Rush re-emerged in the 1980s with a stripped-down sound and new commercial appeal. Even Thin Lizzy reinvented itself, bringing in guitarist John Sykes to provide a heavier, more metallic guitar sound as evidenced on their 1983 album *Thunder and Lightning*.

Young Northern Irish bands faced many difficulties in that era, not least the absence of local musical infrastructure. Getting a record deal often meant having to leave the country. Vivian recalled, 'back in Ireland in the late 1970s there were no record companies. Terri Hooley (of Good Vibrations) was on the up, but they weren't signing metal bands! So, we'd go across the water and open for Lizzy and whoever else, knock on the door and record demos and try to get record and publishing deals.'[20]

Vivian later reflected: 'all I ever wanted to do when I was a teenager was just play angry guitar.'[21] As a self-taught guitarist he was sometimes frustrated that he hadn't mastered some of the technical aspects of the very best rock guitarists, citing Paul Gilbert, Yngwie Malmsteen and Vinnie Moore as examples of 'fantastically technical proficient guitar players.'

Over time, Vivian was able to gain perspective on his ability, both his flaws and strengths. 'Sometimes I think "How the fuck did I do that?"' he chuckled. 'Other times I cringe and think I was bending that note way to sharp or my vibrato was nervous… I couldn't do sweep arpeggios or manage 54th note alternate picking. Now I'm happy that I can't, as my limitations on the guitar, in which there are many as I'm self-taught, helped me craft my own style, sound, and identity which I think are more important than pure technique. As a young guitar player, you get blindsided by technique and try to aspire to that only. With some experience you learn what really makes you stand out is to have something unique.'[22]

Among Vivian's signature moves were accurate and clean fast picking, deep bends, slow vibrato, and hammer-on trills. He was known for fast but tasteful and melodic solos, somewhat similar to Gary Moore's style, but showing influences by the likes of Rudi Schenker [Scorpions].

His approach to soloing was carefully crafted: 'to an extent, a solo is a song within a song,' he explained.[23] He was also proficient in the stock in trade effects of 1980s heavy metal guitarists such as dive bombs and pinch harmonics. His style is based on a strong right-hand technique: 'I generally pick a lot more notes than other guitarists do,' he explained.[24]

In December 1980. *Record Mirror* reported the following Sweet Savage tour dates:[25]

Dec 13 Maysfield, Pavilion
Dec 16 Maidstone, Mid Kent College
Dec 18 Glastonbury, Worthy Farm
Dec 19 Rayleigh, Crocs
Dec 20 West Runton, Pavilion
Dec 21 & 22 Marquee, London

The band played a further gig at Maysfield on April 3, 1981 supporting Motörhead. The set list was 'Sweet Surrender,' 'Prospector Of Greed,' 'Eye Of The Storm,' 'Take No Prisoners,' and 'Killing Time.' That gig was filmed and is, as far as is known, the only professional footage of Sweet Savage that has come to light from that era. Campbell recalls Sweet Savage as a raw band full of nervous energy. Drummer Davy Bates in particular, had difficulty keeping to the correct tempo: 'if we wrote a song that was 120 beats a minute when we played it live it was 150 beats a minute!'[26]

Despite Vivian's comment, footage of the Maysfield show indicates that Sweet Savage played a tight set, with the 19-year-old guitarist showcasing some fast, angry playing. Ray Haller's distinctive vocals also stand out. It's likely his particular style influenced Dave Mustaine and James Hetfield who were both in Metallica at the time. The opening track, 'Sweet Surrender,' clocks in at around two minutes and is a fast-paced rocker with a galloping bass line reminiscent of Steve Harris from Iron Maiden. Vivian plays a speedy solo with fast picking. 'Prospector Of Greed' features a recurring riff and Vivian plays another amazing solo. 'Eye Of The Storm' bears some similarities to fast-paced Judas Priest tracks from that era and also Deep Purple's 'Flight Of The Rat. Vivian plays two aggressive solos. 'Take No Prisoners' sounds a bit like Rainbow's 'Starstruck,' but it's the least inspiring of the five tracks played that evening, lifted only by another tasty solo from Vivian. The final track, 'Killing Time,' has a thrash metal drum tempo, energetic riffs and fast fills.

On August 16, 1981, Sweet Savage enjoyed substantial exposure when they played to tens of thousands of fans at Slane Castle, appearing on the same bill as the likes of Thin Lizzy, U2, Hazel O'Connor, Rose Tattoo, and fellow Northern Ireland rockers Mama's Boys. In August that year, Sweet Savage was invited to play at Phil Lynott's birthday party at the Astoria Ballroom in Bundoran. The band was introduced on promotional advertisements as being 'Direct from Slane Castle,' which indicates the high profile of that appearance.

When Lizzy undertook a UK tour in November and December 1981 to support the release of their *Renegade* album, Lynott invited Sweet Savage to be the band's support act. The tour consisted of 23 performances, mainly in theatre-sized venues in English and Scottish cities, with a sole performance in Cardiff, Wales. The ever-reliable Thin Lizzy Guide fan site provides the following tour itinerary:[27]

| | |
|---|---|
| Nov 11 | Cornwall Coliseum, St. Austell |
| Nov 12 | Colston Hall, Bristol |
| Nov 13 | Arts Centre, Poole |
| Nov 14 | The Brighton Centre, Brighton |
| Nov 16 & 17 | Apollo Theatre, Manchester |
| Nov 19 | Queens Hall, Leeds |

| | |
|---|---|
| Nov 20 & 21 | Odeon Theatre, Birmingham |
| Nov 22 & 23 | Empire Theatre, Liverpool |
| Nov 25, 26, 27, 28 | Hammersmith Odeon, London |
| Nov 30 | Gaumont Theatre, Southampton |
| Dec 01 | Sophia Gardens, Cardiff |
| Dec 03 | Playhouse, Edinburgh |
| Dec 04 | Caird Hall, Dundee |
| Dec 05 | Capitol Theatre, Aberdeen |
| Dec 06 | Apollo Theatre, Glasgow |
| Dec 08 | Apollo Theatre, Coventry |
| Dec 09 | City Oval Hall, Sheffield |
| Dec 10 | City Hall, Newcastle |
| Dec 12 | Lockley Grand Hall, Guild Hall, Preston |
| Dec 14 | Leicester de Montford Hall |
| Dec 15 | The Guildhall, Portsmouth |
| Dec 16 | Gaumont Theatre, Ipswich |
| Dec 17 | Assembly Rooms, Derby |

Music journalist Dave Ling recalls seeing Sweet Savage at the Brighton gig. The band was 'a little on the ordinary side,' Ling decided, 'with only their fiery young guitarist raising himself above the level of mundanity.'[28]

The band also had a regular gig at a Dublin club called McGonagles. Phil Lynott occasionally joined the band on stage to perform a Thin Lizzy song, which Vivian thought helped his band's credibility.[29] Sweet Savage also played five headline gigs in 1982, on February 18 at the Whitla Hall, Belfast; on February 20 at the Main Hall RDS, Dublin; on February 23 at the SFX Hall, Dublin; on April 30 at the McMordie Hall, Queens University Student Union, Belfast; and a follow-up gig at the SFX Hall on October 29 that year. These venues were higher profile than the usual pubs and clubs, but Sweet Savage was not yet popular enough, nor financially secure to be self-supporting.

Only a handful of Sweet Savage studio recordings exist. On December 3, 1980, the band recorded four songs live for the BBC radio programme *The Friday Rock Show*, presented by Tommy Vance. Their session was broadcast on December 19, while the band was on tour in England. These songs were 'Queen's Vengeance,' 'Eye Of The Storm,' 'Killing Time,' and 'Into the Night.' One of those tracks, 'Eye Of The Storm,' appeared on an album also entitled *The Friday Rock Show*, which was released in 1981 on the BBC's own record label. The band also released a cassette which contained all four of the songs they performed for the BBC recording, hoping perhaps to recapture the success of another NWoBHM band, Def Leppard, whose break came when the band released their own self-published EP which then attracted some Radio One airplay. A retrospective review by *Kerrang!* gave *The Friday Rock Show* session its approval: 'It turned out really well — Vivian was obviously a young man who knew what he was doing.'[30]

'Queen's Vengeance' is a mid-paced rocker with an epic feel somewhat reminiscent of Celtic rock band Horslips, not least due to the similarity of lead singer Ray Haller's voice to that of Horslips' co-lead vocalist Charles O'Connor. However, the song is also reminiscent of UFO and at times Vivian seems to be channelling Michael Schenker's fast riffing and solos. The extended guitar solo that forms the song's outro is an impressive example of Vivian's fluid, fast picking. 'Eye of the Storm' begins with a short drum and guitar solo, before a catchy guitar riff kicks in. It features a singalong chorus. 'Killing Time' is two-plus minutes of thrash metal, while 'Into the Night' is riff-heavy hard rocker.

In 1981 Sweet Savage signed to Park Records and in November that year they released their first single 'Take No Prisoners' c/w 'Killing Time.' Only 1,000 were cut, which wasn't unusual for a relatively unknown band. More would follow if the single was successful. However, it failed to chart.

Over the years a few more obscure Sweet Savage tracks have emerged from the Campbell era, but little is known about them. A few fall into the time period just before Campbell joined Dio but were released under a new Sweet Savage line-up. For example, 'Lady Marion' was written by Vivian, recorded in 1979, but not released as a single until 2005, when it was coupled with a track called 'Pity.'

'Teaser,' was recorded in 1980 but was not released until it appeared on a *Radio Times* CD compilation in 2005. Also on that release was a hard rocker with punk influences entitled 'Lady of the Night,' recorded in 1979 and featuring a thrilling solo from Vivian. The tracks 'Reach Out' and 'D.U.D' from a 2006 EP entitled *All That Remains* were supposedly first recorded in 1981.

A demo called 'The Raid,' and another track called 'The Ripper,' were supposedly recorded in 1980 and released in 2005 on an EP called *The Raid*. Finally, 'Ground Zero,' from the *Ground Zero* EP, was first recorded in 1981, and not released until 2005. According to Vivian, there were, in fact, four songs on Dio's debut *Holy Diver* album that originated with Sweet Savage: 'they are songs that have been changed with different vocals. Some just use parts of songs: Lady Marion [is] Rainbow In The Dark practically note for note.'[31]

Undoubtedly 'Lady Marion' is the most interesting of these tracks as one can detect the bones of 'Rainbow In The Dark's A, F G-chord sequence and just a hint in the prototype guitar solo of what would become Campbell's signature piece. It also bears some resemblance to 'Strange World' from Iron Maiden's debut album, as well as sharing some influences from the early 1970s 'Krautrock' scene.

'Straight Through the Heart' features an identical riff to 'Caught in the Middle,' from the Dio album *Holy Diver*. A post-Campbell line-up of Sweet Savage released this track on the Crushed label and it was reviewed by *Kerrang!* magazine. 'Apparently, [Vivian Campbell's] on this single,' said the magazine, 'and it is good, although the production could have been a bit more selective. The rest of the band are competent, but having Vivian Campbell here is clearly designed to attract interest.'[32]

'Teaser' is one of a handful of Sweet Savage songs with lyrics that border on misogyny, although given the time period that's probably fewer than unexpected. The song features Vivian's trademark fast picking but is otherwise unremarkable. 'Pity' is another Iron Maiden soundalike, with similarities to the track 'Remember Tomorrow' from Maiden's debut album. 'The Raid' shares a similar lyrical theme to Thin Lizzy's 'The Boys Are Back In Town.' Pulsing bass, eerie sound effects, and busy riffs make for an effective in uninspiring rocker. 'The Ripper' is a repetitive hard rock track with Vivian once more leading the way with angry riffs and fast licks.

Of the aforementioned tracks, 'Queen's Vengeance' is probably the stand-out effort, mainly as it's a showcase for the precocious guitarist's remarkable guitar skills. It was, apparently, written in 1980 when Vivian was just 19. It begins with a tumble of riffs and features a variety of time signatures and guitar styles, including arpeggiated chords, fast picking, and huge bends and slides. Foremost though is Vivian's stunning solo that drives the song to its playout. It's an exercise in pure speed, with Vivian showing the maturity of a seasoned professional but also the wild exuberance of youth. 'Queen's Vengeance' was finally released with the *Radio Times* compilation CD in 2005.

After Vivian joined Dio he was asked about his old band Sweet Savage: 'They're still going strong with even more line-up changes,' he explained. 'They have now got David Gaynor (from Girl) on drums, but I honestly don't think they're going to do anything, because they sound too like Lizzy. That's the problem, it isn't lack of talent, it's lack of enthusiasm. We did a lot of tours with Lizzy and other bands, but it was a lack of management and Ireland's a very barren country for bands, you have to move over to Britain. I really don't think you're going to hear much more of them in the future.'[33]

Vivian's prediction was partially correct: Sweet Savage hired a replacement guitarist and continued to record and play live, but never managed to raise their profile until Metallica covered the Sweet Savage track 'Killing Time,' which appeared on the B-side of Metallica's 1991 single, 'Unforgiven.' In fact, Metallica found the song so influential in their early days that they took an audition tape featuring 'Killing Time' to the booking agent for the Whisky a Go Go music venue in Sunset Strip where they were successful in securing an opening slot for UK NWoBHM band, Saxon. These were only Metallica's second and third ever gigs.[34] Metallica initially passed off the song as one of their own: however, when they became more successful, they acknowledged its true origin. Since then, Metallica have played 'Killing Time' on stage on many occasions.

Vivian remained close friends with Ray Haller in particular, attending Haller's wedding in March 2017. In 2009 there was a band reunion of sorts when Campbell agreed to perform on a new Sweet Savage album entitled *Warbird*. The album was to feature a cover of the old Lizzy song 'Whiskey in the Jar,' and Vivian recorded a guitar solo for that song in Los Angeles, emailing it to the band. Unfortunately, the album remained unreleased, but the track later appeared on a further Sweet Savage release entitled *Regeneration* (2012).

This recording demonstrates once more the overhanging branches of the rock family tree: Campbell began his career with Sweet Savage, who supported Phil Lynott and Thin Lizzy at the first ever Slane Festival at Slane Castle in Meath. Campbell later performed 'Whiskey in the Jar' on stage in a post-Lynott iteration of Lizzy, before recording a studio version with Sweet Savage. In the meantime, Metallica had also recorded a version of 'Whiskey in the Jar' which appeared on their 1998 album *Garage Inc.* Metallica had previously recorded a studio version of Sweet Savage's 'Killing Time.' In August 1991, Haller joined Metallica on stage at Marler Park in Dublin to co-perform 'Killing Time.' Two decades later, in December 2011, he was a special guest of Metallica when they performed at The Fillmore in San Francisco; and in 2015, Metallica performed 'Whiskey in the Jar' at Slane Castle in, Meath, Ireland.

Campbell would also play live once more with Sweet Savage when he joined them onstage at the Waterfront Hall in Belfast in a show arranged to commemorate recently deceased guitarist Trevor Fleming. Campbell was on tour at the time with Thin Lizzy and a Belfast gig was on Lizzy's itinerary. Campbell was happy to join up with his old friends for a rendition of 'Killing Time' saying of Fleming: 'He was a great musician and a great character as well. It seems like a lifetime ago since we first met but he was too young to die. I miss him a lot.'

However, Campbell found the experience somewhat nerve-wrecking, not just because of the death of Fleming, but also because he was revisiting a track he hadn't played since his late teens. 'It was the first time I'd played that song for nearly 30 years,' he revealed. 'I was more nervous doing that than anything I was playing with Thin Lizzy.'[35]

In 2017, Campbell reflected on his Sweet Savage days when he gave some local radio interviews to mark his appearance at the Oh Yeah music award in Belfast. He told Maurice Jay: 'We did what we could, we wrote our own songs and we opened for every rock band that came over here — Lizzy, Wishbone Ash, Motörhead, Wild Horses — went across to the mainland played with Budgie at the original Marquee Club. I did the Renegade tour with Lizzy all over the UK, did *The Friday Rock Show* with Tommy Vance. We were all young and we tried, we did what we could and it's very flattering that we went on to inspire bands like Metallica... It's bittersweet. It would have been great if Sweet Savage had cracked it and maybe I would've had a career just in one band!'[36]

A similar mix of regret and resignation marked his interview with Gerry Kelly of BBC Radio Ulster. 'We did what we could,' Campbell reflected. 'We opened for every band that came to Belfast. We opened for Wishbone Ash, Motörhead, Thin Lizzy. We performed at the first Slane festival. We were the first band on in 1981. We went to the UK several times; we opened for bands there. We were trying to get a record deal, but I think the focus back then was on new wave music, Terry Hooley, Stiff Little Fingers and the Undertones. We and Mama's Boys were the only two rock bands giving it a go then. It was difficult to get the industry's attention over here, we were a little bit removed from it. We came really close to doing it. We gave it a go.'[37]

# Chapter 2

## Rainbows and Dragons:
## The Dio Years

Ronnie James Dio had one of the great rock voices of the 1970s and 1980s. He enjoyed some initial success with his band Elf, and in the early 1970s Elf opened for British rock band Deep Purple. When guitarist Ritchie Blackmore left Purple in 1975 to form his own band entitled Ritchie Blackmore's Rainbow, he asked Dio to be the lead singer. Other members of Elf took part in the studio sessions for the band's debut album, but either left or were fired by Blackmore after the album's release. Dio, however, continued his collaboration with Blackmore, which led to the breakup of Elf.

Dio recorded three critically acclaimed and commercially successful studio albums with Blackmore, *Ritchie Blackmore's Rainbow* (1975), *Rising* (1976) and *Long Live Rock 'n' Roll* (1978), as well as a live album entitled *On Stage* (1977). Dio shared co-writer credit with Blackmore, providing distinctive fantasy-themed lyrics that proved attractive to young British and American fans looking for escape from ongoing social and political tensions and Cold War fears. The combination of Blackmore's guitar playing, Dio's powerful vocals and arcane lyrics, and the band's visual aesthetic, provided a template for the next generation of rock bands like Iron Maiden, Judas Priest, Queensrÿche and Helloween.

Dio and Blackmore parted company in 1979, with Dio joining Black Sabbath as successor to Ozzy Osbourne. Dio brought to Sabbath his skills as a vocalist and lyricist, and his debut album with the band, *Heaven and Hell* (1980), proved to be one of Sabbath's most commercially successful and critically acclaimed releases. The follow-up album, *Mob Rules* (1981), followed a similar template, but wasn't received in the music press with quite the acclaim of *Heaven and Hell*. By that time Iommi and Dio had begun drifting apart, mainly due to drug use in the band.

When it came time to mix the band's live album, *Live Evil* (1983), Sabbath was dysfunctional. Dio and drummer Vinny Appice quit the band in what *Circus* magazine's Michael Smolen called 'one of the most viciously publicised splits in the history of heavy metal.'[38]

At this point Ronnie Dio's reputation as a vocalist and lyricist was unparalleled. In the year that *Holy Diver* was released, *Kerrang!* magazine's Dante Bonutto called him 'the most accomplished vocalist on the heavy rock scene,' above even the likes of Ian Gillan and David Coverdale.[39]

Smolen called Dio 'the very heart and soul of two of metal's most respected founders Rainbow and Black Sabbath' and a 'role model from whom many of today's vocalists/frontmen draw their very lifeblood.'[40] He had contributed to two hugely successful and influential albums (*Rising* and *Heaven and Hell*) and he appeared prominently and often in the music press.

Given his reputation and fame, it made commercial sense for Dio to start his own band. Apparently, Dio and Appice had discussed this possibility months before they both left Sabbath, so Appice was Dio's first recruit. Dio then asked Jake E. Lee to audition as lead guitarist, but Dio was unhappy with the results and Lee soon departed to join Ozzy Osbourne's band for what would turn out to be two very fruitful and commercially successful albums — *Bark at the Moon* (1983) and *The Ultimate Sin* (1986).

Having already attained commercial and critical success working with British guitarists in Rainbow and Black Sabbath, Dio and Appice travelled to London to look for another. After a fruitless search, Dio contacted ex-Rainbow bandmate Jimmy Bain for advice. Bain had invited Dio to make a guest appearance when Wild Horses played the Lyceum in London, so they maintained a post-Rainbow friendship. Dio tracked him down to a studio in Dublin where he was recording with Phil Lynott and asked if he knew of any available hotshot British lead guitarists. Bain gave some consideration to John Sykes, the ex-Thin Lizzy guitarist, but he dismissed that idea for aesthetic reasons: Sykes was too tall to play alongside the diminutive Dio.

Bain also had in mind the young guitarist from Belfast band Sweet Savage, who had previously opened for Bain's Wild Horses at a gig in London. Bain didn't have Campbell's contact details, but a studio engineer explained that, by happenstance, Campbell was scheduled to be in that studio the next day. Bain met with Campbell and solicited a cassette tape from him with examples of his playing. A few days later Bain met with Dio and Appice in London to play the cassette. Obviously impressed with what he heard, Dio pressed Bain to persuade Campbell to come to London for an audition.

Bain, however, still hadn't found Campbell's phone number so he consulted the telephone book. Campbell recalls the somewhat fortunate turn of events: 'My father's name was Vivian and [Jimmy] looked up Vivian

Campbell in the phone book and there weren't many in Northern Ireland, so he literally woke my father up at two in the morning and I remember my dad coming round to wake me up saying there's a drunken Scotsman on the phone for ye!' Bain told Vivian jr. that Dio was auditioning for a guitar player and asked if he could fly to London later that morning to audition. Campbell agreed, but only after his dad agreed to buy the plane ticket. 'God bless him, he really was my biggest fan,' Vivian would later say.[41]

Campbell met with Bain, Appice and Dio at London rehearsal studios John Henry's. 'The four of us got there, set up and played,' Bain recalled. 'It was just fucking magic.'[42] Campbell remembers playing multiple renditions of 'Holy Diver,' a song Appice and Dio had put together soon after leaving Black Sabbath. 'We started playing and the chemistry of the band was just immediate and undeniable,' Campbell recalled. 'There was just a real connection in the way we all played.'[43]

Dio's impression of Campbell was emphatically positive: 'He was great right off the bat,' Dio recalled.[44] 'His chord playing was the thing. Americans seem to be very fiddly, they don't play big, rousing power chords and have great fields of accent, but Viv has that because he's a British player brought up in a tradition. And as for his solos... as far as I'm concerned, they should put him in the ranks of soon-to-be Guitar Heroes because I think they're brilliant.'

Dio later confided in Campbell why his audition was successful: 'He told me he was looking for someone who had something a bit different. What I came to understand in later years about all these great technical players in LA is that they have great technique but their personality is stifled perhaps or takes a back row seat to the technique, whereas I think a lot of guitar players from this side of the pond, especially in that era, were all self-taught so we had to find our own way and develop a personality as a player, a sound and a style.'[45]

In later years, Dio played Campbell a tape of the audition. Campbell had played all his best licks, everything that he hoped would impress Dio, but it was only when he ran out of ideas and fell back on Chuck Berry rock 'n' roll licks that Dio made up his mind. 'Ronnie pointed at the cassette player,' Campbell recalled, 'and said "That's it! That's when I knew you were the guitar player for me." So basically [it was] when I ran out of ideas and had to go on instinct, making stuff up. I think that's what he liked. It wasn't so "typewriter" you know it wasn't so technical.'[46]

About a month later Campbell flew to Los Angeles and although he didn't know it yet, he was ending one chapter of his musical career with Sweet Savage and beginning a new chapter as rhythm and lead guitarist for one of the hottest bands around.

The situation he suddenly found himself in was both exciting and daunting. He was relatively inexperienced and to that point, mostly out of the public eye. He had toured the UK and Ireland with Sweet Savage, but this was his first trip to the United States. Initially, he was unclear even as to what was required of him. 'I wasn't too sure what my role was going to be,' he confessed. 'I was under the impression that Ronnie was doing a solo LP, using a number of guest musicians and that I'd be playing at most, on half the tunes, before returning to Sweet Savage. But it's all turned out rather differently.'[47]

Furthermore, he was the youngest person in the band and the other three musicians already knew each other from their days in Rainbow or Black Sabbath. He was also a bit starstruck: Ronnie James Dio was a superstar in rock circles, someone Campbell greatly admired. Campbell recalled, 'I was literally listening to *Mob Rules*, *Rainbow Rising* and *Long Live Rock 'n' and Roll*, all that stuff, and then the phone rings and it was Dio.'[48]

He described the experience as 'surreal' and intimidating: 'I didn't feel worthy. I didn't feel secure in my playing or my position in the band I just didn't feel like I belonged there.'[49] In a contemporary interview, however, Campbell expressed belief in his own ability: 'I've every confidence that I'll prove them right in taking a chance on me.'[50] An opportunity had opened up for the young guitarist, but it was risky, and he was well aware it could all end in humiliating failure.

In a 1983 *Kerrang!* interview, Campbell revealed how he was treated in Los Angeles: 'It was strange… people there automatically assumed I was some big new British name, whose fame hadn't yet spread across the Atlantic, simply because everyone thought that Ronnie Dio would only employ the biggest stars around.' This misconception about Campbell's 'stardom' was reinforced by Dio's recruitment of Appice and Bain, both of whom had what *Kerrang!*'s Malcolm Dome referred to as 'distinguished rock genealogies (and the scars to prove it).'[51]

When, many years later, Maurice Jay asked Campbell how he felt about working with 'one of the greatest rock vocalists of all time,' Campbell responded: 'Musically it was great, very dynamic, but I always felt very uncomfortable around Ronnie because I was a fan [but] it was like being in a band with your stepdad because he was very protective of me, trying to protect me from Los Angeles in the 1980s. We had a very strange relationship: he was just about old enough to be my dad. I had so much respect for him professionally.'[52]

The age gap between Campbell and Dio meant they would never be close and was perhaps a factor in Campbell forming an unexpected friendship with Jimmy Bain. Scotsman Bain was in his mid-thirties when the Dio band was formed. He had worked with Dio previously when both were in Ritchie Blackmore's Rainbow. He played bass on the band's studio album *Rising* (1976), which became one of the pedigree hard rock albums of the 1970s, and he took part in the band's subsequent world tour.

However, Blackmore fired Bain early in 1977, after the Japanese leg of the tour, possibly due to Bain's fondness for alcohol and partying. Bain recalled, 'it got wild and wacky in Japan, but we'd been working our asses off for a year. We were winding down.' Blackmore was notoriously controlling and stubborn, while Bain's behaviour was unpredictable at best. Dave Ling called the bass player an 'unrepentant rogue dedicated to the romance of rock 'n' roll.'[53]

The following year, Bain formed Wild Horses, recruiting ex-Thin Lizzy guitarist Brian Robertson, and Neil Carter, who would later play with another ex-Thin Lizzy guitarist, the incomparable Gary Moore. Wild Horses released two albums: the eponymously titled debut appeared in 1980 and demonstrated Bain's musical versatility. He co-wrote all the tracks, playing bass and performing lead vocals on most of them. It was moderately successful, reaching the top 40 of the UK album charts.

A second album, entitled *Stand Your Ground*, followed in 1981. Again, Bain co-wrote all the tracks on the album, played bass and performed lead vocals. The album was not commercially successful, and Robertson quit in June that year. Bain soldiered on for a time with a new line-up, but Robertson's departure essentially put an end to Wild Horses.

Although Bain was never a member of Thin Lizzy, he is inextricably linked to the band. For example, he played bass on the track 'With Love' from Lizzy's 1979 album, *Black Rose: A Rock Legend*. Wild Horses saw him team-up with Robertson, who was part of the classic Lizzy line-up of Phil Lynott, Brian Robertson, Scott Gorham and Brian Downey, with Robertson and Gorham playing dual lead guitar.

Gorham also co-wrote a song entitled 'Dealer,' which appeared on Wild Horses' debut album, while Lynott co-wrote the track 'Flyaway' on that album. Bain also worked with Lynott on the Irish musician's solo albums *Solo in Soho* (1980) and *The Phil Lynott Album* (1982). On the former, Bain co-wrote two songs and played piano and Minimoog. On Lynott's second solo album, Bain co-wrote two tracks with Lynott, 'Old Town' and 'Ode to Liberty (The Protest Song).' He also played bass guitar on the album and sang backing vocals on two tracks.

A further Lizzy link occurred when Bain joined Gary Moore in the studio in January and February 1981 to record tracks that would later appear on Moore's 1983 album *Dirty Fingers*. Bain played bass but didn't contribute to song writing or vocals. Lastly, in 2010-11, Campbell joined

Gorham and fellow Ulsterman Ricky Warwick in another iteration of Lizzy, which meant when Bain joined Campbell's Last in Line band in 2012, he added a further Lizzy link to his rock family tree.

Dio would later insist that his initial plan was simply to ask Bain if he knew any good British guitarists who might have the chops to play in his new band. Dio claimed that when Campbell came to London for a try-out, Bain turned up too, thinking Dio also wanted him as his new bass player. Whether or not that is true, it appears there was immediate understanding between the musicians, and Dio knew better than to interfere with that chemistry. If true, it was a fortuitous misunderstanding that helped cement Campbell's place in the band, because Bain and the much younger Campbell quickly became friends.

At the beginning of 1983, Campbell was only just out of his teen years, whereas Bain was 36, Appice 25, and Dio 40. While one might have assumed that the two youngest members might form a bond, it didn't turn out that way. Dio and Appice were each married, but Bain was single. Furthermore, both Dio and Appice were of Italian-American heritage, so shared that commonality, whereas Campbell and Bain were from the UK and shared some common culture. (The Campbell family name is Scottish and it's likely therefore that Vivian had some Scots-Irish ancestors. Campbell is, in fact, the third most common surname in Northern Ireland. He identifies as Irish Catholic, saying 'I didn't ask for it, but it happened.')[54]

In any event, Dio rented a two-bedroom apartment for Bain and Campbell to share. Campbell was at times shocked by Bain's party antics and drug use, but he found the Scot an affable roommate. 'Jimmy was a generous man who'd give you the shirt off his back,' Campbell later recalled. 'He could be the clown, the drunk, the drug addict, but he had a very kind and gentle spirit.'[55] Still, it was a real culture shock to see Bain free-basing cocaine with strangers in the apartment they shared, and Campbell admitted he would often lock himself in his room so he could sleep more securely.[56]

### *Holy Diver* (1983)

The quartet began recording their debut album in Los Angeles at Sound City music studio, which had a rehearsal room on one side of the building and a recording studio on the other, separated by an external courtyard. Originally, the band only had two songs: Appice and Dio had created the riff to 'Holy Diver,' but as yet it had no lyrics. There was also 'Don't Talk To Strangers,' which would be credited solely to Dio when the album was released, although Jake E. Lee would later claim that he helped write it during his short time with the band. The other seven songs that would appear on the debut album were created and recorded in the studio with

Campbell and Bain. While Dio wrote all lyrics, Campbell was credited as co-writer of the music for five songs: 'Gypsy,' 'Caught In The Middle,' 'Invisible,' 'Rainbow In The Dark,' and 'Shame On The Night.'

Campbell provided some insight as to the creative process: 'we would get together early afternoon and then have ideas to show Ronnie in the evening. Sometimes Ronnie would make suggestions, other times he would listen, look at his lyric book, then 30 minutes later step up to the mic to start singing something.'[57]

Campbell was also appreciative of Ronnie Dio's advice about his guitar playing: 'Ronnie, I must say, was a great help to me... To a great extent, he would let me get on with it, not interfering. But when I'd worked out a solo, I'd play it to him, and he'd make a couple of suggestions that would immeasurably improve it. He certainly brought out the best in me.'[58]

The recording process went smoothly and quickly, and it seemed to be a happy and relaxed time at Sound City. Campbell said, 'We used to go in there every night and we were having a great time. We were smoking a lot of pot; friends would come down. It was a great atmosphere.'[59]

On the album, Campbell used a black Les Paul Deluxe with DiMarzio blade-style humbuckers. This was his first Les Paul, the one he purchased as a teenager, had repainted black, and used in Sweet Savage. (Later in his Dio days he used Charvel super-strats fitted with Seymour Duncan pickups, including one painted with the *Holy Diver* album art.)

Malcolm Dome compared Campbell's technique on the album to Paul Kossoff or a young Jimmy Page, 'but with a distinctive modern buzz behind it. His sound is clean, piercing and coaxing, managing to stay clear of exaggerated tonal qualities and histrionic ebullience.'[60]

*Holy Diver* opens with 'Stand Up And Shout,' which is credited to Dio and Bain. Campbell, however, tells a different story: 'That was a Jimmy riff, although he and I go back and forth because it was similar to an old Sweet Savage thing. But that was stolen from a Gary Moore riff, so it was six degrees of separation.'[61]

It also bears some resemblance to the Def Leppard track 'Wasted' (1980), which Campbell liked, and which was recorded by Leppard at a slower tempo than 'Stand Up and Shout.' The song's back bone is a pacey three-chord riff, similar to the heavy metal riffs of the likes of Mötley Crüe, for example 'Live Wire,' the first track of their 1981 debut album *Too Fast For Love*. Campbell's two short solos cram in lots of notes but remain melodic. If the riffs are reminiscent of Mötley Crüe, then the solos are more akin to the style of Judas Priest's Glenn Tipton.

At nearly six minutes in length, 'Holy Diver' is the longest track on the album. That's partly due to a lengthy keyboard introduction which leads into a main riff comprised of five power chords. Campbell uses palm muting to add colour to its steady rhythm. In the solos and fills, he makes liberal use of string bends and pinch harmonics to add variety and character. While 'Stand Up And Shout' is an energetic album opener, if the title track opened the album instead, and was then followed by 'Stand Up and Shout,' the effect could have been even more dramatic.

Unsurprisingly, 'Gypsy,' which was written by Campbell and Dio, feels like a showcase for Campbell's guitar skills. It's a mid-paced song based on a recurring riff and features an extended bridge over which Campbell plays melodic patterns. The lyrics fall a bit short of Ronnie Dio's usual standard, and the song fades out a bit like a studio jam. Dave Dickson called 'Gypsy' the 'only real bummer' on the album, but admitted it was still 'pretty good.'[62]

'Caught In The Middle' is credited to Dio, Appice, and Campbell, but that is perhaps a bit misleading as the track features an almost identical guitar riff to the Sweet Savage song 'Straight Through The Heart,' making it a likely candidate as one of the four songs on *Holy Diver* that Campbell claimed had originated in his Sweet Savage days.[63]

While Campbell provides some clean riffs and harmony guitars, the performance however, belongs to Dio and Appice. Dio's vocals are powerful and nuanced, while Appice's skilful percussion sets the song apart from most middle-paced rock songs of that era. If it had been released as the third single from *Holy Diver*, its catchy riffs, which are somewhat similar to Pat Benatar's hit song, 'Hit Me With Your Best Shot' (1980), might have made it another hit.

'Don't Talk To Strangers' evokes Ronnie Dio's time with Black Sabbath, particularly 'Children Of The Sea.' Both begin with the guitarist picking the arpeggiated chord of C minor, before launching into power chord riffs. In this instance, Campbell accompanies Dio on acoustic guitar, before an angry electric guitar riff propels the song into hard rock territory. Campbell plays a dynamic solo in the style of Gary Moore that is fast and technically accomplished, but still serves the song rather than just showcases speed and technical ability. The riff bears some resemblance to the title track of Ozzy Osbourne's 1983 album *Bark At The Moon*. That riff was composed by Jake E. Lee, but 'Don't Talk To Strangers' predates it since *Holy Diver* was released about six months before Osbourne's album.

Reviewer Charles C. DuBois of the US paper *Reading Eagle* pointed to 'Don't Talk To Strangers' as an example of Dio's supposedly non-sensical lyrics. In the song, Dubois wrote, 'listeners are advised, essentially, to avoid human contact, dreaming, smelling flowers, even trying to go to heaven because it only causes harm and, presumably, disillusionment.'

DuBois considered Ronnie Dio's lyrics a 'mixture of non sequiturs and angry adolescent paranoia.'[64] In his rush to condescend, DuBois seemed unaware of such concepts as allegory, metaphor, and symbolism, or, like many mainstream critics of hard rock and heavy metal, he simply dismissed the genre as beneath his critical gaze.

The first track on side two of the vinyl album is 'Straight Through The Heart.' Written by Dio and Bain, it shares its name with a Sweet Savage track but does not resemble that song in any way. That Campbell is not given a co-writer credit reinforces the suggestion that there is no musical or lyrical connection between the two songs. Indeed, it seems the riff was based on a song by Wild Horses to which Dio added melody and lyrics. Nevertheless, Campbell claims to have done some uncredited writing on the track but was 'too stupid' to realise his name wasn't included. 'I was also too young and naive to say anything about it when I finally did notice,' he explained.[65]

'Invisible,' written by Dio and Campbell, is a slower song that begins with Campbell playing arpeggiated chords. It appears to be influenced by the 'krautrock' genre of bands such as Amon Düül II and early Scorpions, and it bears some resemblance to Sweet Savage's 'Queen's Vengeance.' The song's middle section is a showcase for Campbell's guitar pyrotechnics, and there are some experimental sounds on this track, including the use of a deflating bicycle tyre. One of Campbell's riffs was inspired by a mistake in the recording studio when the band's soundman ran a tape backwards of the partially completed song. The band, having smoked 'a whole bunch of pot' according to Appice, thought it sounded interesting, so they learned to play the backwards riff.[66]

Campbell claimed that 'Rainbow In The Dark' was based on an old Sweet Savage song called 'Lady Marion' (aka 'Lady Marianne') that he wrote when he was 16. He described how credit for the Dio version was attributed: 'Jimmy, Vinny and I had worked out the basic riff and then Ronnie came in to add his contribution. On the spot, he sang the melody line that eventually appeared on the record! It just came to him. Of course, he had to sit down and write the lyrics, but instantaneously he had turned a rough idea into a great song.'[67]

Jimmy Bain came up with the keyboard lines that add some melody to the guitar-based track. With some exaggeration perhaps, Campbell claimed the band wrote the song in about ten minutes. Whether that was true or not, it does indicate how well Dio gelled together, as well as the good vibes in the recording studio.[68]

Ronnie Dio, however, was not fond of 'Rainbow In The Dark,' saying 'I really hated it when we did it and it's not my favourite song. It's just too poppy.' In fact, Dio didn't even want it included on *Holy Diver*. 'Musically, it's just those same three "Louie Louie" chords with a hook around it.' However, the rest of the band liked it and insisted that it stay.'[69]

Dio made this comment at a time when he was embroiled in a public slanging match with Campbell and it's possible that he was trying to diminish the importance of the track. While it's true that the song's main riff is based on three chords, the same could be said of literally thousands of rock and pop songs, so deriding 'Rainbow In The Dark' for its relative simplicity is a little unfair. Perhaps it annoyed Ronnie Dio that a track so closely associated with Campbell gave the band its biggest hit single.

Moreover, while the basic chord structure is simple enough, Campbell's solo is not. In fact, it's one of the most memorable hard rock solos of the era. It begins with a huge bend, some vibrato, and a slide. The next section emphasises up and down picking with his right hand. It is a straightforward pattern in the A-minor pentatonic scale. However, Campbell rarely just plays a 'clean' simple scale, so he uses some string muting to add colour, while effecting hammer-ons with his left hand to get a trill effect. Most of the following fast patterns are played on just two strings with Campbell using pull-offs rather than picking each note to maximise the number of notes played and to ensure smooth transitions. In the final part of the solo, Campbell plays some single-string runs in a descending pattern and the solo ends with some harmonics played on the fifth fret. The end result is an 'Eastern'-sounding solo that, together with Appice and Bain's solid rhythm, Bain's catchy keyboard lines, and Dio's powerful vocals, helped make the song a hit.

The album's closing track, 'Shame On The Night,' is credited to all four band members. Its backbone is a slow, somewhat ponderous riff that is nevertheless powerful and menacing, and which reflects the song's lyrics about coping with inner demons. In an otherwise scathing review of the album, rock magazine *Creem* singled out the track for a back-handed complement, stating 'only Shame on the Night gets those knuckles scraping pavement.'[70]

### Artwork

Ronnie and his wife and manager Wendy Dio came up with the demonic-looking figure known as Murray, who would soon become synonymous with the band and would appear prominently on Dio's debut album cover artwork. The first iteration was done by musician friend, Gene Hunter, who depicted a priest underwater and suspended upside down on a cross. Although such a sacrilegious image would have made an eye-catching and controversial album cover, Dio disliked the inclusion of a cross, so Randy Berrett was asked to redo Hunter's work and the result of that became the final album cover.

At first glance, Berrett's art appears to depict the demonic Murray using a chain to lash at a drowning priest. It stirred some controversy upon release, receiving a two-pronged attack from religious groups about its implied violence against a religious figure, as well as the inclusion of a demonic figure. However, the theme of good and evil had been inspiration for multiple genres of music for centuries. Moreover, it was particularly associated with the American blues, the genre from which rock 'n' roll emerged. Guitarist Robert Johnson's tale of selling his soul to the devil at the crossroads was particularly influential from the 1960s onwards, and demonic themes became a mainstay of rock music in the 1970s, and of heavy metal music in the 1980s.

NWoBHM band Iron Maiden had been enjoying some success with their demonic mascot known as Eddie. He appeared on their first two album covers and much of their merchandise. When Maiden's 1982 album *Number of the Beast* reached the top of the UK album charts and the top 40 in the US, a host of heavy metal bands copied Maiden's iconology and using demonic imagery to sell music quickly became a genre standard. Dio merely jumped on this bandwagon.

Despite this history of Biblical and demonic themes in their music, rock and heavy metal musicians faced a backlash from religious and conservative organisations, particularly those active in the US. For the most part, heavy metal bands used demonic imagery in an ornamental way, simply to make album covers as striking and colourful as possible. Furthermore, lyricists tended to use such imagery in a symbolic or metaphorical way rather than as a serious expression of support or interest in occultism. Nevertheless, a kind of moral panic at rising levels of violence in the US led to a backlash against heavy metal, as evidenced by organised album burnings, censorship of some records and videos, and court cases against musicians for the harm allegedly caused by supposed hidden messages in their music.

A further response came through the emergence of Christian rock bands such as Stryper, and the formation of organisations such as the Parents Music Resource Centre, whose main activity was to lobby for the censorship of song lyrics and album covers. Although the PMRC was mainly concerned with violent and sexual imagery and lyrics, it also cited two heavy metal bands, Venon and Merciful Fate, as having occult influences, and pointed to sexual, violent or substance abuse themes in the music of other rock and heavy metal bands such as Black Sabbath, Twisted Sister, Judas Priest, Mötley Crüe, WASP and even Def Leppard.

While Ronnie Dio got a certain amount of enjoyment from his new-found notoriety as an alleged Satanist, he did attempt to muddy the water a little, saying: 'On that album cover how do you know the priest isn't drowning the Devil? Just because the priest is wearing a collar doesn't mean he's a good force. These covers mean what anybody wants them to mean.'[71]

On another occasion he explored the concept further: 'the *Holy Diver* album sleeve dealt with this topic: What is good and what is evil? What does evil look like? What does good look like? Everyone said that it depicted a devil drowning a priest. But how do they know? How do they know that the devil wasn't disguised as a priest and vice-versa? That's on the outside — what's on the inside? Are we evil or divine?'[72]

Dio further undercut his critics by providing an origin story for Murray which removed demonic connotations. This backstory was provided in the 1987 *Dream Evil* tour book. Originally known as Murralsee, Murray was the son of Roncanor, leader of a tribe of benevolent ancient giants. Believing a fake prophesy that his son would betray him, Roncanor had his newborn male children killed. However, Murralsee's mother spirited him away and hid him in a cave telling him not to leave otherwise he would die. To keep him alive, she gave him a magic sleeping potion. He awoke eons later, in the present day.

Over time, his physical appearance had been transformed; instead of a benevolent giant, he now looked demonic. Ronnie James Dio, on a spiritual quest, came across Murralsee in his cave and the two slowly became friends. At first, the giant was almost incoherent and Dio interpreted his name as Murray rather than Murralsee. Dio returned to the cave on numerous occasions to hear Murray's stories of the distant past, and these were the inspiration for many Dio songs. Murray agreed with Dio's request to use his image on album covers to introduce the giant to the world and tell his true story: he was not the evil figure of legend but was instead a benevolent sage who shared his wisdom and knowledge with Dio as his storyteller.

Campbell was caught up in these events because of his association with Dio's supposedly demonic imagery, particularly Murray's appearance on the *Holy Diver* and *Last In Line* album covers. However, Campbell wasn't consulted about album artwork, nor how the band was branded.[73] One of the consequences for Ronnie and Wendy Dio was that in retaining this responsibility for themselves, they also became solely responsible for any consequences.

Campbell was further detached from association with this imagery because Ronnie Dio wrote the band's lyrics which, in any event, were not really about the occult. Dio's lyrics had little to do with Satanism, and he made the case whenever he could that his lyrics used fantasy themes to explore the nature of good and evil. In fact, many of those lyrics are an indecipherable mix of romantic medievalism, fantasy, and science fiction.

When Campbell was fired from the Dio band in the year before Ronnie Dio created Murralsee to transform Murray's image, Campbell was left largely untouched by any of the Satanic allegations that could have limited his future musical options.

## Reviews

Despite widespread retrospective assertion that *Holy Diver* ranks among the greatest and most influential rock albums of the 1980s, initial critical reception was mixed: indeed, critics considered it as either great or terrible, with not much nuance in between those polarised views. The most positive reception came from specialised rock and heavy metal journalists. For example, *Kerrang!*'s Dave Dickson called *Holy Diver* 'great, triffic, brilliant, superb, the best Metal album release of the year thus far and it's going to take a Helluva lot of beating.' Dickson concluded: 'Ronnie James Dio is back and has thrown down the gauntlet and set the standard by which all other HM albums of 1983 are going to have to be judged.'[74]

Dickson inferred, however, that Ronnie Dio had prevented Campbell from unleashing the full range of skills, perhaps due to Dio's often negative experiences with Ritchie Blackmore in Rainbow. Rumours had circulated that the two clashed over who was the boss in that band, and perhaps Dio didn't want the same dynamic to unfold in this one. Dickson wrote: 'Campbell's star is never really allowed the chance to shine to its full and obvious potential, but we mustn't forget who's paying the bills this time around...'[75] Nevertheless, Dickson claimed the album tracklist had 'eight gems out of a possible nine' while Campbell claimed: 'Out of the nine tracks I'd say only two can be called "fillers" — and they're not bad either!'[76]

Dave Ling, writing in British pop music magazine *Number One*, was effusive in praise of the new album: 'What do you get if you cross a few Rainbows, Elves and Wild Horses with a Sweet Savage?' he asked. 'One of the finest heavy rock LPs I've heard in a long time... an absolute scorcher... there's plenty of light and shade, with Ronnie Dio's larynx wrapping itself around some superb melodic material. This is a true contender for my album of the year award, but then, with ingredients such as these, that's not surprising.'[77]

In contrast, the *LA Times* gave the album a poor review, saying: 'There may be some complaints about the satanic references on the album cover, but the real sin here is the music. Dio has none of the flair of Van Halen or the sassiness of AC/DC. *Holy Diver* is all crash, bang, boom with Dio yelling over everything.'[78]

Other north American newspaper reviews were equally dismissive. For example, the *Reading Eagle* saw no merit in the album, and reviewer

Charles C. DuBois was scathing of a genre of music he clearly abhorred: 'It's hard not to hose [sic] this album too hard. It begs for it. But to give this stuff the going over it really deserves, only calls more attention to it than it really deserves.'[79] In a similar vein, Canada's *The Leader-Post* called the album 'another unimaginative exercise for metal fans... indistinguishable from any other project by Sabbath or many similar bands.'[80]

Newspapers often employed only a single music reviewer to discuss multiple music genres and as a result, reviewers were often tasked to review bands they either actively disliked or knew nothing about. The dismissive tone of the above reviews may indicate examples of this trend.

Surprisingly, specialist rock magazine *Creem* also disliked the album, singling out Ronnie Dio for particular criticism: '*Holy Diver*… houses the exact same kind of utterly anonymous leadshrieks [sic] that R.J. inflicted upon both Rainbow and the Sabbie [sic] (most appropriately titled track here is "Invisible") and tallies a pathetic 1.7 on the plod-o-meter.' The review went on: 'features back cover credits arranged under the headings "Those Who Created," "Those Who Laboured" and "Those Who Supported." Too bad they left out the category for us listeners — "Those Who Suffered."'[81]

A common theme though was praise for Campbell's guitar work, with *Kerrang!* journalists once again providing the most positive comments. For example, Dante Bonutto wrote that Campbell was 'confident in his own ability and determined to keep a goodly distance from all combos suffering the plague-like scourge of (Eddie Van) Halitosis.'[82] This was something Ronnie Dio appreciated, that Campbell had what the singer considered to be a 'British sound' in comparison to many American guitarists whom he considered as mere clones of Eddie Van Halen.

Malcolm Dome was also enthusiastic about Campbell's playing on *Holy Diver*, claiming the guitarist had 'come up trumps' on the album. Dome also suggested that it was the chemistry between Campbell and Ronnie Dio that made *Holy Diver* a special album. He explained that while bass, drums and keyboards 'have to be right,' 'it's the interplay between vocal nuances and guitar punch that people most remember... Campbell needed to come out of his corner fightin' and rockin' – HE DID!'[83]

Dome then attempted to explain Campbell's style, within a broader description of the impact caused by a great guitar solo: 'More controlled than contrived, more a snapper than a snarler, more intuitive than introspective, his relatively simple and straightforward approach certainly engenders "the primitive rush," a phenomenon that occurs when flesh and mind fuse together transfixed in eerie fascination by an external stimulus, as waves of adrenaline wash over the sense. It's akin to standing in the road, frozen for a mere instant by a perverse sense of unworldly ecstasy, as a car hurtles towards you. It's the moment when the subconscious death-wish inherent in all of us races to the surface before being suppressed. It's the moment when the constant search for a radical thrill takes over. A talented exponent of the electric guitar can just occasionally reach such depths. Campbell is one of 'em.'[84]

**Singles**

The first single from the album was the title track 'Holy Diver,' coupled with a newly-recorded non-album track entitled 'Evil Eyes.' It was released in August 1983 and offered in 7-inch and 12-inch vinyl formats, with the 12-inch version featuring a further album track, 'Don't Talk To Strangers.' There was no attempt to emulate the elaborate album artwork, nor was the demonic 'Murray' anywhere in evidence, but the single was offered in a picture sleeve which had a dark blue background, 'Holy Diver' written in white, and the stylised Dio band title presented in red. The back cover had a dark blue background with a vertical red stripe. The song titles were written in white on this red stripe. The 12-inch release substituted a black background for the dark blue. 'Evil Eyes' was recorded in July 1983 at Sound City studios.[85] Campbell said: 'Phonogram asked us for a B-side and we went into the studio with no idea what to do, and it just came about and we recorded and mixed it in 36 hours.'[86]

The promotional video gives some insight about Ronnie Dio's status in the band, and his relationship with the others. The storyline presented in the video is very much in the 'sword and sorcery' genre. It is set in an arcadian landscape and depicts Dio as a sword-wielding warrior-hero who strikes down another warrior-bandit who has just pillaged a church (in reality, the derelict St Mark's Church in Silvertown, east London).

Murray, the demonic figure that features on the album cover, then appears, raising questions as to whether Dio's violent act is justified. Dio is then presented with a new, freshly made sword before going in search of three hooded figures. Dio exits the church, while Murray's demonic eyes are superimposed onto his. Who is good and who is evil? Aside from the video imagery, what is most notable about this promotional video is the absence of Campbell, Appice and Bain, which leaves it open to question if Dio was an actual band or just a solo project from Ronnie with some hired musicians in tow.

Evidently, Bain and Campbell weren't entirely happy with Dio's solo performance, so for the promotional video to the second single from the album, which was 'Rainbow In The Dark,' Bain and Campbell made their presence felt. The track was released in October 1983, coupled with 'Stand Up And Shout' (a live performance from Castle Donington). Some copies of the 7-inch came with a 'Dio at Donington' sew-on patch. The 12-inch version had an extra track, which was the live at Donington rendition of 'Straight Through The Heart.' Both came in a colourful orange picture sleeve, featuring an illustration of Murray on the cover and a band picture on the reverse side.

*Kerrang!* called 'Rainbow In The Dark' the 'best track on the album' and 'pretty damn amazing.' *Kerrang!* also deemed the live B-side 'utterly brilliant' but speculated that it had some dubs added in the studio.[87] *Music Week* called it: 'No frills hard rock without a commercial kick.'[88] Whereas 'Holy Diver' had been only a moderate hit, reaching the US top 40 and UK top 75 singles, 'Rainbow In The Dark' was more commercially successful, reaching the top 20 in the US and top 50 in the UK.

'Rainbow In The Dark' was boosted into this lofty position by a cheesy but entertaining promotional video, which nevertheless did not go entirely to Ronnie Dio's original plan. Noting that Ronnie had flown alone to London to record the video, Bain and Campbell decided to gate-crash the shoot. Campbell later told *Classic Rock* magazine: 'It was Jimmy's idea. We drove to where they were shooting in Soho. We went to the pub, had a pint, then we walked round. The director's there, and he's like: "Great! You guys should be in the video!" Needless to say, Ronnie wasn't too chuffed, but we thought, fuck it, you know? He didn't say anything, he just gave us that look. Like: "I'm gonna get you…"'[89]

The video is set in central London and its plot alternates between tourist-type scenes of London landmarks, footage of Dio on a rooftop performing the song, and a street-level story of a shady guy following a young woman through the seedy Soho streets. At this point, Campbell appears from a doorway to intercept the man, while the woman returns to dance to Campbell's guitar solo. Bain then appears to accompany Campbell on bass guitar. The man runs off after being deterred by Campbell's physical presence as well as the woman's evident physical attraction to the guitarist. At no point does Ronnie Dio interact with Bain and Campbell, which suggests that their scenes were shot separately and perhaps even that the original plan was simply to have Dio perform on the rooftop while the 'harassed female' subplot was a last-minute addition to accommodate Campbell and Bain's appearance on the scene.

While *Kerrang!* called the promotional video for 'Rainbow In The Dark' 'a disappointment, with neither the story-line nor the visuals matching the epic magnificence of the number,' the short video promo has at least a clear storyline and is visually eye-catching. In addition, Campbell's appearance in the video and his prominence in the subplot, served to boost his profile: for the first time, perhaps, he was in danger of being recognised by the general public![90]

## Holy Diver Tour, 1983-84

The typical gameplan for a rock group in the 1980s was put in place decades before. It went something like this: book studio time; record tracks that were either written in the studio or on the road; choose cover art; decide which singles to release and when; film promotional videos for singles; undertake a promotional campaign of interviews and television appearances to promote the album; put together a touring strategy; choose a set list of songs and alternatives; commission the design of a tour book and tour merchandise, particularly one-off t-shirt designs; undertake pre-tour rehearsals; work with promoters in the required territories to book venues and compose promotional material; put a touring crew together; decide on stage design, lighting rigs, and equipment; hire transport; book accommodation; arrange a further promotional campaign to promote the tour, which normally consisted of radio and press interviews; and — finally — give a great, value-for-money performance to keep fans happy and generate a 'buzz' that proves this isn't just a concert tour, it's an unmissable event.

Together with those practical concerns, for some bands at least came the after-show partying, the groupies, and the drugs. Dio, however, managed to avoid the worst excesses of the drug-fuelled rock star lifestyle. Ronnie Dio frowned on that particular hazard; Campbell, Bain and Appice smoked pot in the studio, but like many who grew up in Northern Ireland in the 1970s, when even a mild drug such as pot was hard to come by, Campbell's main vices were cigarettes, coffee and alcohol. It was Bain who most embraced the rock 'n' roll lifestyle, being fired from Ritchie Blackmore's Rainbow for excessive drinking and developing, as journalist Dave Ling put it, 'a fondness for pharmaceuticals.'[91]

Dio's tours with Campbell mainly followed this formula of recording and touring. *Holy Diver* was released May 25, 1983 and around eight weeks later Dio began a six-month tour that would take the band through North America, the UK, and Europe, before returning to North America in January 1984. From July 23-August 12 the band performed 11 times in North America. They then flew to England to perform on August 20 at the high-profile Castle Donington 'Monsters of Rock' festival before returning to North America for 23 performances from October 1-25. From October 30 to December 6, Dio performed 25 times in Europe, including 12 in the UK. Then from December 10 to 31 the band returned to North America for 15 performances, with the tour ending in January 1984 with a further three gigs in North America.

The first ever Dio band tour began on July 23, 1983 at the 3,000-capacity Barn in Antioch, California. The stage design was modest and economical compared to later Dio tours. The stage was set up on two levels, with Appice's drum set raised at the rear centre stage, while Dio, Campbell and Bain performed on the lower level. The stage backdrop was perhaps inspired by the *Holy Diver* cover art, although it omitted Murray and the drowning priest and featured only the album cover's rocky cliffs, which were rendered 12 foot high in hardboard. A good-quality bootleg of the show indicates the band gave a memorable debut performance, although Campbell remembers it for a different reason: 'I'll never forget it,' he said. 'Jimmy came over during Invisible and went to lean on me right as I turned away and he fell off the stage. He didn't miss a beat he was down but not out.'[92]

The 45-minute set list that day was:

> Stand Up And Shout
> Straight Through The Heart
> Children Of The Sea (Black Sabbath)
> Rainbow In The Dark
> Don't Talk To Strangers
> Shame On The Night
> Invisible
> The Mob Rules (Black Sabbath)
> Holy Diver
> Stargazer (Rainbow)
> Heaven and Hell (Black Sabbath).
> Man on the Silver Mountain (Rainbow)
> Starstruck (Rainbow)
> Man on the Silver Mountain (Reprise)
> Neon Knights (Black Sabbath)

Seven of the nine songs from *Holy Diver* were performed, with only 'Gypsy' and 'Caught in the Middle' omitted. This was Dio's first and only live performance of 'Invisible.' The remainder of the set list was comprised of four Black Sabbath songs and three Rainbow songs.

When Ronnie Dio was asked in the summer of 1984 if he would continue playing legacy songs from his days in Rainbow and Black Sabbath, he revealed that he considered 'Heaven and Hell' a landmark song for him and for Sabbath. He also considered 'Man On The Silver Mountain' something of a trademark of his. However, he revealed he didn't care as much about 'Stargazer' and 'Starstruck' anymore but planned to keep 'some connection with the past,' mainly because both older and newer fans wanted to hear these songs.[93]

Of course, this meant Campbell had to fill the rather large shoes of Richie Blackmore and Tony Iommi. Campbell said: 'I love playing them better than Dio ones, not because I think they're better than Dio songs, but because we wrote, recorded and rehearsed the songs time and time again. It's maybe okay if we didn't play them for a year, but to me it's refreshing to play that Sabbath stuff, as I haven't played it a lot before. Also, there are two reasons we have to play those songs, one is because we're a new band and have to do them otherwise we would have to do the whole LP and I don't think some of it's suitable to play live and the second reason is that I think we have a right to, because we have two guys from both Sabbath and Rainbow and what's more they were songs that Vinny, Jimmy and Ronnie were all involved in, and people want to hear them again. I don't think Ronnie's trying to live on past glories.'[94]

On the tour, Campbell played a very different solo on 'The Mob Rules' compared to Tony Iommi's original. Campbell had previously indicated that he didn't like Black Sabbath's music when Ozzy was the band's frontman, and he only liked the *Heaven and Hell* album because of Ronnie Dio's contribution. He probably wasn't trying to curry favour with Dio: Sabbath found a new generation of fans with their 1980 *Heaven and Hell* album, Ronnie Dio's first as lead singer and lyricist, and Campbell evidently was one of them.

Moreover, Campbell may have wished to put his own stamp on Iommi's solo. On 'Heaven and Hell' Campbell deviates from the original version, using volume pots and pinch harmonics to extract spectral sounds from his guitar. Campbell's playing on 'Neon Knights' also differs from the Iommi version, while staying fairly close to the original. This is also the case for 'Children of the Sea.' The band played a short rendition of Rainbow's 'Stargazer,' which led to a solo from Campbell done in the style of Gary Moore's 'Dirty Fingers,' complete with fast picking and a demonstration of technical expertise.

After Dio's landmark first gig, the band toured in support of Aerosmith, playing a further ten gigs over the course of 18 days in the US and Canada. The first of these was a prestigious event at the Red Rocks Amphitheatre in Colorado, but the venues were mostly small to medium sized halls. When asked how Dio was received, Campbell responded: 'Very well, it was all our crowd, definitely, about 70 per cent of the audience were wearing Dio shirts. They had come to see Ronnie not Aerosmith, the crowd wanted heavy metal and Aerosmith are certainly not that.'[95]

After the Canadian gigs, the band flew to the UK in August 1983 to perform at the Donington Monsters of Rock festival. Howard Johnson of *Kerrang!* magazine predicted Dio might go down well: 'Appearing very early on for such a stalwart and favourite, I wouldn't be surprised to see Dio stealing a lot of (blood and) thunder. A big voice for a big day, with a stunningly good debut behind him as well as a first-rate band... this act could well be the rainbow in the dark. Watch out for fireworks!'[96]

Top of the bill that year was Whitesnake, followed by Meatloaf, ZZ Top, Twisted Sister, Dio and Diamond Head. ZZ Top's *Eliminator* album had been released on March 23, 1983 and was a huge commercial success so it's a little surprising that the Texas 'good old boys' weren't higher on the bill, despite there being some strong competition.

Dave Dickson also thought Dio would steal the show, but the band suffered from sound problems. In particular, the volume of Campbell's guitar wasn't brought up to the correct level until 'Rainbow In The Dark,' the fourth song of the 40-minute set list. Howard Johnson called Campbell's sound problems a 'fiasco' that undermined Dio's otherwise strong set. 'Without sound,' Johnson claimed, Campbell's posturing had a 'comical effect,' making him look 'perfectly ridiculous.' Of course, that would be the case with almost any rock guitarist put in that situation through no fault of their own.

Campbell was asked about the festival experience in general, and Donington in particular: 'It was awful, it could have been so good. I don't like festivals anyway... I don't think they're worth the money because many people can't see or hear. Whitesnake will be okay, because it will be at night and they'll have effects, all the bands before have no chance because everything's hired (Amps, Kits). Vinny's drum kit was rubbish... it's chaotic! I like playing live, but... I prefer playing indoors, I get annoyed because you can't do your best. I would prefer them to see Dio headlining.'[97]

Nevertheless, the band had made a strong impression, playing four songs from Ronnie Dio's Rainbow days, two from his stint with Black Sabbath, four from *Holy Diver* ('Stand Up And Shout,' 'Straight Through The Heart,' 'Rainbow In The Dark,' and the title track), and one Dio B-side, 'Evil Eyes,' which the band performed as an encore. There were also solo spots for Appice and Campbell. Clearly, Ronnie Dio knew how to construct a crowd-pleasing and well-balanced set, which also, and probably not coincidentally, served to remind everyone of his pedigree and why this band was called Dio. Dickson predicted the band was going to be the next supergroup: 'On the strength of this performance,' he pronounced, 'Dio could be back next year as headliners.'[98]

Although there were sound problems on the day that had an adverse effect on Dio's performance, an archive release in 2010 with restored sound is evidence of the quality of a Dio stage show, as well as its impact. An Associated Press review cited the release as an example of the 'raw fury and speed that marked Dio... It races from the gate with guitarist Vivian Campbell's frenetic licks on the classic concert opener 'Stand Up And Shout.'[99]

Campbell played a 90-second neoclassical guitar solo that fell somewhere between Beethoven's Bagatelle No. 25 In A Minor (Für Elise) and Gary Moore's 1983 guitar instrumental, 'Dirty Fingers.' Due to time restrictions this was an abbreviated version of his usual tour solo spot, which usually lasted about a minute longer and involved a little more crowd interaction. Nevertheless, this was Campbell's time to set down a marker and it seemed to be effective. Ronnie Dio realised Donington was a turning point for the young guitarist: 'I'm very proud of Vivian,' he later revealed. 'I was proud at Donington to be able to present a guitar player who had been overlooked as far as I'm concerned, who shall never be overlooked again.'[100]

After Donington, Dio returned to the US for a string of successful performances, including one at the Uptown Theatre in Kansas on October 19 where a thief attempted unsuccessfully to make off with Campbell's guitars.[101] The band then set off on their first full UK tour in October and November, supported this time by Waysted, former UFO bassist Pete Way's new band. For his touring band, Dio had recruited keyboard player Claude Schnell, formerly of Rough Cutt, a band managed by Wendy Dio. Despite the commercial and critical success of *Holy Diver*, the tour was relatively modest. The band played 12 gigs in total, 10 of which were in England and one each in Cardiff on November 4 and Glasgow on November 12. The band played medium-sized theatres and halls with a capacity of a few thousand. The full tour schedule was:

Oct 30 Manchester, Apollo
Oct 31 Bristol, Colston Hall
Nov 1 Hanley, Victoria Hall
Nov 3 Birmingham, Odeon
Nov 4 Cardiff, St. Davids Hall
Nov 5 London, Hammersmith Odeon
Nov 7 Southampton, Gaumont Theatre
Nov 8 Leicester, De Montford
Nov 9 Sheffield, City Hall
Nov 11 Newcastle, City Hall
Nov 12 Glasgow, Apollo
Nov 13 Liverpool, Royal Court Theatre

The Guy Fawkes Day/Bonfire Night gig at the Hammersmith Odeon was the stand-out gig on the tour. For many new bands, the Odeon was an aspirational venue, a step-up from the usual clubs, pubs and small theatres, and it had hosted gigs previously by the likes of Buddy Holly (1958), Rolling Stones (1963), The Beatles (1964-65), David Bowie (1973), Elton John (1974), Queen (1975), Bruce Springsteen (1975), Thin Lizzy (1976), Black Sabbath (1978), Rush (1978), Whitesnake (1978), The Who (1979), UFO (1980), Judas Priest (1980), Ozzy Osbourne (1980), Iron Maiden (1981) and Dire Straits (1983).

This was a landmark gig for Campbell, in particular: while Ronnie Dio, Bain and Appice had all played in successful bands before Dio, Campbell had only been involved with Sweet Savage, who were only big enough to headline small London venues. One reviewer pointed to Campbell's performance as evidence that he was a rising force in the rock world: 'On guitar was the much-praised Vivian Campbell, and after the reviews that he has been receiving there seems little that I can add. Despite his distracting habit of ending a long guitar solo, moving to another part of the stage and starting again, the solo still managed to retain the crowd's interest, containing enough different styles to make it worth concentrating on. His straight guitar playing was a copy of how it is on records, but that, in itself, is an achievement.'[102]

Dio's gig in Utrecht, Netherlands on December 4, 1983, filmed and released in VHS cassette format under the title *Dio: Live in Concert* as the band's first live video and video disc. The front cover features a close-up of Ronnie Dio holding a sword, while a small picture of the band appears on the reverse. With a running time of just 60 mins, the video is a truncated representation of the full Dio set from that period, featuring only the following eight songs:

> Stand Up And Shout
> Straight Through The Heart
> Shame On The Night
> Children Of The Sea
> Holy Diver
> Heaven And Hell
> Rainbow In The Dark
> Don't Talk To Strangers

Reviews of the live release were mixed: *Music Week* was mainly positive, writing: 'The standard of musicianship is very high and the four play well together in a concise and disciplined manner. Their stage show is flashy (literally and metaphorically) but they don't overdo the theatrics.'[103]

Reviewing the video for *Kerrang!*, Paul Roland was less favourable. He claimed, for example, that Ronnie Dio was a better songwriter when he was with Black Sabbath. For Roland, tracks such as 'Holy Diver' and 'Don't Talk To Strangers' lacked the 'melodic hooks' of Dio's previous work, and his lyrics were comprised of a 'moribund set of cliches.' Roland admitted, however, that the Dutch crowd was enthusiastic, and he concluded that this was a 'very well-made video', albeit one aimed strictly at Dio devotees.[104]

Dio finished the European leg of the *Holy Diver* tour in Paris before returning to North America for a series of 18 gigs in the US and Canada. Among these was a performance recorded January 4, 1984, for the Rock Palace television show in Hollywood and broadcast 10 days later. The gig was played in front of an audience of Dio fan club members, which guaranteed a friendly and enthusiastic response. Indeed, one fan was so enthusiastic that she jumped onto the stage, did a handstand, then leaped into Dio's arms, almost causing him to overbalance. It took the show's security staff a while to realise this wasn't part of the performance, but she was eventually escorted offstage with no lasting damage done. Ever the professional, Dio hardly missed a beat. This occurred during the set opener, 'Stand Up And Shout,' and the remainder of the short televised set consisted of 'Straight Through The Heart,' 'Rainbow In The Dark,' and 'Man On The Silver Mountain.'

As well as being a commercial and critical success, the *Holy Diver* album and tour was also a personal triumph for Ronnie Dio. The two most prominent of his former bands, Rainbow and Black Sabbath, also released albums in 1983, namely Rainbow's *Bent Out of Shape* and Sabbath's *Born Again*. Neither achieved the commercial success or critical acclaim of Dio's debut album. In *Kerrang!* magazine's readers' poll for the year, Dio was voted best new band, while Ronnie Dio was voted best singer. *Holy Diver* was second in the year's album poll, while the title track was voted nineth best single. The album artwork came second in its category. The magazine placed each band member in the Top Ten for their instruments, with Campbell placed nineth behind the likes of Ritchie Blackmore, Angus Young and Eddie Van Halen, but ahead of his hero, Gary Moore.[105]

Ronnie Dio had gambled his reputation and his finances in the band and his faith had been rewarded. He had also gambled on a young, almost-unknown guitarist and his instincts were proved right once more. Campbell had his big break, but could he build upon it for the all-important second album?

### *The Last In Line* (1984)

In February 1984, *Kerrang!* reported that Dio was currently writing new songs for their thus far untitled second album, the recording of which would begin in March at a studio in England. Two months later, *Kerrang!* provided updated information to confirm that the album would be called *The Last In Line* and was currently being recorded at Caribou Ranch studio in the Rocky Mountains, Colorado (not the English studio *Kerrang!* previously predicted).[106] Dio's intent was to release the album in June and then tour to support it. This would include an appearance at the Pink Pop festival in Holland on June 11, a potential summer appearance at a major US festival which would also feature Ozzy Osbourne, and a UK tour at the end of the year.[107]

This was welcome news for fans, and for those who were keen to find out if Dio could emulate or surpass the success of *Holy Diver*. Magazine adverts described *The Last In Line* — now due for release on July 13, 1984 — as the 'ear splitting new album' from Dio. In retrospect, that was a somewhat misguided marketing strategy given the band's reputation for melodic hard rock, and Ronnie Dio's particular reputation for thoughtful lyrics. Dio played loud, but it wasn't just noise for the sake of it. Pigeon-holing Dio as heavy metal was an unfortunate misconception as the band then became associated with some of the more unfortunate aspects of that genre.

Of course, Dio had some of the trappings of heavy metal, especially the band's use of demonic imagery, as well as Ronnie Dio's infamous 'devil horns' hand gesture. However, this was a calculated approach to attract a particular fanbase, while provoking controversy and newspaper headlines. In response to interview queries about this, Ronnie Dio often seemed defensive: 'I consider myself a singer, not a shouter,' he insisted[108] while pointing to his musical credentials, complex lyrics, and the musical qualities of the band. Perhaps that would have been firmer ground on which to base the promotional campaign for *The Last In Line*.

The album's opening track 'We Rock' is a fast-paced anthemic rocker written by Dio with Campbell playing speedy power chords that are the song's spine. Its singalong chorus may well have been written with a live audience in mind. *Creem*'s Roy Trakin states, for example, that it 'gathers a flock of true believers and affirms the faith.'[109] *Kerrang!*'s Mark Putterford wrote that 'We Rock' 'gallops along on Vinny Appice's snappy, scuttling skins and Jimmy Bain's broad, bobbing bass. Whipped up by Vivian Campbell's strapping six-string stunts, it makes for stirring stuff.'[110]

The chorus of the Ozzy Osbourne song 'Never Know Why' (1986) bears some resemblance to the chorus of 'We Rock.' When asked if the track was merely a 'simplistic HM anthem,' Ronnie Dio responded: 'The only anthemic part of that song is its punchline. I don't write stupid songs. I don't consider myself to be a stupid writer or a stupid person. It's a song that says: "We rock…" unlike many of its ilk, it's not insulting, it's not condescending.'[111]

The title track was written by Dio, Bain, and Campbell. Ronnie Dio explained that it was about 'people who are looking for the answer to a question: Are we evil or divine?'[112] It begins with Campbell playing a delicate melody, using a finger picking style. Ronnie Dio sings over this delicate melody and then the full band joins in, cued by a powerful high note hit by the singer. The song then progresses with Campbell playing power chords and using some palm muting, pinch harmonics and a big power dive using the tremolo bar.

The pre-chorus sees Campbell riff around the F and G power chords, while the chorus returns to power chord versions of the original notes picked finger style earlier. The solo involves fast picking, pinch harmonics, pull-offs and hammer-ons, deep bends, and wide vibrato. The song has an epic quality that album reviewers found attractive. For example, *Rolling Stone* magazine called it a 'strong, hook-filled contender in any genre' whereas *Kerrang!* adjudged it 'Sabs-slanted' and 'another hefty winner.'[113] 'The Last In Line' was released in June 1984 as the first single from the album.

'Breathless' is another riff-driven song, with Campbell playing a mix of power chords and open chords. It begins with some heavy breathing, and the lyrics suggest a woman in peril. It's an energetic song that is a little too busy to be catchy, while Campbell's solo is a further example of his fast, clean picking style. Michael Lawson of the *Star-Phoenix* wrote, 'the introductory hyper-ventilation bouncing between the left-right channels may prompt you to defog your ears before you get to the good stuff,' but he nevertheless adjudged the track 'a good tune.'[114] In contrast, *Kerrang!*'s Mark Putterford thought 'Breathless' was 'a touch ordinary for Dio's towering standards.'[115]

'I Speed at Night' is a tribute to rock music's fascination with all things fast, including riffs, solos, clothes, women, and motor vehicles (although given Dio's particular fascination with fantasy, perhaps he had a chariot in mind when he wrote the lyrics.) A song about a car may well have been the first rock song, namely 'Rocket 88' (1951) by Jackie Brenston and his Delta Cats, and automobiles have been a staple of rock music since then. Other examples from Dio's era include Van Halen's 'Panama,' Judas Priest's 'Hell Bent For Leather,' Sammy Hagar's 'I Can't Drive 55,' and Rainbow's 'Death Alley Driver.' Of those bands' 'I Speed At Night' sounds closest to Judas Priest.

While the track's subject matter was, therefore, already well-trodden ground, Dio gave it a thrash aesthetic that distinguished it from other automotive songs in the genre. Campbell's two solos are among the fastest he's ever played, and while he uses some tapping, mostly the solos involve fast, accurate picking. *Creem* journalist Roy Trakin wrote that both

'Breathless' and 'I Speed At Night' 'stray from heavy metal's plodding 4/4 to pick up on some adrenaline punk overdrive' while Mark Putterford called 'I Speed At Night' a 'fountain of fury… A positively pyromaniacal frolic, it's the kinda thing most HM bands kill with amateurism, but Dio execute in style.'[116]

The closing track on side one is 'One Night In The City,' a medium-paced rocker based around D and C power chords, with Campbell using palm muting and pinch harmonics to add colour. For the solo, Campbell uses a delay pedal to achieve a melodious echo effect. Putterford called 'One Night in the City' a 'remarkably powerful stomp featuring a marvellous echo-assisted solo from the excellent Campbell. Indeed, both he and Appice are capable of stopping you in your tracks, such is their brilliance at times.'[117]

The opening track of side two is 'Evil Eyes,' which was originally the B-side of the 'Holy Diver' single release but was then re-recorded for *The Last In Line* album. The original version has a rawer feel than the re-recorded version, perhaps because it was recorded quickly to make it available as a B-side. The track is uninspiring, sounding a bit like sub-par Judas Priest, with incomprehensible lyrics and a weak chorus. It is saved from total mediocrity by another dynamic Campbell solo in which he deploys a variety of techniques including pinch harmonics, double stops, bends, hammer-ons, pull-offs, tapping and slides. The more polished version from *The Last In Line* is similar to the original, with the main difference being better recording of Ronnie Dio's vocals. The overall result of the re-recording is that 'Evil Eyes' sounds more like a Journey rocker than Judas Priest.

When Mark Putterford claimed that 'Evil Eyes' was now 'shining brightly with a new lick of paint,' he provided the most accurate assessment of the new recording. Other comments were less insightful: for example, *Rolling Stone* magazine described 'Evil Eyes' as 'a bit of Ozzy-inspired I'm-a-mad-mamajama nonsense,' which may be a reference to the 1981 hit single from Carl Carlton entitled 'She's A Bad Mama Jama (She's Built, She's Stacked).'[118] However, if there is a connection between Carlton's funk track, Ozzy Osbourne, and Dio's 'Evil Eyes' it remains obscure.

'Mystery' is a commercial piece of AOR with a searing solo break from Campbell which, nevertheless, remains melodic and radio friendly. The song's structure is a basic three-chord riff and on the solo Campbell uses such techniques as a fret slide, palm muting, and deep bends. When played live, Campbell made more use of pinch harmonics and tremolo chord bends, but these are mostly absent from the studio version perhaps for the sake of radio-friendly easy listening. As a result of these self-imposed restraints, Mark Putterford predicted 'Mystery' would make a great single,' and that prediction came true when the track was released in September 1984 as the third single from the album.[119]

Dio would later claim that he didn't like 'Mystery's commerciality and despite feeling like he was 'selling out,' gave in to band pressure to include it on the album. The group 'wanted to write songs that could expand our audience. That's where Mystery came in,' he explained.[120] When he introduced the track to the audience at the Hammersmith Odeon gig on October 5, 1984 he was almost apologetic, saying it was 'just a short little song, it doesn't mean all that much really.'[121]

The backbone of 'Eat Your Heart Out' is ascending and descending power chords with Campbell using finger tremolo on the E power chord, together with some palm muting and chord slides. Campbell also plays natural harmonics on the fifth fret, before executing a tremolo arm dive. The solo includes lengthy descending hammer-ons, then some tapping and a tremolo arm divebomb. Like 'Mystery,' it features a radio-friendly fade out at the song's conclusion, which was something many radio disk jockeys appreciated as it allowed them to talk during the fade out.

However, 'Eat Your Heart Out,' would not have made a good single as Dio's lyrics are a tangle of mixed metaphors, and the chorus lyrics are particularly banal. The lyrics concern a duplicitous or evil woman, which, while a major theme of heavy metal music in general, was not one that Dio turned to that often. Nevertheless, critics were harsh in judgement: writing in *Circus* magazine, Roy Trakin claimed 'Eat Your Heart Out' was evidence of Dio's 'Old Testament... misogynistic equation of Eve and Evil,' while *Rolling Stone* claimed the track featured heavy metal's 'obligatory (so it seems) touch of misogyny.'[122]

At just under seven minutes in length, the album's final track, 'Egypt (The Chains Are On),' is also its longest. Its lyrics and character evoke ancient Egypt, and with lyrical references to bondage, perhaps also the Exodus story of enslavement. Egyptology was a common motif in classical and popular music, but not necessarily in heavy metal music. Perhaps the most well-known iteration in that genre was the Iron Maiden album *Powerslave* (Sept. 1984), which had a stylised pyramid as its cover art and the title track made reference to ancient Egyptian mythology. 'Egypt (The Chains Are On)' was not, therefore, a typical Dio or heavy metal song. The song's spine is a pattern played around the D power chord and then descending power chords D, C and A flat, with Campbell sliding from D to A flat when he repeats the descent. Music critics seemed to like the song: for example, Trakin noted its 'arty acoustic interludes and muezzin-like chanting,' while Putterford thought the song 'radiated the country's mystique.'

Nevertheless, the shadow of Orientalism hangs over many musical evocations of Egypt, including the Dio track. The term 'Orientalist' originates in colonial India and its original intent was to identify westerners who took a sympathetic view towards local cultures and religions. In 1979 the word was redefined by academic Edward Said, who argued that western interest and sympathy was often misplaced: westerners tended towards romantic idealisation, and this worked to validate western culture by drawing misleading and unfair comparisons. The west appeared modern, rational, and efficient, whereas the east remained primitive.

Said made the case that, despite appearances to the contrary, Orientalism was not innocent or apolitical, and instead was patronising, and perhaps racist and insulting. Nostalgia for an ancient past served only to remind westerners of their superiority, and such nostalgia failed to acknowledge both the modernity and diversity of eastern nations.[123] Most Western musical evocations of Egypt, from Steve Martin's 'King Tut' (1978) or The Bangles' 'Walk Like An Egyptian' (1986) to the aforementioned tracks by Iron Maiden and Dio, fall into this Orientalist 'trap' regardless of the artists' original intent.

**Artwork**

The album artwork was done by South African sculptor and artist Barry Jackson. Jackson explained how the cover came about: 'The piece was done entirely in acrylic paint. I spoke to Ronnie on the phone before beginning the piece. As I recall he wanted an endless line of people marching off towards a creature he referred to as "Murray." I did the line of people like it was the end of the world, the lady with the shopping cart was my idea. He then sent me reference on what "Murray" looked like and I dropped the image in.'[124]

The imagery provoked more complaints that Dio was dabbling in the occult. In this instance, Murray makes the infamous Dio 'horns' hand signal, while he presides over a parade of agonised, disturbed people. At first glance, the imagery seems to be a representation of Dante's Inferno, with demonic figures herding a line of people towards a fiery portal. Are they lost souls and is Murray the devil? A closer look muddies the water a bit. The futuristic landscape and ruined architecture suggest an apocalyptic event, but not necessarily one in humanity's future. This interpretation is given credence by the fact that behind Murray two planets or moons can be seen in the night sky, suggesting an extraterrestrial landscape. Moreover, not all the figures in the parade are human: some look like monsters, and one has the head of a bird. This is a group of creatures, not people. Yet one non-human figure pushes a shopping trolley, which suggests some connection with our reality.

Although the overall concept art was Dio's, the actualisation was Jackson's responsibility, and he used a degree or artistic license to ensure there was some doubt as to the image's meaning. In so doing, Jackson built on Dio's overall strategy to leave the meaning of his lyrics open to interpretation. Jackson's art was eye-catching and controversial, which meets the basic criteria for artwork designed to promote a commercial product. However, some critics missed that point and insisted on judging the subjective artistic merit of the album cover. For example, journalist Michael Lawson had this to say: 'Dio has spent more time on the new [album] than his artist did with the cover painting. (The art looks like a two-and-a-half-hour job, including an hour off for lunch.)'[125]

**Reviews**

Often the most critical reviewers are the musicians themselves, but the band appeared pleased with *The Last In Line*. For example, Ronnie Dio claimed it was 'twice the album *Holy Diver* was... I'm really pleased with it.'[126] In several interviews, Campbell discussed how well the band functioned in the studio during the album sessions, emphasising the sense of camaraderie and creativity of that time: 'I personally felt more integrated in the *Last In Line* record,' he explained. 'I established how I was working within the band and felt a bit more comfortable.'[127] The result was another commercial hit for the band as *The Last In Line* reached the top 30 of the US Billboard album chart, the top five of the UK album charts, and was a top twenty hit in a number of European markets.

Music critics were almost unanimous in praise of the album. For example, *Circus*'s Michael Smolen predicted that *The Last In Line* was 'guaranteed to scoop up even those headbangers who didn't get in line for last year's... Holy Diver.' Smolen called it 'a great album' and 'definitely a progression for the band.'[128]

He reiterated this point a few months later in a further *Circus* article, saying: '*The Last in Line* shows a much more polished foursome who have worked out a tight metal sound that is decidedly their own.'[129] *Kerrang!*'s Mark Putterford pondered if *The Last In Line* might be the album of the year, calling it 'a classy exhibition of elative diamond-hard rock which stands head, shoulders and torso above most of its so-called competitors' and a 'worthy follow-up' to Dio's 1983 debut album.[130] *Rolling Stone* magazine called the album, 'one of the best heavy records of the year.'[131]

Of the major rock magazines, only *Creem* was unimpressed with *The Last In Line*. For example, reviewer Roy Trakin called it 'mediocre metal' that dealt in stereotypes and 'old hoary cliches.' According to Trakin, the album's 'few' melodies were overpowered by Appice's drumming, and the result was 'a wailing wall of noise.'[132] Given the praise Appice has received over the years from fans and musicians, that criticism has to be considered something of an outlier.

**Singles**

The first single release from the album on June 11, 1984 (about three weeks before the album release) was the title track 'The Last In Line,' coupled with a live rendition of 'Stand Up And Shout' from Donington, 1983. This was an edited, shorter version of the album track, about four minutes in length compared to the album version which was over five minutes. A cut to Campbell's solo accounts for most of this edit. However, the 12-inch vinyl featured the full album version of the title track, along with live recordings of 'Stand Up And Shout' and 'Straight Through The Heart,' both from Donington, 1983.

Oddly, the single was released in North America, Australia, the Netherlands and Spain, but not in the UK, where it was only available as an import. The artwork for the 7-inch single was a zoomed-in section of the album cover, while the 12-inch cover image used the full album cover artwork. *Kerrang!* called 'The Last In Line' single 'prophetic rock 'n' roll… streamlined, gut-punching music. Heavy Metal that's lean, raw and tough. Epic and grandiose are terms too tiny to do justice to this.'[133]

A promotional video for the single relies heavily on the apocalyptic imagery of the album cover for its aesthetic. As with many of the band's videos, Ronnie Dio plays the main character, although the others make cameo appearances. The storyline concerns a teenage bicyclist who enters a deserted building to deliver a package, but also partly to escape a threatening man (played by Claude Schnell!). The boy descends in an elevator whose destination is the landscape depicted on the album cover. Ronnie Dio sings the lyrics while the boy and an odd rabble of humans and human-like creatures are herded towards Murray. One of them is played by Jimmy Bain, who pushes along an empty shopping cart. Along the way, the teenager witnesses a video arcade where players are given electric shocks when they lose. Another room introduces Campbell playing his solo to an audience of tortured souls. Vinny Appice is also shown in a brief cutaway playing drums. Ronnie Dio then helps the boy escape by hitting a demon in the groin with a cattle prod before Dio is captured and led away, presumably to an audience with Murray and an agonising death.

The music video had a budget of over \$100,000 and was directed by Don Coscarelli, who was responsible previously for the horror film *Phantasm* (1979) and fantasy epic *The Beastmaster* (1982).[134] The video served its purpose by being interesting, topical (the video arcade), humorous and memorable. Campbell's single scene, in which he plays his solo, sees him in full 'guitar hero' mode. He is dressed in black jeans and a sleeveless leather waistcoat, and he wears a chunky silver neckless and thick bronze-coloured wrist band. In addition, Campbell plays a dark-coloured Kramer guitar. As usual, Campbell acts with passion, showing awareness that he is not just miming but also performing for the video's audience. Like Ronnie Dio, his facial expressions and body movements are animated, dramatic and eye-catching.

The second single from the album was 'We Rock,' coupled with 'Holy Diver' (live at Donington '83) and released on August 3, 1984. The initial run came with a 30 by 20-inch poster. The 12-inch vinyl also featured a live version of 'Rainbow In The Dark' (live at Donington '83). The cover art of the 7-inch vinyl was another zoomed-in section of the album artwork, focusing on Murray, while the 12-inch cover image replicated the full album cover artwork. *Kerrang!* called the single 'a gas,' proclaiming that Dio 'delivers the goods with the minimum of fuss, displaying a breath-taking economy and a sparkling thrust from the clean and polished armoured guitars of Vivian Campbell.'[135] A promotional performance video successfully captured the live energy of the band and helped the song reach number 42 in the UK singles chart.

The final single from the album was 'Mystery,' coupled with a rendition of 'Eat Your Heart Out' that was recorded live at the Spokane Coliseum, Washington state on July 24, 1984. It was released in the UK on September 21, 1984, and it came with a promotional laminated replica tour pass. The Dutch release had a different back cover featuring a list of European tour dates. A 7-inch picture disc was also made available. The 12-inch vinyl featured a live version of 'Don't Talk To Strangers' and a tour poster. The German release of the 12-inch had the band's European Tour dates on the back cover.

The track is one of the most commercial released by Dio while Campbell was in the band. *Rolling Stone* suggested that the single's chord changes brought to mind a song called 'Love's Got a Line on You,' which was recorded in 1982 by the pop outfit, Scandal. While 'Mystery' does bear some similarity to this track, both use a simple chord structure that makes them similar to thousands of other recordings. However, if the commercial Scandal track did influence the band, it might suggest some awareness of the importance of radio airplay and hit records to promote album sales.

To that end, a promotional video was released. It's notable that the video features only Ronnie Dio and not the rest of the band. It is fantasy-themed and includes scantily clad female dancers. The visuals are, however, handled tastefully, unlike many other depictions of women in heavy metal videos. No one 'smells the glove' here. Murray appears briefly as a man in a mask, while Dio once more wields his almost obligatory sword.

'Mystery' reached number 34 in the UK singles chart, which was an improvement over 'We Rock' which only reached number 42. 'The Last In Line' didn't feature in the UK charts at all because it wasn't released in the UK. Collectively, the singles from *The Last In Line* performed a little better than those from *Holy Diver*, but it was a modest improvement. Perhaps that was the catalyst for a shift in tone in the band's next album, *Sacred Heart*, wherein Dio would insist on a more central role for keyboards to the detriment of Campbell's guitar. That, together with arguments about finances, would result in *Sacred Heart* being Campbell's last recording with Dio.

## The Last In Line Tour

Many rock and heavy metal fans were unconcerned with singles, and instead considered that albums carried more weight. Dio was an 'albums band,' although Ronnie perhaps didn't appreciate that at the time. Moreover, rock and heavy metal bands built their reputation on touring, and Dio therefore toured extensively to promote the album. Ronnie told *Circus* magazine that he recognised the value of live performances as a tool to promote the band, and he considered the Dio was at its best when playing live: 'It's very important to follow up your product,' he explained. 'You simply have to go out and let people hear your music at its best. And that's live, not on record. People talk about the benefits of video, but to me, touring is far more important. I'm not convinced that a band like Dio benefits much from videos. It's more of a help to people like Cyndi Lauper and Billy Idol. I can't say that it's saved me any legwork. We still go out and play for nine or ten months of the year.'[136]

Dio debuted *The Last In Line* tracks 'We Rock' and 'One Night In The City' on June 11, 1984 at the Pinkpop Festival in Gelen, Netherlands. Wang Chung opened the festival, followed by Marillion, John Hiatt, The Pretenders, Dio, Billy Bragg, and Big Country. Reggae artist Jimmy Cliff closed the show.[137] This was, therefore, not a typical Dio audience, nor was their popularity necessarily reflected in their position on the bill. Nevertheless, it was an opportunity to play to a large audience and thereby raise the band's profile.

It immediately became clear that Dio did not look or sound like any of the other musicians on the bill. They mainly dressed in black, while Campbell wore a red sleeveless shirt with a gold sheriff badge on his chest, dark jeans and a studded belt around his waist. He also wore a red scarf around the bicep on his left arm, and a sweat band around the wrist of his right arm.

Whereas the popular memory of rock band stage wear is leather and studs, in actual fact, and as Campbell's outfit evidences, bands wore a variety of stage outfits: while Judas Priest almost single-handedly made leather and studs part of the mainstream heavy metal aesthetic, that look was first adopted in the 1950s by the likes of Gene Vincent and Elvis Presley, in the early 1960s by The Beatles and in the later years of that decade by Jim Morrison, and then in the 1970s it was embraced by the punk movement. Another British band, Iron Maiden, were also influenced by punk music, and promotional pictures from their early era (1978-80) indicate how they used punk fashions to create their band image. For a time in the 1980s, almost every new rock and heavy metal band adopted a studs and leather motif.

As the decade progressed, however, and American hard rock and heavy metal bands such as Van Halen, Poison, Mötley Crüe and Guns and Roses began to gain traction, a new glam aesthetic took hold. Big hair, spandex, ribbons, headbands, and jewellery became the norm. So, while in retrospect Campbell's stage garb may seem atypical of rock bands, it was, in fact, an example or rock's evolving style. It did, however, irritate Ronnie Dio, who told one journalist that Campbell, 'just stood there on stage like one of the Thompson Twins.'[138] (At Pinkpop Dio wore boots with red tassels, a black shirt with silver tassels and lace shoulders, and a black fingerless glove wristband on one hand, so perhaps he wasn't the best arbiter of good taste himself).

As this was a multi-artist music festival, Dio could not use their elaborate stage props and lighting. In fact, the band had to make do with the minimal lighting provided for the event, as well as contend with a hazardous stage drop of 25 feet into the crowd. Of course, the stage set and design weren't essential as it was the music on which the band rose or fell. Aside from playing the two new *The Last In Line* tracks, the remainder of the set list was comprised of tracks from *Holy Diver*, together with legacy tracks from Black Sabbath and Rainbow.[139]

Footage of the two songs from the new album indicates Dio gave a dynamic performance in front of an enthusiastic audience. Campbell played his new black Charvel and gave a faultless performance of heavy riffing and speedy solos. A surviving audio recording of 'Heaven and Hell' reveals that the song was arranged differently to the studio version and that Campbell made little attempt to emulate Tony Iommi's studio solo, instead perfoming his own interpretation.

Music journalist Geoff Barton covered the festival for a piece in *Kerrang!*. Barton revealed that Dio got a great reception from the festival crowd, and he compared Dutch Dio fans to 'a pack of rabid Dobermans on the heels of an escaped prisoner of war… Eyes glazed and glinting with feverish fury, mouths wide open and spraying spittle.'[140] Barton judged Dio 'definitely the success of the fest.'

After returning to the US, the American leg of the tour began in earnest on July 17 in Bakersfield California. Supported in the early days of the tour by David Coverdale's Whitesnake and later by Twisted Sister, Dio performed 31 times in 40 days. The tour ended on August 25, 1984, at the Spectrum in Philadelphia and the gig was recorded for future release. Unlike at Pinkpop, Dio could now unleash their full stage design, which contained, according to *Circus* magazine, 'an abundance of special effects that make Van Halen's killer-watt lights and Judas Priest's Metallain [sic] monster seem soft by comparison.'[141]

The Spectrum performance provides a good look at the Dio stage set as well as their non-festival set list. On the night, the band played 13 songs, five of which came from the new album. The video release features only 10 tracks however, omitting 'One Night In The City,' 'Holy Diver,' and 'Man On The Silver Mountain' segueing into 'Long Live Rock 'n' Roll.' Most noticeable is the stage set designed like a pyramid. When the top of the pyramid was raised, Appice's drum set was revealed, while Bain and Campbell positioned themselves on the stage at its base. Ronnie Dio's entry to the stage was via a tunnel-like entrance to/from the base of the pyramid. After this, the tunnel was sealed by a set of steps that ascend the pyramid. Two sphinx-like props were situated on either side of the stage. At points in the show, the heads of the sphinxes would become animated, belching smoke. Unfortunately, this impressive stage set only appeared on the American leg of the tour, so UK and European fans never got to see it.

The full set on the night was 'Stand Up And Shout,' 'One Night In The City,' 'Don't Talk To Strangers,' 'Mystery,' 'Egypt (The Chains Are On),' [Appice drum solo slot], 'Holy Diver,' 'Heaven And Hell,' [Campbell guitar solo slot], 'The Last In Line,' 'Heaven And Hell' reprise, 'Rainbow In The Dark,' 'Man On The Silver Mountain' / 'Long Live Rock 'n' Roll,' then 'The Mob Rules' and 'We Rock' were played as an encore.

Campbell's stage outfit was red leather trousers and a red sleeveless waist coat. He played a white San Dimas-style Charvel adorned with a graphic of four skull and crossbones images on a red background. However, for 'Heaven And Hell' Campbell switched to a black and white Charvel Explorer, and it was on that guitar and song that he played a lengthy solo. It began as part of 'Heaven And Hell,' with Dio leaving the stage while Appice, Bain and Campbell performed instrumentally. The solo was played rhythmically, based around the chord sequence of the song. Then Appice and Bain left the stage, allowing Campbell to shred up and down the neck with fast and accurate picking, and using some tremolo effects.

During this time, the lights went down and luminous glow-in-the-dark strips on the body and neck of the guitar did their work. When the lights came back on, Appice and Bain rejoined Campbell on stage to find he had ascended the pyramid steps and now stood in front of Appice's drum set. The solo then changed back to a rhythmic pattern matching the 'Heaven And Hell' chord structure, while Ronnie Dio rejoined the stage to make it a foursome once again. Dio sang some well-rehearsed 'improvised' lyrics before the song returned once again to the epic power chord structure of the studio recording.

Campbell reverted to the San Dimas-style Charvel for the following song, which was the title track of the second album. Campbell and Ronnie Dio were on top form at this point, with Dio singing the first verse gently and with feeling, before blasting out the final word of the verse in his powerhouse fashion. Indeed, this was probably the high point of the concert, with Campbell's power chords sounding as apocalyptic as a modern-day Gabriel's Horn, Appice battering his drums mercilessly, Bain never missing a beat, Schnell adding light and shade with his keyboard skills, and Campbell improvising in fiery fashion during the guitar solo.

While that was unfolding, the door to the pyramid reopened to allow a giant three-headed serpent prop to make its way on to the stage, adding more visual drama to the event. But then a bigger surprise! The band had not finished with 'Heaven And Hell' and Campbell led the song to its final conclusion with some heavy riffing and finally a speedy solo that resembled Iommi's studio version enough to be familiar, while still having Campbell's stamp on it.

The band left the stage for a time while the eyes of the two sphinxes lit up, and Murray's devilishly slanted red eyes appeared above Appice's drum kit. Dio thanked the audience before introducing 'Rainbow In The Dark,' one of Campbell's more important contributions to the Dio set list. With Campbell's power chords sounding thunderous, this simple but effective piece of rock-pop took on a new lease of life, and if Campbell perhaps overused pinch harmonics during the solo he can be forgiven due to the excitement of the occasion.

Despite being dynamic and fast-paced, the following track, 'The Mob Rules,' feels a little underwhelming, and this is despite Campbell playing astoundingly fast fills and solos set against a background of exploding pyrotechnics above the stage. This is where the video release ends, but of course on the night the concert ended fittingly with the tried-and-tested showstopper, 'We Rock.'

Reviews of the Philadelphia show are difficult to come by, but the video release received some critical attention. For example, a *Creem* magazine review called Ronnie Dio 'probably one of the best hard rock vocalists going,' with a 'whompin' HM band.' *Creem* told its readers, 'If you like your metal hot, hard and heavy, and you like it on TV, you're gonna pick up this little mother and jam.'[142] This was, however, a flimsy and inadequate summary of the qualities that made Dio such an exciting live draw.

Steve Gett for *Circus* magazine provided better analysis in his review of the August 15 gig at the Nassau Coliseum, Uniondale, New York, where the band played to an audience of 12,000 fans. Gett differentiated Dio from the 'wham-bam-thank-you-ma'am styles' of contemporaries such as Ratt, Mötley Crüe and Quiet Riot, whom Gett dismissed as mere 'anthem-orientated bands,' describing Dio as 'more in the traditional heavy metal vein. Longer, more complex pieces tend to dominate the set, enabling the individual group members to prove their virtuosity.' Gett was particularly impressed with Campbell, claiming that aside from Ronnie Dio, the audience's attention was mostly directed toward the 'young Irish axe-grinder' who unleashed a 'blitz of wild lead-breaks' throughout the show and who proved his 'digital dexterity' in his solo slot during 'Heaven And Hell.'[143]

Dio flew to Europe for three huge gigs in as many days. The first was the Breaking Sound festival in Le Bourget, Paris on August 29/30. Over the next two days Dio would play at two Monsters of Rock festivals in Germany, firstly at Wildparkstadion in Karlsruhe and then another at Zeppelinfeld, Nurnberg. At these festivals Campbell would be sharing the bill with his guitar hero, Gary Moore.

Dio performed in Paris on August 30, day two of Breaking Sound. On that day, Blue Öyster Cult topped the bill, followed by Daytona, Dio, Heavy Pettin' and two other unknown bands. The set list was unchanged from the American tour. 'Dio, of course, won the day,' claimed Derek Oliver, who provided an exuberant review of the festival for *Kerrang!* 'They stamped their majestic superiority over the entire two-day bill. If there's a band deserving of the crown that Zeppelin left behind, then it surely must be Dio. The concept is total. A flashing, magnificent vessel of orgasmic proportions that sweeps the air with incredible ease, engulfing all that stands before it.' Oliver even asserted that Dio's renditions of Rainbow and Sabbath songs 'made the original versions sound insignificant.'[144]

After the Monsters of Rock festivals, it was on to Britain. Dio's UK tour dates for September and October were first announced in April, with plans for a 19-date tour in which Dio would be supported by newcomers Queensrÿche.[145] However, due to popular demand, further dates were added, with the band now scheduled to play two Irish gigs. The first was a homecoming gig for Campbell on September 4 at the Forum in Antrim, Northern Ireland; the second was at the SFX Arena in Dublin the following day. Dave Fanning provide a mixed review of the Dublin gig for the *Irish Times*. Fanning called heavy metal 'musically stagnant' but praised Dio for 'successfully managing to ignore the more repulsive or unacceptable elements of heavy metal while still making sure that they deliver music in that essential aggressive style that your parents hate.'[146]

Fanning was struck too by the Egyptian 'Warlord of Doom' stage backdrop, and Campbell's 'skin-tight red leathers that left nothing to the imagination.' This was, though, not the full stage show that American fans saw earlier in the tour. According to *Kerrang!*'s Paul Suter, high shipping costs and small European stages made it too expensive and impractical for Dio to bring the full set to Europe. Unfortunately, that resulted in European audiences missing out on two of the most striking and effective props — the pyramid and three-headed serpent.[147]

The UK dates that followed these Irish gigs were as follows:

Sep 8 Hanley, Victoria Hall
Sep 10 Ipswich, Gaumont
Sep 11 Portsmouth, Guildhall
Sep 12 Cardiff, St. Davids Hall
Sep 14 Bristol, Colston Hall
Sep 15 St. Austell, Coliseum
Sep 16 Oxford, Apollo
Sep 18/19 Birmingham, Odeon
Sep 20 Nottingham, Royal Concert Hall
Sep 22 Edinburgh, Playhouse
Sep 23 Glasgow, Apollo
Sep 24 Aberdeen, Capitol
Sep 26 Newcastle, City Hall
Sep 27 Hull City Hall
Sep 28 Liverpool, Empire Theatre
Sep 30 Manchester, Apollo Theatre
Oct 1 Sheffield, City Hall
Oct 2 Leicester, De Montfort Hall
Oct 4-6 London, Hammersmith Odeon

Even without the elaborate and costly stage set used in the US, these small to medium-sized arenas would only generate enough earnings for the tour to break even or perhaps make a modest profit. Booking these smaller venues indicated one of two things: that promoters considered Dio not yet a big enough draw to justify booking larger venues; or that Ronnie and Wendy Dio lacked the confidence or financial backing to book them. If, for example, they booked larger venues and the crowds didn't come, Wendy and Ronnie would face a significant financial blow.

The Hammersmith show on October 5 was recorded and broadcast by the BBC, with rock DJ stalwart Tommy Vance compering. Vance introduced Dio as 'one of the tightest rock bands in the world,' predicting that in 1985 they would 'really, but really, explode on the scene.' This show offers further insight as to the band's live performance in 1984. Once again, the set list remained unchanged, and it was becoming clear that Ronnie Dio was too much of a professional, or some may say too set in his ways, to take a risk by introducing new songs into the set mid-tour.

As might be expected from the BBC, the recording quality is top-notch, with drums, vocals, bass, and guitar all clearly heard and mixed, while keyboards and audience noise are kept to an appropriate level. As such, this is a great document of the band in this era. For example, the recording highlights what a great singer and frontman Ronnie Dio was, but also the clarity and accuracy of Campbell's playing. While this is the case for the whole set, it's particularly evident on the opener 'Stand Up And Shout,' and when Dio gives that command, how could anyone resist? Campbell's riffs are tight and accurate, and his tone is big and bright.

Among the outstanding performances is 'Egypt (The Chains Are On),' which segues unexpectedly but neatly into 'Holy Diver' during which Campbell diverges noticeably from the studio version of the solo to produce some Jake E. Lee-style shredding. At one point during 'Heaven and Hell,' there is space in the arrangement for Campbell to play an extended solo that relies less on the speedy picking of the original than it does more rhythmic playing. He also makes good use of volume pots, tremolo and harmonics to provide atmosphere and colour.

The song reverts to the original arrangement for a short time before transitioning beautifully into 'The Last In Line,' with Campbell's delicate fingerpicking leading into Ronnie Dio's magnificent explosion of vocals at the end of the first verse. The following track, 'Rainbow In The Dark,' is another Campbell *tour de force*, spoiled only a little by Bain's out of tune bass. Nevertheless, Campbell nails the solo and Schnell's gentle and understated keyboard accompaniment adds a new dimension to the track. Appice's madcap drumming, leading to the song's denouement, ties all the threads together to create a special moment.

The next track, 'Man On The Silver Mountain,' segues into 'Long Live Rock 'n' Roll,' which is played jam style and thus showcases a different side of Campbell as he 'duels' with Schnell's keyboards. While the encore on this tour usually featured 'The Mob Rules' and 'We Rock,' here only the latter makes an appearance. Its frenetic pace and hard riffing relent only for a few seconds to accommodate a brief drums and vocals-only attempt to instigate some crowd participation, before the song ends in usual abrupt fashion. 'Excellent unit: two Americans, a Scot and an Ulsterman who really know how to do it,' Vance exclaimed.

After the UK tour was complete, Dio travelled to Scandinavia for six shows beginning in Lund, Sweden on October 10 and finishing in Copenhagen eight days later. A further 10 European shows took place, eight of which were in Germany, before Dio flew back to the US to prepare for a 46-date American tour from November 4, 1984, to January 27, 1985 that would take the band as far afield as Honolulu, Hawaii and Anchorage, Alaska. Allowing for travelling time between venues, and a five-day break at Christmas, 46 dates in 85 days was a gruelling schedule, but it seems the band never lost their focus. For example, a newspaper review of the Glenns Falls gig in New York State on November 4 claimed that the 6,000-strong crowd 'sang nearly as loudly as their hero,' while noting that Ronnie Dio's 'magic' rubbed off on Campbell, making the interplay between the two 'among the most dynamic elements of the evening.'[148]

While the logistical practicalities of such a long tour were demanding, the experience did allow the band to further hone their craft, something Campbell in particular, felt he needed to do. In reviewing Dio at the Pinkpop festival, Geoff Barton called Campbell a 'guitar hero in the making.'[149] Campbell was, however, reluctant to adopt the role. He already lacked confidence in his ability, especially compared to more technically proficient guitarists, and he suffered a little from 'imposter syndrome' after being hand-picked by one of the era's great rock vocalists. He would later reflect: 'I don't have that outgoing exhibitionist personality that makes for the best guitar hero. My passion was to play the instrument. Then there is this whole other side of it if you want to do it seriously. To make a career of it, you have to go on stage to perform in front of people and wear a persona that isn't really you.'[150]

However, Campbell's insecurity about his skills was not shared by those who heard him play. For example, journalist Bruce Taylor saw the band perform on July 24 at the Spokane Coliseum and as well as praising Ronnie Dio's 'powerful vocals' he also singled out Campbell's 'fluid guitar work.' According to Taylor, Campbell 'pounded out riffs and slipped into solos with skill matched by few other heavy rock guitarists.'[151] Nevertheless, after paying close attention to guitarist George Lynch of Dokken, the support band for much of the American leg of *The Last In Line* tour, Campbell used the break between the end of the tour and the recording sessions for the next album to work on his guitar proficiency and technique.

### *Sacred Heart* (1985)

By the time the band entered the studio for the *Sacred Heart* sessions, keyboard player Claude Schnell had begun to play a bigger role. Schnell joined Dio in May 1983 to play keyboards during the *Holy Diver* tour. On the album, Bain and Dio played the keyboard parts but Dio felt a dedicated keyboard player such as Schnell would improve the band's live show. Schnell played keyboards on the next four studio albums, but it wasn't until the live album, *Intermission* (1986), that he earned his first co-writing credit, ironically for the only studio track on the album, 'Time to Burn.'

As Dio increasingly turned to Schnell's keyboards, for example on the title track of *Sacred Heart*, 'Hungry For Heaven,' and on 'Rock 'n' Roll Children,' it caused some friction in the band. Campbell later revealed: 'Ronnie was going to write more with keyboards which Jimmy, Vinny and I were not in favour of. We felt the guitar was the main focus of the band as we were a guitar driven band. We thought Ronnie was trying to overly complicate the arrangement particularly with keyboards. They weren't necessarily making the songs better it was just for the sake of having it in the song. It became more difficult to write songs.'[152]

Jimmy Bain confirmed Campbell's recollection of events, claiming: 'The production was watered down with all the keyboards, [and] the songs were not as good because it became harder to satisfy Ronnie's need to complicate arrangement and structure.'[153] When asked to account for increasing use of keyboards in his music, Dio explained, 'for a long time I didn't really like keyboards. I make no bones about being a guitar-voice-meat-and-potatoes man... that's what I like. But I've been steadily bringing keyboards in right from the word go: *Holy Diver* had traces of it in there, then on *The Last In Line* I spoon-fed the songs with keyboards, bit by bit. *Sacred Heart* had more still.'[154]

It was possibly the age difference between Campbell and Dio that accounted for their contrasting views about keyboard-based music. Ronnie Dio had, of course, close links with Deep Purple, one of whose strengths was the iconic keyboard sound of Jon Lord. Keyboards were also intrinsic to the sound of Rainbow while Dio was that band's lead singer. While Dio preferred a guitar-based sound, he saw the value of keyboards and did not consider the instrument at all out-of-place in rock 'n' roll.

However, by the 1980s keyboards, and particularly synthesisers, had developed a bad reputation among rock fans, who increasingly associated the instrument with commercial pop music. Genres such as Disco, New

Wave, and the New Romantics were almost the opposite of rock music, and synthesisers now marked a band as being outside the rock fraternity. Furthermore, the ease with which one could learn and create music with a synthesiser using pre-programmed sounds led to the instrument being associated with lack of musical talent. Rock musicians traditionally earned their reputation by mastering an instrument and paid their dues by playing live. Rock fans considered synthesiser-based pop bands as untalented posers.

Rock musicians were often just as scathing as rock fans. For example, guitarist Gary Moore claimed that 1980s pop stars couldn't play their instruments and were able to fool fans with cool videos and attractive imagery. He thought popular music was at 'an all-time low' and that the BBC's flagship chart program *Top of the Pops* was 'completely unwatchable,' pointing to the likes of Kylie Minogue, Brother Beyond, and Bomb the Bass as examples of style over substance.[155] He was particularly scathing about house music, which he claimed was 'just an excuse for people who can't play to make a record.'[156]

Nostalgia for 1970s-era guitar-based rock helped feed the rise of heavy metal in the 1980s. Yet, older rock bands often suffered a backlash if they attempted to modernise their sound, particularly if they incorporated synthesisers. To a section of their devoted fanbase they were 'selling out.'

For example, Canadian rock band Rush faced a backlash from fans upon the release of their 1982 album *Signals*. The album preceding it, *Moving Pictures* (1981), had already signalled a change in style, with shorter, more radio-friendly songs. However, the album's primary instrument remained Alex Lifeson's electric guitar, and tracks from that album such as 'Tom Sawyer,' 'Limelight,' and 'YYZ' quickly became fan favourites. In contrast, *Signals* relied more heavily on synthesisers and electronic effects and less on guitar-based riffs. Lifeson's iconic, virtuoso guitar work was reduced to mere ornamentation. Drummer Neil Peart admitted that it was a contentious album: 'some will love it, some will hate it,' he explained in a contemporary interview, and the album remains divisive among the Rush fanbase.[157]

Yet *Signals* was Rush's biggest-selling album. For example, it topped the Canadian album charts and within four months of its release, went double platinum in the band's home country.[158] It also reached the top ten in both the UK and US. Other older bands were also able to modernise their sound to great effect. For example, ZZ Top's *Eliminator* (1983) completely changed their image and their fortune. It was a huge commercial success and earned the band a new generation of fans. Similarly, British blues rock band Whitesnake introduced more keyboards and synthesisers to their studio production and while fans of the bands older material were aghast, this culminated in the album *Whitesnake / 1987*, which was a huge commercial success, reaching the top ten in the UK and USA, and selling 8 million albums in the US alone.

It was this crossroads that Dio found themselves at in 1986. Should they compromise their guitar-based formula and embrace a more commercial sound or stick with the tried-and-trusted music that had thus far brought them a degree of critical and commercial success but nevertheless had failed to break them into more mainstream markets. Added to this was confusion between band members as to what even constituted mainstream music. Comments from Ronnie Dio and Appice suggest that Campbell wanted the band to embrace what was going on around it and to modernise its sound in pursuit of more mainstream commercial success.

Ronnie Dio had, however, made it clear that he saw no need to change. In fact, he explained that the Dio band was his attempt to bring to his audience a less complex version of the lyrical themes and musical tone of his writing in Rainbow in the 1970s. 'Lyrically I've become more attuned to people,' he explained. 'I'm giving them something they can understand a little more easily than ['Man On The Silver Mountain'], which is very vague.'[159]

When it became clear to Campbell that Dio didn't intend to change his tune, it was then that Campbell began to look for ways outside of Dio to create more contemporary music. Their contrasting comments about keyboards are perhaps evidence of these musical differences. Dio saw keyboards as part of his rock heritage; Campbell, Bain and Appice thought that keyboards were replacing the guitar-based rock that all parties claimed to be their foremost interest. In contrast, Ronnie Dio claimed that Campbell's outside musical interests were more in line with 1980s pop.

Given these sometimes-contradictory statements, it's difficult to strip the layers away to find the truth. In later years, however, Campbell disowned a lot of his work with Dio, claiming that while it was nice that fans still approached him to praise that era, that music meant very little to him personally. Yet Campbell made those comments in 2010 at the height of his feud with Ronnie Dio, so that might have been a factor in disowning that era of his life. He certainly embraced that time period enthusiastically when he formed his Last In Line band in 2012, naming it after the Dio song and playing old Dio tracks.

In addition to musical differences causing tension, Ronnie Dio had split from his wife Wendy, and although she remained his manager they were now living apart. According to Campbell, Dio was often in a foul mood in the studio, which led to a difficult working environment in the *Sacred Heart* sessions. When writing and recording the band's debut and sophomore albums, studio sessions were normally enjoyable, creative and fruitful; band members usually stayed after their individual parts were recorded to lend support to each other and be involved in the collective creative process. However, the sessions for *Sacred Heart* were often stressful and difficult, and band members tended to make their exit when their parts had been recorded.

Campbell recalled: 'I can honestly tell you that I didn't enjoy *Scared Heart*; I don't think any of us did. There were issues with the Dio band during that time of making the record. That's when things were starting to go wrong personally and creatively. Also, Ronnie had split up with Wendy at the time who was our manager. His mood was exceptionally dark and nobody wanted to be in the studio with him.'[160]

This version of events is corroborated by Ronnie Dio himself: when Dante Bonutto asked him about rumours of problems in the studio, especially band members not being around when they were supposed to be, Dio responded: 'Vivian was there all the time, though there were moments when I needed somebody and he wouldn't be around and by the time he was called up the idea might have gone, I might have lost the passion of the moment, or I might have gotten so damn angry that the person wasn't there that I didn't want to do it and did something else instead.'[161]

If that remark can be taken at face value, and if Campbell was there 'all the time,' then that 'somebody' must have been Bain, Appice or Schnell. Dio's remark therefore contradicts later criticisms he made of Campbell being disinterested and unproductive during this time. Moreover, while Ronnie Dio wrote all the lyrics for *Sacred Heart*, as was the norm, Campbell co-wrote five of the nine tracks on the album, including the opening track, the title track, and the final three tracks on side two. This suggests a level of involvement that goes far beyond Ronnie Dio's retrospective criticism of the guitarist.

On *Sacred Heart* Ronnie Dio's lyrics remained grounded in the medieval fantasy genre of dragons, wizards, magic, and rainbows, and it would soon become clear that critics, fans, and even Dio himself were all growing concerned that these themes were becoming a little stale. Nevertheless, Dio insisted that his lyrics remained a cut above those typically associated with the heavy metal genre. He said: 'On an album like *Sacred Heart*, we're trying to capture the spirit of King Arthur, of chivalry and good values. We're not degrading women in our songs — I sing of being a knight and protecting them.'[162]

The original plan was to record the album at the Record Plant and to be the final band to record there over a period of two months before was scheduled to close later in the year. However, a diary clash with Kiss's

Paul Stanley would have meant cutting short Dio's studio time by half, so Ronnie Dio decided instead to record the whole album at Rumbo Studio in Los Angeles.[163] Rumbo was owned by husband and wife recording artists Daryl Dragon and Toni Tennille (known as Captain and Tennille). Perhaps Ronnie Dio saw the 'Dragon' as a good omen, given his plans to have a dragon on the album cover and use a dragon prop in the live stage set-up.

Not long before the album was released on August 12, 1985, Ronnie Dio was asked what fans might expect. He responded: 'Big drum sounds, big guitar sounds, no ballads.'[164] He could also have added 'transitional artwork' because the cover art saw Murray take a back seat to Dio's new totem, a dragon known as Denzil. Dio commissioned the artwork to Robert Florczak, an artist whose work, according to his website, is characterised by 'an avid interest in historical, literary, and mythological themes of drama and romance.'[165] This specialism made him an ideal candidate for the album. Ronnie Dio liked it so much he kept the original artwork for himself.[166] The design features a close-up of two hands holding a crystal ball, inside of which is a dragon holding a crimson diamond heart. Murray's head can be seen in silhouette behind the dragon. The cover border features a Latin inscription which may translate to the spoken word section of Dio's 'Hungry For Heaven' promotional video: 'Come with me now and discover the magic that lies beyond the sea of dreams. And if you have the courage to cross the rainbow bridge you may find the sacred heart.'

Side one opens with 'King Of Rock And Roll,' an anthemic hard rocker that was likely written with audience participation in mind. Indeed, a 'live' performance video of the song was made to promote the album, and a 12-inch promo was made available to radio stations. Despite the crowd noise suggesting this was a live recording, in fact 'King Of Rock And Roll' was created entirely in the studio with Dio explaining that he added crowd noises to create 'a bigger sound.'[167] The song begins with Campbell playing a brief Chuck Berry-style pattern, then a power slide down the neck introduces the main riff, which is based on D and E power chords with the low E string played open. Campbell deploys techniques such as palm muting and pinch harmonic vibrato.

The title track, 'Sacred Heart,' is next in the running order. Clocking in at nearly six and a half minutes, it is the longest track on the album. Rock journalist Dante Bonutto called it 'probably the best song on the album, an epic emotive sweep across the senses.'[168] The main riff is played at a moderate tempo and is comprised of E, D and C power chords. Preceding the guitar solo, Campbell adds a power slide from the 18th fret to the D power chord position. The solo features some of his stock-in-trade techniques such as fast picking, deep bends, tapping, hammer-ons and pull-offs.

'Another Lie,' written solely by Ronnie Dio, is an uneventful, mid-tempo rocker, with incomprehensible lyrics that seem patched together from other, better tracks. Even Campbell seems not to be trying too hard, with the exception of a power slide wherein he uses his hand as a slide but without pressing down completely on the neck. By just sliding down the strings and 'pick scaping,' he creates a harmonic effect similar to a technique used by Gary Moore in the early 1980s, and thereafter copied by numerous rock and metal guitarists.

The final track on side one is 'Rock 'n' Roll Children,' which is credited solely to Ronnie Dio. He claimed: 'We've never done a song like Rock 'n' Roll Children on any of our albums' and that's probably because this song sees the band firmly in AOR territory with prominent keyboards and a restrained performance from Campbell.[169]

He uses palm-muted power chords to create a chugging rhythm effect reminiscent of Jake E. Lee's playing on the Ozzy Osbourne song 'Shot In The Dark' (1986). The solo begins with a power chord before Campbell presses the tremolo arm five times to get a vibrato effect. He then picks a natural harmonic on the fifth fret and uses the tremolo to bend the note upwards. The next phrase also features tremolo arm vibrato and after that Campbell uses finger vibrato and descending single note slides.

Campbell doesn't pick that many notes, which is unlike his usual soloing style, and instead uses these techniques to add colour to his solo. Instead of playing a fast solo over the top of the song as many heavy metal guitarists tended to do, he composed a slower solo in sympathy to the song's overall mood, albeit he does end with some speedy runs to remind listeners that this is, after all, a hard rock band. Ronnie Dio called the track 'tuneful without sacrificing the intensity that makes Dio special.'[170] It was an obvious choice as the first single from the album. Bonutto described it as 'Undoubtedly a step forward, with interesting keyboard work and rhythm breaks and changes.'[171]

The opening track on side two is 'Hungry For Heaven,' written by Dio and Bain. It's another commercial rock song, based on a three-chord riff and layered with prominent keyboards. Its lyrics are somewhat formulaic in that they fit the mould Ronnie Dio had been using since *Holy Diver*. Its tone is uplifting and triumphant, and although the lyrics inject a note of caution, the inspirational chorus dominates the song. Although it is closer to soft rock than heavy metal, it nevertheless harks back to previous albums in being almost a rewrite of 'Mystery,' and with the lyric 'last of a line' it also invokes a song from the previous album. Campbell even throws in a guitar lick that is virtually identical to one he used in 'Rainbow In The Dark.'

A different version of this song also made an appearance in the 1985 movie *Vision Quest* and on that film's soundtrack album (both released in February 1985). That version was produced by Ronnie Dio at Sound City studios in Los Angeles, and the mix is more commercial than the *Sacred Heart* version, with more pronounced keyboards. Dio revealed that he included it on the album as he didn't like the way the song was mixed for the *Vision Quest* soundtrack album, with too much compression and echo effects added, and that he 'didn't feel the song was going to be given the attention it needed on a compilation album.'[172]

'Like the Beat of a Heart,' written by Dio and Bain, can best be described as 'filler.' It's a generic, plodding rocker enlivened only by Campbell's inability to play a boring solo. This particular solo is replete with bends, pinch harmonics and dive bombs. The track features some backmasking which Ronnie Dio would later admit was an attempt to have some fun at the expense of critics of heavy metal music.[173]

'Just Another Day,' written by Dio and Campbell, is a frenetic hard rocker reminiscent of mid-1980s Judas Priest but with Campbell's guitar sounding more like it did in his Sweet Savage days. Bonutto praised the 'punch and pillage' of Campbell, Bain and Appice, and called the track 'confident and fleet of foot.'[174]

Sadly, the final tracks on the album are mainly filler. 'Fallen Angels' is the kind of generic hard rock that the likes of Cinderella, Poison, Ratt, Mötley Crüe and Twisted Sister were churning out in the mid-1980s. Nevertheless, Bonutto claimed the track 'leaps into action on the sort of guitar riff that has to explode into something special... and does.' Presumably, Bonutto was referring to the guitar solo which is another huge musical statement that Campbell had the skill and technique to compete with the sheer size of Ronnie Dio's powerful vocals.[175]

'Shoot Shoot' is a Sammy Hagar-like mid-tempo rocker that is passable except for Ronnie Dio's lyrics, which were really going stale at this point, and a weak chorus that is repeated far too often. Its chugging rhythm would be monotonous if not for some interesting chord choices from Campbell — a mixture of power chords and open chords punctuated by an occasion descending pick slide and tremolo chord bend. The solo features Campbell's characteristic fast picking, and he adds variety with natural and pinch harmonics as well as some tremolo effects.

## Album Reviews

*Sacred Heart* proved to be a divisive album: while fans appreciated the band's 'more of the same' approach, music critics gave mixed responses, and over time even Ronnie Dio appeared to change his opinion as to the album's merits. Initially, Dio claimed it was 'a bigger sounding album' than the two previous albums, and 'a natural progression. We're not Ratt,' he insisted, 'and we're not Twisted Sister. We pride ourselves on being very good musicians, crossing a line beyond just rehashing everything we've done before.'[176] A few years later, however, Dio admitted: 'In retrospect, I think that *Sacred Heart* sounds kind of hurried, kind of washed out. The truth is I was in a hurry to see the back of Vivian Campbell.'[177]

Of course, these comments have to be taken with a pinch of salt. Even if Dio did believe the *Sacred Heart* was below par, he would never admit that while he was promoting the album and forthcoming tour. When that time had passed, he could be franker about *Sacred Heart*'s shortcomings, as he perceived them: 'It was a disappointing album because it was made at a time of unrest and unhappiness. It wasn't played properly and therefore it wasn't productive... The songs were repetitive, as were the lyrics... it was an album I was doing all by myself.'[178]

There is a noticeable difference in critical reception of *Sacred Heart* on either side of the Atlantic, with North American critics generally offering more positive opinions than British. For example, *Circus* wrote: 'The emphasis on *Sacred Heart* is evenly divided between Dio's chrome-plated lungs and Vivian Campbell's searing leads. The music is out-and-out arena rock; the kind of scorching material that lends itself to audience participation.'[179] *RPM* wrote: 'Dio is superb with his latest work.' Appice, Bain, Campbell and Schnell 'combine with Dio to deliver their style of hard rock.'[180]

*Hit Parader* called the album 'a rocking, rolling collection of metal anthems that cements Dio's reputation as one of hard rock's premier proponents.'[181] *Billboard* gave the album a measured, positive review, describing the release as: 'Hard-driving, crash-and-burn rock that should prove more resistant to radio's recent metal backlash, thanks to the band's avoidance of the genre's more volatile lyric motifs; the playing, however, is typically blood-curdling.'[182]

The St. Petersburgh *Evening Independent* called *Sacred Heart* 'a more melodic record' than its predecessors, and predicted that, like *Holy Diver* and *The Last In Line,* it would go on to sell more than half a million copies each.[183] The *Toledo Blade* said the album's high points were the 'invigorating gallop' of 'King Of Rock And Roll,' the orchestral strings on 'Rock 'n' Roll Children,' and 'Hungry For Heaven,' which the *Blade* called Dio's 'most commercial sound yet.' The paper also praised Ronnie Dio's 'rich vocal prowess' on the album, which, it claimed, was 'frequently drowned out by the head-banging music.'[184]

In contrast to these North American reviews, *Kerrang!*'s Dave Dickson was less than impressed with *Sacred Heart,* and with Ronnie Dio in particular. As far as Dickson was concerned, *Sacred Heart* was more of the same from the band, with no musical progression since *Holy Diver*. Dickson claimed Ronnie Dio was 'locked in a perpetual Time-Warp circa 1970' and his lyrics had become repetitive and stale.

Dickson, however, was complimentary about Campbell's playing on the album, calling him 'quite exceptional,' and predicting Campbell would 'give all headbangers true tennis racket value for money.' In particular, Dickson singled out Campbell's performance on 'Just Another Day' and 'Fallen Angels' as 'staggering.' He concluded that Campbell was 'rapidly turning into a sensational guitarist of major stature!'[185]

*Kerrang!*'s Dante Bonutto also saw Campbell as a rising star, saying that his playing on *Sacred Heart* featured 'a lot of choice picking [with] long, lingering chords and fret-wearing forays.'[186]

UK pop-rock music magazine *Sounds* offered a mixed review of the album. Journalist Paul Elliott wrote: 'there's plenty of hammer on the new Dio album. *Sacred Heart* is a burst of fierce, unfettered power... Spirited stuff, for sure, but in truth not much more than a reworking of Ronnie's former glories, steeped in Seventies tradition, satisfying on a purely gut level but offering little surface evidence of any sizeable growth or development in his songwriting style.'[187]

**Singles**

'Rock 'n' Roll Children' was released in July 1985, coupled with 'The Last In Line,' which was recorded live in Philadelphia on August 25, 1984. The 12-inch single featured live performances of 'We Rock' and 'The Last In Line.' All artwork for the 7-inch and 12-inch singles replicated the crystal ball and dragon from the album, but without the hands holding the ball, nor the Latin inscription. While the 7-inch retained the original colour scheme, the 12-inch was rendered with a blue background.

A conceptual music video was created to promote the single. As with the video for 'The Last In Line,' it used the imagery from the album cover to build a narrative, in this case focusing on the crystal ball. Instead of the whole band, it features only Ronnie Dio playing the owner of a magic shop in which a young couple shelter from a sudden storm. They then enter a portal to another landscape wherein they experience visions of troubling episodes in their lives. In similar fashion to the 'The Last In Line' video, Dio helps the young protagonists escape. In both, he remains the centre of attention as a heroic and benevolent participant in events. This visually striking video, cost around $50-60,000 to produce, and helped the single reach number 26 in UK singles chart.[188]

The second single from the album, 'Hungry for Heaven,' was released in October 1985. The UK 7-inch release featured the studio version of 'King Of Rock And Roll' and the 12-inch included a live version of 'Like the Beat of a Heart' from Dio's September 13 concert in Philadelphia.

The cover art of the 7 and 12-inch singles is a band picture on stage set against a blue background. European releases of both the 7-inch and 12-inch singles featured a different cover image of Ronnie Dio with a different band picture relegated to the back cover. A performance music video was released to support the song, which reached number 72 in UK singles chart.

## Sacred Heart Tour, 1985-1986

*Sacred Heart* sold well, and critical reaction was mainly positive, although there was some criticism that the band had failed to evolve or grow. In addition, some jokes were being made at Ronnie Dio's expense about the repetitiveness of his lyrics. Nevertheless, the band remained a major box office draw, and it soon set out on what was meant to be an 80-date, five-month-long world tour to support and promote the album. In fact, the tour lasted from August 1985 until October 1986 and the band played over 150 gigs — albeit not with the same line-up.

The *Sacred Heart* tour began on August 10, 1985, when Dio performed at the Super Rock Festival in Tokyo. (Also on the bill were Mama's Boys from Northern Ireland.) Each band at the festival performed a much-shortened set than usual, and Dio's consisted of just three tracks: 'King Of Rock And Roll,' 'The Last In Line,' and 'Holy Diver' — one from each studio album. A few days later, the North American leg of the tour began, and thereafter Dio played around 90 gigs in cities across the US and Canada, ending on January 12, 1986, with a gig in Honolulu.

Allowing for a 3-week break in the run up to Christmas, this itinerary averages around five gigs per week, so this was a tough schedule to maintain, but it needed to be that extensive to ensure it generated enough profit to break even. Most of the arenas had capacities between 10 to 20 thousand, although some smaller arenas were also included.

As with album cover art, Ronnie Dio had full control over the tour's stage design and on this occasion, he decided to link the album art with the stage design by introducing a 18-foot tall, fire-breathing dragon into the set. It would also feature a 60 by 40-foot castle, moat and drawbridge, two eight-foot battling knights armed with lasers, a six-foot crystal ball displaying holographic images, a back lit panel displaying fierce-looking flying lizards, and all the usual sound and lighting pyrotechnics and effects familiar to and increasingly expected by rock fans.

Dio estimated the set would costs around $200,000 and all other overheads would amount to $5 million, which meant that the tour would have to earn $250,000 per week just to break even. Dio justified this extravagance and cost, saying: 'I try to give back to the kids some of what they give me; I want them to get value for their money. And… I want this band to be a legend. It's money well spent.'[189] However, these financial considerations also exacerbated some divisions within the band, and by the end of the tour Dio had fired Campbell over a long-standing financial dispute.

Of the new stage design, Campbell said: 'It is a very huge, expensive production, but I don't think that there is anything there that will take the audience's attention away from us for too long. We still have to stay on our toes. In the one and a half hours that we're on the stage, there's plenty of time to check out the dragon, the knights, the backdrops and still hear us make mistakes. So, we don't think of the theatrics as a distraction, but rather as an enhancement.'[190]

Campbell was being ironic about the band's 'mistakes,' but he admitted he still had a lot to learn. He explained: 'I realised last tour that I really wasn't playing as well as I could. I saw other guitarists play like Dokken's George Lynch and I wanted to improve my technique. Playing every night is very helpful to me because I can experiment with new ideas and new sounds.' Campbell hoped that by learning to play guitar 'properly,' as he described it, his playing would be 'faster and cleaner' on this tour.[191]

He also made some changes to his usual live set up for the *Sacred Heart* tour. For instance, he set aside his beloved Gibson Les Paul for a Charvel strat-type custom guitar with a Floyd Rose tremolo and a single Charvel humbucking pickup. He also used a Steinberger GL-2 guitar with a Steinberger transposing tremolo. On both, Campbell used Black Diamond strings.[192]

Campbell explained: 'I had tried steel-wrapped, solid brass-wrapped, gold-plated and a whole bunch of different types of strings and I couldn't find much difference in sound among any of them. It was a matter of durability, so I still use Black Diamond custom strings because I find them the most comfortable.'[193]

As it turned out, reviewers would be divided not so much about Campbell's playing or his choice of equipment but instead about the scale of the stage design and how the music was presented. For instance, a *Circus* reviewer who attended the gig on October 27, 1985, at the Meadowland Arena, East Rutherford, New Jersey, called the *Sacred Heart* tour an 'extravaganza, an hour-and-a-half plus pyrotechnical circus,' a 'fast-paced show that featured some of the finest special effects this side of George Lucas' Star Wars.'[194]

However, a different view came from Martin Morrow of the *Calgary Herald*, who attended the gig on January 4, 1986, at the Stampede Corral venue in Calgary, Alberta. While impressed by the stage effects, he thought at times the band was 'dwarfed by this awesome backdrop, and played second fiddle to the proliferation of fireworks, fire-spouting torches and laser beams.' Morrow admitted, though, that when the music emerged 'it proved primitive and effective.'[195]

The show began with a darkened stage and dry ice before Dio's mechanical dragon appeared, belching smoke. An explosion was the signal for the band to appear on stage. Appice's 360-degree drum set sat atop the stage set castle, while Schnell was positioned on a parapet. Campbell, Dio, and Bain appeared on the stage proper, with Dio positioning himself in front of the castle's laser-lit entrance. Bain was situated on Dio's left and Campbell to the vocalist's right. At one point, lasers encased Ronnie Dio in a pyramid of emerald light, while the backdrop screen changed to an image of a horned, red-eyed creature (probably Murray making a guest appearance).

Before the tour began, Ronnie Dio was asked how he might adjust his setlist given he now had three original albums of material to draw from, and which of the 'oldies' would have to be cast aside. Dio responded: 'we'll probably have shortened versions of a lot of the material. Heaven And Hell won't be as long as it was before.'[196]

This turned out to be the case. In addition, the band played medleys of songs to ensure there was space for crowd favourites and to ensure the show did not overrun. The set list for the East Rutherford gig was:

> King Of Rock And Roll
> Like The Beat Of A Heart
> Don't Talk To Strangers
> Hungry For Heaven
> The Last In Line/Holy Diver
> Drum Solo
> Heaven And Hell
> Guitar solo & keyboard solo
> Sacred Heart
> Rock 'n' Roll Children/Long Live Rock 'n' Roll/
> Man On  The Silver Mountain
> Stand Up And Shout
> Rainbow In The Dark
> We Rock

That amounts to just four tracks from *Sacred Heart*, the album the tour was meant to both represent and promote, as well as three from Ronnie

Dio's stints in Rainbow and Black Sabbath. While any setlist has to strike a balance between promoting a new album and playing hits and crowd-pleasers, Ronnie Dio's heavy reliance on pre-Dio band songs does indicate how he viewed the band and his place in it.

In contemporary interviews he was quick to praise bandmates: for example, he told *Hit Parader*: 'I'm just the singer in the band. I have people like Vivian Campbell... kicking me in the ass every night onstage.'[197] Perhaps that was genuine praise, but in every other respect Ronnie Dio considered his rock pedigree as the band's main selling point. This was Ronnie Dio's band, and despite Campbell going along with this arrangement up until now, Dio's total control over every aspect of the band, including — crucially — its finances, would soon bring the first iteration of the Dio band to an end.

Immediately preceding Campbell's solo at East Rutherford, one of the two mechanical knights emerged from a castle turret awaiting battle. While Campbell performed, laser light beams danced around him. At the end, a purple oval disc ascended upon which an image of Ronnie Dio appeared to announce the next song, 'Sacred Heart.' The dragon reappeared, and a second mechanical knight emerged. While Ronnie Dio 'fought' the dragon with a prop sword, the two knights brandished their weapons to fire laser beams at each other, which emanated from crowns each wore. During 'Stand Up and Shout,' medieval-design pennants descended from the rafters, and the end of the performance was signalled by a pyrotechnics display. The band would return for two encores, the first being 'Rainbow In The Dark' and the finale was a frenetic performance of 'We Rock.'[198]

The following month, on September 22, Dio performed at the Pittsburgh Civic Arena to an audience of 6,591 fans. A newspaper gig review indicates that the setlist remained unchanged. Reviewer Pete Bishop was unimpressed with support band Rough Cutt, whose brand of heavy metal he considered overpowering, but he praised the melodic nature of Dio songs such as 'Hungry For Heaven,' 'Sacred Heart,' 'Rainbow In The Dark,' as well as 'Man On The Silver Mountain,' all of which, Bishop claimed, 'blended muscle, melody and musicianship well.' As for Campbell, Bishop thought he was 'obnoxiously macho at times,' but that his playing 'added a lot' to 'Hungry For Heaven' and The Last In Line.'[199]

Reviews of the concerts on October 23 at the 6,500-capacity Sports Arena in Toledo, Ohio, and on December 7, at the Inglewood Forum in Los Angeles, focused mainly on the stage set and effects. Ralph Kisiel of the *Toledo Blade* called the local gig 'one of the most colossal theatrical concerts in recent memory' and 'one of rock's most lavish theatrical spectacles,' whereas *Billboard*'s Ethlie Ann Vark called the LA gig 'an elaborate, effects-laden production with plenty of speed-freak guitar solos, klaxon vocals and Gothic overtones. When Dio puts on a show, the kitchen sink is the least of what you get,' Vark insisted.[200]

As for the music, Kisiel described it as 'bone-jarring' but 'several notches above conventional heavy-metal fare. It's a sort of sophisticated heavy metal,' said Kisiel, 'the customary thundering volume and booming beat is there, but Dio's songs are more complex and carefully crafted than those generic, simplistic arena anthems that bands like Mötley Crüe are so fond of.' Vark praised the 'melodic crunch' of 'King Of Rock 'n' Roll,' 'The Last In Line,' 'Sacred Heart' and 'Rock 'n' Roll Children,' and noted the 'us against them' theme of some of this material, which connected effectively to the 'camaraderie of headbangers.' Vark pointed to 'Hungry For Heaven' as the anomaly on the set list because of its blatant commerciality. 'Fans ate it up,' Vark noticed, especially Campbell's 'requisite guitar solos.'

In late December, Dio played three gigs in the Pacific Northwest, including one in Spokane, Washington on December 30. The gig at the Coliseum included the full stage set-up, impressing newspaper reviewer Clay Hutto, who attributed such lavish designs to the influence of music channel MTV and the increasing prevalence of elaborate and expensive music videos. 'With such theatricality, who needs music?' Hutto asked. 'But music there was. Or at least screeching guitars, thundering drums and the piercing wail of lead singer Ronnie James Dio.'[201]

Dio played their final gig of 1985 on New Year's Eve at the Coliseum in Seattle, with five more scheduled in early January 1986 in Canada and the United States. This leg of the tour ended on January 12 in Honolulu, Hawaii with a gig at the Blaisdell Centre, a 7,800-capacity arena situated between Downtown and Waikiki Beach, with Punchbowl Crater to the north and beaches and leisure facilities to the south. This was meant only to be the final gig of the North American leg of the tour, but it also turned out to be Campbell's last concert with Dio.

Taking stock, Campbell had travelled many thousands of miles with Dio on a musical journey that had led him from rock clubs in Belfast to exotic Hawaii. During that time, he cemented his reputation as a professional musician and an exceptional guitarist. For example, *Hit Parader*'s Andy Secher claimed that Campbell's playing 'led the way' in creating a 'sonic fury' not found on Dio's studio versions. In Secher's view, Campbell's lead playing, in particular, 'proved he may be the most underrated six-string master on the rock scene.'[202]

**Leaving Dio**

In the break between the North American and European legs of the *Sacred Heart* tour, Dio and Campbell parted ways. The circumstances of that split remain unclear, despite the main protagonists openly talking about it in the music press. Initially, Ronnie Dio claimed that Campbell quit the band, whereas Campbell has always claimed he was fired. The issues that caused the schism between the two men seemed to concern creative differences and financial arrangements. Ronnie Dio accused Campbell of losing interest in the band, and of attempting to form his own. What irked Ronnie the most was that Campbell was working with other musicians while he was still in Dio. Ronnie claimed that Campbell told him he didn't want to be a 'guitar hero' any more and wanted to explore new sounds. Secondary issues, according to Ronnie Dio, were accusations of unprofessionalism, for example, being out-of-tune, and how Campbell presented himself, which Ronnie maintained was not in keeping with the band's image.

Campbell's main complaint concerned his financial situation and role in the band. Campbell claimed Ronnie Dio had broken a promise made when they first met in London that by the time of the band's third album a more equitable arrangement would be put in place. This was mainly a financial arrangement: Dio had the name recognition and would part-fund the band to get it off the ground, and his wife Wendy would act as band manager. However, Campbell's understanding was that band members would have more say in the writing process and the musical decision-making. In addition, Campbell explained that neither he nor Appice were happy when Ronnie Dio decided to make more use of keyboards, which meant giving Claude Schnell a bigger role in the band. Campbell also accused Dio's management company, Niji, which was run by Wendy Dio, of promoting Ronnie Dio's interests over that of the band, and of interfering in the band's musical decisions.

Things got complicated when Ronnie Dio made counter claims that he wasn't keen on using keyboards and that he only agreed to the recording and release of more radio-friendly tracks like 'Mystery' and 'Rock 'n' Roll Children' due to band pressure to go in a more commercial direction. Campbell and Ronnie spoke openly about these claims and counterclaims, and a public feud soon developed. Even the circumstances and timing of the split are contested: Campbell claimed he never quit the band and instead was offered a contract in March 1986 that he couldn't sign. When he failed to do so, Niji informed him he was fired.[203]

However, Ronnie Dio claimed that he and Campbell had heated words at the end of the US tour and it was then that he told Campbell he was fired.[204] A few months after Campbell and Dio parted company, Campbell said: 'I can't say that I didn't see it coming, but I really didn't expect it when it happened. Relations with Ronnie and Niji were never good at any time. I was constantly looking over my shoulder, and it was the same with everyone in the band. We were always treated like second class citizens.'[205]

In April 1986 UK rock magazine *Kerrang!* was the first to break the news that Campbell and Dio had parted company. It wasn't until the follow-up issue, however, that the first public explanation for the break-up came, and it was Campbell who spoke first.[206]

Campbell was, however, wary of revealing too much because Niji and UK record label Vertigo had yet to issue an announcement. Campbell told Dante Bonutto that he was prepared to respond to any statement, if necessary, but in the meantime, he didn't want to become involved in public mudslinging. Campbell's careful response showed a level of maturity and business nous: it wouldn't be the smartest approach at this point in his musical career to allow himself to be painted as a troublemaker or band wrecker, especially when so many Dio fans would be confused and hurt by the demise of the original line-up.

While in later years Campbell would point to a broken promise from Ronnie Dio about more equity in the band, Campbell's first public response cited personal issues between he and Dio, together with his inability to fully express his musical ideas within the Dio band framework. Campbell told Bonutto that he had been 'suppressed as a musician' while working with Ronnie Dio, mainly because Dio wrote mainly with Jimmy Bain. 'I don't write well with Ronnie, I write for him,' he revealed. 'Dio was just highly restrictive for me [because] it's absolutely Ronnie's project, 100 per cent. He's very set in his ways and that meant the band wasn't very forward-thinking.'

Soon after, Sal Treppedi of *The Hard Report* spoke with Campbell, providing this summary of the conversation: 'According to Campbell, it had nothing to do with his playing. It was apparently a personality clash between Campbell and Ronnie... Later, it spread to him also clashing with Wendy Dio. The problems allegedly started several months after Campbell joined the band. But he stuck with it thinking that the situation could be patched up. When he realised it could not be, he left.'[207]

Campbell admitted that due to Dio's restrictive nature he had been writing and demoing new material with a friend from Belfast who was living in Los Angeles. Campbell's intent was to work with this friend if the Dio band came to an end. While perhaps innocent in intent, Campbell's work outside Dio did widen a crack between he and Ronnie, and it was perhaps naïve of Campbell to think otherwise. In public, at least, he remained phlegmatic about events: 'I'm not upset in the least by what's happened, I'm a firm believer in fate,' he explained. 'I don't need the grief and I don't need the paycheque!'

According to Bonutto, however, the split was not as amicable as

Campbell suggested. His read on the situation, after speaking to both musicians, was that some hostility had arisen: 'to say they parted on good terms might be stretching things a bit — in fact, quite a lot.'[208]

An interview Campbell gave in the early days of the band supports this version of events. Campbell said: 'In Sweet Savage I was in charge. I formed the band after I left school, myself and the bass player were the two men who made the decisions, whereas in Dio because I'm the most unknown, I don't generally say a lot. Ronnie makes most of the decisions, I don't resent it either, he has the experience. It's strange coming from a band that is virtually unknown, it's a hell of a leap like cold to hot, it takes a lot of getting used to. The band works really well, unlike a lot of bands I've seen where there has been a lot of tension. So far it works but maybe in five years it'll be a lot different.'[209]

These remarks make clear that Campbell knew he was the 'new guy' and that Ronnie Dio's pedigree was the band's main selling point at that time. Campbell was happy to accept this arrangement, but his remark about how this might change over time suggests some agreement or arrangement was in place at an early stage that Ronnie Dio's total control over the band would diminish over time. His seemingly throwaway mention of five years might actually be an informed guess as to how long it would take the band to reach their third album, which was the point, he later explained, that Ronnie promised a more equitable arrangement between band members would be negotiated.

In later years Campbell provided more details of the financial and equity situation he claimed was agreed when the band first got together: 'That night in London in that rehearsal room… Ronnie sat us down and said, "Here's the plan. This is what we're gonna do." He had promised us all that by the third record, it would be an equity situation, because, basically, we had to work for next to nothing for the earlier records. We earned less than the crew. So, we didn't get any of those… t-shirts [sales], we got none of the ticket sales, we got none of the record sales. But we were working towards that promise which was by the third album it would be an equity situation.'[210]

In retrospect, it seems Ronnie Dio knew during or soon after the recording of *Sacred Heart* and its release in August 1985, that Campbell would no longer be part of the band. In an interview published in *Sounds* that month, he seemed to be preparing the ground for an announcement about Campbell being fired. In the interview he defended his prime position in the band, telling journalist Paul Elliott 'I think I've grown as a writer... in Dio you can see how important my part is. Take Ronnie Dio away and they're not such strong songs anymore.'[211] He rejected the notion that he was responsible for increasing the use of keyboards in the band's music, saying: 'I've not allowed Claude to play with the expertise he has. He's had to play the way I play — like a one-fingered typist. It must be very boring for Claude, but that's the conception of this band. We are not keyboard-orientated.'[212]

Then he made a cryptic comment about Campbell, answering a question that Elliott had not asked. Dio explained, 'I may be the producer and leader of the band, but when I'm on stage, I'm only the vocalist — and if I don't do my job as well as the guitar player, then I've failed. That's why we don't change personnel. We're very happy with each other, and when the time comes when we are dissatisfied, we'll change, but it won't be because Ronnie feels threatened by the success of Vivian Campbell.'

Finally, he provided a less than subtly reminder that he was responsible for giving Campbell his first big break as an internationally well-known and recognised guitarist. 'I don't feel threatened,' he said. 'I feel that I've accomplished my purpose, which was to make each individual in the band an individual star.'[213] In fact, Bain and Appice were already well-known musicians before Dio, and it was only Campbell who was relatively unknown.

Soon after the split was announced, Dio claimed to have spoken to Campbell personally to let him know he was fired, and to explain why. He revealed: 'I had my talk with Vivian — my shout with Vivian — and he may not understand it to this day, but the band has to survive over the whims of one person. I felt Vivian's attitude was wrong, that he didn't care enough about this band, and this band is the only thing I do care about. It's my child and I'm not going to let anyone hurt my child.'[214]

In other contemporary interviews Ronnie gave further examples of how he felt let down by Campbell. He revealed, for example: 'By the second album I could see the shift in personality. After one album I felt he thought he knew more than anyone else... by the third album I found him almost completely non-productive.'[215]

Dio also claimed that when Campbell began working with outside musicians, it resulted in the guitarist having less to contribute to the Dio band. Ronnie claimed, for example, that when it came time to begin work on *Sacred Heart* he asked Campbell: 'We've had four months off, what've you got Viv?,' to which Campbell allegedly replied 'Oh Nothing.'[216] From Ronnie's perspective, his claim that it had become 'a challenge just to motivate [Campbell] to work' may have had some validity.[217]

On the other hand, Campbell had concerns that the band had reached a dead end; worst still, there was some evidence that Ronnie was losing interest in his creation. In post *Sacred Heart* album release interviews,

Dio talked of the band taking some time off to explore solo projects and collaborations. He wanted the other members of the band to do so as well: 'we need to take a little time away from each other,' he admitted. When asked if he had taken Dio's style of music as far as it could go, he admitted that 'might well be true.' He talked about trying to avoid 'being one-dimensional' and investigating 'new frontiers to explore,' like film or being a music producer for a band like Judas Priest. He claimed to be still committed to the Dio band but planned to take some time off to assess the situation.[218]

It's reasonable to assume that Campbell had concerns about the band's future and of Ronnie's commitment to the music they were making. If Ronnie took a hiatus or even broke up the band, he would have left with his name and reputation intact, and also with most of the profits from the band. However, Campbell was financially insecure and unable to weather an extended period of time when he was not earning. If the band were to split, he would have left it with an enhanced reputation but very little of Dio's past, present, or future earnings.

Members of the band also offered their views on the Campbell-Dio split, and their responses indicate a great deal of support for Campbell's position and some unhappiness about how he was treated. The outlier was Vinny Appice, who basically repeated the official line that Ronnie Dio told the press, that Campbell was to blame. In a June 1986 interview, Appice said: 'Vivian had been wanting to play other types of music, to form his own band — and to be in Dio at the same time. But it got to the point where it seemed like he wasn't interested in Dio anymore... Ronnie was dissatisfied with his attitude, we all discussed it — it seemed like the best thing to do was for him to go his own way, and us to go ours.' When asked if it was an amicable split, Appice replied 'Yeah, well — sorta... we're still friends.'[219]

Appice, however, may have felt unable to contradict Dio's official press line. He had been friends with Ronnie since their time together in Black Sabbath: Ronnie even referred to him as his best friend in the Dio band. Aside from that, though, Appice could not afford to upset Ronnie or Wendy since he remained financially reliant upon them.

In 2017, Appice finally revealed what really happened. First, he confirmed Campbell's version of events regarding the broken promise of a more equitable share. 'But then it never happened' he explained. 'We were doing tours in arenas. Back then, one of the tours grossed eight million dollars — that's probably eighty million dollars [in today's money]. But we got nothing out of it — [we only got] salaries... Vivian... called [Ronnie] on it, so that kind of became bad blood with Ronnie. But we all felt the same way — that we're not getting what we were promised and we should be doing better than we're doing. Somebody's making a lot of money here, and it wasn't us.'[220]

Claude Schnell also commented on Appice's financial relationship with Ronnie, while noting that he also felt he was underpaid whilst keyboardist in the band: 'For as much as I was led to believe that what I would get [paid] early on and didn't, as frustrated as I was about it, I found my solace when I found out what Vinny was promised. So as bad as I felt about not getting whatever it was in terms of money, I could only imagine being in Vinny Appice's shoes being promised the world and not getting it. The people who usually speak up the most are the people who have the least to lose.'[221]

Schnell and Bain offer a different perspective to that of Ronnie and Vinny's initial public statements, one more supportive of Campbell. For example, in a 2012 *Metal Hammer* interview, Bain defended Campbell, saying, 'Viv did nothing that warranted his removal from [Dio] in what is still considered to be a cowardly way. For me, firing Viv was the biggest mistake of Ronnie's career.' He thought the issues between the two men could easily have been resolved if Ronnie and Wendy had the will to do so.'[222] For instance, Bain mainly blamed Wendy Dio for the problems in the band, claiming that she was always 'murmuring in [Ronnie's] ear' when he was with Rainbow about leaving the band.

Furthermore, he confirmed Campbell's assertion that when Dio was formed the plan was to split the money equally among band members by the time of the third album. Bain, however, began to worry as soon as everyone met up in Los Angeles and Wendy appeared on the scene as the band's manager. 'I could tell it was all about her and him and fuck everybody else,' Bain recalled.[223] Bain thought Ronnie's unilateral decision to name the band after himself was indicative of the problems to come: 'I thought it was a shit name. I'd rather they had called the band The Carpets than Dio.'

Wendy Dio, however, defended that choice. It was Ronnie whose name was on the record contract, she said, and the rest of the band were therefore rewarded with terms less favourable than he. This was due to the name recognition he had from his success with Rainbow and Sabbath, whereas the others were less well-known (especially Campbell) before Ronnie recruited them.

As for the band's financial situation, Wendy revealed that Rainbow had been financially unrewarding, whereas Dio's stint with Sabbath was more lucrative. Ronnie and Wendy bought a house with that Sabbath money but then had to remortgage in order to finance Dio's solo career.[224] From Ronnie and Wendy Dio's perspective, the band's financial arrangements may therefore have seemed fair and reasonable.

Even if Ronnie had been open to any renegotiation of financial terms, Wendy Dio certainly was not. In a 2011 magazine article, she made clear that it was her and not Ronnie who made the final decision about Campbell's future with Dio: 'Ronnie didn't fire him. I fired him,' she said.[225] This is an important revelation: Wendy has never publicly discussed the deal Ronnie made with the band. In fact, Campbell claimed Ronnie had never even told her about it but didn't have the courage to stand against her because they had recently split up and Ronnie hoped for a reconciliation. Campbell claimed that because Wendy wasn't a musician and didn't understand band dynamics or the creative process, she didn't appreciate the value of Campbell, Bain and Appice. For her, Dio was the star and the main marketing asset, and the others were simply hired hands. For that reason, it's likely that even if she had been aware of the previous verbal agreement she would not have treated Campbell any differently.[226]

In 2018, many years after he parted company with Dio, Claude Schnell helped clear up why Ronnie Dio earned as much as he did from publishing, leaving the others feeling short-changed: 'when it comes to the rights of a song they are based entirely on two things, the melodies and the lyrics. I think and suspect because Ronnie got the short end of the stick in much of the Rainbow credits as well as possibly Sabbath, the omnipresence of Ronnie James Dio on all lyrics and melodies by him was to get it out of the way that it was his project, every word, every note and it was his own band Dio. Ronnie wrote the lyrics and the melodies and as far as the music went everyone in the band would contribute. Most of that stuff qualifies as arrangement.'[227]

Of course, while that makes a certain kind of sense from Ronnie's perspective, it wasn't a tenable strategy to keep everyone in his band happy. If Schnell is correct about Ronnie's motives, it also suggests Ronnie never had any intention of keeping his promise of an equitable band structure.

While Schnell mainly blamed Wendy Dio, he also found fault with Ronnie, claiming that the singer considered musicians in L.A. bands as 'interchangeable parts of a jigsaw puzzle' who would lose their income if they tried to 'stir shit or make waves.' That was Campbell's main issue, Schnell explained. Vivian was not from L.A. and 'came from a wealthy family,' so he was the one in the band most likely to speak out about the band's financial arrangements and to hold Ronnie to his word about equity.

Schnell accused Wendy Dio of wanting to replace Campbell with Craig Goldy, a guitarist she managed when he was in the band Rough Cutt. The inference was that Wendy could get rid of Campbell and replace him with Goldy using the same contractual terms that Appice, Bain, Schnell and Campbell found so galling. Schnell revealed, 'we all felt that Vivian was treated very badly, not so much by Ronnie but it was obvious those decisions were being handled by Wendy Dio. Vivian was basically set up and he was put in a position where the only thing he could do was the exact thing that would get him kicked out of the band. When it came to pass, Wendy was trying to get Craig into the band and Vivian got unceremoniously let go… for no real fault of his own.'[228]

It seems clear, in retrospect, that despite whatever verbal arrangements Dio had made with Campbell and the others, both he and Wendy arguably envisioned the band as a solo project with Ronnie Dio being supported by a backing band of hired guns. The template for this was Sharon Arden-Osbourne's management of her husband Ozzy Osbourne's career. Sharon promoted the artist's solo identity, first by changing the proposed name of his new band from 'Blizzard of Oz' to just 'Ozzy Osbourne.' With this arrangement, the brand name made Osbourne the star while relegating his supporting musicians to a replaceable backing band.

In fact, guitarists such as Randy Rhoads and Jake E. Lee were a significant factor in Ozzy's success. Both had distinctive guitar styles, and both helped write Osbourne's music and provide lyrics which were, at the time, uncredited to them. This meant Osbourne received all royalties and publishing rights, plus the lion's share of touring income and merchandise. The same situation arose for bassist Bob Daisley and drummer Lee Kerslake, with a series of legal battles later ensuing. It appears Daisley, Kerslake and Lee were fired from the band when they asserted their rights, while Rhoads planned to leave the band but died in a plane crash before that could happen.[229]

While this seemed to be the type of arrangement that Wendy Dio had in mind for her husband, there was, however, another more personal reason why Ronnie Dio positioned himself as band leader. As Bain pointed out, both Rainbow and Sabbath were led by influential guitarists with strong reputations, and Ronnie Dio wouldn't accept that situation in his own band.[230] He, in fact, chose an unknown player from an obscure Belfast band which had failed to win a record contract. Given that, it's possible Ronnie wanted the guitarist in his band to feel more insecure and therefore less assertive than were Blackmore and Iommi — two towering figures in hard rock history.

It was these financial and creative arrangements that drove Campbell and Dio apart. In early 1986, before the start of the European leg of the *Sacred Heart* tour, Wendy Dio demanded that band members sign new contracts on the same terms as before. Appice and Bain — despite their unhappiness — agreed to do so as they were in no financial position to walk away. Campbell, however, declined to sign, knowing full well that meant he was out of the band.

In later years, Campbell put the blame more on Wendy than he did Ronnie. The reason he was fired, Campbell claimed, was that he refused to accept a contract that was 'contrary to the original agreement Ronnie had made with Jimmy, Vinny and myself when the band was first formed. Wendy had different ideas for how it was going to be… The original Dio band was a four-piece creative unit and Wendy never understood that. She's not musical. So, Ronnie and I, I think would have been fine. She doesn't know that the sign of a great band is the sum of the parts.'[231]

In the immediate aftermath of the split, both parties were careful not to take part in a public spat or make nasty *ad hominem* attacks. This didn't last long, however, with Ronnie Dio soon making some snide comments to music journalists that found their way to the ears of Campbell, who responded in turn. One of the difficulties of untangling what went on is that there is some degree of contradiction in public statements, so some 'reading between the lines' is required to unpack why the split soon turned nasty.

Further obfuscation comes from whether comments were made at the time or made much later after memories and personal loyalties had faded, and financial circumstances changed. For example, it was a combination of those circumstances that initially caused both and Appice and Schnell to publicly support Ronnie Dio's version of events, while privately agreeing with Campbell. Both lent support to Campbell's version of events only after Ronnie Dio passed away.

Moreover, it's questionable as to how much credence should be given to secondary rather than primary sources: for example, Craig Goldy wasn't present at the events which led to Campbell's exit, yet he was Campbell's replacement and of course heard all the stories from people who were there. Goldy came to the conclusion that to 'piss Ronnie off to the point where he fires you, you've gotta be pretty insulting. So something must have gone down.'[232]

Then again, Goldy owed his break to Wendy and Ronnie and remained loyal to them: besides, as a number of commentators including Campbell have attested to, Dio was mercurial — at times jovial and friendly, but also on occasion in a very dark mood, so perhaps Goldy only saw Ronnie's good side, at least up until the time in 1988 when Goldy himself was fired by Ronnie over nebulous musical differences.

In August 1985, Dio told *Kerrang!*: 'I'm happy with the people in my band. I chose them very carefully and when this group dissolves we'll part as friends, I insist on that, because I don't want to lose contact with people who I care so much about.'[233]

There was probably a degree of truth to Ronnie's intentions. He had, after all, left two previous bands in contentious circumstances and with much public feuding. Yet, he admitted that he regretted the very public spat he had with members of Black Sabbath, in particular, that it had upset him, and he maintained that he 'loved' those involved. Indeed, he would later team up once more with Tony Iommi and Geezer Butler for a new album and to form a new iteration of the band called Heaven and Hell. There was never a reconciliation with Campbell, although in the late 1980s some comments from Dio suggested he was open to the idea.

First, however, was the 'Cold War,' with Dio providing the opening salvo. By September of 1986, Dio had hardened his stance considerably. According to him, Campbell 'wasn't good enough' to be in the Dio band anymore. 'He started reading his own press notices, he was always out of tune and he just stood there on stage like one of the Thompson Twins. He made my life miserable. He didn't want to be a guitar hero anymore, if he ever was one. The rest of the band felt we should finish the last five months of the tour and then deal with Vivian. But I can't perform or even be around someone who makes me feel the way I feel about him. In retrospect, it was a very easy decision. The comments I've been hearing about Craig is that he blows Vivian into the weeds.'[234]

By 1987, Dio was claiming that Campbell 'lost respect' for the band and had come to believe that he was the sole reason for its success. He said: 'You can't justify having such an over-inflated ego that you relegate those around you to second class citizen status, but that's largely what Viv did to the rest of the guys.'[235]

Also that year, Dio claimed that Campbell admitted he didn't 'want to play heavy metal anymore,' and reiterated that Campbell's ego 'just got too big for his own head.' Dio asked, sarcastically, 'Is he still off playing Irish disco music or has he come to his senses? It's a shame what happened to him.'[236]

In a January 1988 interview, Dio then attempted to write Craig Goldy and Campbell out of the creative history of the band. Perhaps in response to a difference of opinion he was having with Goldy at that time, which would lead to Goldy departing Dio in August of that year, Ronnie was asked about the impact the guitarist had on Dio's sound. He replied: 'I don't think it's possible for any one person to have that big an impact on our sound. In fact, I'll go so far to say that no one can alter our sound. That sound is created by Jimmy Bain, Vinny Appice and myself, and it has been that way for a long time.'[237]

Dio was asked in that same January 1988 interview how he felt about Campbell joining Whitesnake. His response was a carefully-calculated, cold dagger to the heart. 'I'm quite pleased for him' Dio said. 'I hope he's had the chance to sit back and think about his own values. What I find a bit strange is that after his harsh words about Craig coming in and playing his parts, he is now in the identical position with Whitesnake. Not only does he have to play John Sykes' guitar parts, he has to share them with Adrian Vandenberg. But I only wish Vivian the best, because I really respect the other members of that band. David Coverdale is a disciple of Ritchie Blackmore's, just as I am, and Adrian is a great guy.'

Note, Dio said Adrian is a great guy, not Vivian. Despite these remarks, Dio claimed he had no 'hard feelings' towards Campbell.[238] In fact, and to Dio's credit, when Coverdale approached him at a rehearsal in early 1987 to — in the words of Dave Ling — 'find out if there was any dirt on Vivian that he should know about,' Dio declined the opportunity to disparage Campbell and to sabotage his opportunity to join Whitesnake.[239]

For a time, soon after Goldy and Dio went their separate ways and just after Dio chose a teenage guitarist from England called Rowan Robertson to fill Goldy's shoes, Dio made some conciliatory remarks about Campbell that suggested he was open to a *rapprochement*. He explained that while he and Appice were listening to audition tapes to replace Goldy, they were disappointed: 'we knew best of all what Dio needed,' Dio explained. 'When we heard Viv Campbell play for the first time, we knew instantly: That's it. Except that we hadn't heard a single Viv amongst all the applicants.'[240] These were the first kind words Dio had uttered in public since the split.

Moreover, Dio revealed that when auditions first began, Campbell's name came up. Campbell had just left Whitesnake and Dio confessed that the idea of a reunion was 'interesting.' He contemplated that 'under the right circumstances' it would even have been worth a try to get Campbell back onboard, although he confessed that he wasn't sure 'whether we would have all been happy in the long run.'

Dio also admitted that Campbell probably would have considered it a step backwards to work with him again.[241] Dio also acknowledged that during the *Sacred Heart* period there were 'many problems with the band,' mainly due to Campbell's 'inability or unwillingness to work the way everyone else wanted to,' but this was the first time Dio acknowledged that Campbell wasn't solely responsible for events, hinting that some of the rumours about others being unhappy, including himself, may have some substance after all.[242]

By 1989, Dio's criticism of Campbell had even become more conciliatory, and the language he used was less harsh. Dio said 'the band threatened to split up on *Sacred Heart*. The balance between Viv and us just wasn't right any more, so the LP wasn't a development on *The Last In Line*.' It's possible to read too much into these comments. Dio had perhaps begun to realise that with Craig Goldy leaving, rediscovering the magic of the Campbell years wasn't going to be easy. However, after Dio hired Rowan Robertson, he declared: 'The good feeling is back, just like it was with Viv, when Dio was a perfectly functioning unit.'[243]

Unfortunately, over the years the feud between the two men escalated instead of receding. In a 2003 interview posted first on the official Def Leppard website, Campbell called Dio 'an incredible talent... But he's an awful businessman and way more importantly, one of the vilest people in the industry.'[244]

In return, and clearly hurt and angry about Campbell's comments, Dio was filmed in 2007 signing autographs after a Heaven and Hell gig at the Radio City Music Hall in New York, whereupon someone in the crowd asked him about Campbell's remarks. Dio responded: 'I hope he fucking dies,' calling Campbell 'a fucking asshole' and 'a piece of shit.'[245]

Grim stuff indeed, However, many years later, and after Ronnie Dio's untimely and very sad demise, Campbell revealed that he regretted the public slanging match. 'I got sucked into making the mistake of saying shit about Ronnie because he was saying shit about me. I'm sure that if Ronnie were still alive, he'd say he regrets that also. No one benefits from that situation.'[246]

Campbell, however, is at peace with his decision to challenge Ronnie Dio to uphold his end of the agreement they made on that first night in London. In a 2017 interview for a Northern Irish radio station, Campbell explained: 'The business side of it didn't work out so well... [But] It wasn't about money, it was about principle. I'm very big on principle. I believe when somebody shakes your hand, looks in the eye and you make it agreement you have an agreement and when people start reneging on agreements, I have an issue with that. I was a squeaky wheel because I wasn't married, didn't have a mortgage. I had nothing to lose. I'm thinking hey you know, a deal's a deal, what's happening here? So, it was easier for Ronnie to just get rid of me; but it is what it is, water under the bridge.'[247]

By the time Campbell and Dio parted company, Campbell had earned an international standing as an exciting and innovative guitarist with many admirers. For example Dante Bonutto wrote: 'live and on record, Vivian has built up a reputation for himself as a guitarist intent on creating his own sound, a guitarist not satisfied simply to fall in line behind all the other Eddie VH clones. Live, he can turn on the thrills when the moment demands, but he's also not afraid to toe the dotted line and smash a chord square and true, standing his ground as it echoes, lingers and dies, resisting the temptation to tack on all the "fiddly bits" so beloved my his US compatriots.'[248] *Circus* magazine readers voted Campbell joint fifth best guitarist of 1985, tied with George Lynch and below Mick Mars in first place, then Yngwie Malmsteen, Eddie Van Halen and Warren DeMartini.[249]

*Metal Hammer* magazine went one further, naming Campbell one of four guitarists of the 1980s who 'made a massive impact on the guitar world.' Along with Yngwie Malmsteen, Steve Vai and Gary Moore, Campbell 'pushed back the boundaries of accepted guitar technique' by 'constantly exploring and developing [their] catalogue of new styles, guitar patterns and sounds, to the level where [they have] broken acres of new ground.'[250] In an age of guitar heroes, this was high praise indeed.

Mainly thanks to Ronnie Dio's harsh public comments, Campbell, however, carried with him some baggage. Was he a diva? Was he a band-wrecker? Did he have a poor work ethic? What would the future bring? Perhaps in the darker moments of losing his role in Dio, Campbell also gave these questions some serious consideration.

**Final Vinyl**

Three final record releases emerged from the Dio-Campbell era. The first was a single written by Bain, Campbell and Ronnie Dio entitled 'Stars' (April 1986), which originated from a charity project idea by Campbell and Bain entitled Hear 'n' Aid; the second was an Extended Player single release called, simply, *The Dio EP*. (May 1986); the third was a (mostly) live Dio album entitled *Intermission* (June 1986).

After Campbell's exit, Ronnie Dio was faced with two immediate, practical problems. Firstly, he needed a replacement guitar player to fulfil the remaining European tour dates beginning in April, so he recruited former Rough Cutt and Giuffria guitarist Craig Goldy. The second practical problem was recording a follow-up to *Sacred Heart*, and it was likely the recording sessions for that would not begin until 1987. That would mean two years would separate *Sacred Heart* and the next studio album. Ronnie was concerned that being out of the public eye for so long might hurt the band, and he therefore wanted to make some product available on the marketplace before the next studio album. That was the main reason why two Campbell-legacy releases appeared in 1986.

*The Dio EP* release featured a track each from Dio's three studio albums, plus one new track. These were 'Shame On The Night,' 'Egypt (The Chains Are On),' and 'Hungry For Heaven.' The new track was entitled 'Hide In The Rainbow,' which at that point was previously unreleased, but would appear a few months later on the soundtrack of the movie *Iron Eagle* (1986). It was written by Ronnie Dio and was the final studio track that Campbell worked on with him. Fittingly perhaps, given the circumstances, Dante Bonutto called Campbell's performance on 'Hide In The Rainbow' an 'example of vintage Viv, the guitarist coming out of his corner with the best recorded sound he's ever had... Way to go, Viv!'[251]

The EP was released as a 12-inch single, as a single and gatefold double 7-inch single, and as a limited edition 10-inch pic disc. Early copies came with a Dio 'family tree' insert which traced Campbell's history back to his Sweet Savage days. 'Hungry For Heaven' from the EP reached number 56 in the UK charts. *Kerrang!* gave the release only a lukewarm review: 'Great voice, no doubt about it. But I've often felt that it's wasted on less-than-adequate songs. The only one you probably haven't heard — Hide In The Rainbow — is actually rather dull. Doomy, a bit gloomy and melodically leaning a bit too much towards the "wicked witch of the north" music you often hear in pantomimes.'[252]

Just after *Sacred Heart* was released, Dio was asked if he had any plans to release a live album. He responded: 'I'd love to, before it becomes too late to include material such as Stargazer and Starstruck, or any part of what has been an important area of my past.'[253]

That chance came in 1986 with the release of *Intermission*, but it was not the definitive live album Dio hoped it would be. Live double albums with eye-catching gatefold sleeves had become something of a statement for rock bands, even an indicator of status. Thin Lizzy's *Live and Dangerous* (1978), Judas Priest's *Unleashed in the East* (1979), Neil Young's *Rust Never Sleeps* (1979), Rush's *Exit Stage Left* (1981), and Iron Maiden's *Live After Death* (1985) set a high bar for live recordings, and Dio wanted to make a similar statement about his place in the rock pantheon.

However, Warner Bros., Dio's record company in North America, had different plans. It wanted a cheap, single-vinyl album in the stores as a stopgap until Dio was ready to release their next studio album. Ronnie was so disappointed with this approach that he named the album *Intermission* to ensure fans knew why it was released. 'Think about that title,' he demanded. 'What do you do in between movies? You have a fag, or you take a piss, and so as the name suggests this became an album that was an interval. It was a product that [Warner Bros.] wanted, it was product that kept us in the marketplace, but that doesn't mean I was happy with the situation.'[254]

The album consists of five live tracks recorded at the San Diego sports arena on December 6, 1985, one of which was a medley of three songs, together with one new studio track entitled 'Time To Burn.'[255] Campbell performed on all tracks except 'Time To Burn,' and he co-wrote the three tracks that comprise side one of the album, those being 'King Of Rock And Roll,' 'Rainbow In The Dark,' and 'Sacred Heart.'

Critical reaction to *Intermission* was mixed, with *HiFi Stereo Review* giving the harshest evaluation. The magazine called the album 'some kind of low-water mark for music — the One Million B. C. of heavy-metal. Ronnie Dio snarls his way through six tracks of mind-numbing, incomprehensible noise. Meanwhile, the heavy-metal guitar bangs away with frightening predictability while Ronnie wails about blood-and-guts and rock-and-roll... anyone can make a mediocre record, but an album this bad doesn't come along every day. *Intermission* is an achievement in the truly awful. As such, it merits a place in any serious rock collection.'[256]

In stark contrast, *Kerrang!*'s Dave Dickson wrote: 'you can't knock quality and this is very definitely quality stuff.'[257] Dickson's praise was not, however, completely unqualified. For example, he pointed to the album cover as 'one of the worst I've ever seen,' and he noticed something odd about credits and the album mix: 'nowhere does it tell you that the guitarist on the five live tracks is the now departed Vivian Campbell. This may explain why the guitar has been mixed down so much — rarely does Campbell get to display any teeth on this record.'[258] In fact, the tonal and volume difference between the clearly-mixed rhythm playing and the more muted guitar solos led some to speculate that Craig Goldy had rerecorded Campbell's rhythm guitar parts on all the live tracks while Campbell's lead solos remained untouched.

**Hear 'n Aid/Stars**

Aside from his musical creations, the Hear 'n Aid project must be considered Campbell's greatest achievement. The context of the project was a horrendous famine in Ethiopia which led to the deaths of at least 300,000 people between 1983 and 1985.

Musicians on both sides of the Atlantic responded by releasing charity fundraising records: In the UK, Midge Ure and Bob Geldof gathered together a group of pop stars to record a charity single. Released in December 1984 under the Band Aid name, 'Do They Know It's Christmas' went straight to number one in the UK charts and was the first multi-million-selling charity single.

In the US, musician Harry Belafonte, inspired by Ure and Geldof, set about organising a similar charity single. Under the banner of USA For Africa, this group of musicians recorded 'We Are the World,' which was released in March 1985 and became one of the biggest-selling charity singles in history. Six months later, at the Live Aid charity event, musicians performed in London and Philadelphia in a televised event to raise money for African famine relief.

Despite the popularity of hard rock and heavy metal, its stars were under represented at these gatherings. This omission was not lost on Campbell and Bain when in February 1985 they contributed to the KLOS Los Angeles 'Rock Relief For Africa' radiothon, with each contributing a guitar for auction. The charity event raised $175,000 and Campbell had a moment of clarity. He told the *LA Times*, 'It's so incredible when you sit back and say, "How much money can be raised?" I know there's a kind of fever right now with everybody getting involved in charity, but then again, why the hell not?'[259]

Campbell and Bain were inspired to produce their own charity record, this time using the talent available in the rock and heavy metal genres. Bain even came up with a name for the project — 'Hear 'n Aid. They took their proposal to the USA For Africa organisation, which was supportive. At that point, the pair asked Ronnie Dio to become involved.[260] Together, they began to organise a charity recording using the template established by 'Do They Know It's Christmas' and 'We Are The World.' With Dio's support and his connections, a recording session was booked on May 20-21, 1985.

Some of the cream of heavy metal music were invited to take part. 'Initially it was going to be a local thing featuring a few L.A. bands,' Campbell revealed. 'Then it grew and grew.'[261] Among those who accepted the invitation were members of Dio, Judas Priest, Iron Maiden, Mötley Crüe, Twisted Sister, Blue Öyster Cult, and Journey, as well as solo artists like Yngwie Malmsteen and Ted Nugent. Fittingly, perhaps, members of the heavy metal parody band Spinal Tap also took part, demonstrating the truism that life often imitates art.

'We're the people who weren't invited to USA For Africa,' said Bain, 'but we still wanted to help.'[262] Ronnie Dio made the same point: 'Hear 'n Aid was a response to being excluded from USA for Africa. Hear 'n Aid came from Jimmy and Viv. They wanted to take our participation [for world hunger relief] from a local to a national level. They thought, "Let's find some of those people who play the music we do and see if they'd be interested in putting a song together."'[263]

A *Back Stage* article about the video release *Hear 'n Aid: The Sessions* put the release into its political and social context: 'With heavy metal currently the particular target of Washington D.C.'s Parents Musical Resource Centre for allegedly promoting violence, sexism and Satanism through music, the Hear 'n Aid documentary is an unexpected yet sincere portrait of a group of recording artists who came together with a common purpose.'[264]

Campbell confirmed that these attacks on heavy metal music and musicians influenced his decision to develop the project, telling *Back Stage*: 'Maybe Hear 'n Aid shows that what is bad is not always bad. We may appear to be the bad boys of rock 'n roll, but it's just an image, an extension of an act. We do care and we are doing something about it.'[265]

The recording session was productive, and artists contributed their musical talent to a track called 'Stars,' which was written by Dio, Campbell and Bain. Campbell contributed backing vocals on the track and recorded a guitar solo. Despite the array of guitar talent in the studio, Campbell claimed not to be nervous, mainly as he recorded his solo separately from everyone else. 'It was very enjoyable,' he revealed. 'There were no ego problems at all, and I learned a lot from watching the other people play.' When asked who most impressed him, Campbell singled out Journey's Neal Schon. 'I'd never heard him play like that before. I was amazed; it was so much off the wall. Journey isn't much of a showcase for his talent. That was probably my favourite solo on the record.'[266]

The original plan was for 'Stars' to be released as a single and that artists would contribute live and studio tracks from their own catalogues to an album released under the Hear 'n Aid banner. However, due to legal contractual issues, the single wasn't released until April 1986 with the album following in May. Campbell appeared on the Dio band's sole contribution to the album, a live version of 'Hungry For Heaven' which was recorded at Dio's September 13, 1985 gig at the Spectrum in Philadelphia. When Campbell was asked if the project arrived too late to have maximum impact, he responded positively, saying: 'I don't think that charity begins or stops at any certain date. I think it's an ongoing thing.'[267]

Despite such noble sentiments, it is nevertheless likely that the delay between recording 'Stars' and its subsequent release nearly a year later meant the project was unable to take full advantage of the outpouring of publicity and goodwill that greeted the UK and US charity records.

In addition, some controversy arose when Phonogram press officer Suki Pardesi tried to organise a press event for the single launch at an Ear, Nose and Throat Hospital in London, and to supply promotional press kits in the shape of a hearing aid. Critics considered this was poor taste and the idea was quickly abandoned. The launch took place instead at London's Hard Rock Café.[268] Campbell, perhaps feeling he had every right to take part in the launch despite being fired by Dio a few months beforehand, was present.

The circumstances of Campbell's appearance are unclear, but a few months earlier Ronnie Dio insisted that he wanted Campbell and Bain to get proper recognition for the project they started. 'Vivian and Jimmy were behind the Hear 'n Aid record Stars and they deserve the credit for writing it,' Dio said. 'Those two guys really put themselves fully into it, so of course, I like to see them get the credit.'[269]

Still, it was an awkward time for Campbell, partly because his replacement in Dio, Craig Goldy, was in attendance and gained some publicity by offering a guitar to the Hard Rock Café which had promised to give $2,000 to the Hear 'n Aid cause in return for every guitar gifted to them.[270]

*FMQB*, an American radio and music trade magazine, was perhaps the most effusive in its praise for the 'Stars' single, although that's unsurprising given the magazine's nature. *FMBQ* wrote: 'Finally, a 'superstar line-up charity song made with Rock Radio in mind!… To say the song is one of the best Ronnie James Dio (along with band-members Jimmy Bain and Vivian Campbell) has ever written would be an understatement. More importantly, the cause (world-wide famine relief) is still a worthy one; and with Stars you have a song that fits the format. In other words, if there were no cause, it would stand up to practically anything you currently have on the air!'[271]

*Kerrang!*'s review of the single was almost as extravagant, although not as elegant. *Kerrang!* called 'Stars' 'Shit hot… the most blessed Heavy Metal 45 in some time' which 'beats seven shades of shit out of either We Are The World or Do They Know It's Christmas.'[272] *Kerrang!*'s combative words are evidence of the grievance hard rock and heavy metal audiences felt at being omitted from previous music charity projects.

In the first weeks of its release, 'Stars' sold 100,000 copies and the album 125,000.[273] However, 'Stars' reached only number 26 in the UK singles chart, while the album barely charted. While there is little evidence that it rescued the image of Heavy Metal from those who would always link it to Satanism, hedonism, sexism and degenerate values, the charity project was nevertheless a worthy effort that raised money for a good cause.

Sharon Wiesz, who sat on the Hear 'n Aid Board of Directors, told *Billboard* she hoped the endeavour would eventually raise £20 million. A year after the project was launched, however, Ronnie Dio expressed some disappointment that it had only raised one million dollars thus far.[274] Many years later, Wendy Dio suggested that the final amount was nearer Ronnie's figure than Wiesz's. Nevertheless, $1 million was still a significant amount.[275] Furthermore, all money raised from the 'Stars' single, the *Hear 'n Aid* album, the *Hear 'n Aid: The Sessions* video documentary and merchandise sales were distributed through the charity organisation USA for Africa to fund famine relief projects.[276] For those who benefited from it, this aid was undoubtedly a rainbow in the dark.

October 25, 1983,
White Beacon Theatre,
New York, USA.
© Frank White Photography

August 15, 1984,
Nassau Veterans Memorial
Coliseum, New York, USA.
© Frank White Photography

November 5, 1984,
Brendan Byrne Arena, East
Rutherford, New Jersey, USA.
© Frank White Photography

September 19, 1992,
San Diego Sports Arena, USA.
© Tom Wallace

September 19, 1992,
San Diego Sports Arena, USA.
© Tom Wallace

August 27, 1996, San Diego Open Air Theatre, USA.
© Tom Wallace

# Chapter 3

## Snakes, Dogs, and Kings

After the split with Dio, *Circus* magazine's Nick Bowcott revealed that Campbell had returned to Ireland and formed his own band, which he called Trinity. 'We can be expecting something from them shortly,' Bowcott promised.[277] Campbell told Dante Bonutto that Trinity was the side project he had been working on while in Dio, and it had become a bone of contention for Ronnie, perhaps even the straw that broke the camel's back in their strained relationship.

Bonutto wrote: 'With sights set firmly on the future, the guitarist, it seems, turned to writing and demoing fresh material with a friend who was living in Los Angeles for four years but is now back in the bosom of Belfast, as indeed is Viv. For a while now it's been the intention of the Campbell clansman to work with the music in question… if and when Dio called it a day, though in light of recent events his plans have suddenly been thrown into a higher gear.'[278]

Bonutto called Trinity 'a three piece in the classic mould — guitar/bass/drums — with the bassist doubling up on lead vocals.' He revealed, 'Viv's old songwriting sidekick is part of the team, and the three are already hard at work in the studio with a view to starting a debut album next month. With finance coming from Viv himself and a US publishing company, the band are in no great hurry to sign a record deal; they're currently debating whether or not they should work with a producer on the project — perhaps just to provide an objective opinion — the plan being to record the tracks in Ireland then take them to the record companies as a finished product. Negotiations of this sort will be handled by the US-based manager who Viv has been signed up with for over a year.'

While Campbell was initially coy about revealing the names of his band, in time it became known they were his close friends, bass player Davey Watson and drummer Pat Waller.[279] As for the music, Campbell explained: 'This band has a broad base; it isn't heavy guitar-influenced, though there's still a lot of searing solos. It's a different-sounding band, an open band, open to ideas. We're not aiming for any particular market, we'll just create a market for ourselves, a new category. I've absolute faith that this band will succeed.' The following year Campbell revealed a little more about his new band's musical direction, telling *Circus* magazine, 'We're not afraid to utilise sequencers, so we've got a very big sound for a three-piece. We've got a strong soul feeling, but we're still a melodic hard rock band. We're sort of a Free [Paul Rodgers' band] for the '80s.'[280]

Campbell told Bonutto, 'I've been suppressed as a musician for so long that right now I just want to go over-the-top!' and that seemed to explain the range of instruments the trio had been using in the studio, which included keyboards, piano, acoustic instruments, and saxophone. Evidently, there was some truth in Ronnie Dio's remark that Campbell was no longer interested in being a 'guitar hero.'

After completing a number of demos, Campbell told Paul Gallotta that he had 'showcased' his new music to record companies and 'impressed a lot of people.'[281] In retrospect, Campbell's optimism can be explained away as mere wishful thinking. How many new bands successfully create their own market, the 'new category' that Campbell referred to? In reality, Trinity soon disbanded because it failed to secure a record deal, and none of the music demoed at the time has ever come to light.

**Whitesnake 1987-1988**

Given that Campbell had been the sole lead guitarist in Dio, a popular and successful rock band with a number of hit singles and albums behind them, as well as critically acclaimed and well-attended live tours, his ousting from the band, and the failure of Trinity to get off the ground, must have been a sobering moment. Was he destined to be just another hotshot guitarist who wouldn't find a popular audience outside the framework of an already-popular band? That was the fate of a number of his contemporaries: for example, Jake E. Lee was never as popular again as he was when working with Ozzy Osbourne; Steve Vai's solo albums never surpassed the popularity and sales of his recordings with Frank Zappa, Dave Lee Roth, and Whitesnake; and when Brian May and Eddie Van Halen collaborated on a mini album entitled *Star Fleet Project* (1983), it garnered only weak sales and harsh reviews.

However, the trajectory of Campbell's rollercoaster music career was soon on the rise again. A call from John Kalodner, an A&R man with Geffen Records, soon had Campbell hooking up with David Coverdale's Whitesnake. Coverdale had given Kalodner a list of musicians he would like to work with and Campbell was on the list.[282]

Campbell was familiar with the singer from when Whitesnake supported Dio on the US leg of Dio's 1984 *The Last In Line* tour. Managed by Kalodner, the band had just had a massive worldwide hit with their self-titled album released in 1987. Outside of the Americas and Japan it was referred to as *1987*. Coverdale fired the line-up that worked on the album and recruited a new touring band from scratch. Campbell was a direct replacement for lead guitarist John Sykes, who had co-written most of the album tracks with Coverdale but would have to share the stage with Dutch guitarist Adrian Vandenberg, whom Coverdale had also recruited mainly for his potential as a future song writing collaborator.

Coverdale explained how the new line-up came together: 'It was like Zen and the Art of Forming a Band. I'd spent a brutal winter in Germany [and] I'd lost all perspective on the album, because of the grief that had gone down with it. I'd gotten ill. It was difficult to listen to, but I had nothing else to do, and I wrote on a piece of paper who I'd like to work with. Literally, the people I wrote down are exactly who I'm working with now. Nobody crossed out, nobody approached who wasn't interested.'[283]

What was it that attracted Campbell to Whitesnake? Campbell said that when he spoke to Coverdale he found the singer's attitude 'really refreshing.' It seemed Coverdale had given the guitarist some assurance that the band would be a more equal affair than was Dio. Campbell said: 'After leaving Dio, I had enough of being in that [kind of band situation], where you don't get an equal say in the music. I could have joined Ozzy if I just wanted a steady paycheque, but that wasn't the case.' Besides, he looked forward to working with the new band line-up, saying: 'I didn't think you could ever find better players... I couldn't have hand-picked a better band.'[284]

These were confident statements from a man who must have wilfully ignored Whitesnake's turbulent history of hirings and firings with 14 personnel changes thus far, or perhaps he was just saying what was expected of him for the benefit of the press.

Coverdale had considerable pedigree, which is perhaps why those musicians, including Campbell, were eager to work with him. In 1973, he replaced Ian Gillan as the lead singer for Deep Purple, working with the likes of Ritchie Blackmore, Glenn Hughes, Jon Lord, Ian Paice, and Tommy Bolin. When Deep Purple disbanded in 1976, Coverdale embarked on a solo career before forming his own band in 1978, after the release of his second solo album, 1978's *North Winds*. He named this new band Whitesnake, which is a variation on the title of his first solo album, entitled *White Snake* (1977). The band quickly developed a solid reputation among rock fans, releasing six popular studio albums and one critically acclaimed live album from 1978 to 1984, before reaching worldwide fame with the release of the *Whitesnake / 1987* album.

When Campbell was recruited soon after the recording of that album, he was joining a band in flux: in its early days, Whitesnake could be categorised as a blues-based rock band, very much a product of 1970s musical fashions. However, by the mid-1980s, and after Coverdale had realised that most of the band's success came solely in the UK, he began writing for American audiences with his songs now falling more into the heavy metal, glam metal or hair metal style rather than blues-rock.

Campbell said: 'the band had sort of fallen apart, there was only David Coverdale and this record [*Whitesnake / 1987*] was poised to be released and so they put together this super group [consisting of guitarists Campbell and Adrian Vandenberg, bassist Rudy Sarzo  and drummer Tommy Aldridge] and the first thing we did together was shoot three music videos… before we played a note together and that set the tone for the band. It was the '80s, huge hair, shoulder pads, shaking your arse… it was a very image driven band.'[285]

Journalist Mark Madden provided a colourful description of the band's transformation: 'Once a home for old bluesers like Aynsley Dunbar and Deep Purple keysman Jon Lord, Whitesnake '87 is young, hot and loud.'[286]

Coverdale's new focus on the American market began to take shape as early as 1982 when the singer fired his band after disillusionment at the way the *Saints & Sinners* album had turned out. At the time, Coverdale claimed his all-star band was merely coasting, 'cruising along on gold status and I'm hungry for platinum.'[287]

However, the real turning point came with 1984's *Slide It In* album. Bonutto had predicted that due to Coverdale's new deal with Geffen Records, and a new and fresh band line-up, the album might be the one to break Whitesnake in the United States (or as he put it, 'breaking down hard-to-fathom colonial resistance').

In fact, two versions of that album were released, the original for the British market and a second for the American. The British release reached number nine in the UK albums chart and generated two moderately successful singles. However, Geffen asked that it be remixed by experienced sound engineer Keith Olsen, and that the two current members of Whitesnake's touring party, John Sykes and Neil Murray, re-record the album's guitar and bass parts.[288]

The result was mixed: the album reached the *Billboard* top 40, which Geffen and Coverdale likely found a little disappointing. However, it did stay in the charts for an extended period and eventually achieved gold sales status. In addition, two eye-catching promotional videos for the singles 'Slow An' Easy' and 'Love Ain't No Stranger,' set the template for the huge success to come with *Whitesnake / 1987*.

An indicator of how much Coverdale's views had changed in just a few short years can be found in an interview the singer gave to *Kerrang!* in 1982. When asked about potential new recruits for a revamped version of Whitesnake, Coverdale replied: 'That Dutch guy Vandenberg was actually under consideration as one of the guitarists — but they all sound the same to me.'[289] By 1987, however, Coverdale would recruit Vandenberg in an attempt to break the American market.

It was an odd situation for Campbell: he hadn't played on the album but was asked to perform on the promotional videos for the first three of four singles from it, namely, 'Still Of The Night,' 'Is This Love,' and 'Here I Go Again '87.'

'Still Of The Night,' released in March 1987 in the UK, was Campbell's introduction to the world as a member of Whitesnake. It is mainly a performance video of the band onstage, but that description hardly does it justice. It is, in fact, a visual tour de force, and one of the iconic promotional videos of the era. Director Marty Callner placed each band member on a riser, with Coverdale situated centre stage rear, against a backdrop image of a large and brightly lit full moon. With dynamic lighting and liberal use of dry ice, Callner paints a dynamic and dramatic portrait not simply of musicians plying their trade but of rock stars being rock stars. Campbell performs the song's main guitar solo, with both guitarists sharing the visuals for the remaining riffs and hooks.

'Still Of The Night' was one of the most requested videos on MTV, garnering 'Hip clip of the week' honours, which helped the single reach the top twenty in the UK and 79 in the US Billboard singles chart.[290]

These were encouraging stats for a song which was more of an album track than a natural single release. The video's main achievement, however, was to promote the album and the band: the album reached number two in the US and was near the top of the charts for seven months, selling over four million copies by the end of the year; moreover, Coverdale was no longer a shaggy blues singer and instead was now transformed into a major rock star and sex symbol.[291]

The second single from the album, 'Is This Love,' benefitted greatly from the popularity of the 'Still Of The Night' music video. Because all three promotional videos for the singles were shot within a short space of time, it has the same aesthetic, albeit at a lower intensity as befitting the song's power ballad nature. Released in May, it reached the top ten in singles charts in the UK and USA. Campbell acted out the main solo in the video. The third single from the album was an older song called 'Here I Go Again,' with '87' added to the end to distinguish it from the original version. It was recorded initially for Whitesnake's 1982 *Saints & Sinners* album, and Geffen executives convinced Coverdale to re-record it in line with Whitesnake's current sound and image. Released in June, it features another dynamic performance video, with Vandenberg performing the main solo.

In all three of these promotional videos, with the exception of Coverdale, the musicians are mostly backlit, which results in their faces almost always being in shadow or dimly lit. The effect of this, deliberate or otherwise, is to make them merely a backdrop to Coverdale's performance, as well as his on and off screen relationship with American actress and model, Julie 'Tawny' Kitaen, who features memorably in all three videos.

If the video editor favoured one guitarist, it was Vandenberg ahead of Campbell. Chiselled, tanned, and with a mass of blond hair that mirrored Coverdale's new blond highlights, Vandenberg was the more camera-friendly of the two. (In fact, Campbell was the only dark-haired member of the band, with Sarzo and Aldridge also adopting the blond 'poodle perm' look of hair metal.)

The Dutchman may also have been given a more visible role than Campbell as he had actually performed on the album, playing some rhythm guitar and recording the solo on 'Here I Go Again' in place of Sykes. Coverdale had, in fact, discussed future arrangements with Vandenberg before Campbell came on the scene. Vandenberg therefore expected to be the sole guitarist on the tour and was surprised when Coverdale also recruited Campbell.[292] As late as September 1987, *Hit Parader* was reporting that the new Whitesnake line up consisted of Coverdale, Vandenberg, Sarzo and Aldridge, with no mention of Campbell.[293]

The final single from the album, 'Give Me All Your Love' (Jan. 1988), stands out from those that preceded it in that it was released mainly to promote the band's US tour rather than the album. The single mix features Campbell's sole studio contribution to Whitesnake, when he recorded a new solo specifically for this release. This was a radio edit so the primary purpose of Campbell's new recording was to shorten the solo while still providing something flash, fast, and memorable.

The music video is relatively low budget and simple compared to the promotional videos for the previous three singles. Tawny Kitaen is noticeably absent too. However, Campbell featured more prominently than before. The video begins with footage of a private plane flying the band between gigs. It shows the band walking across a runway at an airport, then it skips forward to some backstage footage at the venue, which in this case was Meadowlands Arena in East Rutherford, New Jersey. Campbell is in the foreground of this backstage footage, looking happy and keen to get on stage.

The remainder of the video features the band performing the song on a concert stage rather than the studio stages of the first three music videos. Campbell sings backing vocals and plays the first part of the guitar solo before Vandenberg joins in with some harmony guitar patterns. Perhaps a little Whitesnake fatigue was setting in at this point, or singles from the album were beginning to suffer from the law of diminishing returns, because the single barely broke the top 50 in the US and top twenty in the UK.

In late 1987, Coverdale told *Circus* magazine that Campbell, Aldridge, and Sarzo were hired initially for the 'Still Of The Night' video, with no guarantees made of further collaboration. However, when the album proved a success, as Coverdale told it, 'A booking agency was waving money under my nose to tour,' so with financial guarantees in place, he contacted Campbell *et al* to secure their services for a tour.[294] Suddenly Coverdale's 'vidkids,' as he called them, were his new touring band.[295]

So, in June 1987, Coverdale's Whitesnake set off on its first arena tour of the US as special guests on the Mötley Crüe tour. However, as the album became increasingly popular, and especially when the 'Here I Go Again' single topped the charts, by October Whitesnake was the headline act, 'bringing one 20,000-seater arena after another to its knees.'[296] Vandenberg recalls that the initial plans were for a three-month tour, which ended up lasting 18 months.[297]


**On Tour, 1987-1988**

Whitesnake's debut live performance in the US was at the Cotton Bowl in Dallas on June 20 at Texxas Jam, an annual rock festival that had been running since 1978. The band was billed beneath Boston and Aerosmith, but above Poison and Tesla. Two years previously, the festival was headlined by Coverdale's previous band, Deep Purple, so this was something of a triumphant return for the singer who had last toured the United States with Deep Purple in the 1970s. This was a significant moment too for Campbell, as his previous band, Dio, had been high on the festival bill in 1986.

This was a huge opportunity for Whitesnake to impress but the band was also under scrutiny: could their live show emulate their dynamic promotional videos, and could they replicate their studio sound in a live setting with new musicians? They certainly chose an impressive set list, opening with 'Bad Boys,' then performing tracks that would go on to become live crowd favourites — 'Give Me All Your Love,' 'Here I Go Again,' 'Love Ain't No Stranger,' 'Slow An' Easy,' and 'Crying In The Rain.' The set ended with their most well-known song, 'Still Of The Night.'

After 'Slow An' Easy,' Coverdale introduced 'magnificent guitarist'

Campbell to the crowd to perform a short solo slot. Campbell proceeded to play a solo that would have been familiar to any Dio fans in the audience, featuring his signature Gary Moore style neo-classical shred, which morphed into some atmospheric bends that soon segued into 'Crying In The Rain.' During that song, Vandenberg also played an extended solo to showcase his talents. However, he also made an error, coming in early with the 'cello' part of the song before Coverdale had finished his vocal lines. Given this was a new line-up playing together for the first time, such errors were to be expected.

When asked many years later how it felt to share the stage with Campbell, Vandenberg said: 'I didn't mind because it was another adventure and I enjoyed playing with another player, I just prefer being by myself, not for ego reasons, but because all the bands I grew up on like Queen, Free and Bad Company were three-piece bands with a singer.'[298] Nevertheless, concert reviews singled out the duel guitar approach as one of the band's strengths, and suggested that Campbell and Vandenberg gelled well together. For example, a *Pittsburgh Press* review of the gig at the Pittsburgh Civic Arena talked of the guitarists fusing on 'Guilty Of Love' 'in a hot dual lead.'[299]

In addition, while many dual guitar bands create some fake stage drama by performing a set piece 'guitar battle' purporting to be spontaneous and improvised, in reality there is usually no rivalry between guitarists and theirs is a purely professional and well-rehearsed performance. On this tour, however, with both Campbell and Vandenberg uncertain of their future with Coverdale after the tour ended, each tried to impress. 'There was a certain rivalry in the air,' Campbell would later reveal, a situation Coverdale encouraged by introducing Campbell's solo with a phrase used in boxing, 'and in the blue corner…'[300]

Preceding 'Crying In The Rain' at the Pittsburgh gig, both guitarists gave short solo performances. 'Campbell had the unenviable position of following Vandenberg's barrage of diverse scales and modes,' wrote the *Pittsburgh Press*. The result? 'It was a standoff.'[301]

In a contemporary interview, Campbell explained his approach to playing Sykes's guitar solos: 'I want my solo to project as much personality as possible. It's not like singing, where you can use words and dynamics to bring yourself across. It's very hard to interpret notes. You have to use loud, soft, hard, fast, high and low to convey expression. I like to think of myself as melodic — not concentrating too hard, not just playing with the fingers. Music must come from the head and heart.'[302]

When asked how he coped with sharing the guitar spotlight with Vandenberg, Campbell admitted it took getting used to. 'It's not an ego thing,' he insisted. 'It's just that two guitar players in the same band can get in each other's way a lot, because they're both pretty much doing the same thing. Our only rule of thumb was that we split solos 50-50, and we try to keep it that way. This is a healthy competition.'[303]

While Whitesnake didn't quite steal the show at the festival, which had a strong line-up of American bands, their appearance was a major success. They put on a dynamic stage show and generated a positive audience response in sweltering heat. Coverdale's voice was magnificent, the band looked great, and they proved capable of performing creditable live versions of the album's studio sound.

Primarily, however, the band lived up to the image they created in their promotional videos. That image could have proved an anchor around their necks but Texxas Jam, and the subsequent tour, proved otherwise. Sarzo attributed Whitesnake's success to three main things: first was the great album the previous line-up had delivered; second was the band's new image, created by the promotional videos; and third was that the group could 'deliver onstage what the videos promise.'[304]

In order to fully exploit Whitesnake's popularity, the *Whitesnake / 1987* tour was extensive: from June 20 to October 15, the band performed at 74 venues across the US, mostly in large arenas and stadiums. The touring party then proceeded to Canada, where the band performed on a further seven occasions, before returning to the US once more to begin their headline tour in Saginaw, Michigan on October 30. This consisted of another 26 gigs which would take them up to early December.[305] At that point the original plan was to return to mainland Europe to perform. However, Coverdale was suffering from an intestinal virus and those dates had to be cancelled.[306]

Nevertheless, Coverdale recovered quickly enough that Whitesnake was able to undergo a short UK tour that lasted from December 29 until January 8, 1988, during which the band played a total of nine gigs at four venues, which were Wembley Arena, Birmingham NEC, Newcastle City Hall and Edinburgh Playhouse. Notably, the Wembley Arena and Birmingham NEC venues were the two largest indoor venues in England, much bigger than earlier incarnations of Whitesnake was able to fill.

In late January the band returned to the US for another 49 gigs ending at the Los Angeles Forum on April 7. A short tour of Japan followed from June 11-21. After returning to North America the band played a further 33 concerts in the US and Canada. Some of these had been rebooked from earlier after Coverdale suffered a serious injury, a slipped disc that required surgery.[307] The tour ended with a gig at the Portland Memorial Coliseum in Oregon on August 15.

**Concert Reviews**

Indicative reviews suggest that Whitesnake were a popular touring act, and that most fans left arenas happy. As for the unspoken rivalry between bands on the same bill, Whitesnake also held their own as headliners, and sometimes stole the show when they weren't topping the bill.

For example, at the 'Day On The Green' event on October 10, 1987 at Oakland-Alameda County Coliseum, Whitesnake were second on the bill, behind headliners Mötley Crüe but billed ahead of Poison. A reviewer for the *Union Democrat* paper was less than impressed with the headline act, reporting that of the bands performing that day, the crowd reacted most passionately and noisily to Whitesnake. While the reviewer focused mainly on the Whitesnake frontman, he also wrote that Campbell and Vandenberg 'put Crüe's [Mick] Mars to shame without blinking, providing tasteful solos and a mid-set duet that was simply superb.'[308]

Bruce Haring of *Billboard* reviewed the band's sell out show on January 31, 1988 at the East Rutherford Meadowlands Arena in New Jersey. As with many reviews of this tour, the focus was mainly on the charismatic Coverdale, but Haring also offered some incise commentary on what made Whitesnake a great live draw. Pointing to Whitesnake's stripped down stage production, Haring claimed the band had 'decided to let the music do the talking [with] 90 minutes of... melodic pop metal.' Haring called the encore, which was a cover version of the ZZ Top song, 'Tush,' 'a winking nod to Whitesnake's sexually-charged image.'[309]

Peter B. King reviewed Whitesnake's February 3, 1988 gig at the Pittsburgh Civic Arena for the *Pittsburgh Press* paper, where the band was supported by Great White. King praised Whitesnake's brand of melodic hard rock, arguing that both guitarists 'give the band its stamp,' reeling off 'stinging, lightning quick, melodic breaks' and 'amazing chops.'[310]

Journalist Mark Madden also reviewed that Pittsburgh gig. Madden, a self-confessed Coverdale fan, naturally focused much of his review on the singer. However, he also praised Campbell and Vandenberg, claiming that their sound 'was the musical touchstone, cutting through the night with alternating dexterity and abandon.'[311]

Not everyone was a fan though. Eric Snider of the *St. Petersburg Times* wrote a scathing review of Whitesnake's February 20, 1988, gig at the Sun Dome in Tampa, calling it '90 minutes of just about every hackneyed rock cliche ever invented.' Snider directed most of his ire at 'smug and pompous' Coverdale, criticising his vocals as a 'strained, nasal screech' that fell short of the bluesy, soulful tone of his studio recordings. Snider also claimed the band lacked the chemistry required to perform the studio tracks properly. Snider gave Campbell the edge in the rivalry between the two guitarists, saying: 'Adrian Vandenberg's solo feature was composed of tired riffs that showcased fast fingers and effects; Vivian Campbell, the other six-stringer, followed with a stronger effort — he mixed in chords and bluesy lines and built the solo to a climax.'[312]

*Cash Box*'s Gary Starr reviewed Whitesnake's performance at the Los Angeles Forum on April 07, 1988, which was the band's final show in North America before flying to Japan. While the focus was again on Coverdale, Starr praised Campbell *et al* for giving the singer 'strong and complimentary support.' He called Whitesnake 'one of the strongest touring bands currently on the scene,' concluding that the band 'rocked The Forum for nearly two hours using a combination of great musicianship and vocals, interspersed with relaxed wit and humour between songs.'[313]

When Craig MacInnis of the *Toronto Star* reviewed the band's gig in the city on July 11, 1988, he thought it was 'as 'dated and ritualised as a Manilow gig.' He called the performance a 'hoary juggernaut of 1970s hard-rock escapades and crotch-thrusting cliches' and accused the band of delivering a 'hectic hybrid of stock riffs and lyrics that span the gap from the trash metal of "Slide It In" (thank you, Mötley Crüe) to the wild-in-the-streets angst of "Bad Boys" (thank you, Bon Jovi).'[314]

MacInnis's views proved to be an outlier, however. In the main, Whitesnake performed in large venues, including sports arenas, and to sold-out audiences. That audiences and reviewers usually went home happy was proof that the band was capable of delivering a classic rock show, and this was despite using a toned-down stage set with a minimum of pyrotechnics. The band let the music do the talking, and it proved to be a successful tactic. The tour also demonstrated that the Whitesnake image created by the music videos was based on a solid musical foundation.

## Live Recordings

Only a handful of professional recordings exist from the tour. Given the album and tour's high profile, this is perhaps a little surprising. However, further line-up changes occurred before the next album was released and it's possible Coverdale did not want to release a live performance from an older version of his band. Moreover, Coverdale did not release many live albums in this era, perhaps feeling that 1980's *Live...In The Heart Of The City* could not be outdone.

Whitesnake gave a high-profile performance of 'Still Of The Night' at the MTV Video Music Awards at the Universal Amphitheatre in Los Angeles, which aired live on September 11, 1987. Coverdale performed live vocals while the remainder of the band mimed to the studio recording. Vandenberg looked more than a bit foolish writhing on the floor as he mimed the cello part on his guitar with a violin bow. Campbell mimed the main solo. Also performing that evening were Whitney Houston, Madonna, Bon Jovi and David Bowie, so Whitesnake was among the cream of pop and rock royalty at this event, which helped raise their profile even further.

The 30th anniversary release of *Whitesnake / 1987* came with bonus material including live recordings from the 1987-1988 tour. One version featured a bonus CD entitled *Snakeskin Boots*, which offered eleven tracks recorded on the tour, plus Campbell and Vandenberg's co-performed guitar solo.

In addition, a handful of bootleg recordings exist, which give a sense of how the band performed at different stages of the tour. For example, there were a few errors at Texxas Jam, which was to be expected as the band only had two days to rehearse before setting out on the road. As the tour progressed, however, the band began to gel and performances became tighter. Conversely, and again as to be expected, Coverdale's best vocal performances were early in the tour before the demands of performing led to some wear and tear on his voice.

Aside from the opening gig at Texxas Jam in June 1987, and at the 'Day On The Green' event in October, when Whitesnake played shortened sets to meet festival requirements, the band's setlist remained consistent throughout the tour. Coverdale mainly chose songs from his latest couple of albums, with one or two others from earlier albums, and one cover version as an encore. An indicative setlist from the earlier part of the tour while Whitesnake was a support act is this one from the gig in Des Moines on July 12, 1987:

> Bad Boys / Children Of The Night
> Slide It In
> Here I Go Again
> Love Ain't No Stranger
> Guitar Solo
> Crying In The Rain (Including drum solo)
> Still Of The Night

As support act, the band played for around 45 minutes. However, when Whitesnake began their headlining tour, a longer setlist was required to fill the 90-minute time slot expected of the main act on the bill. An indicative example of the headliner setlist is this one from the gig in Detroit on February 13, 1988:

Bad Boys / Children Of The Night
Slide It In
Slow An' Easy
Here I Go Again
Guilty Of Love
Is This Love
Love Ain't No Stranger (fade out)
Guitar solos
Crying In The Rain
Drum solo
Still Of The Night
Give Me All Your Love
Tush
We Wish You Well

There were some minor variations: for example, on occasion 'Children Of The Night' wasn't played at the beginning of the concert, or Tush (a ZZ Top cover with alternative, more obscene lyrics) was dropped as an encore. In addition, Coverdale added 'Ain't No Love In The Heart Of The City' from the 1978 *Snakebite* EP, possibly because it was a live favourite from Whitesnake's 1980 release, *Live... In the Heart of the City*.

With a fixed setlist, Campbell and Vandenberg's main task was to decide which harmony parts to play on songs like 'Bad Boys' and 'Guilty Of Love,' and who would perform solo and rhythm guitar parts on each song. In addition, after the Texxas Jam gig, where the pair played separate 'duelling' guitar solos, Campbell and Vandenberg practised some guitar arrangement so that after their solos they would play as a duet in a show of band unity rather than rivalry.

Campbell's solo bears some similarity to the on-stage solos he performed while with Dio, and that solo itself bears some similarity to Gary Moore's instrumental guitar work out, 'Dirty Fingers' and may have meant the similarity as a tribute to the Belfast guitarist. Campbell was certainly more than capable of composing and performing a variety of solos, as demonstrated in instructional videos such as the *Hot Guitarist* Video Magazine Premiere Edition (1991) and the *Hot Licks* Vivian Campbell Lead Master Class (1988), or the track 'Sixgunz' that Campbell composed and performed for the instructional CD *Guitars Practising Musicians* (1991).

Indeed, Campbell's solo at the Buffalo Memorial Auditorium gig, New York, was noticeably different to his normal solo on the tour, which was basically a showcase of neoclassical speed metal. In Buffalo, however, while Campbell began his solo in familiar fashion, he transformed it into arpeggiated chords and phrases that were steeped in the blues tradition. This, however, was a one-off: there was only so far Campbell could push the boundaries of the new-look Whitesnake, and Coverdale clearly wanted to relegate Whitesnake's earlier, blues-based sound to the past.

It is worth considering some of Coverdale's stage banter, especially when introducing his guitarists. Some of his comments were clearly part of the act and were in keeping with the band's image. For example, on various occasions he referred to Campbell and Vandenberg as 'dangerous,' 'horny,' or 'horny bastards.' At the Albuquerque gig on November 24, 1987, Coverdale raised (or lowered?) the bar even further, introducing Campbell as an 'unbelievably horny bastard.' At the New Haven gig on January 23, 1988, Coverdale described Campbell as 'somebody we only release from his cage on the night of the show.'

Yet on other occasions, Coverdale's comments were perhaps more meaningful: for example, at the Wembley Arena in London on December 29, 1987, Coverdale introduced the guitarist as: 'A remarkable young man'; a few nights later at the same venue, he introduced Campbell as a 'wonderful guy'; and at the Newcastle City Hall gig on January 5, 1988, Coverdale introduced Campbell in his cod-aristocratic accent as 'the delightful young man from Belfast.'

Among the torrent of ribald comments from Coverdale directed to the audience, these more thoughtful remarks stand out, suggesting a degree of affection and respect from the singer towards the guitarist. Campbell seemed to reciprocate: during the tour he only had positive and respectful things to say about Coverdale. For example, Campbell said: 'The musicianship [in Whitesnake] is first rate and there is no way anyone could accuse us of being a backup band. The key word is respect amongst the whole band. There is a strong personal bond stemming from that respect. Working with Whitesnake is so refreshing. David has confidence in the people around him. He lets us do what we want and doesn't feel a need to oversee everything. He gives us the freedom and respect we deserve.'[315]

Vandenberg said much the same thing about Coverdale's approach towards this new group of musicians: 'David is very open to giving everyone the creative room they deserve. Had this not been the case, he would not have been able to keep the group together. As we get more familiar with the material, we reach a freedom to experiment. David encourages everyone to bring in ideas.'[316]

But, of course, it all went wrong both for Campbell and for Whitesnake, who would never again reach the dizzying heights of *Whitesnake / 1987*. Even while the tour was ongoing, journalists were keen to discover if Coverdale would reemploy the extant touring band to record the follow-up album. The reason for this curiosity was, of course, Coverdale's reputation for hiring and firing, all of which made good headlines. Moreover, the remarkable success of the album was as much due to the visual image of the new line-up as it was the musicians who created the album.

In response to these queries, band members seemed cautiously optimistic. When asked in late 1987 if the next Whitesnake album would feature the same extant personnel, Coverdale responded: 'there are no guarantees about anything... I've learned from enough past mistakes to know that not even I can look into the future... Having said that, though, I would be greatly shocked if any of the present band did decide they wanted to leave and move on. Personally, this is the best line-up of Whitesnake I've ever played in. There are no ego problems, everyone in the band seems to have the same positive attitude I do to the business of keeping Whitesnake successful, and at the same time everybody is making a lot of money out of the band right now, which tends to keep the old machine rolling along very nicely indeed, thank you.'[317]

By the spring of 1988, Coverdale remained optimistic. When asked again if this line-up would record the next album, Coverdale responded: 'Absolutely. I don't want people to get the impression that I keep changing band members just for the fun of it. All I've ever tried to do was put together the best group possible and hope everyone got along... This unit is the best version of Whitesnake. We all get along famously and everyone seems enthused about going into the studio as soon as we finish tour commitments.'[318]

Sarzo also suggested that the group would stick together to record the follow-up album, saying: 'We're really looking forward to doing the next studio album and fulfilling the potential this band has — the strength really is in the band. We've all been through those negative situations and know how to avoid them.'[319]

In June 1988, Campbell revealed that he had been writing in preparation for the next album, which he predicted would be 'very big-sounding... very rock 'n' roll, and it's gonna have a lot of dynamics — like "Still of the Night", but an album's worth of that... A lot of soul, a lot of fast-slow, stop-start, high-low.'[320] This level of detail suggests the writing process was well advanced, and at this stage Campbell was heavily involved and fully expected to contribute to the new album.

As for Vandenberg, he considered the tour hugely successful and personally gratifying, saying: 'It was such a blast to play "Still Of The Night" and "Crying In The Rain" every night, it was a roller-coaster... it was amazing.'[321] It also became clear that he and Coverdale had been writing together on the road. When Coverdale was asked who would help him write the next album, the singer replied: 'on the one or two jams we've got into at soundchecks and things I would imagine it would be me and Adrian [Vandenberg] who actually sit down together. I've admired his writing for a long time anyway. He's got some very strong ideas for songs, and I think together we could make an interesting partnership.'[322]

However, Coverdale insisted he was open to other contributions. He told *Kerrang!*'s Mick Wall, 'songwriting should never be a closed shop anyway. Ultimately, I'm up for working with anybody who interests me when it comes to writing. Who it is that writes the numbers is never the most important thing, it's whether the songs you have at the end are any good or not that counts.'[323]

After the tour ended, Coverdale and Vandenberg started working together on new material. Coverdale said they had been 'putting together bits and pieces' and he explained why he hoped the collaboration would prove successful: 'One reason I'd wanted to work with Adrian,' Coverdale revealed, 'was that I've been an admirer of his songwriting for many years. In a lot of his work I see a very close parallel to what I do.'[324]

This collaboration, of course, left Campbell out in the cold and this was much the same situation that had left him alienated from Ronnie Dio. In fact, it was even worse: in Dio, Campbell had co-songwriting credits on every album, but on the next Whitesnake album it must have seemed to Campbell that all the songwriting credits would go to Coverdale and Vandenberg. While this would have been to Campbell's financial detriment, his unhappiness was compounded by the knowledge that Whitesnake would not be a genuinely collaborative creative project, and that he would be reduced to just being Coverdale's guitarist.

Many years later, Campbell summed up his feelings about Whitesnake, saying: 'It was never to my ears personally and no disrespect to any of the players in the band — all fantastic players — but I don't feel that we ever really gelled and certainly not in the way that the Dio band was musically just so connected.'[325]

In addition, Campbell was never entirely comfortable with the media attention the band attracted, nor with certain media obligations that came with being in a band such as Whitesnake. For example, during the tour, MTV asked the band to take a 'Snake Train' along with 50 contest winners from Charleston to Daytona Beach, Florida to guest at MTV's Spring Break celebrations. When asked if he enjoyed the promotional trip, Campbell responded: 'It was fine, but I feel a little bit guilty about it. I felt I should have enjoyed it more, because it's part of my job to be a performer as well as a musician. But that's the part of my job I don't always feel comfortable in. To be cast into this situation where you're so popular that everyone's just tuggin' at you and expects so much of you... Whitesnake is very, very professional, and an image-conscious band. And Dio never was. Maybe that's why I feel a little uncomfortable sometimes. When it becomes a 24-hour day thing. I find it difficult to cope with.'[326]

Vandenberg revealed that Campbell was involved in initial rehearsals for the next album but was 'really moody.' Vandenberg speculated that it was at that point that Coverdale decided to oust Campbell from the band because 'he didn't want to work in that atmosphere.'[327] In December 1988, an official press release announced that Campbell had left Whitesnake in what Coverdale described as 'an unfortunate but amicable parting.'[328]

There may have been another contributing reason, however. Rumours abounded that Campbell's girlfriend fell afoul of Tawny Kitaen, who forbade her from being part of the tour party. While Campbell never spoke about this at the time, he perhaps hinted at it more obliquely. For example, when *Circus* magazine asked if Whitesnake's success had changed his life, Campbell responded that it 'made a huge difference' financially, but that he missed his parents whom he hadn't seen since the tour began, and also his girlfriend of two years, a photographer's stylist named Saskia, who 'comes over every now and then.' In addition, Vandenberg's girlfriend was also not part of the touring party: she continued to live in Holland and Vandenberg had only been back there two weeks out of the last ten months.[329]

Stories about Kitaen's alleged behaviour reached legendary proportions. For example, *Metal Hammer* speculated that Whitesnake's pre-Christmas European tour was cancelled not because of Coverdale's ill-health but instead because Kitaen did not want the band to perform in West Germany, where Coverdale's ex-wife lived.[330]

In any event, Campbell confirmed the rumours decades later in explaining why he and Coverdale parted company: 'It was a very uncomfortable situation,' he recalled, 'along with the fact that my ex-wife and Tawny Kitaen, David's wife at the time, just didn't get on at all so that added to the drama.'[331]

Perhaps it wasn't all due to Kitaen's alleged diva mentality: many years later, Vandenberg claimed that Campbell's partner was 'a pain in the ass to everybody — to the sound guy, to the light guy, to the management, to everything.'[332]

Whitesnake never again reached the heights of the *Whitesnake / 1987 album*, and the Coverdale-Vandenberg writing partnership was a bittersweet experience for Vandenberg. During the recording process for *Slip of the Tongue*, the guitarist injured his hand and was only able to record a few guitar parts. To finish the album, Coverdale brought in Steve Vai, who had gained a reputation for virtuoso playing during his time with Frank Zappa, and a reputation for rock star excess when working with Dave Lee Roth.

Vai was one of four guitarists cited by *Metal Hammer* magazine in 1989 as pushing the boundaries of guitar experimentation, the other three being Yngwie Malmsteen, Gary Moore, and — somewhat ironically — Vivian Campbell.[333] Vai also had a solo album (entitled *Passion and Warfare*) to promote, and he saw Whitesnake as a vehicle to gain further exposure. Vandenberg didn't recover in time for Whitesnake's tour to promote *Slip of the Tongue*, so Vai took his place. After the tour, Coverdale disassembled the band and took a three-year break from music. Vandenberg wouldn't play with Whitesnake again until the band's 1997 album, *Restless Heart*.

Despite Geffen's press release claiming that the Coverdale-Campbell split was 'amicable,' there was some bad blood between the two. While they never indulged in the bitter public name-calling that characterised the Campbell and Dio split, Coverdale nevertheless advised Campbell to ask himself why he had now been fired from two superstar bands, while Campbell said a few months after the announcement that he and Coverdale parted company because the vocalist 'only offers a large amount of cash [but] no artistic freedom.'[334]

Of course, money was a factor and song writing credits have traditionally been a source of dispute for bands. However, in Campbell's case it really does seem that Campbell needed to feel part of a band in which his creative impulses were respected, and his contributions acknowledged. He has spoken enthusiastically and with passion about how the members of Dio struck sparks when they played together. They all knew that together they brought the best out of each other and that the sum was greater than the parts. In contrast, he said of Whitesnake: 'I don't really think of [it] as being part of my career because I never got to write any new songs with them... That line-up of Whitesnake never really gelled musically… it doesn't mean an awful lot to me from a musical point of view.'[335]

In the years that followed, Campbell described his relationship with Coverdale as 'strange,' mainly due to the way they parted company. Coverdale left it to his management and record company to break the news to Campbell, which was something the guitarist did not appreciate. Nevertheless, they did eventually make up. When Def Leppard and Whitesnake first toured together in 2008, Campbell and Coverdale spoke about the manner of Campbell's departure from the band. Campbell revealed: 'David was very apologetic and pointed out that he was in this bad relationship, living in an ivory tower, having people do things instead of doing those things by himself.'[336]

In 2015, when Def Leppard topped the bill on a UK tour with Whitesnake and Black Star Riders, Campbell was asked if he would enjoy catching up again with Coverdale and Tommy Aldridge. He responded: 'It will be good to see those guys again. I didn't realise Tommy was back with Whitesnake again. I can't keep track of who's where these days but yes, I'm looking forward to seeing them on the tour.'[337]

In fact, Coverdale invited Campbell to make a guest appearance with Whitesnake during the final show of their tour, so on December 19, 2015, at the Sheffield Arena, Coverdale introduced Campbell on to the stage, saying: 'Ladies and gentleman, with great pride and great honour, once a snake, always a fucking snake, on the guitar Mr Vivian Campbell.' Campbell performed 'Still Of The Night,' sharing rhythm and lead parts with Joel Hoekstra and Reb Beach. It was the reconciliatory moment Campbell never got to have with Ronnie Dio: he was, however, determined not to repeat the mistakes of his youth, and his reconciliation with Coverdale meant a lot.

## Lou Gramm

Campbell's involvement with Whitesnake ensured the years 1987 to 1988 were among the busiest and most lucrative of his career. Despite his departure from the band, the following couple of years proved almost as busy, although much less lucrative. Campbell first worked with singer Lou Gramm on his 1989 album *Long Hard Look.* Gramm, described by *Kerrang!* as 'one of the great rock singers of all time,' was the vocalist for the platinum-selling American-British rock band Foreigner. However, he was increasingly growing estranged from the band, and from guitarist Mick Jones in particular. *Long Hard Look* was his second solo album, and in May 1990, as he was preparing the album's promotional tour, he announced that he and Foreigner had parted company. Gramm and Campbell met during the recording sessions for the album when producer Peter Wolf asked Campbell to perform on some tracks. Gramm said, 'I really liked the way he played and we hit it off personally.'[338]

*Long Hard Look* was released on October 13, 1989. Campbell featured on three songs, playing electric guitar on the tracks 'Broken Dreams' and 'Day One,' and lead and rhythm guitar on 'Hangin' On My Hip.' 'Broken Dreams' begins with atmospheric bends and guitar effects from Campbell before revealing itself as a mid-paced pop song punctuated throughout by Campbell's melodic guitar runs. 'Hangin' On My Hip' is a riff-driven track on which Campbell's guitar tone bears some resemblance to that of Mick Jones in any number of Foreigner rock tracks. Campbell's speedy guitar solo elevates it above similar upbeat rock tracks. It begins around the two-minute mark and continues until the song ends 100 seconds later. On an otherwise pop-themed album, Campbell's fierce playing really stands out. 'Day One' is a three minute, moderately paced pop song with an upbeat theme about love and devotion. Campbell plays a repeating descending pattern after each verse. Toward's the song's end, that changes to an ascending pattern which Campbell repeats as the song plays out.

*Long Hard Look* was a top 40 US Billboard hit and its success encouraged Gramm to organise a tour to further promote the album. Dann Huff, who had also played rhythm and lead guitar on *Long Hard Look*, was the touring guitarist and Campbell was not involved. Some clue as to why Gramm would later seek out Campbell to work with once more comes in a *Kerrang!* review of Gramm's live show at the Universal Amphitheatre in Los Angeles. Reviewer Brian Brandes Brinkerhoff, a self-confessed Gramm fan, wrote: 'Lou's singing was great, but save for [bass player Bruce] Turgon the rest of the band just weren't happening in the looks, image and stage presence area... Where Lou needed a roaring fire, his band delivered just an occasional spark... If Lou wants to rock, then he and Turgon better find the band that can really roll.'[339]

Gramm would later say that he had 'good fortune' that Campbell was available to play on the album, that they 'struck up a friendship and talked about working together at some point in the future.' However, at the time Campbell was involved with a band called Riverdogs so there were no firm plans to collaborate again in the immediate future.[340]

**Riverdogs, 1989-1990**

When Campbell parted company with David Coverdale, the blow was softened somewhat by his ongoing involvement with a Californian band called Riverdogs. They were up and comers without a record contract, and Campbell had been giving guitar lessons to their then-guitarist, Nick Brophy, as well as helping the band produce some demos.

At that time, the band consisted of Rob Lamothe, who sang vocals and played acoustic guitar, Marc Danzeisen on drums, and Nick Brophy on lead guitar. The more Campbell heard of the music, the more he wanted to be involved. Singer Rob Lamothe recalled: 'The night before [Campbell] was to leave to begin pre-production for [Whitesnake's] *Slip Of The Tongue*, he called and asked if he could join my band. Label interest was there... and having Vivian didn't hurt that.' The label in question was Epic and Riverdogs drew the attention of its president, Tony Martell. A recording contract soon followed.

It was agreed that Campbell would take over lead guitar duties and Brophy would play bass on the album, while Mike Baird and Allen DeSilva would share percussion duties. Nevertheless, on the album cover and on promo singles, the band is photographed as a trio of Campbell, Lamothe and Brophy, rather than a four-piece. 'The Riverdogs record was really something I wanted to do,' Campbell revealed, 'because it was a departure from Dio and Whitesnake. It was a rock band that had a hard edge. It was guitar driven but it wasn't a heavy metal band. It was very song oriented and blues influenced.'[341] Of course, Campbell also knew his future wasn't going to be with Coverdale, so it must have seemed that Riverdogs was a chance to start afresh with a new group of musical collaborators.

Recruiting Campbell would, however, turn out to be a double-edged sword for Riverdogs: on the one hand, as Lamothe indicated, Campbell brought his considerable guitar skills and reputation to the band, thus ensuring that the unknown Riverdogs would attract interest from the music press. On the other hand, Campbell had gained his reputation playing hard rock, so initially Epic tried to market Riverdogs as part of that genre. 'Epic actually suggested we put a pack of wolves on the album cover with blood dripping of their fangs,' Lamothe recalled. 'I had to ask them if they even listened to the record.'[342]

The eponymously titled album was produced by Michael Frondelli, who had worked previously with the Rolling Stones, and it was mixed by Jeff Glixman, who had worked with the likes of Gary Moore and the Georgia Satellites. Campbell is credited as co-writer of four tracks:

> 'I Believe' (Campbell/Lamothe/Brophy/Allen DeSilva)
> 'Water From The Moon' (Campbell/Lamothe)
> 'Rain, Rain' (Campbell/Lamothe/Brophy/DeSilva)
> 'America' (Campbell/Lamothe)

The promotional single of 'I Believe' credits the lyrics to Lamothe and the music to Campbell, so it's likely the credits on the album reflect a similar division of labour.

The opening track, 'Whisper,' begins with some brooding guitar sounds and arpeggios from Campbell, before the song's main riff kicks in. It's immediately clear that Lamothe's impressive vocals set Riverdogs aside from the pack, and the combination of guitar tools Campbell has at his disposal, together with Lamothe's vocals, make this track a memorable and classy opener.

'Toy Soldier' is perhaps Riverdogs best known track. It was released as a single, together with a promotional video. Its elegiac lyrics, together with Lamothe's Steve-Earl-like vocals, had potential to latch on to the downbeat mood of Gen X, but whatever combination of good promotion, radio airplay, catchy hooks, MTV exposure and good fortune is required to get a hit single were to fail Riverdogs on this occasion. Perhaps the reason can be seen in the promotional video, which is an on-stage band performance of the song. Although the band's music was a mix of folk-rock and AOR, its visual aesthetic was typical of glam metal acts such as Cinderella and Bon Jovi, and although no one knew it at the time, the era of glam metal was coming to an end.

'Big House' is a mid-paced track with a country-rock vibe. Its lyrics are suggestive of an abusive relationship from which one of the participants ends up in gaol. However, in truth, the lyrics are a hodge podge of well-known phrases arranged into rhyming couplets, and it's therefore open to multiple interpretations.

At first listen, 'Holy War's lyrics suggest its theme is conflict in the Middle East, but Lamothe again draws upon well-known phrases that obscure meaning, so the song can be interpreted more broadly as a physical conflict in any location, or even an interpersonal battle. Its musical structure is arpeggiated chords played on an acoustic guitar, before Campbell switches to an electric to play heavier, fuller chords. His guitar solo on this track is perhaps the heaviest on the album and is reminiscent of his Dio days.

'Baby Blue' is a mellower track similar to the melodic rock of UK band The Cult in this era. Campbell's playing is almost a tribute to Billy Duffy and his Gibson Les Paul. As the song progresses its tone becomes heavier, and it begins to take on an epic feel before fading out.

'I Believe' is done in the kind of funk-rock style that US band Extreme were popularising at that time. Campbell shares lead vocals and sings backing vocals. Unlike the restrained style of 'Baby Blue,' Campbell is let off the leash on this track, which features very fast picking and heavy-rock style pick squeals.

'Water From The Moon' is another rock track that mimics the heavier side of Foreigner or Boston. Lamothe called it the 'rockin-est tune on the record.'[343] It relies almost entirely on guitar riffs, arpeggios, and fills for structure and colour, and an innovative guitar solo is enhanced by Campbell's liberal use of the tremolo arm.

'Rain, Rain' is a mid-tempo rock track with chugging rhythm guitar and colourful fills. It is pleasant enough, but somewhat uneventful — not quite filler, but not a stand-out track either. Campbell performs another killer solo that is both melodic and technically accomplished.

The lyrics to the album's penultimate track, 'Spooky,' indicate that its subject is an injured war veteran ('Tommy') who struggles to cope with civilian life. The verses tell the story via third-person narration, while the chorus is narrated in the first person to allow us to hear Tommy's thoughts and inner struggles. Its structure and tempo, together with Campbell's squealing guitar fills, and lyrics that deal with an urban working-class man who gets a raw deal, are comparable to Bon Jovi's 1987 hit single 'Livin'

On A Prayer,' but without that song's hopeful optimism.

'America' tells the story of the American Dream, and the promise of freedom and prosperity handed down from generation to generation. Lamothe compares that to the reality for many working-class people, which is a lifetime of hard work for little or no reward. Campbell plays clean arpeggiated chord patterns, without distortion, on an electric guitar that is then overlayed with acoustic guitar. This is a kind of singalong track, comparable to Bruce Springsteen's 'Born In The USA' or even Woody Guthrie's 'This Land Is Your Land' in the sense that a rousing chorus lulls the listener into believing it is a celebratory patriotic song, until the lyrics reveal otherwise.

Campbell deployed his full bag of tricks on this album, using alternate picking, palm muting, power slides, tremolo and finger bends, trills, hammer-ons, pull-offs and pinch harmonics to add a spectrum of colour. He also used a range of effects such as flange, reverb, distortion, wah-wah and chorus to provide variety and atmosphere. The *Riverdogs* album is therefore somewhat of a showcase for Campbell's many skills: depending on the needs of the song, he is at times restrained, holding back from picking too many notes, or he shreds in a heavier rock style.

Given the variety of techniques at his disposal, he was likely encouraged by bandmates to showcase his talent to the greatest extent, but in general, his playing is more restrained than in his earlier career. Nevertheless, Campbell felt he played too much guitar on the album, saying 'while I was making that record I wanted to turn the corner, but I didn't want to turn the whole way so I had a tendency to overplay and when I listen to the record it sounds a little bit overdone to me.'[344]

Two promo singles accompanied the album release. These were 'Toy Soldiers' and 'I Believe.' Promotional material for the latter supports Lamothe's belief that Campbell would bring the band more media attention. For example, text on the promo CD packaging reads: 'Dear radio person. You may not have heard of Riverdogs, but I'll bet you've heard of one of its members: Vivian Campbell. That's right, Vivian Campbell from Dio and Whitesnake.' In addition, adverts for 'I Believe were placed in industry magazines with the following text: '145 AOR reporters believed in "Toy Soldiers", from the Top 20 LP by The Riverdogs. Now comes "I Believe", the powerhouse rocker spotlighting the intense guitar playing of Vivian Campbell. To hear is to believe.'[345]

Epic would, however, only give 'Toy Soldiers' a commercial release, with 'Water From The Moon' on the B-side. Despite its promotional performance video, the single failed to chart.

Album reviews were positive and enthusiastic. For example, the *Los*

*Angeles Times* called Riverdogs 'a hot new L.A. rock band' whose bluesy rock 'n' roll 'packs a real punch.' The paper claimed the album stood out from other hard rock releases due to its 'passion, substance and lyrical integrity.'[346]

The radio subscription magazine, *CMJ: New Music Report*, also gave the album a positive recommendation, claiming that it 'comes out swinging with inspirational and accessible radio-ready hard rock.' It continued: 'the band splices commercial metal with a heavy dose of the blues' and it praised Campbell for 'melodic chops and runs [that] transform the simple folk songs into bluesy power tracks.' In particular, the magazine singled out 'Water From The Moon,' 'Holy War' and 'Baby Blue' as 'red, white and blue' songs that would appeal to the American market.[347]

In summer 1990, the band made a number of radio appearances to promote the album. For example, on June 22-24, 'Vivian Campbell/ Riverdogs' (as they were advertised), appeared on *Metalshop*, which was billed as 'the only national program devoted to metal' and 'the only show with teeth.'[348]

Then in July and August 1990 Campbell and Lamothe undertook a promotional radio tour, performing live acoustic versions of their album tracks, as well as a cover of 'The House Of The Rising Sun,' a song sometimes referred to as the first folk-rock hit, making it a perfect fit for Riverdogs. The tour featured at least 11 performances across the US, taking them to radio stations and clubs in Sacramento, Dallas, Cleveland, New York, Detroit, San Francesco, Los Angeles, San Jose, Milwaukee, Philadelphia, and Pittsburgh.

These performances were audio recorded and a selection from each appeared on a promo CD called *On Air* (1990), and then 15 years later on a remastered and reissued 2-CD version of the debut album. Both releases included a non-album track entitled 'Pennsylvania.' The *On Air* version is a live acoustic rendition with Campbell sharing lead vocals. *On Air* is a further example of Campbell's versatility. Although best known for his electric lead playing and heavy riffing, here he demonstrates his skills on acoustic guitar, especially playing rhythm and adapting the studio-recorded solos to a live setting. In addition, he shares tasteful lead and harmony vocals with Lamothe.

This promotional acoustic tour represents a considerable investment of time and money by Epic in that it took a substantial amount of planning and coordination with local radio stations and record shops. This demonstrates the faith Epic initially had in the group, and its optimism the album would launch the band towards national recognition.

At least one further live gig followed these summer acoustic performances, namely a Halloween night gig in San Jose, California. This was not 'unplugged,' and along with their own tracks, Riverdogs played an electric version of Led Zeppelin's 'Rock And Roll.'

Despite selling 200,000 discs in the United States, Riverdogs fell victim to corporate infighting. Epic's Tony Martell was deposed and without his support the band found themselves in limbo. 'We were doomed before our record even came out,' Lamothe said. Without the backing of their label, and with no further promotion in the pipeline, 'it was like we fell off the face of the earth.'[349]

Soon after, reports began to appear that Campbell had left Riverdogs.[350] Not long after that, Riverdogs and Epic parted company, with the band asking the label to release them from their contract 'due to numerous personnel changes at key positions at the label, and a difference in opinion regarding musical direction.'[351]

Campbell would later reveal that he left for financial reasons: the record label wasn't supporting the band and there was little prospect of making any immediate profit from Riverdogs. Because he was the only member of Riverdogs not drawing a salary from the recording budget, he had been supporting himself financially for 18 months and, as he put it, he 'couldn't afford not to work.'[352]

Retrospective discussions about the band and album tend to express surprise that neither were commercially successful, and to reflect on what might have been. The album was a powerful expression of melodic rock, but in retrospect it seems clear that the band arrived on the scene at the tail end of the popularity of that genre. Unfortunately for Campbell, his next collaboration would suffer much the same fate.

## Shadow King, December 1990-April 1992

By the end of the year music magazines such as the UK's *Kerrang!* and USA's *Radio & Records* were reporting that Campbell and Gramm had formed a new band together entitled Shadow King. It would also feature Turgon on bass and Kevin Valentine on drums. Gramm told *Kerrang!*'s Paul Elliott that the band's name derived from a song still unfinished at the time about a huge, decadent, apocalyptic city with the lyrics, 'I'll be there when the sun goes down/Welcome to the world of the shadow king.' Gramm liked the name Shadow King, which he considered 'dark and powerful.'[353]

In that same contemporary interview, Gramm said: 'I've surrounded myself with performance-orientated people... When I was putting a band together, Viv's band, Riverdogs, was falling apart.' Gramm would later reveal in his autobiography that he was 'going to stay solo, but then the opportunity arose to form a new band. Vivian was available, his only condition was that the group not be the Lou Gramm band but rather a collaborative effort, and I was fine with that.'[354] Campbell's one proviso, that the new endeavour be a collaborative experience, supports the assessment that Campbell's main driving force was not financial, but instead he needed to be an equal partner in a band that would allow him to express his musical creativity.

The band's self-titled debut album was completed by the summer of 1991 and had a scheduled release on the Atlantic label in October. It featured ten tracks, nine of which were written by Gramm and Turgon. Campbell co-wrote only one song, which is a little surprising given his stipulation about collaboration and his previous troubles with Dio and Coverdale. However, Gramm and Turgon were already an established songwriting team, with Turgon having been involved in the writing process for Gramm's two solo albums.[355]

Furthermore, at least some of the tracks that would appear on *Shadow King* had been written by Gramm and Turgon before Gramm and Campbell had agreed to work together in this new band. In a filmed interview for MTV's *Headbanger's Ball*, which was held on the day of the band's first and only live gig at the London Astoria, Gramm explained that after Shadow King had played together more, and as they all grew to know each other better, both Campbell's singing and writing would develop, and he would play a larger role in the band's future.[356]

The opening track of the album was almost an iteration of this idea. It begins with keyboard, bass, percussion and vocals before Campbell's introduction with a build-up of feedback that launches into clean and melodic riffs. Campbell's playing is restrained throughout, playing a mixture of arpeggiated patterns and tasteful fills. The overall effect is of a smouldering band ready to burst into life.

In keeping with that idea, 'Anytime Anywhere' is more upbeat and Campbell's riffs drive the song along. His fills are heavier and faster than on the opening track. *Hard Report* called 'Anytime Anywhere' a 'rocker that grabs you from the beginning and rocks you 'til the end.'[357] The end, in this case, is a polite fade out that actually undoes some of the earlier rock impact.

The keyboard-led 'Once Upon A Time' juxtaposes the fairytale-inspired title with hard-boiled lyrics about trying to survive in a tough urban landscape. Campbell's sparse chords, which are played clean without distortion or effects, seem to be marking time until his first solo, which features discordant notes that create atmosphere, and then the second solo where he takes the reign to play some tricky patterns which continue as the track plays out.

'Don't Even Know I'm Alive' is a brooding power ballad on which Campbell's riffs are low in the mix. Hot guitar fills punctuate the track, although the absence of a proper solo demonstrates the melodic rock credentials of, and perhaps the weakness in Gramm and Turgon's writing partnership. While radio friendly, the song is not very dynamic: it is evenly paced and fails to build to a climax. Nevertheless, *Hard Report* called 'Don't Even Know I'm Alive' a 'trademark Lou Gramm vocal with that great Vivian Campbell guitar to make it soar.'[358]

'Boy' is another classy AOR track, with Campbell playing in this new, restrained style. However, he does unleash a heavy and fast solo, tempered only by its ending which features some delicate harmonics. Gramm revealed that the song was a simple reflective statement: 'this is what I am, take it or leave it.'[359]

Campbell opens 'I Want You' with a powerful chord which he lets ring. However, the track unfolds into the type of power pop that was executed so successfully by the likes of Foreigner and Bryan Adams in the 1980s and early 1990s before grunge swept much of that genre off the airwaves. 'I Want You' was released as a single in Autumn, 1991. Kent Zimmerman of *The Gavin Report* described it as '4/4 medium tempo, pounding,' with Gramm relying on 'sheer blues power and pushing his vocal range up an octave and a half without resorting to a Heavy Metal shriek' and Campbell 'doling out some grinding chords that are sanded around the corners.'[360]

A promotional video shows Campbell looking muscular and sexy in a tight, crimson-coloured gilet/waistcoat. The video adopted the template set by Whitesnake four years earlier, consisting of a fully permed and pretty band performing on a rooftop while in the loft apartment below a beautiful woman dances provocatively. It's doubtful Campbell's presence in the band led to this style of video; it was just another example of the style many genre bands adopted after Whitesnake had such demonstrable success with this look and style. Despite the commercial potential of this radio-friendly, power pop song, and the promotional video, the single failed to chart.

'This Heart Of Stone' is a keyboard-driven, commercially-minded piece of power pop. Campbell embroiders the simple power chord structure with neat and tasteful patterns. The solo is a further example of the new style he had developed, picking less notes and relying on bends and melodic feedback rather than just speed to make the solo interesting.

'Danger In The Dance Of Love' is the heaviest track thus far on the album, with some distortion added to the guitar to give the riffs more crunch. Campbell plays some fast, repeating patterns as if to remind the rest of the band of his credentials. Together with Gramm's dynamic vocals, this is a harder side of Shadow King that rarely came to the fore.

Keyboards introduce 'No Man's Land,' then Campbell plays some heavy power chords. As the song develops, Campbell mixes those power chords with arpeggiated chords which contribute to this song's radio-friendly AOR vibe character. This track features a range of dynamics from heavy rock to quieter playing from Campbell which evokes a sad and thoughtful mood tying in to the lyrical theme of the loneliness caused by a broken relationship.

The final track of the album, and the sole track co-written by Campbell, is the gentle 'Russia.' It began when Campbell first played Gramm a cassette tape with the acoustic guitar pattern. Gramm would later reveal that he found the guitar line 'so haunting and the mood of the song very ethnic that it can either be interpreted as a personal relationship or a call to another country. It's really wide open, it works any way.'[361] The lyrics were co-written and came quickly after he heard Campbell's demo, Gramm revealed. 'Russia' was to have been the second single from the album had not the band split up soon after.[362]

One further Shadow King track was released, not on their debut album but instead on the soundtrack of the film *Highlander II: The Quickening* (1991). The movie was an attempt to emulate the successful format of the original, which featured a rock soundtrack by the band Queen. On this occasion, multiple artists provided songs for the soundtrack, including ex-Deep Purple man Glenn Hughes, and Shadow King, who are, however, listed on the album credits as Lou Gramm and the Lou Gramm Band. The song is called 'One Dream' and it stands out as the heaviest track Campbell recorded with Gramm. On this occasion Campbell returned to his trademark high gain guitar sound, with plenty of pinch harmonics and pick squeals.

## Reviews

Reviews of *Shadow King* were mixed, although a common theme was praise for Gramm's vocals and for Campbell's playing. For example, *Billboard* wrote: 'New power quartet helmed by Lou Gramm sounds like, you guessed it, the old Foreigner. Gramm always sounds best when he's pushed on such standard rockers as "Anytime Anywhere" and "Boy" and he's in fine vocal form here. Ex- Dio and Whitesnake guitarist Vivian Campbell is impressive as always. The material doesn't have the kick of Foreigner, but fans of the group might prefer this to that band's current line-up.'[363]

In contrast, *New Sunday Times* was mostly unimpressed, calling the album 'run-of-the-mill hard rock' and bemoaning the 'predictability of standard AOR.' While Gramm was trying to put Foreigner behind him, comparisons between both bands were inevitable, with the *New Sunday Times* favouring Foreigner's mainly successful body of work: 'There are a couple of songs that sound like Foreigner fare,' it opined, 'but these are not enough to make up for the shortcomings.'[364]

Perhaps the most positive review was from *Kerrang!* magazine's Paul Elliott, who called the album 'high quality.' The urge to compare Shadow King to Foreigner is understandable, with Elliott noting Shadow King's similarity to the 'hard-rocking Foreigner of 1991.' He continued: 'Ultimately, Foreigner will never make another album as great as *4*, but Lou Gramm and Shadow King might. With this debut, they're getting there.' Elliott also noted how Campbell had toned down his usual playing style to better fit Shadow King's soft rock stylings: 'Campbell exhibits his customary flash on "Once Upon A Time," but elsewhere he plays with restraint, notably on the delicate "Russia." The riff on "Anytime, Anywhere" is a killer, but Viv leaves it clean and simple, where a few years ago he would have squeezed in a bunch of squeals and hammer-ons at every turn.'[365]

When Elliott interviewed Gramm before Shadow King's Astoria gig, Elliott put it to Gramm that Campbell had changed his playing style for Shadow King: 'Once brash, Campbell now plays with a genuine understanding of simplicity and space,' he opined. Gramm responded: 'Viv can play all day on a song: he'll come up with a myriad of things. It's new for him to leave spaces and he's enjoying it. We suggested it to him; we loaded him up with all the Free albums and he rediscovered Paul Kossoff, who's the guy for space.'[366]

In addition, Campbell explained that he felt he overplayed on the 1991 *Riverdogs* album and he didn't wish to repeat that error on *Shadow King*. 'I'm very cognisant about... what's appropriate for the song. And in the case of Shadow King the songs are basically all really melodic just with a guitar edge. So, if anything, I'd rather be understated than overstated particularly for this first record... I don't consider that I was too subdued on the record. There's maybe one or two songs where I cater to the less rather than more school, it's just a question what's appropriate for the record, what's appropriate for the band.'[367]

A further positive review came from *Circus* magazine, who wrote: 'the music is sweet and this album may be a sleeper... Once a name, always a threat... Gramm may have the goods with this one.'[368]

James Gaden wrote a retrospective review of the album for *Fireworks* magazine, calling it 'an absolute beast of a record... a superb record [that] deserves to be spoken about in the same breath as other one-off classics like Coverdale/Page and Hughes/Thrall. In short, this is fantastic!'[369] Gaden suggested a few reasons why the album 'flew under the radar' when first released, including lack of support from the record label, failure of a single to make an impact, and that the band only played one live show.

The key selling point for the band and album was the involvement of Gramm and Campbell, as indicated by the magazine adverts which featured a picture of the four band members but had a tagline which only mentioned Gramm and Campbell: 'The brand-new album featuring Lou Gramm, the melodic rock vocalist and ex frontman with Foreigner, and Vivian Campbell, ex guitarists with Dio and Whitesnake.' Sheila Rene of *The Gavin Report* called the band 'the world's best kept secret,' indicating that she expected the combination of Gramm and Campbell would be a commercial success.[370] In contrast, *Hard Report* was even clearer in pointing to Campbell as Shadow King's main draw when it urged its readers to 'Watch for Vivian Campbell and Shadow King to perform on Arsenio' on February 27, 1992.[371] In a similar vein, in a *Kerrang!* review of the album, Paul Elliott listed the group line up and referred to Campbell as 'doubtless the one they'll all talk about.'[372]

**London Astoria, December 13, 1991**
Shadow King played only one concert, at London's Astoria Theatre on December 13, 1991. This was part of an 'American Dream' series of concerts that also featured shows on different nights by the bands Badlands, Scream, and Warrior Soul. For this gig, Gramm employed keyboardist Rick Seratte to fill out the band's sound. Gramm told Paul Elliott that he might play some older tracks such as Foreigner's 'Dirty White Boy' and 'Juke Box Hero,' and a song from his first solo album, *Ready Or Not* (1987), entitled 'Midnight Blue' — 'songs I feel are personal,' the singer revealed.[373]

Gramm was confident that Shadow King tracks would stand up well in a live setting. He told Elliott, for example, that every song on the record 'was rehearsed on a small stage, so they translate well live.' It came as no surprise, therefore, that the majority of songs on the set list for the Astoria gig were from that album. This is the set list based on Neil Jeffries' *Kerrang!* review:[374]

I Want You
Danger In The Dance Of Love
Boy
Don't Even Know I'm Alive
Anytime, Anywhere
Once Upon A Time
What Would It Take
Russia
No Man's Land
Ready Or Not

Dirty White Boy
Midnight Blue

Encore:
Tin Soldier
Fire and Water

In total, nine out of ten songs before the encore were from the *Shadow King* album, and only 'This Heart of Stone' is missing; 'Ready or Not and Midnight Blue were from Gramm's 1987 solo album; and 'Dirty White Boy' was from Foreigner's 1979 album, *Head Games*. The two encore songs were cover versions of the Small Faces' 'Tin Soldier' and Free's 'Fire and Water.'

While Foreigner fans may have been disappointed by the absence of that band's many popular hits, Gramm was keen to turn the page on Foreigner and to promote his new musical vehicle. At the same time, the set list reveals that the singer was not completely renouncing his back catalogue, whereas the encore songs were a tribute to some of Shadow King's influences.

According to Jeffries, the first part of the show was marred by issues with Campbell's guitar sound, and it was only after 'Once Upon A Time' that the sound improved. 'Previously,' wrote Jeffries, 'whenever Vivian Campbell had delivered an otherwise cracking solo, what should have been a piercing lead break was little more than an annoying squeak.' While Jeffries praised Gramm's vocals, he was keener on the singer's older songs than he was the new Shadow King material. According to Jeffries, it was only when the band played 'Ready or Not,' 'Dirty White Boy,' and 'Midnight Blue' that the band 'suddenly… sounded very special indeed.'

Jeffries also bemoaned the show's brevity — 'Only a one hour set then an encore' — because a longer set would have left space for more of Gramm's back catalogue. Of course, Jeffries had missed the point: Gramm was doing no more or less than Ronnie Dio did in including a scattering of Rainbow and Black Sabbath songs in the Dio set list, or as David Coverdale did in the later years of Whitesnake in incorporating Deep Purple songs into the band's set list.

Footage exists of four songs played that night, namely 'Danger In The Dance Of Love,' 'Boy,' 'Don't Even Know I'm Alive,' and 'Anytime, Anywhere.' The band lined up in the traditional way, with Campbell positioned front of stage right, Gramm centre stage, and Turgon stage left. Behind them on a raised stage were Valentine stage left and Seratte stage right. Campbell was dressed in a decorated waistcoat and faded blue jeans, with a necklace and bracelet. Together with Turgon, he sang backing vocals and the mixture of all three voices proved powerful and harmonic. *RAW*'s Dave Ling claimed that the band's performance at the Astoria was evidence, in particular, of the chemistry between Campbell and Gramm.[375]

Like most AOR bands, Shadow King's live show had a harder edge with all of the studio production and effects stripped away. This is particularly evident with 'Anytime, Anywhere': on the studio version, Campbell's playing is a little low in the mix to avoid overwhelming the other instruments and vocals, but when heard live and with a higher monitor mix, his soloing is exceptionally heavy. In fact, earlier in the day, Campbell told MTV's *Headbanger's Ball* that in contrast to his studio work, 'tonight when we play live, I will probably play a little bit more aggressively.'[376]

When asked if the band had plans to come back to Europe, Campbell responded: 'We'd like to, as soon as they'll have us.' Gramm revealed: 'We've just signed with an agency and they've promised us something pretty good for 1992 and we're going to need all of that to establish this band but we don't know what it is yet.' Campbell also said that he hoped the Astoria gig would be the start of many by the band. It seemed, therefore, that both were committed to Shadow King at least through 1992.[377]

In fact, Campbell said joining Shadow King was the best thing that happened to him in 1991, enabling him to come to Europe (and to visit his family), 'having a good time, being allowed to do what it is I do, because if I didn't do this, I don't know what I'd do. Thank God for rock 'n' roll!'

Indeed, three gigs were scheduled to take place in California in March 1992, including two nights at the Coach House, San Juan Capistrano on the 11th and 12th, and a further gig on the 14th at the Ventura Concert Theatre.[378] However, the end for Shadow King came before that when US rock band Cinderella lured away Kevin Valentine, and Campbell started rehearsing with Def Leppard.

Gramm responded graciously to the news saying, 'I wouldn't blame Vivian if he left because the kind of support we're getting from the label doesn't look too promising. If I had a chance to join Def Leppard I would too, let's face it, they're the world's premier Rock band.'[379] Gramm also said he would welcome Campbell back to Shadow King if it didn't work out with Def Leppard.[380]

When asked many years later why Shadow King ended, Gramm responded: 'because we got no support from Atlantic [Records].' Gramm claimed the album should have been a hit but Atlantic didn't promote it. He claimed he couldn't find the album in record stores. He said the Astoria gig 'went down a storm' and the band deserved more than a single gig. He inferred that Mick Jones collaborated with Atlantic to ensure Shadow

King wasn't a success, because if it were, Gramm would never return to Foreigner.[381]

Over time, however, a different story emerged. After Campbell joined Def Leppard, he explained: 'Ostensibly [Shadow King] was to be a band project as opposed to a solo record 'cause I had also played guitar on his previous solo record. And it turned out it was nothing like a band. It was another Lou Gramm solo record, so I basically wrote one song, played a bit of guitar and left.'[382]

This is, however, a truncated and simplified version of events. Campbell had been enthusiastic about Shadow King while it was his only vehicle to play professionally. However, when the chance to join Def Leppard cropped up, and in the knowledge that they were a proper band and not just a big-name singer who needed some backing musicians, Campbell eagerly embraced the opportunity, leaving Gramm somewhat adrift. The 'pull' factor from Def Leppard was stronger than the 'push' away from Shadow King, which — not withstanding Gramm's allegations about Atlantic Records — may well have continued as a touring and recording act had Campbell not so abruptly left for greener pastures.

Of course, when relying on press statements one has to be cognisant that musicians sometimes support a cover story to avoid bad publicity for themselves or those around them. Sometimes an unpalatable or damaging truth is only revealed many years later. In this instance, long after the facts about Gramm had already come to light, Campbell explained his real reason for leaving Shadow King: 'I quit,' he said, 'cause Lou was just having massive, massive problems with cocaine addiction, and there was no future with that.'[383]

# Chapter 4

## 'All I ever wanted to do was play guitar in a Rock band': Def Leppard

The strengths of Riverdogs and Shadow King were also their weaknesses. While one can point to individual circumstances in both bands that resulted in them being commercially unsuccessful, such as troubles with their record labels, it was also the case that both bands were on the cusp of a seismic shift in the public's taste for rock music. It's usually easier to see the wider picture in retrospect, but writer Douglas Coupland figured it out in real time by identifying a 'Generation X' of Americans, mostly younger people coming of age in the late 1980s, who were so disillusioned with the previous generation of 'baby boomers' that they blamed that generation for most of America's ills.

In America, and to an extent in the UK, the 1980s was an era of economic prosperity that came crashing to an end at the end of the decade. 'Gen X,' as they came to be known, blamed the crash on the selfishness of 'boomers' who benefitted from the greed of the decade's rat race, but left only a few scraps from the table for the next generation. Gen X responded as the punks did in the previous decade, by rebelling. This was reflected in popular culture, in novels, comic books, television, cinema, fashion, and music. One particular genre of music — grunge — best reflected that sense of rebellion and disillusionment.

Grunge originated in northern California and became associated, in particular, with the city of Seattle in Washington State, and with bands such as Mudhoney, Pearl Jam, Stone Temple Pilots, Alice in Chains, Soundgarden, and Nirvana. With its emphasis on stripping away excess and focusing on generational angst and disillusionment, grunge swept away most of the successful rock and heavy metal artists of the 1980s and crushed the hopes of those up-and-coming artists hoping to join the party — bands such as Riverdogs and Shadow King.

Just as punk's aesthetic in the 1970s was anti-virtuoso in rejecting the musicianship of artists such as Pink Floyd, Yes, Genesis, Emerson Lake and Palmer, and Queen, the grunge aesthetic was to reject the guitar heroes of the 1980s and instead to strip back solos to mere repetition of the main vocal melody. Kurt Cobain's solo on Nirvana's most iconic song, 'Feels Like Teen Spirit,' is a prime example of this. While grunge's 'back to basics' approach didn't quite 'kill the guitar solo,' as journalist Will Byers alleged, it did undermine the commercial value of 1980s guitar heroes like Campbell.[384]

It is deeply ironic, therefore, that after the commercial failure of his previous two bands, and the shift in the wind that left '80s rock bands still in the water, that Campbell would proceed to join Def Leppard, who might be considered not only the ultimate boomer band but were also emblematic of the type of guitar-based rock whose time had surely come and gone.

Leppard was a product of the New Wave of British Heavy Metal, a label that still carries some weight even if it was, like grunge, more a record label marketing ploy than a term musicians used to describe themselves. After attaining moderate success with their first two albums, Leppard was thrust into the spotlight after their 1983 album *Pyromania* became a commercial and critical success. The follow-up, *Hysteria* (1987), was a worldwide hit and for a few years Def Leppard was probably the biggest rock band in the world.

The release of *Hysteria* was delayed due to a car accident in which drummer Rick Allen lost an arm. Remarkably, over a period of years, Allen relearnt his craft with a specially made set of electronic drums. It would be another five years before Leppard's next album, *Adrenalize* (1992), hit the shops. This time the delay was caused by a mixture of circumstance including the ongoing success of *Hysteria*, which generated seven hit singles in the US, but also by guitarist Steve Clark's continuing battle with alcohol addiction.

In that time, grunge had changed the musical landscape. Although *Adrenalize* was a commercial success, and its leading single 'Let's Get Rocked' peaked at 15 in the Billboard Hot 100, its lyrical content, as well as the band's visual identity, left them appearing archaic compared to the likes of cool new grunge bands like Nirvana and Pearl Jam, or even 'alternative rock' bands such as Faith No More. At the time, it seemed like Campbell had jumped from one sinking ship onto another. Grunge was the future and bands like Leppard were the past.

On the plus side however, Leppard remained commercially successful. They were a household name and were respected as a band comprised of talented musicians with an enviable back catalogue. Moreover, unlike

Riverdogs and Shadow King, Leppard was an ongoing concern. Campbell explained why he found joining the band an attractive proposition: 'Def Leppard's commitment to their music and to each other has been well-documented over the years. These two factors have never gelled for me in previous associations. I therefore consider it to be a great privilege to be a part of a band who, as a fan, I have watched grow from young hopefuls into a bona fide rock institution. The music's a gas, and that level of commitment has been felt already.'[385]

Campbell also spoke about a more intangible attraction, a fellowship that Def Leppard seemed to have, unlike Dio and Whitesnake: 'People need to feel a part of something… When you've got a small group of people and they're creating… something as ethereal as music, something as intangible as being a rock band, they really have to get something out of it... to be a band, you have to have more in common than just playing instruments and making music. There has to be some kind of a bond there… some kind of understanding that goes deeper.'[386] In a *Los Angeles Times* interview, Joe Elliott revealed that Campbell 'wanted to join us because he saw that we were the same guys who had been together 15 years. He liked that.'[387]

Clark's alcohol-related death before the release of *Adrenalize* was a sad time for the band, and the rock world lost a fine musician. However, there was no question of Leppard disbanding. As a group, they had come through past traumas and line-up changes and, although tragic, Clark's alcohol addiction meant his death was not entirely unexpected. So, the band soon began looking for a replacement.

Joe Elliott confirmed that the musicians had spoken to six guitarists about auditioning for the role. Rumours linked the band to John Sykes of Thin Lizzy, who had sung some backing vocals on *Adrenalize*, former Ozzy Osbourne guitarist Jake E. Lee, and Gerry Laffy, who had previously played with Phil Collen in his pre-Leppard band, Girl.[388] Adrian Smith from Iron Maiden was also rumoured to be the one to fill Steve Clark's shoes.

All were excellent guitarists, but Collen indicated that personality was just as important to the band. The replacement would need to have the right temperament to fit into the collective character of the band. Collen said: 'We just want someone who'll blend in with our personalities, who won't do loads of drugs or be rude to people because we just ain't like that. It's got to be someone who's a similar age, too.'[389]

Before they met him, Campbell maybe wouldn't have been the band's first choice, with Campbell reflecting: 'Prior to joining Def Leppard, I had been with Dio and I had been fired. I had been in Whitesnake and been fired. I had a reputation in the industry of being difficult to work with and not being able to keep a job.'[390]

However, Elliott knew that reputation wasn't accurate: in fact, as Campbell explains, the two had crossed paths before, and Elliott had already raised the possibility of Campbell replacing Clark: 'I've known Joe Elliott for a few years. He lives in Ireland, where I'm originally from, so I would see him every time I'd go there — we have a lot of mutual friends. And a couple of months after Steve had died, he had said that they were gonna continue, that they were gonna finish the [*Adrenalize*] record as a four-piece, but that they were eventually going to look for a new guitar player — and that he would like it to be me.'[391] Elliott later revealed that his discussions with Campbell were 'never totally serious,' but 'by the time the tour came up, we had to get serious.'[392]

Elliott told the *Los Angeles Times*: 'We mulled some names over and in January we started playing with a few people. One of the main things, outside of musical ability, was that we were looking for a relatively ego-free person, someone who we all liked and someone who wouldn't behave like an obnoxious, self-absorbed jerk.'[393]

Campbell auditioned in Burbank, jamming with the band on a Thin Lizzy song. Two days later they offered him the job.[394] Campbell explained how the audition unfolded: 'We just got together and played and sang and talked. Talked more than anything. I think personality was the key determining factor, much more so than guitar-playing ability.'[395]

In the end, the band chose Campbell because he was a good fit in a few keyways. For example, Elliott said: 'Def Leppard wanted someone with a British passport, a good guitar, decent voice and a great personality. In Vivian Campbell, we exceeded our wildest expectation. We found a great player, an excellent singer, a terrific human being and a British and Irish passport holder! A perfect fit.'[396] Rick Allen said: 'Viv was the perfect choice. His playing is so tight, and that's what he's like as a person — solid.'[397]

The band knew from Campbell's musical pedigree that he had the technical skills to replace Clark. However, what mattered most to them was Campbell's character: they did not want anyone with drug or alcohol problems because they didn't want to go through the same trauma they had with Clark. Many years later, Elliott said bluntly: 'Vivian was the perfect fit. He brought his own thing to the band. And the one thing Viv's always given us is a feeling of he's not going to wake up dead in the morning. Steve for the previous five years always gave that impression.'[398]

Moreover, they wanted someone who would be at ease in the high pressure and demanding musical world they inhabited — someone in whose company they were comfortable, and who they could hang out with during long tours and studio sessions. Elliott later explained: 'When you're on the road, you're only on stage two hours a day. The rest of the time you're with this person on a bus, or whatever, so actually his personality is more important than his playing. We would have settled for someone who was less a player if he fit into that family unit. But with Vivian, we were able to get both.'[399]

Basically, the guys in Leppard wanted someone just like them so that the transition from 'life with Steve' to 'life after Steve' would be as painless as possible. On a professional level, they wanted someone who could play, sing, and perform, but on a personal level they wanted a buddy. After Campbell's experiences with Dio and Whitesnake, it's possible that Campbell felt the same way.

The big question was, would it turn out that way? Collen and Clark were particularly friendly and were, in fact, known as the 'terror twins' because of their antics together. A few months after Campbell was recruited, Collen spoke fondly of his old bandmate: 'I could say stuff to him that I could never say to anyone else. We used to sit there for hours and just discuss stuff. I miss having that type of friendship.'[400]

Musically, it was important that Campbell find a way to fit into Leppard's current musical style. That meant continuing his journey towards a 'less is more approach,' as he had attempted with Shadow King. It also meant accepting Collen as the lead player, while Campbell took the less prominent role in the band's dual guitar approach. But how would his personality gel with Allen, Savage, Elliott and Collen, especially given the 13-year relationship Clark had with the band. And would Campbell and Collen, in particular, get along?

Moreover, Clark wrote or co-wrote over 90% of Def Leppard's songs, including those on the *Adrenalize* album, which was released after his death. Could Campbell make a similar contribution to the band? Collen had taken on some songwriting responsibility after replacing Pete Willis, and was, in fact, listed as co-writer for every track on the hugely successful *Hysteria* and *Adrenalize* albums. Campbell had already demonstrated songwriting ability while a member of Sweet Savage, Dio and Riverdogs, but it remained unclear if he would be able to contribute as Clark and Collen had done, or even if the band wanted him to.

Campbell made his live debut with the band on April 15 at a Dublin club called McGonagles in front of approximately 600 people. This is the same club where, many years previously, Campbell's Sweet Savage played a regular set. The show was almost two hours long and featured a mix of old and new songs. It went well: Elliott said, 'When we played our first gig, it was like Vivian had always been in the band... I would be very surprised if the fans didn't accept Vivian.'[401]

Campbell's reaction was even more enthusiastic. He revealed: 'I was excited, but I wasn't at all nervous. That show was absolutely steaming. The band was really, really good. I'm really going to enjoy this tour. Def Leppard plays good music. The band feels good. The songs too... they feel very fresh on it. I feel that no matter what happens that this will be the last band I play with.'[402]

His next gig one week later was the Freddie Mercury Tribute in front of an audience of 72,000. Leppard performed 'Animal' and 'Let's Get Rocked,' before Brian May joined them onstage for a rendition of the Queen song, 'Now I'm Here.' On both the Def Leppard songs, Campbell played rhythm guitar while Collen played the lead lines. However, on the Queen song, Campbell played rhythm and took the lead solo. This was Campbell's introduction to the world as a member of Def Leppard and it therefore represented a new start for the band.[403] Campbell admitted to being 'incredibly nervous' ahead of the show, but that was not evident in his performance.[404]

It was, however, a strange event, part festival, part memorial, part an Aids charity fundraiser, and subsequently the tone was uneven throughout. With some exceptions, the list of performers was more representative of Brian May's musical heritage then of Mercury's. Indeed, it's hard to know what Mercury might have made of the likes of Metallica, Def Leppard, Extreme, Slash, and Axl Rose, playing his music, although he no doubt would have enjoyed Lisa Minelli singing 'We Are The Champions.'

As for Leppard, this was an opportunity to promote their new single, 'Let's Get Rocked.' However, while the band received a good reception from the audience, it was almost as if their daylight performance exposed some hard home truths, particularly that they were representative of a genre that had aged badly in a short space of time. The song's lyrics were cheesy, even for a band that five years previously had written 'Armageddon It' and 'Pour Some Sugar On Me.' Back then, the lyrical content of those songs came across as jovial and singalong, but now what self-respecting rocker was going to sing 'Let's get rocked' or 'I suppose a rock's out of the question?' In the age of grunge, a comical wink was easily misinterpreted as an offensive leer.

Even Elliot's designer ripped jeans seemed out of place and out of time after *Nevermind* and 'Smells Like Teen Spirit' (September 1991). Of course, the band wasn't known for its deep lyrics and it had previously made a virtue of that fact. Fans accepted their lyrics as tongue in cheek and funny. As Elliot would later say, the band's lyrical content was less Bob Dylan and more 'hubcap diamond star halo,' quoting a lyric from the Marc Bolan song 'Get It On' as an example of lyrics that sound good within the context of the song in contrast to lyrics that are deeply profound.

Even in 1992, Elliott didn't think much of the lyrics to 'Let's Get Rocked': 'I'm 33,' he said, 'and… can look at the lyrics to a song like Let's Get Rocked and say: "That's really stupid." But it's intended to be stupid. For four minutes, I'm playing the role of Bart Simpson.'[405]

Campbell also defended the lyrics, saying: 'Def Leppard always gets hammered from the press for not taking a stance on socio-political issues or whatever, and just being "Let's get rocked", kind of adolescent in nature. But that's what Def Leppard has been, and that's what Def Leppard is. It's about escapism, it's about entertainment, both on record and especially when you see the band live.'[406]

Nevertheless, the young record-buying public was more into the introspective, somewhat gloomy lyrics of new grunge bands, and to them the lyrics of 'Let's Get Rocked' came across as archaic and naff rather than tongue in cheek. What was cool to a certain audience in the 1980s, was now uncool, and it felt like Def Leppard was a band of the past, not the present, and certainly not the future. However, the real question was not just how the music critics saw the band but also how their fans would respond to new music and — crucially — would they accept Campbell in place of their beloved Steve Clark?

## Promotional Videos

Partly due to the absence of a studio album release since *Hysteria* in 1987, which created a lot of fan expectation, and partly due to media coverage of Steve Clark's headline-making death, *Adrenalize* was highly anticipated: when released, it went straight to the top of the UK album chart and the US Billboard chart. In addition, the album spawned six singles, four of which were top 20 hits in the UK with two reaching the Billboard top 20. 'Let's Get Rocked' was the biggest chart success in the UK, reaching the number two spot, whereas 'Have You Ever Needed Someone So Bad' was the biggest chart success in the US, reaching number 12. The flip side of the 12-inch picture disc of that single featured a picture of Campbell, which was unusual since he hadn't played on the album, albeit he was firmly established in the band by the time the single was released.

Campbell appeared in five of the six promotional music videos made for these singles. In the main though, he is in the background and is never a central 'character.' His first appearance was in the performance video for 'Make Love Like A Man': if the band was determined to make a new start, they showed it in this video in which everyone seemed to be enjoying themselves. It's one of those 'good times' videos, with lots of laughter, guitar poses, and activity. At one point, Savage put his arm around Campbell, who had adopted the rock star look of wearing cool sunglasses indoors. And at one point Campbell did the 'rabbit ears' finger symbol behind Elliott's back, something he would never dare do with Ronnie Dio, which indicates how comfortable he was with Def Leppard. This song was written around the same time as 'White Lightning,' which was Leppard's tribute to Clark. It's title was not meant to be taken at face value and instead was meant as a fun distraction from Clark's death.

In the promotional video for 'Have You Ever Needed Someone So Bad,' Campbell appears mostly in the background, and he limited his activities to swaying, holding his guitar, and singing the chorus. 'Stand Up (Kick Love into Motion)' has a moody promotional video that is part story, part performance-based. The camera focuses mainly on Elliott with Campbell and other band members in the background and in shadow. Campbell first heard this track while he and his wife had been separated for 12 months and in that context, he thought the track was 'a really positive love song.'[407]

The promotional video for 'Heaven Is' features digital effects in the style of Aha's landmark 'Take On Me' video. Once more, it is part story, part performance, with the band playing on stage and shot mainly via a series of quick edits. When the camera does linger for more than a split second, it does so on Elliott and Collen. Collen performs the guitar solo, which is not unusual since he composed and recorded it. Campbell features only briefly during the quick edits, on one occasion miming backing vocals. 'Tonight' is a monotone performance video with some storyboard elements. It mostly focusses on Elliot and Campbell appears only fleetingly.

While Campbell makes only brief appearances in these five videos, while not featuring at all in the video for 'Let's Get Rocked,' he wasn't involved with the *Adrenalize* album, which was conceived and recorded before he joined Def Leppard. For that reason it would have been incongruous if he were more centre stage, and the fact that Collen plays all the solos in the videos mirrors the real-life creation of the songs. It was a similar situation to the *Whitesnake / 1987* album, where Campbell was hired initially just to record promotional videos for songs written and recorded before he joined the band.

The real test came when Campbell embarked on a colossal world tour with Leppard and he and Collen needed to work out how to perform these songs live in front of thousands of fans. After all, and as Elliott pointed out in pre-tour interview with the *Los Angeles Times*, while the McGonagles gig went 'as well as could be expected for a warm-up date… Vivian still has to learn to play with us live. Doing rehearsals is one thing. Live shows are another.'[408]

**Adrenalize '7-Day Weekend' World Tour, 1992-93**
The *Adrenalize* World Tour was colossal in scale and ambition, comprising 241 dates unfolding over 17 months. The first leg was a European club tour which began after the Freddie Mercury Tribute at Wembley Stadium. These intimate club gigs would help the band shake off some rust and give them an opportunity to try out some of the newer songs in a live situation. They would also help Campbell embed into the band. On the most basic level, Campbell had to learn how to form a tight rhythm section with Savage and Allen, as well as work out rudimentary physical aspects of playing in a new band such as where to stand on stage and how to avoid being in each other's space. He was literally 'finding his feet.'

As a seasoned live performer, these challenges would not cause too many problems for Campbell. Working with Collen might, however, prove less straightforward. Collen and Clark had been playing together for nearly a decade, and they were close friends. All indications were that it would take time for Collen and Campbell to develop a working relationship. However, time was in short supply due to the forthcoming tour. The main challenge was for Campbell to learn all the songs; and the second was how to condense multiple guitar parts into something that could be performed live on stage by just two guitarists.

In an October 1992 newspaper interview, Collen explained how he used to work with Clark and how he and Campbell figured out how to play together: 'How me and Steve used to do it was, we'd decide based on whether one person played a particular part better than the other one. Basically, Vivian and I have done exactly the same thing. What you do is, you make a collage. There's two of us, and there's eight parts here on the record. But only really three or four are very apparent; the other stuff is just there for atmosphere or whatever. So, you take the most prominent parts, and that may mean making a combination part that's not exactly what's on the record, but close to two of the guitars that are on the record. Then the other guy takes the other two.'[409]

Campbell mainly played Clark's parts, learning them by relistening to the albums. He explained: 'A lot of what Steve did was very thematic. It's very much part of the song, so I tend not to vary from that too. It's what people expect to hear. It's what they want to hear, and I think it works fine.'[410]

Then, of course, Campbell had to learn the vocal harmonies which were one of the band's signature characteristics. Given that all of Campbell's early influences were guitarists who could sing, such as Marc Bolan, Rory Gallagher, and Gary Moore, this dual role was a challenge Campbell was eager to take on. He had been denied that prospect by Ronnie Dio. However, things changed when Coverdale gave him the opportunity to perform backing vocals. But he really developed his backing and lead vocals while recording and performing with Riverdogs. He also performed backing vocals on the *Shadow King* album, and during their sole stage performance.

Campbell had also demonstrated his capability as a lead vocalist during a 1991 live performance at the Guitar Institute Of Technology, when he sang lead vocals on Jimi Hendrix's 'Little Wing' and 'Purple Haze,' Stevie Wonder's 'Superstition,' and Thin Lizzy's 'Don't Believe A Word.'[411] Journalist Richard Paton speculated that Campbell's attraction to Def Leppard partly stemmed from the 'opportunity he had been given to sing with [them], something other bands didn't want him to do.'[412]

As well as a musical learning curve, Campbell also had to learn the ins and outs of each band member's off-stage routine: did they like to horse around between gigs, did they need their own time and space at certain points, what did they do for recreation and was he going to be part of that? This band had been together for most of the 1980s, after all, and Campbell was the new initiate. Nevertheless, the experience of touring was familiar to him, all of its trials and tribulations, as was the camaraderie of being a professional musician playing alongside other young men. In fact, these experiences would make his introduction into Leppard almost seamless.

Billed as 'The 7-Day Weekend Tour,' the club part of the itinerary began in Madrid on May 19 and ended in Amsterdam on June 17. During that time, Leppard performed 13 times in nine countries, making this a gruelling schedule of almost daily gigs with lots of travelling in between. Towards the end of June, the tour raised in intensity when the band played ten arena gigs in the UK and Ireland, including a homecoming gig for Campbell in Belfast on July 3.

For this tour, Leppard chose once again to roll out their famous circular stage. First used during the *Hysteria* tour in 1987, the stage could only be used in large, modern arenas which could accommodate the heavy lighting rig equipment that needed to be hung from the roof. On the *Hysteria* tour, for example, this weighed 32 tons. While the stage layout gave the audience the best view of all five band members, it also caused practical issues such as how to get the band to and from the stage. In the early days, this was solved when the musicians were secreted in laundry baskets that roadies would transport back and forth.

The riser upon which Rick Allen's drum set was situated, would mechanically revolve so that fans on all four sides of an arena could get a clear view. While the 32-ton stage remained static, the layout allowed almost total freedom of mobility for those on stage, with the exception being static microphone stands. Whether that was a positive or negative depended on one's point of view. Journalist John Street claimed the layout gave Leppard freedom to 'canter round with unhindered, if ungainly, enthusiasm, adopting all the usual rock poses.'[413]

In contrast to this back handed compliment, many fans found this a new and exhilarating experience, and they appreciated the band's efforts, at considerable expense, to provide the best possible experience in the barn-like arenas in which the band often played.

For the *Adrenalize* tour, the overall principle of a round stage remained, but the stage setup was modified and updated. For example, the centre stage area was now a star-shaped designed, and was cleared of all speakers and amps, while the drum set riser could now rise around six feet and move across the stage as well as revolve. The visual aesthetic was also updated to reflect *Adrenalize* album imagery rather than the computer circuit board imagery of *Hysteria*.

The circular stage was introduced at the Dublin Point on June 19 and travelled around the world with the band. However, when Def Leppard returned to Europe in late April 1993, they reverted to the traditional concert layout of placing the stage at one end of an arena, and that arrangement continued until the end of the tour. The band also discarded most of the elaborate lighting effects seen earlier on the tour and began to present a stripped down, more back-to-basics rock show. This was a reaction to the ongoing shift in the rock music scene, with Collen referring to it as 'the best thing we've ever done.'[414]

The set list was, of course, comprised mainly of songs from Leppard's back catalogue, and mainly from *Hysteria* and *Pyromania*, with only a handful of tracks from *Adrenalize*. 'Stagefright' normally opened the show, and the performance tended to last somewhere between 120 and 150 minutes, including encores.

Towards the end of the tour, as the band tried to protect their voices, the majority of shows were two hours in length.[415] On most North American dates an acoustic interlude provided a mid-set break. The band introduced the acoustic section as 'Def Leppard Unplugged,' and they played either 'Bringing On The Heartbreak,' 'Tonight,' or 'Two Steps Behind,' as well as a medley of songs by artists such as Led Zeppelin, AC/DC, Metallica, Nirvana and the Rolling Stones.[416]

Occasionally the band would play just snippets of other artists songs: for example, at the Don Valley Stadium concert in Sheffield on June 6, 1993, Leppard broke into a rendition of Ram Jam's version of the folk-blues standard 'Black Betty,' a song often credited to Huddie "Lead Belly" Ledbetter, before transitioning into 'Armageddon It'; and at the same gig the song 'Rocket' transitioned into a few bars of Led Zeppelin's 'Whole Lotta

Love.' After Mick Ronson's death, Leppard paid tribute to the guitarist by performing an acoustic rendition of David Bowie's 'Ziggy Stardust' as well as Ronson's solo track, 'Slaughter On Tenth Avenue,' at their Stockholm gig on June 30, 1993.[417] The November 3 gig in Landover, Maryland coincided with the election of President Bill Clinton, and in recognition of that the band played Alice Cooper's 'Elected' as an encore.

On October 27, 1992, Jon Bon Jovi and Richie Sambora joined the band on stage at the Brendan Byrne Arena in East Rutherford, New Jersey to perform Bad Company's 'Can't Get Enough,' while in Paris in May 1993, Bryan Adams made a guest appearance to perform the same song. However, these were one-off guest appearances and not usual practice for the band. Normally during the set, space was reserved for both Campbell and Collen to play a solo piece which would last around five minutes each. In Campbell's case, his solo would usually transition into the Leppard track 'Gods of War.'

John Street's *Times* review of the Earl's Court' gig provides a broad summary of how the band was viewed at the time. Calling Leppard a 'triumph of unfashionability,' Street noted the band's 'schoolboy humour,' devotion to untrendy 'denim jackets and bared chests, fluorescent shorts and chromium shinpads.' As for their music, Street wrote that it 'steers clear of current tastes, with no whisper of rap and only discreet concessions to new technology.' He also noted the contrast between 'critical disdain' for their music and fashion and their huge popular success, with *Adrenalize* topping the charts in eight countries.[418]

After the Belfast gig in early July 1992, Leppard flew to Australia where they performed eight times in 18 days in five different cities across the country. Between the penultimate and final Australian gigs, the band travelled to New Zealand for two performances at the Supertop in Auckland. The band then set off for North America for a colossal series of shows that would take them through the US and Canada, beginning in New York on August 10 and ending in Halifax, Canada on April 6, 1993.

The North American leg of the tour began with a statement gig at Madison Square Garden, when the band joined a prestigious list of British rock bands that had performed there such as Cream, Blind Faith, the Rolling Stones, Led Zeppelin, Ten Years After, Jethro Tull, The Moody Blues, Emerson, Lake & Palmer, Deep Purple, Bad Company, Black Sabbath, Paul McCartney and Wings, Queen, Electric Light Orchestra, Genesis, Pink Floyd, The Who, Rainbow, Iron Maiden, Judas Priest, and Dire Straits.

While in New York, Campbell and Collen took time away from the band to do some promotion with New York City radio station Z-100 (WHTZ). To celebrate the nineth birthday of the station's 'Morning Zoo' programme,

Collen and Campbell joined singer Richard Marx, actor James Woods and Olympic gold medallist Lea Loveless in presenting a $40,000 cheque to the Big Brothers and Big Sisters of New York City charity, photos of which were published in the *Gavin Report*.[419]

After these early highlights, a problem soon arose with Elliott's voice. This became clear at the August 14 gig at the Philadelphia Spectrum, where 17,000 fans heard the singer struggle through the opening few songs before he apologised and asked everyone to help by singing along. Elliott made it through the show with the aid of Campbell, Savage and Collen's backing vocals, while the music and spectacle ensured fans remained full of goodwill. *Billboard* journalist Melinda Newman described the scene: 'Elliott, guitarists Collen and Campbell, and bassist Rick Savage ran amuck like colliding satellites orbiting Rick Allen's drum kit. Basically, the members played Chinese fire drill for two and a half hours while running through a top-notch selection of the British band's well-crafted, catchy rock songs.'[420]

'The question on everyone's mind,' claimed journalist Louise King in her review of the December 16 gig at the St. Louis Arena, 'was how newcomer Vivian Campbell, who replaced the late Steve Clark on lead guitar, would fit in with this tight ensemble.'[421]

Of course, there would be many comparisons between Clark and Campbell on this tour, with one journalist citing the Philadelphia Spectrum performance in August as evidence that Campbell 'fits in well' with his new bandmates, 'racing about on stage and dropping to his knees for a brief, blistering solo, just like Clark used to.'[422] Another, viewing his performance in October at the Brendan Byrne Arena in East Rutherford, wrote: 'the Irish guitarist filled Clark's shoes nicely.'[423]

Fears that there would be a backlash against Campbell, or that he would be made to feel unwelcome, soon proved unfounded. From the early shows and throughout the tour, fans gave Campbell a warm reception and responded well to his solo performances. Moreover, the music journalists who were so critical in shaping public opinion were mainly on Campbell's side. For example, in his review of the sold-out Salt Lake City, Utah gig on September 11, Scott Iwasaki wrote: 'Campbell shot out his own style of finger-flying and blasted the crowd with an emotional, melodic solo, which introduced Gods of War. The ex-Dio, Whitesnake axeman proved an asset to Def Leppard when the crowd wanted more of an edge.'[424]

It was inevitable, of course, that as well as comparisons with Clark there would also be comparisons with Collen, and those critics who offered an opinion tended to side with Campbell. For example, John McCarthy of the *Lewiston Tribune* was not a fan of Def Leppard and wrote a scathing review of their gig on September 30 in Pullman, Washington State. He called Collen's guitar solo 'a joke,' saying: 'The riffs carried no melody and worked no new electronic wizardry with his feedback and fuzz.' McCarthy, however, was more complimentary of Campbell's solo, grudgingly admitting that he 'knew his guitar' and 'played some coherent lines.' However, McCarthy was unable to raise a positive point without qualifying it with a complaint. For example, he grumbled that 'every time [Campbell would] begin to develop a melodic fragment, he'd up and dash off to another side of the stage.'[425]

By his own admission, most of McCarthy's ire came after the *Lewiston Tribune*'s staff photographer had allegedly been kept waiting and then denied a press pass for the concert. Luckily two other local newspaper reviewers were in attendance to provide a more balanced viewpoint, Dennis Huspeni of the *Moscow-Pullman Daily News* and Valerie Buck of the *Spokesman-Review.* In contrast to McCarthy, Huspeni enjoyed the performance, the stage set-up, the lighting effects, and the set list. He was particularly impressed by an acoustic rendition of an older track, 'Bringin' On The Heartbreak' and also Campbell's ten minute solo which, Huspeni claimed, 'proved his axe worthy of Def Leppard.'[426]

Valerie Buck's review was more positive than negative. While noting that the set list was similar to the *Hysteria* tour, Buck still found the show entertaining. Like Huspeni, she singled out 'Bringin' On The Heartbreak' for particular praise. However, Buck called Campbell's guitar solo 'grinding' and thought Collen's solo displayed a 'more technical style' than Campbell's.[427]

Journalist Louise King praised Campbell's performance at the St. Louis Arena in December, claiming that his 'licks,' and personality, gelled well with the remainder of the band. On 'Hysteria,' King insisted, Campbell and Collen 'seemed of one mind as they closely approximated the multilayered guitar parts of the original recording with fretwork that sought to complement, rather than compete with each another.' According to King, Campbell's guitar solo slot 'showcased his agility and deft fingering technique but also his wry sense of humour.'[428]

In contrast, when journalist Jim Hutchinson reviewed the October 21 Toronto gig, he was less than impressed by the band's performance, and was particularly uncomplimentary about both guitarists' solo spots, which he called 'nothing more than ordinary — never really breaking new ground.' He complained that Campbell's solo lasted 'five tedious minutes' but did at least acknowledge that his opinion wasn't shared by the audience who 'didn't seem to mind.'[429] Hutchinson also criticised the band's stage wear or 'standard heavy metal uniform,' as he called it, of 'far too tight Spandex pants, sleeveless shirts, knee-less jeans and long, over-permed hair,' as well as Collen going 'bare-chested with a heavy cross and other medallions dangling pendulously around his neck.'[430]

It was, however, the Albany *Daily Gazette*'s Michael Hochanadel who more accurately identified Campbell's role in the band at that time, and more importantly, perhaps, his relationship with Collen. In his review of the gig at the Knickerbocker Arena in Albany, New York, Hochanadel wrote: 'Blues-influenced, via Jimi Hendrix, Campbell was generally a supporting player, with Phil Collen usually soloing as chief guitar strangler. Clark and Collen had a more even balance, but a member for just nine months, Campbell proved an adept team player and a stronger singer than Clark.'[431]

During this North American leg of the tour, Leppard took part in what was back then one of the cultural events of the year, the MTV Video Music Awards. As it turned out, this particular show was also one of the cultural events of the decade, an event that marked a seismic change in the tastes of music listeners, and became a litmus test of cultural changes in a decade that would witness the Rodney King beating, the L.A. Riots, the Clinton era, the murders of Nicole Brown and Ron Goldman, and the murder trial of O.J. Simpson.

The event aired live on September 9 from UCLA's 12,000-seat Pauley Pavilion and Leppard was scheduled to perform 'Let's Get Rocked.' On the day of the performance, Campbell said: 'We're a little apprehensive because Def Leppard is not considered very current. We're the token hard rock band shoulder to shoulder with cutting-edge bands.'[432]

That was something of an understatement: also scheduled to perform were the likes of Nirvana (playing 'Lithium,' a song about depression and religion), Pearl Jam (playing 'Jeremy,' a song about a school shooting), Red Hot Chilli Peppers (playing 'Under the Bridge,' about heroin addiction), and The Black Crowes, as well as 'boomer' rock bands like Guns 'n' Roses and Bryan Adams, and commercial mainstays like Elton John and Eric Clapton. Award winners came from all of these groups, and included the likes of Annie Lennox, U2, Metallica, Prince and Van Halen. Red Hot Chilli Peppers won the most awards (8) and Nirvana picked up a 'Best Alternative Video' award for 'Smells Like Teen Spirit.

Evident also was that rap and hip hop were represented, in part at least, by the likes of MC Hammer and Marky Mark and the Funky Bunch, while more political and controversial artists from those genres had been ignored. Of course, in the aftermath of the acquittal of police officers involved in the Rodney King beating, and the subsequent L.A. Riots, more political, more controversial rap would increase in popularity because, like grunge, its subjects were the real-life concerns of that generation's youth. Hammer's

'2 Legit 2 Quit' would soon be superseded by the likes of Body Count's 'Cop Killer' and the Gangsta Rap subgenre.

The 1992 Awards were a changing of the guard — a moment when one era ended and another began. Grunge was the future and arena rock was beginning to fade in popularity. This was exemplified by a notorious backstage argument between Axl Rose, the lead singer of Guns n' Roses, Kurt Cobain of Nirvana, and Cobain's partner Courtney Love. Rose lost his cool while the duo taunted him for being sexist and aggressive. It was a collision of cultures, and while no one was hurt, Cobain and Love came out on top. Campbell was correct when he said Def Leppard was a token hard rock band at the event. In comparison to the grunge/alternative rock bands on display, they were as uncool as Axl's temper tantrum.

However, Leppard had been invited to the event because they sold a lot of records and concert tickets, and underneath MTV's uber-cool visage, money remained the driving force in the music business. Elliott didn't help matters by reminding *Kerrang!* magazine that Def Leppard was about escapism and that critics didn't understand that 'Let's Get Rocked' was intended to be funny.[433] 'If you want misery, then go listen to Soundgarden,' he told them. What Elliott didn't understand though is that critics were aware of its humorous intent, but for them the joke had fallen flat. Leppard was nominated for four awards but lost in every category.

Whether or not Leppard was uncool and passé, the band continued to sell millions of records and to play to sold out audiences. John Mackie reviewed their October 3 gig at the Pacific Coliseum, Vancouver, and was able to catch a glimpse of their appeal: 'If you're looking for music that goes into realms no band has entered before, well, you'd best look elsewhere. But if you want radio rock, '80's and '90's style, Def Leppard offers a textbook example of pop metal at its best.'[434]

A few days later the band performed at the Calgary, Saddledome with reviewer James Muretiche calling the show a 'rock 'n' roll circus… a three-ring spectacular tailor-made for fist-pumping fans who can't get enough of power chords, sing-a-long harmonies, insidiously infectious melodies and who maintain the youthful belief that life should be a "seven day weekend" with arena rock as its soundtrack.'[435]

However, it wasn't only the band's music that fans found appealing, it was also their personas: *Hollywood Reporter*'s Daina Darzin reviewed the band's October 27 performance at the Brendan Byrne Arena in East Rutherford and left with the impression that 'Elliott and company come off as such unpretentious, appealing people, one can't help but hope for their continued success.'[436]

In April 1993 Leppard travelled back across the Atlantic for a European leg of the tour that began on April 30 in Stockholm, with a further 21 performances in 14 countries. The tour culminated in a showcase outdoor stadium gig on June 6 in the Elliott and Savage's hometown of Sheffield in England. Not everything went according to plan on this leg of the tour, however. In June, *Kerrang!* reported an altercation between Campbell and singer Glenn Danzig backstage at a festival in Germany. Danzig's self-titled band were a minor support act on the bill. *Kerrang!* reported: 'Vivian Campbell allegedly squared up with Glenn Danzig leading to the latter storming off, muttering something about how he didn't want to hit anyone from Def Leppard in case they sued him.'[437]

More details emerged when both parties issued statements about the incident, with each blaming each other. Elliott, it seemed, was more aggravated by Danzig's press statement than he was the actual altercation, so he gave *Kerrang!* a fuller explanation of what occurred. According to the singer, there was an altercation at the Nürburgring, Rock Am Ring Festival on May 30 when Danzig was rude to the band and to Campbell's wife. Danzig apparently bumped into the band while carrying some food, spilled his soup, and then became aggravated.

Elliott claimed that Danzig called Campbell's wife a 'fuck-head' and Campbell squared up to him. Both Elliott and Collen — a black belt in karate — became involved, and at that point, Elliott kicked Danzig in the backside, followed immediately by Campbell doing the same.[438] What's interesting about this incident, which was a minor skirmish in the history of rock 'n' roll escapades, is that Campbell's band mates stepped in to support him, which indicates that the guitarist was now a firmly established member of the Def Leppard family.

The Sheffield stadium gig was a high point of the tour, not just because of the scale and nature of the event, but also due to the amount of media attention it garnered. Moreover, it was filmed, and a highlights show was broadcast. Furthermore, BBC Radio One recorded the entire gig, broadcasting most of it. The first chance Campbell got to showcase his soloing skills was on the old Leppard song 'Hit And Run.' Dressed in light blue shorts and a sleeveless white t-shirt with the logo 'Virginia Tech' emblazoned in red letters on the front, Campbell played a speedy run on his red Charvel guitar before switching to a wood grain-coloured Charvel for the solo. In fact, Campbell played most of the patterns on this track with Collen taking a rare back seat to allow Campbell to demonstrate his talent.

Campbell then played the opening riffs to 'Too Late For Love' and then a solo, before the usual routine of sharing riffs returned with 'Hysteria,' whereupon Collen played the main solo. Campbell switched to a blue Tom Anderson Stratocaster to play the opening arpeggiated chords to 'Foolin'' and then picked up his red Charvel again to swap licks with Collen on 'Rocket,' which was extended to allow both guitarists to play short solo pieces. Campbell also played a prominent role in the ever-catchy 'Armageddon It,' which is something of a show-stopper when played live. Of note too is Campbell's slow and melodic solo on 'Love Bites' which is about as far away from his playing in his Sweet Savage days as it is possible to be, and which demonstrates considerable growth in his playing.

The overall impression from this filmed performance is of very professional musicians, well-rehearsed, playing tight, and singing close harmonies. It's also evident that they were all having fun and that there was real camaraderie among the band with, for example, Campbell and Collen sharing a microphone stand to sing backing vocals, Campbell pretending to play Collen's fretboard while Collen was playing a solo, and Campbell playing a single note on Savage's bass guitar.

*Kerrang!*'s Dave Reynolds called the event, which also featured Terrorvision, Ugly Kid Joe, and Thunder, an 'extravaganza' and 'a real success,' saying of Campbell: 'After years as a hired gun in other acts, Viv really has found his true vocation in the Leppard family. And no disrespect to the late Steve Clark, but it is almost as if the Irishman has been in the band all his life.'[439]

After Sheffield, the band flew to Japan for seven gigs, including one in Hiroshima and three in Tokyo, before once more returning to North America for another extensive leg of the tour which saw them play the opening gig in Camrose, Alberta, Canada, and then perform a further 53 times across Canada and the US, before the tour finally came to an end with three gigs in Mexico on September 25, 28 and 29. It was, by any standards, a remarkable journey and a resounding critical, financial and musical success, the latter being evidenced by the band's remarkable ability to approximate their studio recordings on stage without the use of pre-recorded tapes. The musicians were able to arrange and perform those tracks in a way that captured the essence of the original.

Of course, no rock tour of this scale passed off entirely without incident and Leppard had some challenges to overcome, but all came within the usual boundaries of a touring band's travails such as illness, vocal problems, crowd behaviour, and transport issues.

For instance, at Binghampton, New York on October 22, Elliott explained to the audience that the show started late due to problems with US customs at the Canadian border that led to a 6-hour delay. Elliott also suffered some health issues. For example, on the airplane to Hershey, Pennsylvania for the band's November 8 gig, Elliott suffered chest pains and subsequent X-rays showed he had a pleurisy in his lung which meant that evening's show, and the next few, would prove difficult for him. In fact, in Duluth on November 14 'Photograph' was cut from the encore to ease the strain on the singer's voice. However, Elliott soldiered on, and the pain gradually eased through both gigs.[440]

There was also an issue at one arena where fans were injured. This occurred at the September 5 gig in Bismarck, North Dakota. Around 8,500 fans attended this sold-out show but unfortunately some fans at the front of the stage suffered crush injuries and had to be carried out of the arena. In addition, the parents of two fans in the audience had been injured in a car crash and during Campbell's solo, tour manager Malvin Mortimer passed Elliott a message from the police asking him to make an announcement to that effect. As a result of these issues, the performance that evening lasted almost three hours.[441]

Finally, on December 8 in Green Bay at the Brown County Veterans Memorial Arena, two roadies were injured while moving equipment into the arena. Overall, however, these setbacks were temporary and soon put behind them.

The tour also ended with something of a disagreement among the band as to their immediate future. Promoters offered them further dates in South America and Elliott and Collen wanted to stay on the road. However, Allen, Savage and Campbell wanted to bring the tour to an end.[442]

Campbell was especially keen to begin work on the next Leppard album, saying: 'the schedule in the States has been five shows a week, and 70 per cent of the tour's been in America and Canada. It's the same every week, and we play the same set every night. It's hard to be charged up when you're doing that often without a break. Also, I'm playing someone else's music, which is exactly what I did with Whitesnake and that was a 14-month tour. I'm ready to go make a record! I love writing songs, and it's been so long since I made a record which I was really involved in.'[443]

Nevertheless, if *Kerrang!*'s Alison Joy is to be believed, Campbell was having the time of his life. Joy reviewed the December 8 gig at the Brown County Arena, Green Bay, Wisconsin and couldn't help but notice how Campbell responded to the many pretty girls in the audience: 'Campbell is positively basking in the attention, sashaying to the far reaches of all the stage's ramps and gyrating his guitar in a very suggestive manner to the girlies at the front. The grin on his face suggests a 12-year-old who's just found out what his dick really does.'[444]

At the tour's conclusion he was still in a happy mood as attested to by *Kerrang!*'s Paul Elliott who wrote: 'Guitarist Vivian Campbell enjoys himself in Def Leppard. In Monterrey, he fools around continually, taking the piss out of Phil when the latter indulges in a brief solo.'[445]

When Campbell joined the band, his on and off-stage relationship with Collen was key to his success. That the two were still clowning around right at the end of the tour was a good sign.

Both the music scene and Def Leppard had changed by the end of the '7-Day Weekend' tour. Hard rock and heavy metal had dwindled in popularity among general music fans with only the likes of Guns n' Roses, Metallica and a handful of others remaining successful. Grunge and alternative rock were now the genres championed by the music press. Mid-tour, Leppard saw which way the wind was blowing and modified how they presented their music to audiences. They stopped using the round stage and updated their stage wear to more everyday clothing that was more in line with grunge fashion. They also drastically cut the amount of lighting and lasers in their production.

'There are few frills about Def Leppard these days,' observed Paul Elliott in reviewing the band's antepenultimate gig in Monterey, Mexico. He also noted Elliott's 'flatter post-Seattle' hairstyle.[446]

There was unanimous agreement within the band as to these developments. As the tour progressed it was impossible to ignore how the musical backdrop was evolving. Collen said of these adjustments: 'I wish we'd started this tour the way we're doing it now. We go onstage like this [indicating his tatty denim cut-offs] we don't have stage clothes. Our whole attitude is totally different these days. Without lasers and shit, people focus on the band. Before, I thought we were putting on a great show, but we just got slagged for it, and as soon as we lost all that stuff and did some European festivals, we started going down 10 times better!'[447]

In reviewing the tour, a handful of recurring themes cropped up in the music press. The first was, of course, Campbell replacing Clark. However, music journalists tended to use that as a jumping off point to discuss the band's supposed ill-luck. Was Def Leppard cursed? The band's image hardly warranted their inclusion in the devil-worshipping branch of the rock family tree. However, the past tragedies of Rick Allen's accident and Steve Clark's death made good headlines.

Another recurring theme questioned why the band was so successful. Most critics disliked Leppard's 1980s-style glam rock stylings, claiming they were now behind the times, but there was grudging appreciation of the band's ability to write catchy tunes. Another factor that helped mitigate the worst criticisms was the band's working-class background and down-to-earth attitude. As one critic pointed out in reviewing the band's November 11 gig at the Dane County Coliseum, 'it's hard to hate a well-meaning band for having some cheesy fun.'[448]

The tour passed off about as well as Campbell might have hoped. He quickly found his feet on stage and was able to form an effective 'twin guitar attack' with Collen, albeit with Collen performing the majority of solos. Campbell made some adjustments to accommodate to his new circumstances.

For example, he amended his usual guitar solo to a style more in keeping with his current band. He no longer tried just to play fast, and his solo was more melodious and refined. There were still echoes of Gary Moore's blistering, passionate playing, but by now Campbell had developed his own distinctive style. For example, footage of his solo on May 19 at a gig in Milan shows that Campbell used a delay effect to create a double echo on his solo, and also that he moved his left hand down to the end of the neck while tapping with his right hand to effectively change the position of the nut.

It was, however, Campbell's successful bond with Collen during the tour that was his most crucial achievement. Campbell said of Collen, 'he's very inspirational for me, because you tend to get a little jaded after you do this professionally for a few years. And there's none of that childish gibberish [sic] that goes on between guitar players that I've experience in other bands.'[449]

Collen was also complimentary of Campbell, comparing him favourably with Steve Clark. He revealed: 'Steve and I were really close. I thought playing with someone else was going to be really weird. But the way Vivian approached it was really natural, really comfortable. He's very tasteful, you don't have to worry about him playing something out of context.'[450] One reviewer even suggested that Campbell's presence 'inspired' Collen 'to a higher level of lead playing.'[451]

Moreover, Campbell's tasteful backing vocals helped reproduce the studio vocal harmonies that were one of the band's trademarks. In fact, Campbell was at ease throughout the tour. At the beginning he revealed: 'I feel so comfortable on stage with this band it's sick.' At the end he still felt the same, saying 'The vibe's so easy going. All I do is make the tea.'[452]

Not only did it feel good to be in Def Leppard, it also offered him more freedom to express himself while playing live. He revealed: 'I can do whatever I want onstage. I can be goofy, whatever, or even play something funny, like a Beatles riff. If I'd done that in Dio, I would have got Ronnie's glare of death! I really feel my personality can come out a lot more in this band.'[453]

Reflecting on the tour, Elliott said, 'for some reason... it's been a lot easier... since Vivian's been in the band we haven't had to deal with a personality like Steve's, which was so erratic. It put everyone on edge... Now it's on a more even keel... it makes life a bit easier when you don't have to deal with those kind of things. This tour has been a real hoot.'[454]

Nevertheless, while the tour helped establish Campbell as a great fit for the band, he was still an unknown quantity in the studio. 'The challenge on the next record is to see how Viv's songwriting fits with ours,' Elliott admitted.[455]

Clark had written for and played on the band's biggest two albums, and the question remained, not least because Campbell asked it himself, would he be able to write with and for the band? And how would fans respond to Campbell-penned songs?

## Songwriting

Since *Adrenalize*, Def Leppard have released a further six studio albums — discounting various 'Hits' and live releases, plus one covers album — and Campbell has writing credits on five of those. Of the 77 songs on these six albums, Campbell has 24 writing credits, most of which are co-written with Elliott, Collen and Savage. On only four tracks — 'Turn It In' from *Slang* (1996) and 'Cruise Control,' 'Only The Good Die Young,' and 'Gotta Let It Go' from the 2008 release *Songs From The Sparkle Lounge* — is Campbell listed as sole writer. And on only two tracks — 'To Be Alive' from the 1999 release *Euphoria* and 'Wings Of An Angel' from the 2015 release *Def Leppard* — is Campbell given co-writer credits with one other person, the former being P. J. Smith from a Campbell side project band named Clock, and the latter with Phil Collen. Campbell therefore contributed to the writing process of almost a third of the band's studio output in the last three decades.

Before fully committing to the 'Vivian recording era,' which would begin in earnest with 1996's *Slang*, Def Leppard first had some unfinished business with recordings from the past. While touring in support of the *Adrenalize* album, band members had the idea to release a rarities and B-sides album. There were two main reasons for this: first was to tie up loose ends from the Steve Clark era; second was to experiment with recording at a quicker pace than before. Nearly all the songs were rerecorded or remixed in spare moments during the '7-Day Weekend' tour, with the band taking no longer than one day to record each track.

Elliott explained that these recordings were done in the looser and more spontaneous mode of Alice in Chains and Pearl Jam, and that the quicker recording process 'helped bring the band into the '90s.'[456]

He also explained why the album needed to be released now, before any new recording with Campbell could begin: 'We didn't think it would have been morally right to push those songs on Vivian, so this was a way to wrap up the Steven era and give fans a souvenir.'

The album was released in 1993 and was entitled *Retro Active*. With those tracks released, Def Leppard could now start afresh. Nevertheless, this album marked the first time Campbell recorded with the band, playing electric and acoustic guitars and singing backing vocals.

Four singles were released from *Retro Active*. The lead single, 'Two Steps Behind,' is a power ballad that reached the top five in Canada and top twenty in the US. *Cash Box* praised Campbell for providing the song's 'simple yet highly effective acoustic foundation.'[457]

Campbell featured in the promotional video for the single, playing acoustic guitar while Collen performed the acoustic solo. 'Desert Song' was also released as a single. It is an instrumental that was left over from the *Hysteria* sessions. When it was rerecorded with lyrics, Campbell sang uncredited backing vocals, which makes it the only Def Leppard track on which both Clark and Campbell play.[458]

Campbell also featured in the promotional video for 'Miss You In A Heartbeat,' which was the fourth single from *Retro Active*. He plays electric guitar (a Fender Stratocaster) to Collen's acoustic. Campbell plays the electric guitar solo in the video, while Collen performs a short acoustic solo.

Before *Slang*, Campbell also performed on two new tracks entitled 'When Love & Hate Collide,' which appeared on the band's 1995 *Vault* release (*Vault: Def Leppard's Greatest Hits (1980-1995)*), and 'Can't Keep Away From The Flame,' which appeared on the Japanese release of that album. Campbell was credited on *Vault* for guitars and backing vocals, as well as being given a producer credit.

The promotional video for 'When Love & Hate Collide' provides evidence of the band's recent image change. All are dressed in black, with Elliott wearing a round neck sweater, and with his hair styled shorter and straighter he now bore a passing similarity to Kurt Cobain. Both Collen and Allen sport short beards, and Campbell even had his trademark locks trimmed considerably. While the song is traditional Leppard, and in fact sounds more like Bryan Adams than Nirvana, the band's visual presentation seemed more than a little influenced by the grunge aesthetic.

Lastly, Campbell features prominently in the performance video of Leppard's cover of the 1975 Sweet song 'Action.' The video mostly features footage of the band performing on stage during the '7-Day Weekend' tour, but some scenes were filmed later, as evidenced by Elliott appearing in some shots with his post-tour goatee beard. Campbell's scenes mainly involve him larking around on and offstage, including kicking a football in one of the tour's sports arena venues.

### *Slang* (1996)

At the end of the '7-Day Weekend' world tour, the prospect of writing and recording a new album seemed nowhere near as daunting as it had for the previous album. As painful as Steve Clark's death had been, the band no longer had to cope with the stress and uncertainty of the guitarist's addictions. Campbell's integration into Leppard had been a smooth process, and everyone knew he wanted to write. In January 1994, Elliott told *Kerrang!*: 'Vivian is a musician who's capable of writing any sort of music he wants, but this is the first opportunity he's really had to do that.' Moreover, Campbell had shown enough during the recent tour to suggest that new material would come easily. Elliott said: 'Phil and I used to get really fired up by some of the huge riffs that Viv would hurl out in soundcheck, and we'll definitely be using a few of those!'[459]

During the tour Campbell told an interviewer: 'I'm looking forward to working [on the next Def Leppard album], although I hope we don't spend four years recording it. I think there's a happy medium between serviceable and musically perfect songs.'[460]

In actual fact, while the new album would not take four years to record, there was still a four-year break between it and *Adrenalize,* mainly due to the length of the tour and the release of *Retro Active*. In January 1994, Joe Elliott told *Kerrang!* that his New Year's Resolution was to have the new Def Leppard album recorded by the end of the year, ready for a 1995 release date.[461] However, various personal issues would undermine everyone's ambitions for a speedy recording process.

Over the next 15 months Elliott gave a series of updates on the new album and also helped prepare fans for a new 'no frills' way of recording and songs dealing with darker themes. For example, Elliott explained that the sound the band was going for on both *Hysteria* and *Adrenalize* was futuristic. However, he said that the next album would be 'the first one we've done where we've consciously aimed to make it sound current.'[462]

In Spring 1994 Elliott told *Kerrang!* that using new 8-track digital recording technology had resulted in the band having 70% of the album already written before going into the studio. Elliott also let it be known that Mutt Lange would not be involved and instead Pete Woodroffe would produce the album.[463]

Elliott explained that pre-Grunge *Adrenalize* sounded the way it did because at that time it was 'really cool to write happy songs, but we're going through a phase now where it's not.'[464] He promised the new album would feature songs that would be 'perceived as more serious' than the likes of 'Let's Get Rocked' and 'Make Love Like A Man,' songs whose lyrical content would be more introspective and less upbeat.

In March the following year, *Billboard*'s Melinda Newman reported that the band had recorded 16 tracks for the album, which was due for release in Autumn 1995.[465] As it turned out, the new album, entitled *Slang*, would not be released until May 1996. This was due to a series of personal crises among the band. Elliott and Collen were going through divorces; Allen was found guilty of spousal abuse; and Savage was diagnosed with Bell's Palsy, a condition which affects facial muscles. In addition, Savage was dealing with the death of his father.

This was a frustrating and worrying time for Campbell, sitting on the sidelines while the band appeared to be falling apart around him. However, Leppard's long, chequered history provided enough evidence to indicate that collectively they would get through these crises and come out the other side, if not exactly stronger, but certainly wiser than before.

To record the new album, the band hired a house in Marbella, Spain, and brought their own equipment to use. Elliott revealed that Allen played an acoustic drum set for the first time since before his accident, which was set up on an Indian rug on the floor of the Marbella house.

Recording took place there intermittently from May 1994 through to December 1995, with some recording also done at Bow Lane Studios in Dublin. To get the new sound they were looking for, the production was much lighter than before: Elliott told the *Irish Times*, 'multi-layering is passé' and the band was going 'back to basics.'

According to Elliott, this enabled Campbell and Collen to 'pull out the Marshalls, the wah-wah pedals, plug in the Les Paul and go for it.'[466] In addition, the band recorded the tracks while playing together live in the room. This was a radical approach for them as on the previous three albums they tended to record their instruments individually. This new approach meant band members spent more time in each other's company and were present in the studio at the same time to discuss musical ideas.

*Slang* was the first full studio album of new material to feature Campbell, and as well as writing, he was credited for electric and acoustic guitars, dulcimer, and vocals. Campbell wrote or co-wrote two songs that ended up on the album and demoed three others. His main writing contribution was the track 'Work It Out,' and he co-wrote 'Truth?' with Collen, Elliott and Savage.

'Truth?' is the album's opening song. Campbell said the band had been listening to the Soundgarden album *Superunknown* (1994) while recording *Slang* and evidence of that can be found in 'Truth?' with its heavy riffing and Indian-flavour guitar patterns. While open to multiple interpretations, the lyrics can be understood as Campbell, Collen, Elliott and Savage's reaction to the new wave of Grunge and alternative rock music, with the band pondering if they still had a place in the new musical landscape that was shaped by the likes of Soundgarden, Alice in Chains, Pearl Jam and Faith No More.

Campbell is credited as sole writer of 'Work It Out,' a sombre song whose lyrics deal with a sense of dislocation and doubt, but it nevertheless has an uplifting chorus: 'We show the world a brand-new face/We get to work it out.' Dale Martin of the *Victoria Advocate* called Campbell's lyrical skill 'above exceptional' on this track.[467]

Campbell resisted the opportunity to write a lengthy guitar solo for himself to play. In fact, the track doesn't have a lead guitar solo at all, and instead there is a short bass solo from Savage. Collen revealed this was due to Def Leppard being influenced by the likes of Red Hot Chilli Peppers and Stone Temple Pilots where the bass 'is almost like a lead instrument.'[468]

The *Chicinner-citye*'s Dean Golemis described 'Work It Out' as 'Def Leppard's attempt at a sound steeped in a more modern, inner-city groove,' while *Q* magazine's David Quantick called the track 'perhaps the world's first and only attempt to suggest what Robert Palmer might sound like singing with Pearl Jam.'[469]

'Work It Out' was the second single release from *Slang*, coupled with 'Truth?' and with an accompanying performance video. The band also performed the song live on *The Tonight Show* with Jay Leno. It was a minor hit in the UK, reaching 22 in the official singles chart, and it reached the top ten in Canada, but it failed to make a significant impact in the US. Paul Elliott insisted that 'Work It Out' should have been the first UK single release from the album, being 'something new and different to make people really sit up and take notice.' Elliott called it 'exactly the kind of thing Def Leppard should be doing in 1996. It's got all the pop suss of their biggest hit singles but has a more contemporary feel — a post-grunge consciousness.'[470]

A non-album instrumental track entitled 'Led Boots' appeared on the B-side of the third single released from *Slang*, which was 'All I Want Is Everything.' Written by Max Middleton, 'Led Boots' originally appeared on Jeff Beck's 1976 album *Wired*. Campbell's adaptation first appeared on a Jeff Beck tribute album entitled *Jeffology - A Guitar Chronicle* (Jan. 1996) and was arranged and played by Campbell with no other member of Leppard involved. Campbell doesn't entirely try to imitate Beck and instead puts his own stamp on this track, which is in the jazz-fusion genre and features two-time signatures. It demonstrates the versatility of Campbell's playing, confirming once again that he did not want to be pigeon-holed as just a rock player.

Campbell was involved in the writing process for at least three more songs during the *Slang* era. The first was 'Burn Out,' which Campbell co-wrote with Allen, Collen, Elliott and Savage. It did not appear on *Slang* and instead was used as a B-Side for the single 'Goodbye' from Leppard's 1999 *Euphoria* album. It is a mid-paced, guitar-based rocker with little to recommend it. The guitars provide generic riffs and the lyrics are unmemorable. It's little surprise really that it was held back from the *Slang* album and used only as a B-side.

When a deluxe version of *Slang* was released in 2014, two more Campbell-penned demos were revealed. These were the power ballad 'All On Your Touch' and 'Move On Up. The structure of the former bears some resemblance to the 1992 song 'Creep' by Stone Temple Pilots. Elliott sings vocals on this classy track, although as it's entitled '2012 revisit' it's unknown how much of it was completed by 1996. Campbell sings lead vocals on the demo of 'Move On Up,' a slide guitar-based blues rocker. It's far from the traditional Def Leppard sound, which possibly explains why it wasn't released previously.

*Slang* generated four singles, three of which were accompanied by promotional music videos. These were 'Slang,' 'Work It Out,' 'All I Want Is Everything,' and 'Breathe A Sigh' (which didn't have a video). Campbell features prominently in those three videos. 'Slang' is a performance video which is set against a computer-generated background. Like Collen and Savage, Campbell assumes a variety of guitar poses. He is a striking and expressive individual, and the director made good use of those attributes via close-ups. The music video for 'Work It Out' is an on-stage band performance, with a shirtless Campbell trying out a new hairstyle for the occasion — brushed back at the top and slicked in close at the sides.

Elliott wrote the album's third single, 'All I Want Is Everything,' which is a solemn love song with a mainly monotone video. It focuses mainly on Elliott, with Campbell a background character along with the rest of the band. However, he does perform the main guitar solo, which is tasteful and melodic.

Despite these promotional videos, none of the singles released from *Slang* made a huge impact on public consciousness. Both 'Slang' and 'Work It Out' were minor hits in the UK, with the former reaching the top twenty and the latter the top thirty, but the final two singles failed to reach the top thirty. The singles performed more poorly in the US, with none making the top 100. This may have been because the songs the band selected as singles did not reflect Def Leppard's traditional sound. However, the main factor, more likely was lack of media exposure. MTV essentially stopped playing Def Leppard music and stopped promoting the band. Moreover, many radio stations declined to give them airplay. Without this exposure, it became increasingly difficult to make casual fans aware that the band even had new music available.

Having stated that the ability to express himself through song writing was the main reason he left Whitesnake, and the opportunity to do that was one of the reasons he joined Def Leppard, it's a little surprising that Campbell is only credited for two songs on *Slang*. Nevertheless, it is a creditable number given that he offered the band a few more which never made it onto the album.

Given Leppard's extant, proven songwriting partnerships it's not unusual that some of Campbell's songs were rejected. A few years later, Campbell provided some insight about his role as a song writer in the band. He admitted: 'it's a bit of a struggle for me to write for Def Leppard. It's not really my natural inclination to write Leppard-like songs… I'll say to myself, is this going to work for Joe? On my demos I tend to be more of a soul-type singer. I've come to realise that Joe doesn't naturally follow the same thought process in terms of the melodies. I'm not a good enough songwriter where I can write to order... It's a painful process for me.'[471]

*Slang* was the first Leppard album not to reach platinum-level sales in the US. However, their changes in style and image had brought them to a 'damned if you do, damned if you don't' situation. The album also reflected some of the personal strife that Elliott, Collen, Allen and Savage were experiencing at the time.

*Slang* was evidence of a more mature band that was attempting to shed its 1980s 'big hair' image, and the band considered it a worthwhile change in direction, even if that resulted in weaker sales. Collen's comment that '80s-style rock is done, dusted, completely over' was the band's new mantra.[472]

Campbell called *Slang* 'a very cathartic record for a band that was so formula-driven,' and he asserted that it gave the band the chance to experiment with new sounds and simpler techniques.[473]

### *Euphoria* (1999)

By 1999, the Grunge fad had faded and audience tastes moved on. In the UK, the guitar-based rock of Oasis, Ocean Colour Scene, The Verve, and Radiohead, and the sunny pop of The Spice Girls dominated the airwaves and the charts; in the US, pop and dance music had become the most popular music genres, while 'hair metal' bands like Poison, Dokken and Cinderella, and melodic rock acts such as Boston and Foreigner were popular live draws once more, driven more by nostalgia than the popularity of any new music they were releasing.

Urged on by their record company and manager to 'make a classic sounding Def Leppard album,' *Euphoria* saw the band return to their pop-rock roots.[474] For example, they turned once again to Mutt Lange to help with songwriting, and the songs they wrote together featured the band's signature harmonies and catchy hooks, with a big, polished sound. Even the album name and design were a throwback to the 1980s with the band once more using their trademark Def Leppard logo, familiar and colourful graphic art by Andie Airfix who had designed *Pyromania* and *Hysteria*, and choosing a one-word title ending in 'ia.'

The bulk of recording was done at Elliott's home and recording studio in Dublin. The studio sessions took place over a period of ten months from May 1998 to March 1999 and, unusually for this band, everything went smoothly and came in under budget. In fact, Collen said *Euphoria* was 'probably the easiest and smoothest recording process the band has experienced' while Elliott called the process 'one of our least traumatic albums to make.'[475] Campbell was co-writer of six of the album's 13 tracks. He described the song writing process: 'the band spends a great deal of energy on each song… One member will come up with a song, the band will try it, put a melody to it, then it will get rewritten and chewed up again in the recording process.'[476]

The album's opening track 'Demolition Man,' which Campbell co-wrote with Collen and Elliott, is a barn-storming hard rocker and an effective statement of intent for the album. It also has the distinction of being the only song written by Campbell to feature a guest appearance by a Formula One motor racing champion when Damon Hill, who was a friend of Elliott and lived close by, played some guitar on the track. In his review of *Euphoria*, Gerald Martinez called 'Demolition Man' a 'big, brash, bombastic chest-beater of a number.'[477]

Campbell co-wrote 'Paper Sun' with Collen, Elliott, Savage, and Pete Woodroffe. Its subject is an infamous terrorist bombing that occurred on August 15, 1998, in the small town of Omagh in County Tyrone, Northern Ireland. Struck by the tragic nature of the event, in which 31 people were murdered including two unborn twins, and its significance in attempting to undermine the Good Friday Agreement that brought an end to the Irish Republican Army's 30-year campaign of political violence, the band sat around Elliott's kitchen table to write the song the day after the bombing.[478] Its accusatory lyrics are addressed directly to the bombers for the pain and suffering they caused.

'It's Only Love,' which Campbell co-wrote with Elliott, Lange, and Savage, is a pop ballad with arpeggiated chords and the band's familiar harmonies. It is classy and elegant, factors that differentiate it from the overwrought heavy metal power ballad song genre.

'To Be Alive,' co-written by Campbell and P.J. Smith, is a ballad Campbell wrote for his side band Clock. Clock came about due to the long gaps between Leppard recording sessions, which allowed Campbell a vehicle for artistic expression without threatening his place in the band. This was basically the arrangement in 1985/86 that so infuriated Ronnie Dio that it drove a wedge between the singer and Campbell. Campbell, however, clearly had a better relationship with Elliott, Collen, Allen and Savage than he had with Dio. A demo exists with Campbell singing lead vocals, but on *Euphoria* Elliott sings the song.

'Guilty,' written by Campbell, Collen, Savage, Elliott, and Woodroffe, comes closest to being the only power ballad on the album. However, it's really another power pop song with beautiful harmonies, catchy hooks, and tasteful guitar fills. It wasn't to everyone's taste though: in reviewing *Euphoria* for the *Dayton Daily News*, Tim Tresslar called the three ballads on the album 'toothless pop-radio fodder,' which 'weaken an otherwise strong album.'[479]

'Day After Day,' written by Collen, Elliott, and Campbell, is a track that might have come from Leppard's 1980s classic period. It is trademark Def Leppard, with a slight nod also to the Nu Metal genre. It begins with arpeggiated chords that lead into the song's main riff. The chorus features some of the big harmony vocals that the band is known for, and the lyrics concern an old relationship partner that the narrator cannot quite relegate to the past.

**Singles and promotional videos**

The album generated three singles — 'Promises,' 'Paper Sun' and 'Goodbye' — while 'Day After Day' was released as a US Tour promotional single. 'Promises' was released in May 1999 and, depending on the release format, it was coupled with 'Back In Your Face' or 'Worlds Collide,' together with a cover of the Alice Cooper track 'Under My Wheels.' It was released as a double A-side in UK. The promotional performance video was filmed partly at the Griffith Observatory in Los Angeles. It is a laser-filled spectacle, which used to be a trademark of the Leppard live show, until that approach was dropped midway through the '7-Day Weekend' tour. The video is therefore something of a throwback to the band's earlier era. However, it is not all nostalgia: both Savage and Elliott sport new shorter haircuts, leaving only Campbell with long 'rock star' locks. While the single didn't break into the UK top 40, it did reach number one on Billboard's Mainstream Rock chart.

It's unclear if 'Paper Sun' was given a commercial release or if it was only sent to rock radio stations in the US for airplay. A promo poster exists which suggests the latter, as does a promo CD featuring both 'Promises' and 'Paper Sun.' However, 'Promises' was given a separate commercial release, and while a promotional video was recorded for 'Promises,' none was shot for 'Paper Sun.' The ballad 'Goodbye' was released in September 1999, coupled with 'Burn Out' which is from the *Slang* era, and a track called 'Immortal.' The promotional video portrays the band performing on a New York subway platform, while the story aspect of the video focusses on the emotions and experiences of everyday train passengers. 'Goodbye' reached 54 in the UK singles chart.

*Euphoria* reached 11 in the Billboard album charts and achieved gold-status sales, which emulated sales of *Slang*, but still fell far short of sales for previous albums. Critical reviews were mostly positive, with, for example, Brian Logan of the *Guardian* claiming the album as 'a return-to-form' for the band, while Campbell and Collen also received praise for their 'chops-heavy performances with lots of chunky rhythms and flashy leads.'[480]

Despite average sales of both the album and its singles, *Euphoria* nevertheless reestablished the trademark Def Leppard sounds of big production, vocal harmonies, and catchy hooks. Campbell was involved in more co-writing than before, and that trend would continue on the next album, their first of the new century, 2002's *X*.

## *X* (2002)

The band's next album marked 25 years since Joe Elliott joined the band. However, a more relevant anniversary was that it marked 10 years working with Campbell. It was also their tenth studio album, if including *Retro Active* and *Vault*. Naturally, it was entitled *X*. The band took six months off after their *Euphoria* tour and then convened at 'Joe's Garage,' the recording studio in the basement of Elliott's home in Dublin. For this album, song writing credits were shared among the band, with three also shared with Aerosmith's songwriting collaborator Marti Frederiksen, and two with producer Pete Woodroffe. The band spent two weeks in Los Angeles with Frederiksen, perhaps hoping to emulate the success of Aerosmith's 2001 hit album *Just Push Play*, and that album's lead single, 'Jaded.'

Additionally, the band travelled to Sweden to work with Andreas Carlsson and Per Aldeheim, part of the phenomenally successful Cheiron Studios set-up that had produced numerous hits for the likes of Britney Spears, NSYNC, Boyzone, Westlife and Backstreet Boys. Campbell said of this collaboration, 'we wanted to get some perspective on the sounds that would be accessible for radio play. Some people thought it was sacrilege, but if you listen to our work, our vocals are complex. Pop music is strong on vocals. We're not that far from the Backstreet Boys — we've just got more guitars.'[481]

Furthermore, Max Martin, who is credited for co-writing one track on *X*, had co-written the platinum-selling, Grammy-nominated Bon Jovi hit 'It's My Life' (2000), which resurrected Bon Jovi's career in the new millennium. Elliott explained the band's approach: 'We wanted to mix this album up. Phil said why don't we try something new... why don't we throw a spanner in the works?'[482]

Besides, song writing collaborations were not new to the band: they had collaborated as early as 1980 with a friend of Elliott named Andrew Smith to produce the track 'When The Walls Come Tumbling Down,' which appeared on their debut album *All Through The Night*; their collaboration with Mutt Lange contributed in particular to the success of *Pyromania* (1983) and *Hysteria* (1987); and they had written with Woodroffe on *Euphoria*. However, the nature of the collaboration on *X* suggested the album would lean more towards pop music than rock, and that indeed turned out to be the case.

These circumstances gave rise to an unusual decision by the band to attribute song writing credits to all band members, rather than individual members. Elliott said: 'It's like a mother and four midwives in the studio to help deliver... That takes the pressure off. Everybody is credited as writers, so there is no personal agenda — there's no "my songs aren't making it on the album." But we have to be brutal because we want the best songs to be on the record.'[483] That approach resulted in Campbell being credited for 11 out of 13 tracks on the album.

It's unclear whether that decision made any practical difference to the song writing, but symbolically it resulted in an album that is much of a muchness, with little individuality apparent. Its main theme is love and its consequences, and that mono-narrative results in one song blending into another in rather wearying fashion.

Elliot revealed: 'We did jokingly call it the love album in the beginning,' but he claimed that it was also about a range of human emotions, including 'hate, greed, distress, envy, addiction.'[484]

Unfortunately, those other emotions don't immediately come to mind, perhaps obscured by the lavish production values and syrupy backing vocals.

'Now' is the album's opening track and was its first single release. Its poppy nature sets the tone for the rest of the album. It is catchy and pleasant, with a memorable chorus hook. In an otherwise scathing review of X, *Billboard*'s Michael Paoletta called 'Now' the 'only noteworthy track' on the album.[485]

'You're So Beautiful' is a mid-paced ballad that rambles along pleasantly without reaching the heights of their previous ballads. The short guitar solo seems to mark time rather than punctuate or elevate the track.

Nevertheless, it is typical Leppard material from this era, in that it's a band in search of a hit but are not willing to take enough risks to get it. It's likely that sense of familiarity that led to Neil McKay of the *Belfast Telegraph* calling 'You're So Beautiful' a 'classic pop/rock anthem stuffed with memorable choruses.'[486]

'Everyday' is a simple, 3-chord track with a verse-chorus structure. The main melody is carried by a strummed acoustic guitar, with some electric guitar fills and a brief solo. *Billboard*'s Michael Paoletta claimed that 'Everyday' and 'Four Letter Word' were 'virtually indistinguishable' from each other, citing their 'overproduced, play-it-safe soft metal banality with more overdone harmonizing than all boy-band records combined.'[487]

However, 'Four Letter Word' is more ambitious than 'Everyday' with bluesy riffs, some 'Hysteria'-like arpeggios, and a little nod to AC/DC's 'Back in Black' in one of the fills. The *Sunday Life*'s John McGurk called it, 'a cheekily worded rock romp with a pummelling, all persuasive rock hook,' while Alan Sculley of the *Boca Raton News* considered it 'a punchy rocker with... crunchy guitar sound'[488] However, Adrian Roberts of the *Morning Star* condemned it as 'the weakest track on their new album.'[489]

McGurk seemed to be of a rather sunny disposition when he reviewed the album, perhaps favouring the band due to Campbell's local connection. For example, he cited 'Torn To Shreds,' 'Let Me Be The One,' and 'Scar' as 'refreshingly assured slices of commercial rock,' which is a fair assessment, while lauding 'Love Don't Lie' for its 'raucous rock guitar and trademark walled harmonic chorus.'[490]

'Cry' begins with a chunky riff that acts as the song's backbone, broken up only by a mellow musical interlude featuring arpeggiated chords. 'Girl Like You' is as close to the 'boy band' sound as Def Leppard ever got, and while the band's harmonies are normally a tuneful addition to the song, here they are overdone and detract from the song's otherwise melodious ambience.

'Gravity' is perhaps the album's most experimental track. It's in the dance pop genre, lacks a guitar solo, and has a distinct tonal change towards the end. Its lyrics are a little undercooked, however; an *Associated Press* review claimed they were 'straight out of adolescent angst poetry.'[491] However, it still sounds like Leppard, particularly when the guitars occasionally kick in.

**Singles from *X***

By the turn of the century, singles were becoming less important in terms of sales and chart positions, and were now relevant mainly as means to promote an artist's new music. Bands like Leppard increasingly took control over their music and image, running their own websites and social media pages.

Promotional videos played the same role as always in advertising new music, whereas radio airplay, while still important, was being challenged by other vehicles for the band's music. Physical product started to become less popular than downloads, and CD sales began to fall as consumers preferred the ease of downloading and practicality of storing music digitally.

So, while *X* generated three CD single releases, and each had a promotional video, these formats were less relevant than earlier in the band's career. Of course, their success or failure still mattered, but gone were the days when if a single failed to chart it put the band's future in jeopardy. Leppard was now selling more concert tickets than CDs of their new studio albums, while their compilation albums remained bestsellers.

'Now' was released in early August 2002. The promotional video is part narrative, part performance. The storyline follows the journey of a Def Leppard Union flag t-shirt as it passes from person to person over the course of decades. It is symbolic of the band's decades-long career from teenage newcomers to heritage act, with the t-shirt's journey ending when it is sold at an online auction to a fan from today's generation. John McGurk of the *Sunday Life* called 'Now' the band's 'comeback single' which 'opens with modern programmed percussion and electronic bass.' However, McGurk expressed surprise at its choice because it lacked a 'killer chorus,' and was 'curiously subdued for such an important single.'[492] The single peaked at 23 in the UK charts and did moderately well in Canada and across Europe. It was a top 30 hit in the *Billboard* rock chart in the US, having only been released to rock radio stations as a promo single.

'Four Letter Word' was released in late November as a promo sent to rock and AOR radio stations. For that reason, no promotional video was recorded. It reached the top 30 in *Billboard*'s rock chart. 'Long, Long Way to Go' was released mid-April 2003, a full eight months after the album's lead single. Campbell features in the promotional video, dressed in black and playing his favourite black Les Paul. It is mainly a performance video, shot in subdued lighting to suggest candlelight. It is, of course, another love song, as demonstrated in the video by the inclusion of a beautiful woman who is the focus of Elliott's attention, and to whom he addresses the lyrics. At one point, Campbell and Collen are shown playing beautiful acoustic guitar patterns. It is charming and elegant, but unfortunately the single barely scraped into the UK top 40 and made no impact in the US.

*X* was a commercial flop, performing poorly in all the major markets. It reached only 14 in the UK charts, and 11 on the Billboard album chart, before quickly dropping back in both. It was the first Def Leppard album that failed to achieve Gold sales status. Critical responses were generally unfavourable: *Billboard* called it a 'musical disappointment,' concluding that '*X* does not mark the spot.'[493] An *Associated Press* reviewer wrote that *X* was a 'pale echo of the group's sexually charged rock 'n' roll past, and its songs could be lesser B-sides to the more popular singles. Virtually every song is a hopeless collage of cliches, whining for love or warning about the power of love. *X* has little to offer that countless glam-rock albums of the past haven't already expressed.'[494]

A more even-handed review from Melissa Ruggieri of the *Richmond Times Dispatch* who adjudged the album 'solid, if not astounding,' while perhaps the most positive review came from the *Morning Star*'s Adrian Roberts, who considered *X* 'their strongest... in a decade.'[495]

Campbell defended the album, blaming a factor outside the band's control for its lack of success: 'We worked really hard on that record,' he explained, 'and when we finished it we were very pleased with it. But from the point of view of sales, it's been a turkey. It's just very hard for us to reach a new audience when radio won't play our music.'[496]

This explanation falls a little short of the mark. Campbell revealed, for example, that while working on the album, the band listened to Linkin Park 'for the production quality of their songs' and listened to the Backstreet Boys for the vocal harmonies, which were an essential part of Def Leppard from their early days.[497]

Perhaps a closer listen to Linkin Park for their 'Nu Metal' musical style would have been more helpful, while Leppard already knew the ins and outs of vocal harmonies and didn't need to associate themselves with manufactured pop bands like the Backstreet Boys. Nine songs on the album don't have guitar solos, which, for a band with two guitar aces, seems akin to locking leopards in a cage.

Critical comments suggested that the album didn't have any stand-out tracks and was somewhat monotonal. Moreover, in addition, 'Now' was a poor choice for the album's leading single, and that was the band's decision, not their record company (Island/Def Jam). Whatever the album represented, what it was not was another *Pyromania* or *Hysteria*. However, it didn't need to be. While the writing partnerships suggested that the band really wanted the album to generate some hits, sales of the aforementioned albums, as well as the continuing success of compilation albums, meant both the band and their record company were sitting pretty in the financial sense.

Indeed, Campbell believed their record company wasn't that interested in promoting new material because of the ongoing success of the band's back catalogue. He explained that it took over a million dollars of promotion for a record to garner enough airplay to boost sales, and their label was not prepared to invest that amount when sales of the band's back catalogue was bringing in around $750,000 per annum.[498]

This situation continued with the impending UK release of the compilation album *Best of Def Leppard* (2004) and the US release of *Rock of Ages: The Definitive Collection* (2005). The former included two tracks written or co-written by Campbell, 'Work It Out' and 'Now,' while the latter featured three tracks, namely 'Work It Out,' 'Now,' and 'Paper Sun.'

The success of these albums caused a delay in the release of the band's next studio album, a collection of cover versions entitled *Yeah!* that was ready for release in 2005 but held back by the record company until the following year.

### *Songs From The Sparkle Lounge* (2008)

*X* left the band's fans and critics in a bit of a muddle. The likes of Linkin Park, Evanescence, and My Chemical Romance had proved there was a market for rock music that incorporated harmonious vocals and modern sounds from other genres like hip hop and electronica. Instead, Def Leppard had chosen a different path by searching for a pop hit. The *Hollywood Reporter* claimed *X* delivered mixed signals about the band's future: 'Will they follow the mellow line to the middle of the road or continue to crank it up and mine the metal they helped make famous?'[499]

It seemed the band was also uncertain which path to follow because their next studio album of original material, 2008's *Songs From The Sparkle Lounge*, arrived a full six years after *X*. In those intervening years, Leppard toured extensively to promote their latest compilation albums, and *Yeah!,* their album of cover versions.

Elliott revealed: 'At this moment in our career there is the challenge of being relevant after 31 years. We're determined not to be like Nazareth and a lot of bands out there who just play the nostalgia circuit and it slowly goes down until they are playing bowling alleys... I am desperate to avoid any association with that stuff. I want to get in with The Rolling Stones, Zeppelin, The Who, The Stones and The Beatles... With *Songs From The Sparkle Lounge* we wanted to make something that makes people think we can still cut it.'

The temptation to name the album *XI*, or perhaps even *XIV* if including *Yeah!* and the two compilation albums, must have been strong. However, in the end they decided on *Songs From The Sparkle Lounge*, which was a reference to a backstage area known as The Sparkle Lounge on Leppard's 2006 tour where the band bounced ideas around for new music.

Collen revealed: 'We went into this little area... it's backstage, could be anywhere. It's been a trailer; it's been a bathroom. The Sparkle Lounge has an electronic drum kit and some stuff in there. It worked out really well. We certainly got the feel of the album while we were on tour, and it was just a matter of finishing it off between tours.'[500]

The album was recorded in 2007 during month-long stints at Elliott's Dublin studio. A few years later Campbell provided song rare insight as to how the band recorded, particularly the creative process between he and Collen: 'With Leppard, we totally do everything separately,' he explained. 'In recent years, for *Songs From The Sparkle Lounge*, Phil and I would record together. There is one track where we actually recorded the guitar solos live because we trade off in a couple parts. That was the first time we had ever done that. Other than that, everything is one guy at a time. It's very piecemeal and it's a very tedious process.'[501]

Campbell was credited as sole writer of three of the album's 11 tracks. From one perspective, this is his biggest writing contribution to a Leppard album: while he had co-writing credit for 11 tracks on *X*, it's unclear how much involvement he had in each of those. For example, coming up with a single sentence or phrase might have been enough in a cooperative and brotherly band like Def Leppard to earn a co-writing credit. On the new album, however, three credits as the solo songwriter was a substantial contribution.

'Cruise Control' is a rare diversion into politics from Campbell. The lyrics describe the reasoning behind a man choosing to become a suicide bomber. The track itself is a little monotonal, although the chorus is almost uplifting in tone, despite the song's troubling subject matter. The song structure is verse/chorus/bridge, with a discordant guitar solo to create a slightly unsettling tone. Indeed, the guitar riff that forms the song's backbone is also played using suspended chords for a similarly eerie effect.

The instrumentation and lyrics of 'Only the Good Die Young' suggest this is a Beatles tribute song. The organ that begins during the first verse is very similar in tone to that used by The Beatles in 'Strawberry Fields Forever' and the line 'Like a diamond in the sky' of course is a reference to 'Lucy In The Sky With Diamonds.' This ties in with the album cover art which is done in the style of the Beatles' *Sgt. Pepper's Lonely Hearts Club Band* with a montage of the faces of the band's family, friends, and crew members.

Campbell uses a wah-wah pedal throughout and during the solo, which is aggressive and tuneful. There is nothing in the lyrics to suggest this song is dedicated to anyone in particular: Steve Clark is a potential candidate, although Campbell never met Clark and it would be odd to dedicate a song to a person who died 17 years previously. Moreover, the band had already recorded a tribute to the guitarist with 'White Lightning' from their 1992 *Adrenalize* album. More likely, it was a generic tribute to musicians who have died young, and perhaps metaphorically to an era of rock music that also seemed to be dying off.

'Gotta Let It Go' is a melodic hard rock track with some great vocals by Elliott. Its structure is verse/chorus/bridge, and there is a short, impactful guitar solo. The song builds to an aggressive climax over which Elliott sings the song title repeatedly.

**Singles & Promo Videos**

Released in April 2008, the album's first single was 'Nine Lives,' which was co-written and sung by country singer Tim McGraw. It seemed like an unusual collaboration, but Rick Allen's brother was McGraw's tour manager at the time, and the band was keen to push musical boundaries. The promotional video features McGraw and the band performing the song on stage. Campbell remains mostly obscured in the video, throwing guitar shapes and looking cool, but not unexpectedly the camera focuses mainly on Elliott and McGraw, while Collen performs the solo. Music journalist Lynn Saxberg described 'Nine Lives' as 'a meat-and-potatoes rock song made even meatier with McGraw's voice.'[502] While an interesting collaboration, it wasn't the most radio-friendly song and wasn't a huge hit, charting only in Canada.

The album's second and final single was 'C'mon C'mon,' which was released as a special UK tour edition 12-inch picture disc. The cinematic promotional video is mainly a band performance with images projected digitally onto international landmarks such as the Arc de Triumph and the Taj Mahal. In one memorable scene, Campbell's image is projected onto the Colosseum in Rome.

The band promoted the release of the new album with a number of high-profile television performances, for example on ABC's *Dancing With The Stars* (April 29), *The Ellen DeGeneres Show* (April 29), and *Jimmy Kimmel Live* (April 30).

Later in the year, Def Leppard performed with Taylor Swift on the *Crossroads* television show. However, despite these high-profile appearances, and some promising initial sales figures of 55,000 units sold in the US in the first week of release, *Songs From The Sparkle Lounge* was not a huge success, albeit it did reach the top 10 in the UK, US, and Canadian album charts.

Critical reaction was also mixed, with no consistent themes emerging. For example, Thomas Ki of the *Lodi News-Sentinel*, called the album 'heavy with paint-by-numbers hard rock that exhibit too little of the inventiveness in which the band once specialised.' Yet Ki also praised Elliott's 'gravelly bark' and Collen and Campbell's 'propulsive guitar pyrotechnics.'[503]

Nathalie Baret of the *Albuquerque Journal* called *Songs From The Sparkle Lounge* 'a tasteful and tuneful album of 11 airtight tunes,' while the *Albany Herald*'s Wayne Parry adjudged it 'Def Leppard's best effort since *Pyromania*.'[504]

### *Def Leppard* (2015)

In 2011, Campbell predicted the band would release its next studio album of new material the following year, and that it would likely be a mini-album. He said: 'I don't see the point in putting out full-lengths since the goal posts have shifted. People are not interested. It used to be 10-12 songs the record company wanted. Now, people don't have time to listen to a full album. Very few will do that, so we want to give people quality.'[505]

He was, however, wrong in both predictions: the next studio album wouldn't appear until 2015, and it was a full-length, full blown, self-titled Def Leppard affair. More ominously, however, it was also overshadowed by Campbell's health concerns.

Campbell's disillusionment with full-length albums was likely inspired by the digital age of legal and illegal downloads, as well as content sharing websites such as YouTube and Spotify. In a relatively short period of time, consumer demand for music had changed considerably: sales of physical product had fallen, and those consumers who preferred digital release tended to download single tracks rather than full albums, creating playlists tailored to their own personal tastes. While this meant consumers no longer had to tolerate 'filler' tracks on an album, it was jarring for musicians like Campbell who had come of age in the pre-digital age.

In some ways, the music industry was simpler in the 1970s and early 1980s. A typical rock band experience was first to play live, perhaps earn some money, but mainly in hope of generating buzz for their music. A good live band might catch the eye of a talent spotter. Demo recordings might follow, and then a recording contract. Supported by a promotional video, the lead single from their debut album might be a hit, which would act as a catalyst for album sales. The band would then tour to further publicise the album and to generate income. In the pre-digital age, this, or something akin to this, was the experience of almost every rock band that achieved any level of popularity.

Of course, this business model was open to corruption and exploitation at every stage: the music industry is rife with infamous tales of corrupt managers, exploitative record contracts, loss of publishing rights, and being ripped off by promoters. A band could have a hit single and album, while playing to full houses every night, yet still be virtually broke or deep in debt.

When the digital age arrived, these practises continued to one extent or another, but there were also opportunities for younger, more aware artists to use this technology to their advantage. For example, they no longer needed a record contract to release their music as they could do it themselves at little or no cost. However, when Campbell made his comment about not releasing a full album, the future seemed bleak. Digital music was so easily copied, bootlegged, and distributed via file-sharing platforms that neither the physical compact disc nor digitally released album were proving financially feasible methods of making music available to the consumer.

In the years between their last studio album of new material and the new album, Def Leppard had spent much of their time touring. The band was on the road for most of 2008 and 2009 in support of *Songs From The Sparkle Lounge*. Then from 2011 to 2014 they toured every year in support of albums such as *Mirror Ball* (2011 and 2012 tours), as well as stand-alone tours in 2013 in 2014, which also included a residency in March through April 2013, at the Hard Rock Hotel and Casino in Las Vegas.

Elliott revealed that the band planned to use their days off between shows in Las Vegas to write material for its next album: 'The downtime will not go to waste,' he maintained. 'Two of the guys in the band live in Dublin and the other three live in California. This is a great opportunity for a band that has decided to live all over the world to be in one room at one time, to look each other in the eyes and to come up with ideas.'[506]

Nevertheless, these lucrative tours beg the question as to why Leppard bothered to record new material at all. A few years after the *Def Leppard* album was released, Campbell revealed: 'I think there's a few things that keep bands vital. For Def Leppard, one of those things is that we continue to occasionally make new albums.'[507]

In 2014, Elliott said: We've been working on and off on a new Leppard record. We're just extremely flattered that people care enough to want us to keep making new music so hopefully we'll have a new album out for next spring.'[508]

The album was written through 2014 and 2015 and recorded in Joe's Garage and Collen's home studio in Los Angeles, which was known as Phil's Sweat Shop. Elliott described the first band meeting: 'We got together in February 2014 for a month with the full intention of... just recording a couple of songs, maybe putting out an EP. By the end of February, we got 12 songs written, so we (were) like, "Oh, ahh, I think we've got an album here," by accident rather than design.'[509]

The band set up to play live, as it had done two decades previously during the recording of the *Slang* album. Campbell was present for two of the three sessions in which the album was recorded, each lasting four to six weeks. 'I was there for the first session,' he revealed, 'and I was there for the third. I missed the second session and, in a way, I'm glad I did. It was the toughest.'[510] Campbell called this section 'analytical,' which meant figuring out arrangements, recording overdubs, and working out how the album would flow.

He was credited on the album for guitar and backing vocals, as well as co-lead vocals on 'We Belong,' on which each band member took turns singing lead vocals. Campbell co-wrote two songs, 'Wings Of An Angel' and 'Blind Faith,' but overall his contribution to the album was minimal as he was dealing with serious health concerns which had already caused him to miss some live performances in 2014, with a replacement guitarist (Steve Brown of the band Trixter) standing in.

Campbell explained: I didn't have involvement in the record for several reasons, primarily my health; I've been dealing with cancer for the last few years. I wasn't able to contribute to that record as much as I'd like.[511] Elliott said, 'Viv wasn't here for the writing session, because we wanted him to concentrate on what he's doing.'[512]

In 2013, Campbell had been diagnosed with Hodgkins Lymphoma, and for much of the next few years his main priority was ongoing medical treatment including three rounds of chemotherapy which resulted in him losing his trademark long, curly hair, a side effect he called 'probably the single most difficult thing for me.'[513]

This treatment was initially successful, but he relapsed in 2014 and subsequently underwent stem cell treatment and then a course of treatment called immunotherapy, which involved taking a new experimental drug called Pembrolizumab.

Campbell, who had lost his mum in 2009, and then his dad in 2010, had also been going through a break-up with his wife during this time, that was finally resolved in 2014 when the two divorced. Campbell revealed the break-up unfolded over five difficult years, calling it 'a very long drawn-out painful process.' Combined with the death of his parents and his ill health, Campbell later explained that he considered those years, 'the roughest of my life.'[514]

The band chose an eponymous title for the album. While Campbell claimed that the musicians were simply too 'lazy to think of an album name,' Elliott offered a more plausible explanation: 'It's just called *Def Leppard* because that's what it sounds like. It doesn't sound like any one specific era of Def Leppard. It's got everything.'[515] Collen claimed that was his idea because 'the album represents us. We didn't record is as a business venture, we did it for us and the fans.'[516]

'Wings Of An Angel' began as a Collen demo during the band's time in Las Vegas, but it really started to take shape in Joe's Garage when Campbell had an idea to play baritone guitar, an instrument bigger and more sturdy than a normal guitar, with a longer neck and more frets, to facilitate it being tuned to a lower pitch. It's a guitar normally used in country music, but also features in some heavy metal music when a lower or dropped tuning is required.

Rick Savage wrote the lyrics, so it's possible that baritone guitar idea was enough to earn Campbell a co-writing credit. The arpeggiated chords played throughout the track are tuned lower than concert pitch so were likely played on the baritone guitar. Campbell played the main guitar solo, while Campbell and Collen played the closing guitar licks. The atmospheric arpeggiated chords give this track an 'alt-rock' vibe.

Elliott wrote the lyrics to 'Blind Faith,' saying it was about the futility of organised religion. He pointed particularly to news stories about abuse in the Catholic church he learned of while living in Dublin. Campbell plays acoustic guitar on the track, while he and Collen share the closing guitar solos. The song has a psychedelic, Beatlesque vibe; however, given the song's lyrical content, it's likely the band was trying simply to evoke the sound of a church organ.

Campbell is also credited for guitar and backing vocals on the album, as well as co-lead vocals on 'We Belong,' a track on which each band member took turns singing lead vocals. With no disrespect intended to Allen, Savage and Collen's vocal ability, when this song is performed live it confirms the impression given by the studio version, that only Elliott and Campbell really sound like lead vocalists.

Campbell participated in all four promotional videos for the album's singles. The videos have a shared visual theme of computer-generated stories that play out in a futuristic setting and are interspersed with band performance. Unfortunately, the computer-generated imagery looks very old-fashioned even for that era and did little to make the band seem contemporary. The main, recurring guitar riff on 'Let's Go' evokes that of 'Pour Some Sugar On Me,' and the track features trademark Leppard harmony vocals and catchy hooks. Campbell and Collen are shown playing both lead and harmony guitars. Campbell also plays the lead guitar solo in 'Dangerous,' a typical Leppard rocker with great chorus vocals.

'Man Enough' is a funk/disco track reminiscent of Queen's 'Another One Bites The Dust.' The bass line is similar, and the percussion is almost identical. However, the guitar lines seem more influenced by the Queen track 'Fight From The Inside,' which is a kind of funk-punk hybrid with catchy riffs. Campbell did little in the promotional video but wear sunglasses and look cool, which is all he needed to do given this is a bass-driven song. Finally, the 'Hysteria' soundalike 'We Belong' continues the dark and moody theme of the three preceding music videos. As it did with other band members, the camera focuses on Campbell while he sings his lines. Its emotional impact makes it probably the most effective of the four promotional videos.

*Def Leppard* reached 11 in the UK album chart, 10 on Billboard, 11 in Canada, and 4 in Australia. None of the singles charted, but that was now virtually irrelevant to either the album's success or the band's reasons for recording it: 'we do it for two reasons,' Campbell explained. 'We do it primarily for ourselves because it validates who we are and what we do. We have to exercise that creative muscle as a unit as Def Leppard. But we also do it for the hardcore fans that care, that actually will buy this record... If we didn't put our record out it wouldn't have any effect whatsoever on our bottom line with regard to touring. We'd still sell just as many concert tickets.'[517]

Reviews of the album were mainly positive: at this point, Def Leppard seemed to have passed from irrelevant has-beens to a major live draw with guaranteed hits on their setlist, and perhaps critics took note of that. But Leppard was more than a heritage act: suddenly the band was cool again. Campbell noted: 'There seems to be a genuine excitement about Def Leppard again.'[518]

Much of that can be attributed to a younger generation sharing their music online and using social media to remind everyone of the band's undoubted class. Moreover, the band noticed that their audiences were now multigenerational, with many younger fans in attendance alongside their parents.

*Total Guitar* magazine claimed the album showed the band was 'far from a spent force,' and it astutely identified the reason for the band's renewed popularity, that Campbell and Collen's sound was 'as slick and polished as ever' and 'unmistakably Leppard from the first note.'[519]

Elysa Gardner of the *Chicago Sun-Times* claimed the album 'offers enough decent hooks and muscular, arena-friendly arrangements to keep fans happy.'[520]

*Digital Journal* wrote that the band 'can still rock out on their latest studio album. Joe Elliott soars on lead vocals, while Vivian Campbell and Phil Collen nail the lead guitars.'[521]

*Billboard*'s Richard Bienstock said the album delivered a 'characteristic collection of hooky, vocal-harmony-laden rockers and ballads.'[522]

*The Sun*'s Dave Donnelly claimed *Def Leppard* 'encapsulates all of the classic Def Leppard features — booming guitar riffs, shout-along choruses and slick vocal harmonies — it's not an album that sounds dated.'[523]

Finally, *The Day*'s Rick Koster called the album 'a remarkably strong work in which the band continues to mine their post-glam/metal sound... and this recording is a celebration of five musicians who are completely confident in their abilities and the joy it brings them.'[524]

Band members were also happy with the album: Campbell said, for example: 'I can honestly say I think it's the best record that Def Leppard has put out in the twenty-four years I've been with the band.'[525]

Collen went even further, claiming that it was 'the best thing we've done since *Hysteria*.'[526]

Elliott told one interviewer, 'Thirty-five years into our career, we've done what we consider one of the best records we'll ever make because we weren't planning on making it. Everything about it was completely, 100 per cent natural — it's the most organic album we'll ever make.'[527]

Elliott also said in that same interview that *Def Leppard* could be the band's final album. 'God willing, it's not the last album,' he explained, 'but who knows where you're going to end up?' Campbell was a little more optimistic about the band releasing new music and he indicated that the success of *Def Leppard* might act as a catalyst for new recordings. Campbell said, 'I think we'll see another record a hell of a lot sooner than the time between this one and the last one.'[528]

As it turned out, both were wrong: there would be another studio album, but it would take seven years for it to appear when the band found itself in Marc Bolan territory once again with their 2022 album *Diamond Star Halos*.

### *Diamond Star Halos* (2022)

In the years between the release of *Def Leppard* and the subsequent tour to promote the album, and the release of a further studio album of new material, the band released two compilation albums (2018's *The Story So Far* and 2020's *Early Years 79-81* box set), two live DVD/Blu-ray/CD collections (2017's *And There Will be a Next Time – Live From Detroit* and 2020's *London to Vegas*), three reissues box sets entitled *The Collection* Volume 1, 2 and 3) and a 30th anniversary *Hysteria* box. They conducted three world tours (2015, 2018 and 2019) and two summer tours of the United States (2016 and 2017).

In 2018, they conducted a massively successful tour of the US with Journey, playing arenas and stadiums, and reaching over a million fans. In 2018, the band announced a second Las Vegas residency and revealed also that they had resolved their royalties dispute with Universal Music Group, which resulted in the Def Leppard's discography being made available for the first time for streaming and digital download. The results were immediate, with a nearly 400 percent surge in catalogue sales on the first day and appearances in the iTunes Top 10 charts in over 30 countries.[529]

There was also an individual honour for Campbell when, in 2017, he was the recipient of Northern Ireland's Oh Yeah Legend Award, joining the likes of The Undertones, Stiff Little Fingers, Gary Moore, Therapy?, Snow Patrol, Ash, Terri Hooley, and, more recently, Paul Brady. And on March 29, 2019, Queen's Brian May inducted Def Leppard into the Rock and Roll Hall of Fame. Past members Pete Willis and Steve Clark were inducted, as was 'newcomer' Campbell, who at this point had been with the band for 27 years and six studio albums.

In 2018, Campbell appeared in the band's promotional music video for the track 'Personal Jesus,' which Leppard had covered for the *Story So Far* compilation. Campbell called it, 'the sort of classic song that can be interpreted in many ways and as Def Leppard has always been the kind of band that can blend genres, it was an easy choice for us.'[530]

Presented in black and white, and using quick edits, Campbell is shown playing the song's main riff on his black Gibson. Originally recorded by Depeche Mode, Johnny Cash's cover of the song is arguably its defining performance, and with all band members dressed in black, and a monochromatic uncoloured video, this seems to be the band's tribute to the original 'Man in Black.'

Campbell also appeared in the promotional video for a new song recorded for the *Story So Far*, which was entitled 'We All Need Christmas.' The band appear at the start of the video hugging, chatting and laughing, and at the end of the video everyone sings the lyrics. In between those moments are short videos of fans performing the song from their homes. Campbell looks particularly happy in the video, very aware of his good fortune and good health at this point of his life. His little dog Stu also made an appearance.

In July 2019, Campbell revealed that the band could be in the studio in 2020 to record some new music, but he wasn't sure what form it would take or when that music might see the light of day. Campbell said: 'There's some new songs being kicked around. I don't know when it is we'll actually get around to getting the five of us in the same place to record it — I assume that would be some time early next year — and I don't know what it's going to be, if we're just going to aim for doing a couple of songs or a full album... there's always something on the go.'[531]

While Campbell's illness affected his contribution to the previous studio release, a health event of global significance played a role in shaping the band's next album, *Diamond Star Halos* (2022), and that was, of course, the Covid pandemic. In December 2019, the band announced a Summer 2020 Stadium Tour with Mötley Crüe, Poison, and Joan Jett. Early in 2020, Leppard were also due to continue work on their next studio, but Covid put paid to those plans. Elliott explained: 'Everyone was due to come to my studio in Dublin the day lockdown kicked in [March 2020 in the UK]. We made the decision to record remotely because we had no option. We had seven songs to start with and we wrote eight more and not once did we see each other.'[532]

The band hadn't planned to write and record a full album and were only going into the studio to work on a few songs before embarking on the Stadium Tour. However, the Covid lockdown left them with plenty of time to compose and record remotely. 'We spoke on the phone more often than we have in the previous 40 years,' Elliott recalled. 'The lines of communication were open wider. It freed us up and made us more expressive. We talked, old-fashioned on the phone, and did emails. We didn't do Zoom once.'[533]

Collen and Elliott provided the lion's share of material for the album. Savage is the only other band member listed in the writing credits, although Collen collaborated with other songwriters on three tracks. In contrast, Campbell has no writing credits and is credited on the album only for his guitar playing and for backing vocals on 'Take What You Want.' Campbell later explained why he had no writing credits: 'I just wasn't prepared for the record, to be honest, but I don't think it's a bad record as a result. I mean, the songs are great. There's 15 of them and it covers a lot of different musical spectrums. I think we're good. So having said that, I do feel bad because I feel like I just wasn't prepared. I didn't do my homework.'[534]

Campbell added that he had expected to be doing the Stadium Tour and hadn't written anything at that point. Moreover, he didn't have a home recording studio like Elliott and Collen, and he was still dealing with his ongoing health concerns. Campbell said that Elliott, Collen and Savage were writing songs thick and fast so there was little need for him to contribute. This was confirmed by Collen, who revealed that during Covid he and Elliott 'experienced the most creative period artistically that we've ever had.'[535]

Nevertheless, it remains difficult to reconcile Campbell's explanation that he 'didn't do [his] homework' given that he said in 2019 that some new songs were being 'kicked around.' It's possible that Campbell had been writing but had kept those songs aside for his Last in Line project. If this was the case, and the members of Def Leppard were aware of it, none of the band members or band insiders have commented publicly about that potential conflict of interest.

The end result of all this work was *Diamond Star Halos*, Leppard's twelfth studio album of original songs, which was named after a line from T. Rex's 1971 UK hit, 'Get It On.' Elliott said: 'The whole album is a '70s sort of vibe, it could definitely have been in the charts in 1973. Glam is what introduced us to music so it's gonna leak into our DNA at some stage.'[536] It also features two songs, 'This Guitar' and 'Lifeless,' with bluegrass singer Alison Krauss.

Although Campbell didn't write anything for the album, he was heavily involved in the recordings. For example, on 'U Rok Mi' Campbell and Collen trade solos, with Collen doing the first and third, and Campbell doing the second, before both guitarists finish the song with a two-part harmony. Campbell also played slide guitar on 'This Guitar,' which Collen called 'the tastiest playing I ever heard.'[537] Collen was also complimentary of Campbell's Telecaster playing on 'Lifeless,' calling it 'my favourite Vivian guitar solo.'[538]

The album generated three singles, all of which appeared before the album's scheduled release date, and which were made available only as digital downloads. Released in May 2022, about three months before the album, 'Kick' came with a carnival-themed promotional video that evokes memories of the circus-themed 'Animal' promotional video from 1987. The band's 'stage' in this instance is a Wall of Death, thankfully minus the motorcycle.

This is mainly a performance video with Campbell playing his Rick Nielson Gibson Les Paul Goldtop and Campbell is adorned in a snazzy black dress jacket with red pinstripes. In June the band released 'Take What You Want,' with a promotional lyric video only. A few weeks later, 'Fire It Up' was released. Its promotional video is fast-edited, colourful, and flashy. It is basically a no-frills band performance with special effects added to accentuate some moments of excitement. Campbell is dressed in black and plays his Les Paul Silverburst signature model.

*Diamond Star Halos* was something of a rarity for Def Leppard in that it garnered almost total praise from music critics. For example, *Classic Rock's* Neil Jeffries claimed it was 'comfortably the best album by this line-up.' In press interviews, Collen, Elliott and Campbell said much the same, with Campbell calling it 'a fantastic record' to take on tour.[539]

*Guitar World* called it 'the spunkiest and most vibrant sounding record the band has made in some time,' while the *Irish Independent* claimed that *Diamond Star Halo*s sounded 'every bit as epic, theatrical and downright thrilling as their very best work.'[540] Most agreed with Dave Gil de Rubio of the *Atlanta Journal-Constitution* that *Diamond Star Halos* marked a 'creative rejuvenation' for the band.[541]

*Guitarist* magazine rated the album, singling out Campbell and Collen for particular praise: 'there's a 15-course banquet of uplifting rock to enjoy here,' it asserted, with the band placing emphasis on 'sonic grandeur and lush orchestration.' The magazine commended Campbell and Collen's 'girthy and three-dimensional' overdrive tones, and 'absolutely on-point' soloing, the result of which became 'Leppard's love-letter to six-strings.'[542]

As for Campbell, despite not contributing to the song writing process, he was more than happy with his guitar playing, saying 'I do feel that my playing is better than ever and certainly more comfortable. I have a lot less anxiety about it, probably because I'm doing it so much.'[543] Campbell was, of course, referring to the fact that as well as playing in Def Leppard, he was the sole lead and rhythm guitarist in Last in Line, the group he started in 2012 with ex-Dio collaborators Jimmy Bain and Vinny Appice, and vocalist Andrew Strong.

In Def Leppard, Campbell found the band dynamic that best suited his particular demands. He wanted an outlet for his guitar playing and song writing, and to have more equality in the decision-making process. Furthermore, after experiencing the large egos of two overbearing frontmen in Dio and Coverdale, Campbell quickly befriended the no-nonsense Yorkshireman Joe Elliott, a man with similar tastes in music and culture.

Nevertheless, if social media fan comments are to be believed, many fans hark back to his days in Dio as his best work. A typical complaint is that for three decades Campbell has been taking a back seat to Collen, playing well within his ability, content just to earn a pay cheque. So, when Campbell announced, he was planning to resurrect the Dio band and take it on the road, there was much anticipation that he might rediscover his 'gunslinger mojo,' once more putting the full range of his talents on display. But before that, Campbell hooked up with another band from his past, the legendary Thin Lizzy, and to some music from his past, when he announced plans to record a blues-influenced solo album.

# Chapter 5

## Clock, Two Sides Of If, Thin Lizzy, and Last In Line

As well as making guest appearances on other musicians' work while remaining a member of Def Leppard, Campbell has been a member of four other bands. In the late 1990s he was involved with a pop band called Clock, for which he wrote new material in the hope of getting a recording contract.

After Clock failed to get off the ground, Campbell recorded a solo blues album entitled *Two Side Of If* (2005), which featured guest appearances by ZZ Top's Billy Gibbons and solo artist Joan Osborne. He also formed a band in Los Angeles called Sir Sodoff & The Trainwrecks, which was a hobby band that played live covers in small clubs in the area. Apparently, Campbell did this just for the sheer enjoyment of playing live.

In 2011 he performed as a 'stunt guitarist' (his words) on a European tour for heritage band Thin Lizzy, playing alongside original members Scott Gorham and Brian Downey. And he remains a founding member of Last In Line, a band Campbell put together as a tribute band playing covers of old Dio songs, but which subsequently developed into a recording act that has currently produced three studio albums of new material and remains an ongoing concern.

That the other Def Leppard members would not only allow this, but actually encourage it, says much about the supportive relationship of band members. Moreover, Campbell wasn't the first to work on a musical side project. For example, Elliott remains part of the all-star cover band Kings of Chaos and the Down 'n' Outz, and he and Collen have performed with the surviving members of the Spiders from Mars in a band called Cybernauts.

Collen has also been in a side project called Man Raze, working with ex-Sex Pistol Paul Cook, and he is guitarist in a blues band called Delta Deep.[544] Furthermore, Rick Allen's wife Lauren Monroe is a singer, and both Allen and Campbell have performed with her onstage.[545]

These side projects and collaborations not only demonstrate the nurturing and friendly relationship between band members but are also proof that Campbell's musical activity outside of Def Leppard was not a sign of displeasure or disillusionment with Leppard but simply a desire to play music in the often-lengthy periods of Leppard downtime when the band wasn't touring or recording.

It's also true, however, that his work with Thin Lizzy and Last In Line allowed him to play some of the harder rock guitar that made him such a significant 'guitar hero' earlier in his career, whereas his solo album was an outlet for the kind of pure blues that would never be heard on a Def Leppard release.

**Clock**

After the *Slang* tour, which ran from April 1996 to May 1997, and while Def Leppard was on one of their extended breaks, Campbell formed a side band in Los Angeles called Clock. It featured Campbell on vocals and guitar, P. J. Smith on vocals and keyboards, Mark Schulman on drums, and Sascha Knutson on bass. At its core, Clock was a pop band, like an alternative version of Def Leppard without that band's hard rock edge.

The band wrote and recorded one album, entitled *Through Time* (2006). A track from that album called 'To Be Alive' was re-recorded by Def Leppard and appeared on their 1999 *Euphoria* release.

A few years later, Campbell explained the fate of the album and the band: 'Clock was never pursued because we never had a record deal. We recorded some demos, but it was just for the fun of it. It's on the net and exists as a peer-to-peer fan thing, but it's not currently an active project and never really was. It was just something to do and it was great fun. As much as I'd like to, I don't think we'll do that again. Musically, it was totally different. It was power pop and I managed to fuse my guitar into it somehow. In the Clock thing, I was singing maybe 30 or 40% of the material.'[546]

In some ways, Clock was a continuation of the direction Campbell was headed in when he left Dio. Disillusioned somewhat with heavy rock, particularly Dio's brand of fantasy rock, Campbell was listening instead to soul and pop music. He also noted the success of U2, a new wave Irish band that had embraced pop music and achieved massive worldwide success. Riverdogs was Campbell's attempt to move in a new pop-rock direction, while Shadow King was an unapologetic attempt to achieve chart success with easy-listening rock tunes. The planned Clock album was eventually released in 2006 and the tracks on it reveal a similar hybrid mix of rock and pop.[547]

However, having created the opportunity to write and perform in this style, Campbell found it difficult to make a mark on the genre with his guitar playing. He revealed: 'I've always loved pop which is why I got into the Clock thing. I love melody and I love the structure and simplicity of pop music, but as a guitar player it's really awkward. It's like a square peg in a round hole. It's hard for me to fit what I do as a guitar player into the pop genre.'[548]

Campbell became convinced that a more comfortable home for his playing, as well as his gravelly voice, would be found in the blues genre, and he therefore revisited an older plan to record and release a solo blues album.

### *Two Sides Of If* (2005)

Campbell first considered releasing a solo album in the early 1990s, before he joined Def Leppard. The album was to be released on the Epic label. 'I have some of the tracks for it done,' he told *Kerrang!*'s Alison Joy at the time. However, when he joined Def Leppard his immediate priorities meant it was impossible to continue with his solo album as originally conceived.[549]

Campbell later revealed: 'I was still under contract to CBS/Sony at the time, as a result of the Riverdogs record, so I was writing with co-writers around the country, and I'd amassed quite a body of songs, and I'd been taking singing lessons for years and really working on my voice. I was quite content to just be heading down that road of gonna do a solo record… There were no great expectations. I didn't think I was gonna be a pop star or a rock star. But it was fulfilling to me; I was very content doing what I was doing.'[550]

While Campbell revealed that he mostly listened to soul singers rather than rock vocalists, it's not known what style these new songs were, and none of these tracks have ever been made public. It was, however, still a surprise to many fans that Campbell would choose to record a blues album. Partly, it was because his wife at the time had been encouraging him to record that style of album, but also because Campbell was a huge fan of Rory Gallagher and Gary Moore, the latter of whom had inspired a blues revival in the 1990s after the success of his album *Still Got The Blues* (1990).

Not only had Campbell modelled his guitar playing on Gallagher and Moore, but Moore's crossover success with that album proved there was a commercial market for the blues, and Moore had somewhat paved the way in transitioning from rock to blues, which was a challenge relatively few white artists had risen to.

Campbell said jokingly: 'It's been a long time coming. After playing in various bands for my entire adult life, I have finally gotten the opportunity to put out something with ME at the mic!'[551]

However, Campbell provided a more serious answer on the CD album booklet, saying: 'I believe in the reverence of the blues, and I don't subscribe to the misconception that just because you can play guitar you can play the blues. It can be especially woeful to hear rock guitar players play blues with bags full of technique but hearts devoid of soul. I also believe that as simple as the blues can seem, there's a certain intangible that can't simply be written into the three-chord formula, and as such I wish to bide my time and take the path to learning more about that intangible and hopefully, in due course, I'll write within the genre myself. Still, there's always been plenty of room for interpretation of roots music, and that is all I attempted to offer with this record.'

Campbell's approach to the album was different to that of recording with Leppard. For example, he used borrowed amplifiers and guitars and changed from metal to Tortex picks. These are made of a synthetic material that mimics the feel of tortoiseshell picks, which have long been banned from use. The guitars he used on the album, which Campbell borrowed from the Gibson company, were an L-5 Custom hollow body acoustic guitar normally used to play jazz, a 335, and some Les Pauls with P-90s instead of humbucker pickups.

However, the guitar Campbell called the 'shining star of the record' and the one he used most of the album' was a new hollow-body Yamaha AES1500 with a Bigsby tremolo system.[552]

In addition, the recording process for *Two Sides Of If* was very different to the way Campbell recorded with Leppard. For the most part, the musicians in Leppard did not record live as a band and instead performed and recorded their parts separately. However, for this project Campbell and his band played and sang live in the studio, with mixed results Campbell admitted. 'Not only was I cutting all the guitars live,' he revealed, 'but I was also cutting the vocals at the same time. When I listen back to it, it's hard for me to listen to sometimes. I'm always thinking about my performance. If I'm singing, I'll say, Oh, I'm a little flat there or That guitar was a little sharp. If it was a rock record or a regular record, you could fix it. To me, there had to be a certain integrity to it. It had to be live.'[553]

To further add to this spontaneity, the album was recorded quickly, taking only three days to lay down at Ocean Studios, Burbank from April 11 to 13, 2004. This included guest appearances from ZZ Top's Billy Gibbons and singer Joan Osborne, who had a hit a few years earlier with the song 'One Of Us.'

In addition, Campbell recruited ex-Frank Zappa drummer Terry Bozzio to the project, which, given the circle of hard rock drummers Campbell moved in, was an interesting decision. Zappa's music rarely, if ever, leaned on the blues, although Bozzio's experience playing jazz and jazz fusion certainly made him more than qualified to play the blues.

Campbell admitted that, as well as being a talented musician, Bozzio was a friend of his and he couldn't afford to pay him for his work. He also admitted the reason for the speedy 3-day recording schedule was not just to capture the moment, but also because three days was all he could afford.[554]

Campbell revealed how his approach to playing the blues differed to playing rock music with Def Leppard: 'You really have to find the right mode and the right expression. It's not about technique. Whereas when you play rock music, there's almost that sense of urgency that is driving your arms. You want to overplay, for want of a better expression. That's what I really, really like about the blues. It's not so much about technique... it's more about trying to find the right expression.'[555]

In this respect, Campbell was mirroring the approach of his hero, Gary Moore who took the advice of blues legend Albert King to play fewer notes and leave space between his phrases. 'Think ten notes but play five,' King advised, and that was an approach Campbell embraced on *Two Sides Of If.*[556]

Campbell listened to blues albums for about a year before going into the studio. He revealed, 'It's been very educational for me to go back to find where my guitar heroes learnt their trade from. Listening to Muddy Waters and Jimmy Rogers from the Chicago blues era of the late '40s and early '50s and you hear note for note — Eric Clapton guitar licks, Jeff Beck licks, Jimmy Page licks and where they came from.'[557]

It's no surprise, therefore, that Campbell included a number of standard blues tracks that were either written by or made famous by the likes of Clapton and Beck, as well as a couple by Rory Gallagher.

The album's opening track, 'Messin' With The Kid,' was written originally by Melvin London, and was the opening track on Rory Gallagher's 1972 album *Live! In Europe*. It's likely for this reason that Campbell chose it as the opening track on his own solo album.

As Campbell has mentioned many times, it was the first album he ever acquired, and Gallagher was the first artist he saw play live. 'Messin' With The Kid' is a standard blues track that has been covered by numerous musicians, professional and amateur. Like most traditional blues it has a simple three-chord structure, with a memorable descending guitar pattern after each verse that is the song's main hook. Campbell plays it much in the style of Gallagher, adding his own embellishments such as an instrumental crescendo at the start.

Campbell also recorded 'Calling Card,' a track written and originally recorded by Gallagher. It's closer to jazz than blues, with a cool, relaxed vibe. The main riff is played on piano with lead guitar fills, and a piano solo. As with many of the songs on this album, Campbell never strays far from the original recording, which is a sign of respect to the artists involved.

Campbell claimed, 'every rock guitarist owes an allegiance to Muddy Waters,' and it's perhaps for that reason he recorded 'I'm Ready,' which was written by Willie Dixon and first recorded by Muddy. Although the instrumentation is different, Campbell retains the song's basic structure. Instead of the bass line propelling the song, as it did in the original recording, an electric guitar does it here. Campbell also replaces the original harmonica solo with a guitar solo. However, in a nod to the original, Michael Fell joins in on harmonica as the song plays out.

The album features two more tracks written by Willie Dixon, 'I Ain't Superstitious' and 'Spoonful.' However, Campbell likely chose them not because they were penned by Dixon but instead because they became blues classics that were covered by some of his favourite guitarists.

For example, Jeff Beck recorded 'I Ain't Superstitious' for his 1968 debut album, with Rod Stewart providing vocals. Campbell's version is heavier than Beck's, omitting the psychedelic effects that Beck provided using a wah-wah pedal. Instead, Campbell plays two guitar lines that harmonise with each other. Campbell also omitted Mick Waller's drum solo found towards the end of Beck's recording.

The third and final track penned by Dixon is 'Spoonful,' which was first recorded by Howlin' Wolf in 1960 and covered in the late 1960s by the British rock group Cream, with Eric Clapton on guitar.

Just as Cream reinterpreted 'Spoonful' to make it more contemporary, Campbell's version is also a reinterpretation. It retains the main riff but rather than try to emulate either Howlin' Wolf or Cream's version, Campbell plays slide guitar and that gives the song a more Delta blues feel. Soulful vocals here are provided by Joan Osborne, making this the only track on the album where Campbell doesn't sing.

Campbell recorded two songs written by legendary 1930s blues guitarist Robert Johnson, 'Come On In My Kitchen' and '32/20 Blues.' With the sole exception of 'Spoonful,' there is no evidence in Campbell's playing, or in interviews, that Campbell was ever influenced by Johnson's Delta blues style so it's possible he chose these two tracks because Clapton recorded them both on his 2004 tribute to Johnson, *Me And Mr. Johnson*.

Clapton's version of 'Come On In My Kitchen' is upbeat, done in 'boogie woogie' style, with Clapton playing electric slide guitar. Campbell's rendition is more restrained. He mainly uses the Gibson L-5 Custom hollow body acoustic, with some tasteful electric slide to add colour, together with haunting harmonica phrases. The song is one of Johnson's most celebrated and Campbell pays it due respect.

The upbeat and cheerful pace of Johnson's '32/20 Blues' belies its dark lyrics about controlling a woman through violence, with Johnson making liberal use of double entendre and euphemism to avoid being censored by radio stations.

Clapton's version accentuates this cheerful beat, again using boogie woogie piano to carry the song along. This version almost celebrates the song's inherent violence. Unfortunately, Campbell's version repeats Clapton's mistake. While likely thinking he was being respectful to the original, a complete reimagining might have brought out the darker aspects of the song.

A further Clapton link comes with 'Reconsider Baby.' It was written by Lowell Fulsom, but the most commonly known cover was recorded by Clapton on his 1994 *From The Cradle* album. This album of cover songs marked a return to the blues for him and is often cited as an example of the rebirth of the blues in the 1990s. Clapton plays it with a shuffle beat and uses the familiar call and response of soulful vocals answered by hot guitar licks. Campbell's version is similar, although the fills are provided mostly by harmonica until Campbell's spicy solo kicks in, played on a Gibson ES335.

'The Hunter' was first released on Albert King's 1967 album, *Born Under A Bad Sign*, which is one of the most influential blues albums of the late 1960s. King was one of the 'three kings' of blues, along with Freddie and BB King, all of whom greatly influenced the likes of Clapton and, later, Gary Moore. Campbell's version has a strong, driving beat, and he used a Gibson Les Paul '56 Goldtop reissue to perform the solo.

'Good Or Bad Times' (not to be confused with the Led Zeppelin track 'Good Times, Bad Times') was written by James 'Snooky' Pryor. It features the call and response technique with vocals providing the 'call' and the response comes from drums, harmonica, and guitar. It remains faithful to the original recording, with no variation or improvisation.

'Like It This Way' was written by Danny Kirwan and performed frequently by the Peter Green-era iteration of Fleetwood Mac. Billy Gibbons is guest guitarist on this track. Its format is traditional three-chord blues with a walking bass line. It uses call and response at the beginning with one guitar answering the other, then develops into a structure of Campbell singing a line which then instigates a single guitar response. At the end it returns to the two guitar call and response. Campbell played a Gibson Les Paul Classic on this track.

Gibbons also featured on the album's final track, entitled 'Willin' For Satisfaction.' Gibbons wrote the song, finishing it only a few minutes before the recording session. He played guitar on the recording, with his distinctive tone being unmistakable on the fills and solo. The track is a mid-tempo boogie, with the 'down 'n' dirty' feel that marks much of ZZ Top's later blues tracks.

Campbell said he had no plans to tour in support of the album because it wasn't financially viable: 'To take four or five guys on the road is expensive and it's the blues... and I don't want to pay for the privilege.'

However, he did perform an album release show on September 28, 2005, at the Mint in LA. Unfortunately, footage of only one song exists, Campbell's rendition of the Billy Gibbon's track, 'Willin' For Satisfaction.'[558]

Campbell also performed 'Come On In My Kitchen,' 'Willin' For Satisfaction,' 'Spoonful,' and 'Messin' With the Kid' at a gig by his Los Angeles-based side band, Sir Sodoff & the Trainwrecks at the Baked Potato jazz club in Studio City, Los Angeles on October 10, 2012. The whole show was recorded by audience members, providing tantalising evidence of the dynamic live tour to support the album that unfortunately never happened.[559]

Reviews of the album are scarce, but there was some local interest in the release. The *Sunday Life* (Belfast) wrote of the album: 'Cue inevitable comparisons with Gary Moore, another local guitar hero who has been this way, and Campbell stacks up well. Like Moore he won't win any prizes for his singing, but he gets the job done reasonably well, and while the choice of material is overly familiar (though good to see a couple of Rory Gallagher tracks included), Campbell tackles it with enthusiasm, sensitivity and a feel for the songs.'[560]

Campbell professed to be content with how the album turned out, saying 'nobody knows me as a singer, and some people who think they know me as a guitar player will be surprised, as well. I'm not the same guitar player I was 20 years ago. I've come a long way since then.'[561]

**Thin Lizzy**

Ironically, Campbell would go back once more before moving forward. Thin Lizzy was a legendary rock act in the 1970s but by the late 2000s it had become a heritage band, playing the band's back catalogue to nostalgic fans. Still, it had a great line-up of musicians including Scott Gorham, who had been with the band since 1974, Tommy Aldridge on drums, Marco Mendoza on bass, Darren Wharton on keyboards, and John Sykes on vocals and guitar.

In 2009, however, with a UK tour booked in support of AC/DC, Aldridge broke his collarbone, and then Sykes announced he had quit the band. Gorham wondered if he should continue but by September 2009, and after encouragement from ex-Lizzy drummer Brian Downey, he decided to put a new line-up together. Gorham was aided in the process by his friend Joe Elliott, who mentioned that former Almighty singer, Belfast-born Ricky Warwick would be a good fit for lead vocalist. In a further phone call, Elliott told Gorham that as Def Leppard's *Songs From The Sparkle Lounge* tour had just ended and the band would be inactive for a while, Thin Lizzy fan Vivian Campbell was at a loose end and might be interested in teaming up.

In May 2010, Gorham announced Lizzy's new line-up which featured Campbell on guitar and backing vocals, Warwick as lead vocalist, alongside Gorham, Mendoza, Downey and Wharton. Campbell's loyalty remained with Def Leppard, however; the arrangement was that Campbell was welcome to play with Lizzy when his commitments to Leppard allowed him to. And since Leppard would be off on a major US tour with Heart in June 2011, Campbell's time with Lizzy would be necessarily truncated.

Campbell later revealed that when he realised Leppard might take a whole year off, he 'personally hated that,' so when Gorham called, Campbell jumped at the chance to join a band whose music he had grown up with.[562]

In truth though, Campbell felt he was going a little stale in Def Leppard, that the guitar parts were not a challenge, and that he needed a busman's holiday to refresh his interest in playing guitar. Campbell said: 'Being in Leppard is very challenging because it's a very vocal-oriented band, so the challenge is in performing and being part of that unit. But guitar-wise, it's pretty simple.' In contrast, he said that with Thin Lizzy, 'every song has something interesting to play... either riffing, soloing, or doing a bit of both.'[563]

He set about the task with renewed enthusiasm, changing much of his on-stage gear so his sound and tone was more in keeping with Thin Lizzy's style of music. While he continued using his Les Pauls, he also bought a Yamaha SG1802 which he called a 'very tuneful guitar — the kind of thing that would get lost in a Def Leppard mix because there, it's not really about tone.'

It was fitted with P90 pickups and the plan was to use it for 'Still In Love With You' and 'Whiskey In The Jar.' He also switched back to a guitar lead rather than use the wireless set up he was familiar with while playing with Leppard, mainly because he didn't like what a wireless set up did to the tone of his guitar. Of course, no one in Lizzy used a wireless set up, so it might have been difficult to continue with that anyway.

Campbell also explained that his live guitar sound with Leppard was more 'processed' than Lizzy's, so he switched from using his usual Bradshaw rack on stage to a simpler set up that had less interference in the signal path between his guitar and amplifier. His new set up featured only a Crybaby wah-wah pedal, a Fulltone tube tape delay, an Angry Troll boost pedal, and a Mojave Scorpion amp.[564] Campbell later claimed he made no money playing with Lizzy as he spent his fee on equipment to try to get a more authentic Thin Lizzy-type sound.[565]

When it came to choosing the set list, there were few disagreements. Some essential songs such as the hits and fan favourites from the well-regarded 1978 *Live and Dangerous* album, were pencilled in first. A second shortlist was made up of songs that got the most votes from band members. Then there was a list of alternate songs that might be played as the tour rolled on to shake up the set list a bit.

For example, Campbell wanted to play 'Opium Trail' because 'it's got all the riffs — which is why it's so fun to play,' but when they rehearsed it, Brian Downey objected on the grounds that it was too complicated. Ricky Warwick wanted to include 'Chinatown' but, according to Campbell, 'we didn't all do our homework' for the rehearsals so it was dropped.

When appropriate, the running order followed *Live and Dangerous* because that's what fans expected. For instance, 'Massacre' followed 'Dancing in the Moonlight,' as it did on *Live and Dangerous*, and 'Cowboy Song' led immediately into 'The Boys Are Back In Town' for the same reason.

The band also chose some songs that the Phil Lynott-era Lizzy rarely played live, such as 'Romeo And The Lonely Girl,' 'Killer On The Loose' and 'Wild One.' Then the song list would be trimmed to ensure gigs didn't overrun: a typical set would have around 18 songs, and would last between 90 to 105 minutes, depending on the venue and occasion.

Campbell explained that he rehearsed most of Brian Robertson's parts because 'I do like my wah-wah!,' although on occasion Gorham and Campbell would switch: for example, and for reasons unclear, Gorham played Robertson's harmony part on 'Massacre' and Campbell played Gorham's. Campbell even stood on the same side of the stage as Robertson used to so that Gorham could retain his usual, iconic, stage left position.[566]

Campbell was, however, not willing to defer to Gorham in every aspect. In fact, due to Campbell being such a huge Lizzy fan, he was able to reinstate some original Lizzy harmony licks that Gorham had changed or forgotten about over the years. Campbell said, 'I'm a bit of an anorak when it comes to the band's music — so much so that some of the parts Scott was playing were, in my view, wrong. And I've told him so! Over the years Scott's combined some of his guitar parts and some of Brian's parts but I know them all so well I can tell where he's changed things. I was very, very well-rehearsed even before I joined the band and I don't know whether

Scott knew what he was letting himself in for.'[567]

The 2011 tour was due to begin in Dublin on January 4 to mark the 25th anniversary of Lynott's death. According to the tour press release, it would feature many guest appearances and performers. Unfortunately, this date clashed with the annual 'Vibe For Philo' event, which was an established and popular tribute to Lynott. As this caused some controversy, the gig was cancelled, and the tour's opening show occurred instead at Aberdeen's Music Hall venue on January 6.

While the controversy was not the start the band wanted or needed, it turned out to be a minor hiccup in an otherwise very successful tour. The strength of the band was the quality of the songs, as demonstrated by the opening tracks played in Aberdeen — 'Are You Ready,' 'Waiting For An Alibi,' and 'Jailbreak' — a run of three classic Lizzy songs that was a reminder of the band's legendary status. A series of crowd favourites followed, until the show ended with another incredible run of songs, 'The Boys Are Back In Town,' 'Rosalie,' and 'Róisín Dubh (Black Rose): A Rock Legend.'

From January until the end of May, 2011, Campbell played 44 gigs with Thin Lizzy in the UK, Europe and the US. Reviews are scarce, but a common theme was how well the band performed, albeit with the shadow of Lynott looming large over events. For example, while *Times* journalist David Sinclair bemoaned guitars cranked up to heavy metal levels, which sometimes drowned out Ricky Warwick's vocals, he also praised how the guitarists 'meshed together in that sweet, harmonised sound that was part of Lizzy's musical signature.'

For Sinclair, though, Thin Lizzy was 'all about the voice and the words and the personality of Lynott.'[568] The *Scotsman*'s Fiona Shepherd called this iteration of Thin Lizzy, 'a decent meat-and-potatoes tribute to their original incarnation, functioning as loyal custodians of their back catalogue and the memory of their late frontman, Phil Lynott.' According to Shepherd, the band provided merely a 'fairly rote rock performance, often lacking the innate groove which marked Thin Lizzy out from their more hidebound 70s rock peers.'[569]

In contrast, the *Newcastle Journal*'s Simon Rushworth called the band 'Lizzy's finest line-up since the late 70s' and praised the band for delivering 'one of the best live shows you'll see all year' and for 'breathing new life into a bunch of singalong hits.' Will Stones of the *Morning Star* thought the band's London shows demonstrated that the 'spark and chemistry that held together the first line-up is obvious for all to see.'[570]

Rushworth called Campbell's guitar parts 'crystal clear and beautifully executed' and praised the guitarist for playing with 'pure emotion and a genuine feel for Robertson's very best work.'[571]

Perhaps the most positive review was that of journalist Dave Craig, who attended the tour's opening gig in Aberdeen. Craig said that the band delivered a 'stunning tribute to Lynott' with a 'high-octane' set of Lizzy favourites. He concluded: 'it's clear something special is going on' with this line-up.[572]

Some concerts were recorded by a company called Concert Live. They specialised in recording live performances, burning them to disc, and selling them to audiences immediately after the show. This was done entirely legally, and with agreement of the band and their management. These concerts were also made commercially available online.

Both January London gigs were recorded and made available on double compact discs. The set lists for both nights differed slightly, with, for example, 'Hollywood' being played at the Indigo2 on January 23, but not on the previous night. Many fans and reviewers had issues with the tour concept, believing that despite Gorham and Downey's involvement, without Lynott this was merely a tribute band. 'Why is this really necessary?' one reviewer asked. 'It's hard to top the two classic live Lizzy releases that were recorded in their prime. And both of those albums have the real deal on vocals in the form of Lynott complete with his on-stage quips.'[573]

It's a valid question, but it also misses the point that even the greatest and most commercially successful rock bands have continued to perform after the original line-up changed. Def Leppard is probably the best example of this, becoming a massive commercial success only after original guitarist Pete Willis had left the band.

On an artistic level, one could argue that the Rolling Stones were a more cohesive and professional unit after Brian Jones' death led to Mick Taylor joining the band, with critically acclaimed albums *Sticky Fingers* (1971) and *Exile on Main St.* (1972) to follow. Arguably, replacing a lead singer is the most difficult challenge, but successful examples include the likes of AC/DC, Marillion, Black Sabbath, Rainbow, and Iron Maiden.

Nevertheless, Campbell was not part of these arguments: he joined Thin Lizzy not as a permanent replacement for Brian Robertson or John Sykes, but mainly for the enjoyment of playing songs that he loved live on stage and with some of the original members of Lizzy accompanying him. The same reviewer who questioned why this release was necessary also noticed that Campbell was 'having the time of his life doing this gig' and that the whole band was having a 'cracking good time playing Hammersmith and doing all those old Thin Lizzy songs.'

While some of the band's summer festival performances were video recorded, such as the June performances at the Hellfest rock festival in France, the Download festival at Donington Park, and the band's performance on July 23 at the High Voltage festival in London, Campbell had left the band by then. Therefore, no officially-released video record of his performances exist. However, some fan-recorded footage remains, which provides evidence as to Campbell's approach to these gigs.

For example, a lengthy audience recording of the February 1 gig in Bologna indicates that Campbell was concentrating hard and taking care to play his parts correctly, while, judging by the smile on his face, he was also enjoying himself immensely. On 'Do Anything You Want To' he played an African-style drum beat with Warwick and Gorham, emulating Gary Moore who did the same on Lizzy's original promotional video for the single and also when the band replicated that on stage during the *Black Rose* tour in 1979. Campbell also acknowledged with a wave a generous round of applause for his performance of Gary Moore's famous guitar solo in the song 'Still In Love With You,' a track Moore co-wrote with Lynott but for which he was uncredited on Lizzy's 1974 *Nightlife* album.

Campbell played the introduction and solo to 'Whiskey in the Jar,' parts that were performed originally by another Belfast guitarist, Eric Bell. Additionally, Campbell took on Moore's parts of 'Róisín Dubh (Black Rose): A Rock Legend,' including the fast Irish jig section.

This was always a song Gorham struggled with, but Campbell mostly nailed it, with just some minor timing issues. He certainly had more of a feel for the song than John Sykes did. Despite being a talented guitarist, Sykes played it like it was a heavy metal song, and it was mostly unlistenable for that reason.

In fact, when asked how well the Campbell-Gorham partnership replicated the Robertson-Gorham partnership, Gorham responded: 'Well, I think it gets a lot closer than it did with John Sykes and that's not to say anything against him. What happened with John was it started to sound metal-sounding. We always said this is an Irish rock band not a metal band. With Vivian, it's been easy to pull it back to what we originally wanted sound wise.'[574]

In April 2011 the band announced that Vivian Campbell would be leaving to rejoin Def Leppard after one final gig on May 28 at Slane Castle. This was another anniversary gig for Campbell, having played Slane decades previously with his band Sweet Savage. For Campbell, the Lizzy tour marked something of a rebirth in his relationship with his instrument. 'It's really re-energized my passion for playing guitar,' he explained, 'because it is like being a teen again.'[575]

It was not all good memories on tour though: on February 6, news came through that former Lizzy member Gary Moore had died. A few days later, Campbell told a Belfast journalist, 'Another of my guitar heroes has died. At one stage in my life he was a huge guitar influence.' The band were scheduled to play Belfast's Waterfront Hall on February 16, and they decided to dedicate the performance to Moore. There is some bitter irony in the fact that the tour was meant to mark 25 years since Lynott's death and instead it became a tribute to both Lynott and Moore. At the Waterfront Hall gig, Warwick dedicated 'Róisín Dubh (Black Rose): A Rock Legend' to both men.[576]

It was also a bittersweet moment for Campbell when he took to the stage earlier in the evening for a guest appearance with his old band Sweet Savage on the track 'Killing Time.' Campbell's friend, and Sweet Savage bandmate Trevor Fleming, had died just a few months earlier in October 2010. Campbell said, 'It was the first time I'd played that song for nearly 30 years. I was more nervous doing that than anything I was playing with Thin Lizzy. And obviously having just lost Trev, it was even harder. He was a great musician and a great character as well. It seems like a lifetime ago since we first met but he was too young to die. I miss him a lot.'[577]

Nevertheless, the experience of playing with Thin Lizzy was very positive for Campbell. 'I came off that tour really, really energised and reconnected with my guitar again,' he revealed.[578] Phil Collen also saw the impact on his band mate. 'He loved it... he's Irish, and Thin Lizzy evoked that spirit of the Irish artist, the songwriter, the rebel, all that stuff.'[579]

Campbell called his time as a 'stunt guitarist' in Thin Lizzy, 'one of the highlights of my career... It was so much fun, playing with Scott Gorham and Darren Wharton on keys, just playing the songs of my youth, it really took me back to being a teenager again. It really helped my guitar playing because I came off that tour really enthused again about playing guitar in a way that I hadn't been in many, many years.'[580]

As for Thin Lizzy, they went from strength to strength in 2011-2012, performing live on over 150 occasions. Such was the creative spark in the band, particularly from main songwriter Ricky Warwick, that out of Thin Lizzy came a new band called Black Star Riders, who released five successful albums and toured relentlessly over the next decade.

Although he would see his Lizzy bandmates a few more times in 2011 when the band went out on tour with Def Leppard, Campbell never rejoined. Instead, his creative talents took him back even further to his Dio days and a new band called Last In Line.

## Last In Line

Def Leppard's *Mirrorball* tour lasted from June 7 to December 14, 2011. There were no immediate plans for any further studio albums or live performances, which once again left Campbell with time to spare. Since 2010, Campbell had scratched this itch by forming a hobby band called Sir Sodoff & the Trainwrecks, a covers band consisting of Kara Grainger on guitar, Michael Fell on harmonica, Lou Castro on bass, and Glen Sobel (from the Alice Cooper band) on drums. The band played live gigs in clubs in and around Los Angeles. Their set list was comprised of songs from Campbell's solo album, a handful from Def Leppard, and a mixed bag of songs from bands that had influenced him.

For example, the set list from the December 10, 2010 gig at the Baked Potato jazz club in Studio City, California consisted of one Def Leppard song, four from Campbell's solo album, three by Thin Lizzy, four by ZZ Top, and one each by Crowded House, Otis Redding, Horslips, Rolling Stones, and U2. One final song, 'King of the Fairies,' is an Irish folk song that Campbell played on electric guitar, evoking memories of Gary Moore's playing on Thin Lizzy's 'Róisín Dubh (Black Rose): A Rock Legend.'

It's interesting that Campbell chose not to play any Whitesnake or Dio songs. However, in 2011 and 2012, Campbell made a few guest appearances on stage with the American parody metal band Steel Panther, performing either Dio's 'Rainbow In The Dark' or 'Holy Diver.' Ronnie Dio died in May 2010, without ever reaching a *rapprochement* with Campbell. That Campbell would choose to revisit two old Dio songs with Steel Panther is, therefore, a significant moment in his musical career. A combination of circumstances, from playing with Thin Lizzy, forming his own live covers band, and the Steel Panther performances, helped Campbell rediscover his love of playing guitar.

In 2011, Ronnie Dio's ex-wife and manager, Wendy, formed a tribute band called Dio Disciples. It consisted of ex-members of the Dio band, and a rotating group of musicians including Tim 'Ripper' Owens of Judas Priest. In early 2012, Campbell contacted Jimmy Bain and Vinny Appice to ask if they wanted to meet up for a studio jam. Both agreed, and when they got together there was immediate chemistry, as there had been when they first met many years before. Together with a vocalist called Andrew Freeman, the musicians decided to perform some gigs under the name Last In Line, which was also the name of Dio's sophomore album.

It's unknown if the two events were connected, although over the next few years both bands would exchange barbs as to which carried the most authority as the genuine heir to the Dio legacy. For example, in 2011 Appice called it 'disgusting' and 'weird' that Wendy had organised this within a year of Ronnie's death.

In 2016, Campbell said the band had 'zero credibility' and was 'not in the same league' as himself, Appice and Bain who were the original musicians in the Dio band and who wrote and performed all the tracks on Dio's first three albums, which were the band's most successful releases.[581]

Campbell explained the circumstances of his reunion with Bain and Appice. 'I came off of that [Thin Lizzy] tour just wanting to play more guitar. I called Jimmy and I said you know let's just go in the rehearsal room and play and we did and it had been 27 years at that point since we played together and it could have been 27 minutes it just was immediate when we started playing and I got goosebumps and everyone got so excited and one thing led to another.'

Appice suggested Andrew Freeman, the former singer for Lynch Mob, as a possible singer for the group's studio jams, and when they got together Campbell realised Freeman was not only a 'really powerful rock singer,' but also someone with his own style and not simply a Ronnie Dio clone. Campbell began to formulate an idea: 'this sounds very interesting,' he explained. 'You have the unmistakeable sound of the original Dio band. When Jimmy and Vinny and I played together we had this certain chemistry and you have a singer who is powerful and passionate… I said well, you know Ronnie's gone we were literally the last in line… let's just go out under the name Last In Line and play songs from those early Dio albums.'[582]

Last In Line rehearsed at Mates Studios in Los Angeles, where the original Dio band had rehearsed decades earlier. By this point, Campbell had also invited former Dio keyboardist Claude Schnell to join the band, Schnell having joined Dio for their second album, *The Last In Line*, and subsequent tour.

Campbell decided once more to use the Gibson Les Paul he had bought as a teenager, and the one he used to record *Holy Diver*. The band's first gig was at The Slidebar in Fullerton, California in early August. This was really a warm-up performance to detect and fix any problems before the tour began in earnest at the Limelight club in Belfast on August 9. A further three gigs followed at the Bloodstock Festival in England on August 10, bookended by performances in Glasgow and London. The band then returned to the US for a couple of gigs in Las Vegas on October 8, and Ramona, California on October 12. They then flew to Japan for a final gig on October 20 at the Loud Park 13 Festival in Tokyo.

If the itinerary seems a little unusual, that was due to Campbell's health issues. He explained in an interview recorded at the Bloodstock Festival that the European part of the tour was meant to begin in July in Romania, but his cancer diagnosis and treatment schedule meant it had to be delayed and shortened.[583]

In fact, Campbell had his first chemotherapy treatment the day before he flew to Britain. It must have come as a surprise to fans to see Campbell perform with a completely bald head and no eyebrows, but the physical manifestations of his cancer treatment had no impact on his playing. He was focussed and determined to play each song note for note with the original recordings, as if he had something to prove.

Incidentally, Dio Disciples had played at the Bloodstock Festival the previous year, and Last In Line's performance gave the audience and media a chance to compare the two. It's probably no coincidence that in this interview Campbell argued that his line-up had more credibility than tribute bands like Dio Disciples because, he said passionately, 'it's the real fucking deal' and 'we wrote the songs.'

An indicative festival setlist, for example that played at the Bloodstock Festival, featured 11 tracks, six from *Holy Diver*, four from *The Last In Line*, and one from *Sacred Heart*. However, non-festival gigs were a bit longer with, for example, the London gig on August 11 featuring 16 songs, comprised of all nine songs from the *Holy Diver* album, five from *The Last In Line*, and two from *Sacred Heart*. When one considers that just a few years earlier, Campbell didn't own a single Dio record and would turn off the radio if a Dio song was playing, this was a considerable turnaround.

Critical opinion of the tour was positive. For example, Andrew Johnston of the *Belfast Telegraph* reviewed the opening gig at Belfast's Limelight club, writing: 'To see four-fifths of the iconic outfit cranking out gem after gem from the classic *Holy Diver*, *The Last In Line* and *Sacred Heart* albums was quite a treat for the assembled headbangers. Truthfully, Dio's commanding presence and charismatic delivery were missed. Still, you can't blame Campbell and Co for wanting to reclaim material they helped create, and musically, it was astounding.'[584] In addition, the tour sold well, and footage from gigs suggests that audiences responded enthusiastically.

The tour's success also led to an unexpected offer: soon after the band played Tokyo, Italian hard rock label Frontiers called to ask if they would be interested in writing and recording new music. Campbell said, 'at that point we haven't really thought about that because everyone has a day job… and we just had limited ambition.'[585] The band agreed to the deal — 'Why the hell not?' — Campbell, exclaimed, but as each band member had their own music project outside Last In Line, not least Campbell's commitment to recording new music and touring with Def Leppard, as well as his battle with cancer, it would be February 2016 before the album, now called *Heavy*

*Crown*, saw the light of day.[586]

### *Heavy Crown* (2016)

The first news about the album came in Spring 2014 when Northern Irishman Steve Strange, co-founder of X-ray Touring, agreed to be Last In Line's European music agent. The band's dynamics were strong, and songwriting went smoothly. Appice said: 'It's gone great... fantastic. We've got about five tunes written, and they're really cool, and they sound like us... It's very interesting how quickly it came together. And we're happy about it, we're having fun down there exchanging ideas. It's nothing where there's any attitudes or egos or anything like that... There's no quarrels, there's no attitudes. It's really cool.' Appice also revealed that the band had booked studio time in April to record a couple of songs.[587]

By April the following year, the full album had been recorded and was now being mixed in preparation for an early 2016 release. Campbell was happy with the progress being made, saying: 'It sounds amazing, it sounds like a modern-day *Holy Diver*.'[588] Campbell said the writing and recording process was 'absolutely effortless.' Initially, Campbell, Bain and Appice would 'lay down a bed' of music playing live and together in the studio, before sending a digital copy to Freeman in Las Vegas to add lyrics. This was the same method they used during the early Dio years. 'We knocked out that record really quick,' Campbell revealed. 'It's such an exciting record for me, because it's really brought me back to having to wrestle with my Les Paul again in a way I haven't had to in almost 30 years [to] play some really, really angry guitar.'[589] In fact, the album was essentially finished by April 2015, but the band delayed its release until the schedules of all five members allowed them to tour in support of the album.[590]

By the end of 2015, the band announced that Claude Schnell had left Last In Line. He did so without having taken part in any recording sessions. The reason given was that Campbell, Bain and Appice wanted to proceed as a four-piece, as they had been during the *Holy Diver* era, 'thus keeping the emphasis on guitar-driven songs.'[591]

Song writing on *Heavy Crown* was attributed to all four members, which is essentially how Campbell thought writing in Dio should have been. Instead, because Ronnie Dio wrote the lyrics and did the arrangements, he received much of the song writing credit, along with the resultant royalties. While the album title may have hinted at the absence of Ronnie Dio, the lyrics to the title song cannot be interpreted in that way, suggesting instead a broken romantic relationship. There does not, therefore, appear to be any link between the title and Campbell's past, and this is not, therefore, an apostolic album.

Campbell revealed in an album commentary video that the opening track, 'Devil In Me,' began as a studio jam between himself and Appice, with Bain having arrived late into the studio that day and adding his bass lines only after the bedrock of the song had been laid down.[592]

In fact, this was Campbell's preferred way of working. Freeman revealed, for example, that the guitarist didn't like to come into the studio with ideas prepared. Instead, he would rather jam with Appice and Bain to see what develops. Freeman said: Sometimes they will jam some obscure Gary Moore song for fun and it will trigger something else.'[593] 'Devil In Me' is based on an open chord riff pattern, and it marked a return for Campbell to the squealing pinch harmonics of his Dio days.

'Martyr' is a short (less than three minutes), fast-paced rocker, featuring heavy drums and a lengthy guitar solo. It was based on a Bain riff and was known at the demo stage as 'Jimmy Fast F-sharp' until Freeman came up with lyrics and the song was given a proper title. 'Starmaker' is a track with dynamic range. It features tasteful arpeggios and atmospheric patterns with some slides from Campbell that contrast with heavier playing during the chorus.

The origin of 'Burn This House Down' was Appice laying down the drum tempo upon which Campbell and Bain added the riffs. It's the track that sounds closest to a Dio number with some melodic riffing from Campbell that catches some of the flavour of Dio's 'Caught In The Middle.'

'I Am Revolution' began life as a song with a much slower tempo but some studio experimentation led to it developing a hard-driving, Punk-like aesthetic but one that was closer to the likes of The Offspring than 1970s punk. Freeman called Campbell's solo on the track 'smoking,' and Campbell said the song had 'real punk energy.' The earlier, slower-tempo arrangement can be heard at the end of the finished song, and while both sound good, the punk version has more of an individual identity.[594]

The origin of 'Blame It On Me' was a Bain riff that Appice and Campbell then developed. Bain was influenced by Led Zeppelin's 'Kashmir,' leaving open space between the chords, and at over six minutes in length it has an epic feel. However, the finished product sounds less like Zeppelin and more like Soundgarden, with Freeman singing in a lower register than normal and sounding a little like Chris Cornell, while Campbell chugged away in Kim Thayil-like fashion. Along with 'Curse The Day,' it was one of the last two songs written for the album. The band had come up with ten tracks and thought the album was complete until their manager reminded them their contract stipulated an album 12-tracks in length.

'Already Dead' was another of those four original tracks written for the album. It features crunching riffs and Ozzy-like sinister lyrics. Campbell uses the pinch harmonics technique effectively on the solo, and he also uses a wah-wah effect to add some variety and colour. 'Curse The Day' is an Alter Bridge-like song which begins sedately with arpeggiated chords before a shift in dynamics into harder, melodic rock. In the solo Campbell works hard to wrench some tortured bends and screams out of the Les Paul.

'Orange Glow' was among the first songs written and recorded for the album. Campbell said he felt like his riff had ripped off Phil Lynott and Thin Lizzy, although the song bears more similarity to the vibe of Slash and Myles Kennedy. Campbell came up with the title, saying that orange glow was what he saw when he approached any big city in America. He gave Freeman that idea, and when the singer was done with the lyrics, 'Orange Glow' had become about his home city of Las Vegas.

The title track 'Heavy Crown' opens with arpeggiated chords similar to those Tony Iommi composed for Black Sabbath's 'War Pigs.' It was one of the first songs to be demoed for the album. It began with a just a verse and chorus, but Appice thought it needed a pre-chorus so wrote one based on the verse from the Dio song, 'The Last In Line.' Appice said this was a conscious decision to reconnect with their past on this track rather than accidental plagiarism. Campbell played the intro riff in the studio, which Appice liked and encouraged him to record. The band picked one of Freeman's lyrical phrases, 'Heavy Crown,' as the album's title.

The album's final track, 'The Sickness,' is another uplifting Alter Bridge-style track with an exciting solo from Campbell in which he deploys multiple techniques to provide light and shade. It has an epic feel to it and was probably chosen last in the running order for that very reason.

Another track entitled 'In Flames' was provided as a bonus track on the double vinyl album release. It was one of the four original songs written for the album and it began with Appice playing the distinctive rhythm, and then Campbell working out which key to play it in. By the time of the later writing sessions, 'In Flames' had fallen a little out of favour and it was therefore used just as a bonus track. Whether deliberate or not, Appice's staccato riff sounds like Morse Code. The band was not the first to utilise this effect: for example, the riff to Rush's YYZ is basically the Morse Code pattern for those letters. However, it's still a novel and effective idea. Campbell uses a wah-wah pedal in the solo, which features some fast picking.

Two promotional videos were made for the tracks 'Devil In Me' and 'Starmaker.' The former was released as a single preceding the album on November 17, 2015.

The band released lyric videos for 'I Am Revolution,' 'Blame It On Me,' and 'Already Dead.' By that point, lyric videos had become commonplace and were often unconnected to single releases. Lyric videos tend to be released during a tour to provide social media content and publicity or are released for the same purposes long after commercial sales of the album have dropped off.

'I Am Revolution' is a hybrid lyric/performance video, with new footage shot of, for example, Campbell singing the chorus. It's an effective method of conveying the song's energy and message. The 'Blame It On Me' lyric video is more straightforward, featuring only images of band members that have been slightly manipulated to suggest movement. In contrast, 'Already Dead' uses illustrated images of skulls, graveyards and crows all set on a crimson background to provide an eerie and gory backdrop to the lyrics.

'Starmaker' and 'Devil In Me' have performance videos featuring new footage of the band. In both videos the band is dressed mainly in black, suggesting this is the visual identity it is seeking to project. 'Devil In Me' features an on-stage performance set against a backdrop of flaming band logos. Laser lighting and dry ice help create atmosphere, while fast editing provides the illusion of action. The 'Starmaker' video is monochromatic until the chorus when the video explodes into full colour for the first time. In this instance, the editing isn't as quick as on 'Devil In Me,' allowing the viewer to absorb the images more fully. The overall tone of this video is dark and serious. Taken together, these videos offer a different vibe to those of Campbell's 'day job' band, Def Leppard, whose videos are usually more colourful and less serious in tone.

While Campbell insists that the new band sounds like a modern-day Dio, in fact crystal clear production techniques and some modern sensibilities from Freeman and Campbell in particular, mean Last In Line would not be out of place among alt-rock bands of the 2010s including the likes of Five Finger Death Punch, Avenged Sevenfold, Disturbed, Three Days Grace, Halestorm, Shinedown and Alter Bridge. Only an occasional track, riff, or solo is reminiscent of Dio in the 1980s. However, Campbell's playing is a lot closer to his Dio days than it ever was with Def Leppard. He is simply not required to play angry and aggressive licks with Leppard as that's not their sound. On *Heavy Fire*, however, some of that fire and passion is in evidence. Campbell claimed the album helped him to reconnect with his past and also to his 'original passion' of 'getting angry' with his Gibson Les Paul.[595]

## Reviews

Album reviews were mainly positive and encouraging. For example, Steve Swift of *Fireworks* magazine called *Heavy Crown* 'one of the best rock albums so far this year' with 'an amazing collection of songs.' Swift also praised Campbell's playing, which was also the theme of a number of reviews. Swift claimed Campbell's guitar tone was 'clean enough to eat your dinner off but soulful enough to make you take them to your heart.'[596]

While the *Columbia Chronicle* considered that the album relied a little too heavily on trying to emulate the vintage Dio sound, it also praised the band for making 'fine music in their own right,' singling out Campbell in particular for sounding 'fresh and vital in ripping up the fretboard after years of cashing a pop paycheque with Def Leppard.'[597]

This was an allegation that had dogged Campbell over the years, the insinuation being that the guitarist had abandoned the innovative virtuoso aspect of his playing on which he built his reputation in return for guaranteed financial security. For example, while praising Campbell's playing, Rob Laing of *Total Guitar* magazine made an unflattering comparison between Last In Line and Def Leppard, saying, 'it's really striking just how much Dio's former backing band... pick up their past here especially Vivian Campbell who comes out Les Paul blazing, leads biting — you wonder how he doesn't doze off in Def Leppard when he can roll back the years with this kind of hard rock.'[598]

While many fans might agree with this criticism, Campbell, Bain and Appice were more than just Ronnie Dio's 'backing band.' Furthermore, Laing's analysis lacks insight as to Campbell's character and motivations. On numerous occasions, especially after his experiences in Dio and Whitesnake, Campbell made it clear that he wanted to be in a band situation where he was treated as an equal member, where his voice would be heard, and in which his creative talent would be appreciated. While finances were obviously a consideration, they were not the guitarist's primary motivation.

Campbell was also clear about his motivation for forming Last In Line: he was content for Collen to play most of the showcase solos while on stage with Def Leppard because it was now mainly a heritage band and Collen had helped write and record most of the band's hits.

In fact, Campbell found Def Leppard's live vocal arrangements more of a challenge than his guitar parts. However, Campbell so enjoyed the challenge of playing live with Thin Lizzy that it helped him reconnect with his guitar. It brought back happy memories of his earlier years, which is why he reached out to Bain and Appice. While fans and critics may feel a sense of loss or perhaps even unfulfilled potential with Campbell's role in Def Leppard, his motivation was personal and musical, and not primarily financial.

While most reviews of *Heavy Crown* were positive, an occasional outlier offered a different view. For example, Simon Rushworth of the *Newcastle Chronicle* referred to it as 'a mediocre album,' although he did consider that when performed live the studio tracks were 're-energised.' Rushworth claimed that on those tracks Campbell played 'with the same glint in his eye that marked the guitarist's short but sweet stint with Thin Lizzy.'[599]

As for Campbell, he was excited by the album and the band. He reflected: 'I knew it was gonna be good, but it exceeded my expectations, I'm happy to say, particularly Andrew and his lyrics. Jeff Pilson as a producer was a godsend; he was the perfect producer for this band.'[600]

That Campbell was keen to share the plaudits with his bandmates and the album's producer is further evidence that he valued the importance of the right musical formula and chemistry over any individual praise he may receive.

## Tour

Last In Line joined Def Leppard on their *Hysteria on the High Seas* concert cruise from January 21–25, 2016 and played at the Official Pre-Cruise Party at Magic City Casino in Miami on January 20, where they debuted new songs from the album. However, tragedy soon struck the band when Jimmy Bain died suddenly in his cabin aboard ship. Although his bandmates knew he was a recovering alcoholic and that he had been suffering from pneumonia for a few weeks, Bain had never revealed that he had terminal lunger cancer, so his death came as a shock to everyone. Campbell made the announcement on social media saying: 'It was Jimmy who gave me my first big break in the music industry and for that I am forever indebted.'[601]

The video for 'Starmaker' was first aired on board the cruise liner during a memorial tribute to Bain. Last In Line naturally had to cancel their scheduled performance and instead the remaining band members addressed the audience from the stage with memories of Bain.

Campbell later expressed anger when he told the audience that Bain's death had been reported in the music press before his family had been informed. He shed a few tears as he told the audience that Bain had been sober and productive in the last 18 months, warning therefore that no one — especially the press — should jump to conclusions about the cause of his death.

The album was released on schedule, partly as a tribute to Bain. Campbell said, 'We owe it to ourselves and to Jimmy's memory to do something with it. We're all really, really proud of this record — Jimmy was, too. We all really believed in it. We knew it was gonna be good and we were super thrilled that it came out even better than our expectations. It would be sad to just let it go, so we'll see what the future holds.'[602]

The band took some time to consider if and how to proceed. In the immediate aftermath of Bain's death, former Cinderella bassist Eric Brittingham stepped in to play bass so that the band could complete their part of the *Hysteria on the High Seas* concert cruise. This included a performance of the Rainbow classic, 'Man On The Silver Mountain' as a tribute to Bain.

They decided to honour two festival commitments at the Frontiers Festival during April in Milan, Italy, and at Rocklahoma in the US at the end of May, but all other plans were put on hold. However, the band soon made a collective decision not just to continue with the tour but also to carry on as a band. There were multiple reasons for this, including not wanting to disappoint fans who had already bought tickets. In addition, there was a good response to the album, which entered the Billboard Top 200 at 188, and at six on the Hard Rock chart, selling over 4,000 units within a month of Bain's death.[603]

Moreover, the band had obligations to promoters and venues, and there would be financial penalties if the tour did not proceed. But above all, Campbell, Appice and Freeman believed the band had creative energy and musical integrity, and they did not want to lose that. They therefore made the difficult decision to replace Bain with Phil Soussan, who was formerly with Ozzy Osbourne and had written Ozzy's big 1986 hit, 'Shot In The Dark,' and the tour proceeded as scheduled. Soussan had to learn the Dio songs that still comprised the majority of the set list, and also a handful of new tracks from *Heavy Crown* including 'Starmaker,' 'Devil In Me,' 'Martyr,' and 'Blame It On Me.'

The band played the two festivals in April, then three gigs in the United States in May. Campbell returned to Def Leppard June through October to fulfil that band's tour obligations, so the Last In Line tour picked up again late October with a further six US gigs, before the tour party travelled to the UK for the Hard Rock Hell festival in Wales on November 10. A European tour followed, with a further nine gigs in November in Holland, France, Germany, Austria, Poland and the Czech Republic. The final eight dates of the tour in November and December were in the UK, with the tour ending in Belfast at the Limelight Club that, a few years earlier, had hosted the band's first UK gig.

### Last In Line II (2019)

While three years would pass before the band's second album, *Last In Line II*, was released, writing and recording had begun much earlier: By March 2017, six songs had been written. While the band was back in the recording studio in September that year, Last In Line's live commitments, as well as Campbell's involvement in Def Leppard's Summer 2017 US Tour, and its

2018 World Tour, left him with limited time to work on the album during that time.[604]

In fact, Last In Line spent a lot of time touring in those years, taking advantage in Campbell's case at least, of the long periods of Def Leppard inactivity between tours, added to their lengthy gaps between studio albums. For example, Last In Line performed 34 times in 2017, with seven shows in the US in March and April, and a further eight in July.

The band then performed 12 shows in UK & Europe from late July to August, including gigs in Holland, Germany, Italy, Spain, Switzerland, Belgium and all three of the Scandinavian countries. A further six shows in the US took place in September and November, before the band returned to Northern Ireland for a one-off gig on November 11 at the Mandela Hall in Belfast to celebrate Campbell winning the Oh Yeah! Northern Ireland Legend Music Award.

The following year, the band performed 18 gigs in the US from January to May, playing in a mixture of venues including theatres, halls and clubs. That tour finished with a prestige performance at the M3 Rock Festival in Columbia, Maryland.

In the month before its release, Campbell told *Classic Rock* magazine to expect some changes on the new album: 'Its songs are more developed,' he explained, 'with more parts and more experimentation.'[605] This was reflected in the album title which, Campbell revealed, was meant to signal a fresh start for the band. This was their second album of completely new material and their name — which Campbell chose in the spur of the moment six years earlier when his only ambition was to perform old Dio songs — now seemed too much to be looking back instead of ahead. Campbell expressed a hope that the initialism LIL, a stylised version of which made up the band's logo, might become more recognisable than the band's full name.

The album was released in February 2019, with cover art featuring only the band's monument-like logo and name, set against a predominantly dark background, with just a hint of light shining through. This was in stark contrast to the cover image used for the debut album, which featured an uplifting image of Andrew Freeman's son. Nevertheless, that hint of light is important: Soussan said, 'look at the album cover and you see this ancient architectural cold record and there's that light that you see that comes through there that really represents what the album means… and there is a very positive element to this record.'[606]

Listeners would soon discover that the sombre cover image perfectly reflected the downbeat and serious tone of the album. It was thematically dark and focussed on the political, social, economic, and emotional disposition of the times. The context was marked most significantly by the Trump presidency and his subsequent impeachment, the migrant crisis on America's southern border, the breakdown of nuclear talks between the US and North Korea, continuing tension in the Persian Gulf and Middle East, the ongoing Brexit negotiations between the UK and Europe, a US-China trade war, and the environmental crisis of Global Warming/Climate Change. Soussan said, 'the subject of the album is a reflection on some of the challenges and difficulties that everyone has been experiencing over the last few years.'[607]

The album begins with a short instrumental Intro of discordant sounds, before the opening track 'Black Out The Sun' announces itself with what Campbell called a 'very simple, old-school riff with a feel that's reminiscent of classic rock bands of the 1970s and early '80s.'[608]

However, Campbell only plays the riff during the chorus line, while during the verses he plays open chords and arpeggios that allow some space for Freeman's lyrics to sink in. Those lyrics include the words 'misery,' 'lie,' 'enemy,' 'fear,' 'weapon' 'suicide,' 'apathy,' and 'spite,' and this sets a tone for the remainder of the album. Campbell, however, plays a melodic, medium-paced solo that comes as a welcome relief from the otherwise very dark tone of this track.

Freeman said the immediate inspiration for the lyrics was a total eclipse that had occurred the year before, and it sparked an idea that natural events like this are often used by the government of the day to distract citizens from what the government doesn't want them to see or think about. Freeman would return to this idea later in the album with the track 'False Flag.' *Fireworks* magazine called 'Black Out The Sun' a 'tough-as-nails offering [that] will pound your senses into submission.'

Appice explained that 'Landslide' came after he heard Campbell experimenting with guitar effects, including toggling his pickup selector switch. Appice thought that could form the intro to a new song. When completed, Appice described the track as: 'Fast verses into a big giant chorus with Andy storming over the top, killing it! Another earth-shaking guitar solo.'[609]

*Fireworks* magazine reviewer Ian Johnson also singled out Campbell's 'superb' solo as evidence that he 'really seems to be stoked on this release; he plays with a passion and fire that I haven't heard from him in many a year.'[610]

Appice revealed that the origin of 'Gods And Tyrants' was a riff composed by Campbell. Appice called it 'strange' because it seemed to be in an unusual time signature but was 'a cool riff to play.'[611] The entire song is based on the guitar patterns Campbell improvised, and after Campbell plays a sizzling outro solo, the riff is reprised until the end of the song, this time accompanied by some eerie wails from Freeman.

Once Freeman began writing lyrics, the demo 'Boxcutter' developed into 'Year Of The Gun,' a fast-paced rocker with a legato riff reminiscent of Angus Young on tracks such as 'Riff Raff' from AC/DC's 1978 *Powerage* album. Campbell also utilises legato techniques for the solo, which he plays at a different tempo to the rest of the song. He prepares listeners for that tempo change by playing a walkdown transition, so the change is not too jarring. Freeman's lyrics were influenced by the October 2017 Las Vegas mass shooting which took the lives of 60 people who were attending a music festival. Campbell said, 'Some people have incorrectly interpreted this song as taking a stand on the gun debate. It's simply an artistic reflection on the times that we live in. It's always been the artist's role to hold up a mirror to the real world.'[612]

Freeman called 'Give Up The Ghost' his favourite track on the album, saying it was a 'mid-tempo music track that has a fast vocal line on top of it, which creates the energy of an up-tempo song.'[613] It is a little too busy, with too many ideas squeezed in to be a really effective and memorable track. Campbell's choppy riffing and general guitar clutter leaves it sounding a little too much like a demo that lacks a firm direction.

According to Soussan, 'The Unknown' was written mainly by he and Freeman and was based on a 'modern post-punk/grunge idea of cool complex chording with a figured bass line under to inspire melody.'[614] Campbell is mainly in the background in this track and doesn't attempt anything too innovative or overwhelming. Despite this, *College Media Network*'s Jake Doetkott thought he heard a 'borrowed riff' from the Dio-era Rainbow track 'Stargazer' and a borrowed lyric — 'On and on and on ' — from the Dio-era Black Sabbath track 'Heaven and Hell.'[615]

Freeman said of the epic-sounding 'Sword From The Stone' that it's a 'classic Vinny Appice signature groove. Nobody plays like him, and when Vivian and Phil lock in it's just magical.'[616]

Lyrically, it harks back to that era of 1970s rock which often turned to fantasy and mythology for its lyrical and visual inspiration. Freeman said, though, that he had a simpler metaphor in mind, that the lyrics harked for an Arthurian-type hero to pull Excalibur from the rock and save everyone. Ian Johnson of *Fireworks* magazine called it a 'goto song' and noted its Dio/Rainbow-influence and Ritchie Blackmore-esque riff. Johnson concluded, 'this track sums up just why we all love Hard Rock so much.'[617]

According to Soussan, 'Electrified' was the first song this new line-up wrote together. It began with Appice and Soussan playing a Led Zeppelin 'Black Dog'-style riff, before Campbell joined the session and it then became more up-tempo. Soussan said it was a moment of epiphany for him personally, and for the band when they realised, they could write together and therefore move on from the Jimmy Bain era.

'Love And War' is another in-your-face rocker with a melodic middle eight during which Campbell uses a delay effect. The middle eight gives way to some hard riffing and a typically tuneful Campbell solo. Appice said of the track: 'A serious groove sets this boy up, with some tasty vocal effects over it. The chorus is a bit à la Dio retro. A very interesting middle eight that seems to melt and take you away to another universe and back again, keeping the groove pumping to the end of the song.'[618]

'False Flag' is a melancholy, slightly unsettling track. Appice begins with a half tempo introduction with Campbell playing arpeggiated chords. A more up-tempo chorus section then gives the track an energy boost. Freeman's lyrics explore the idea of so-called false flag events which divert attention onto an imagined enemy and distract attention from the actions of those who are meant to protect us.

Soussan said that the album's final track, 'The Light,' was a symbol of hope in an otherwise dark and unsettling album. It was placed at the end to suggest that optimism will overcome pessimism, and that despite everything the band had faith in the triumph of the human spirit. Soussan said the music structure came from 'modern post punk' influence, while praising Freeman's vocals and Campbell's 'classic guitar soloing' that reminded Soussan of Paul Kossoff.[619]

If, as Soussan suggests, the final track was meant to suggest optimism, it unfortunately does not live up to its task. The melody is carried along by the bass and drums, which are not uplifting enough to raise the heavy weight of the previous eleven songs.

Four singles were released from the album, none of which made it onto the mainstream charts. However, that was not the main purpose of a single release in this era. Singles were intended to promote the album, and while a successful single would do that, lack of chart success didn't necessarily mean a single was unsuccessful in acting as a promotional tool. This genre of rock is now a niche market, and if a single made it onto the rock charts or rock radio, or if it became popular on any of the social media platforms, it had served its purpose.

All three singles arrived in advance of the album being released. For example, 'Landslide' was released in November 2018; 'Year of The Gun' in January 2019; and 'Blackout The Sun' in February 2019. 'Landslide' came with a performance video, in which the band is made to look like they are playing in an old warehouse. It is mostly monochromatic, with occasional splashes of colour, with Campbell and the band once more dressed in black.

'Year Of The Gun' is a hybrid performance and lyric video. Shot mainly in black and white, with intrusions of colour at select moments, band members perform individually in the foreground while the lyrics appear as newspaper headlines in the background. The result is effective and interesting, and it possibly owes something to the 1987 promotional video for Queen's 'Scandal' single, which used a similar technique.

'Blackout The Sun's performance video situates the band in what appears to be a medium-sized school or town hall, as evidenced by a hanging American flag in the background. It is shot with a constantly moving camera, which is an effect normally used to make the footage more immersive and engaging. For a few seconds, footage of the Earth from space is shown, perhaps to give the viewer some relief from the claustrophobic confines of the video shoot; however, it is also in keeping with the song title.

## Reviews

Album reviews were mainly positive, and a recurring theme was that the band had grown since recording *Heavy Crown*. In a review entitled 'Ex Dio-ites find their own style,' stalwart rock supporter and music journalist Malcolm Dome wrote, 'with *II*, they've truly got their range and momentum… *II* showcases a band thrusting forward.' Dome described Last In Line as a band that deliver songs with 'British hard rock grit and an American sophistication.'[620]

Ian Johnson of *Fireworks* magazine also viewed the album as a progression, saying: 'With this latest release, Last In Line have moved away from the more obvious Dio-isms and instead recorded a fine Hard Rock album with a strong identity all of its own.' Claiming that *II* was 'well worth smashing the piggy bank for,' Johnson called it 'a great second album' and he expressed hope that the band would 'continue building upon its foundations which in turn will keep them growing as a band, thus showing all the youngsters just how the older guys do it.'[621]

Paul Davies of the *Daily Express* gave perhaps the most enthusiastic review, calling it 'barnstorming,' with a 'cracking mix of heavy songs by some of the best players in the current hard rock scene.' Davies singled out Campbell for particular praise, and for 'playing out of his skin throughout.' With more than a hint of nostalgia fuelling his review, Davies said this 'solid and hard rocking' album reminded him of 'an old school back in the day rock release when bands played for the total love of the music through stacks of amps and thunderous drums.'[622]

In contrast, Jake Doetkott of *College Media Network* in the US gave the album its weakest review, mainly because he insisted on comparing it to the work of Ronnie Dio, including his stints in Rainbow, Black Sabbath, and his own self-titled band. Doetkott considered the album 'an above-average modern hard rock venture' but compared Freeman unfavourably to Ronnie Dio, not just his vocals, which the reviewer claimed, 'lack real tenacity,' but also Freeman's lyrics, which he claimed, 'tiptoe around current political issues' because they are 'too vague to leave any lasting impressions.' As a result, Doetkott claimed, 'people who like to really dive into lyrics or song interpretations may be left stranded.' As for Campbell, Doetkott praised his 'tasty solos' but called his riffs 'generic.'[623]

Doetkott was a self-confessed Ronnie Dio fan and his insistence in comparing Freeman to Dio misses the obvious point that this was an album of new music, and as such it should be judged on its own merits. As for his comments about generic lyrics, Dio was certainly a great lyricist, but his lyrics were hardly clear and precise. He utilised symbolism and metaphor, whereas his themes were based on fantasy and mythology.

In contrast, Freeman prefers a more direct approach, and his topics on this album are based on the world he sees around him rather than Dio's dragons, knights, and rainbows. While some of Doetkott's criticisms have a patina of truth, it might be argued that Last In Line had grown and were now looking towards the future, whereas the reviewer remained rooted to the past.

## Tour

The band began touring in January 2019, a few weeks before the album was released. The tour began in the US and over the next four months the band performed on 30 occasions, mostly in small to medium-sized venues. The touring party then travelled to the UK to play the prestigious Download Festival at Donington Park on June 14.

Def Leppard were one of the headliners, so Campbell would play twice at the festival. A few days before, Last In Line played a warm-up gig in London at the O2 Academy Islington, which has a capacity of 800. When they played Download, the audience was, therefore, much larger than what they were accustomed to thus far on the tour.

It was, then, a bold decision to play a set comprised almost entirely of new material at the festival. The set of six songs included 'Landslide,' 'Year Of The Gun,' 'Give Up The Ghost,' 'Black Out The Sun,' and 'Devil In Me.' Only one song came from the Dio back catalogue, the ever-popular finale, 'Rainbow In The Dark.'

The *Nottingham Post* called it a crowd-pleasing set 'complete with a masterful performance from guitarist Vivian Campbell.'[624] This development was symbolic in that it demonstrated that Last In Line was ready and able to step out of Dio's shadow and to move forward under their own steam.

Nevertheless, this was a festival appearance with a short set, and for the rest of the tour the band continued to play a majority of Dio songs: out of their normal 14-song set, there remained an 8/6 split in favour of Dio tracks as opposed to original Last In Line songs.

The tour continued in the US in September with three headliner gigs, and then in October the band played a number of support slots for UFO and Def Leppard. From October 15 to 31, the band performed 13 times, eight of which were in support of UFO; then on November 2 the band joined Def Leppard on what was the last night of Leppard's US tour.

This gig took place at the Toyota Amphitheatre and served as the Grand Opening Concert for the nearby Hard Rock Hotel & Casino. Last In Line opened the show, followed by Don Felder, and then came headliners Def Leppard. This was only the second time that Last In Line had opened for Leppard, and Elliott marked the occasion during the Leppard set by introducing Campbell in a special way: 'We've borrowed this boy from this young and up and coming band called Last In Line. You saw them open the show right? Will you make some noise please for the boy who puts the fast in Belfast Mr. Vivian Campbell.'[625]

Last In Line's tour continued with a further four gigs in the US before the band embarked on a 13-date UK and European tour in November through December. This included another gig at the Limelight in Belfast, and a festival appearance at Planet Rockstock in Wales. The tour ended on December 14 at the Poppodium 013 club in Tilburg, Holland. However, the band began touring again in February 2020, with three shows in the US that month, one in Nashville and two in Florida. By that time, eight out of 16 songs on the setlist were original Last In Line creations. Further gigs were planned in the US through May, with possible festival appearances in Europe on the cards. However, these plans were cancelled due to the Covid pandemic, so the February 23 gig in St. Petersburg, Florida was the final Last In Line gig of 2020.

Despite the disruption to touring plans, the release of *Last In Line II* marked a considerable step forward for the band. It was their second album of entirely new material and their first writing and recording with Phil Soussan. The album received mostly positive and encouraging reviews, and the subsequent tour in 2019 included a prestige performance at the Download festival.

The band was confident enough in their new material to showcase it at the festival, and the positive response to that setlist further cemented their reputation as exciting 'newcomers' no longer regarded only as a Dio tribute band. As for Campbell, his playing was almost universally praised. For example, Soussan said, 'what Vivian did was tremendous. There's very little smoke and mirrors on his playing in this album, it's just pure guitar playing and it's incredible to see how much expression can be put into these parts.'[626]

Most importantly, Campbell was content with the band's direction of travel. Although it was his side project, he took it seriously: despite its stop-start trajectory and haphazard touring schedule, much of which was due to his primary commitment to Def Leppard, it was proving to be a success. On a personal and professional level, Campbell was content, saying: 'My playing on the album is much better even than the *Heavy Crown* [album].' I feel a lot more confident about my guitar playing as a result of doing all the shows when we were promoting [*Heavy Crown*] so I really feel like I'm at the top of my game as a musician and guitar player. I'm very happy.'[627]

### *Jericho* (2022)

The band had recorded six tracks at Steakhouse Studio in North Hollywood, Los Angeles before the Covid pandemic intervened. The remaining six tracks weren't recorded until early 2022, this time at Desert Moon Studios in Las Vegas. While the band had limited opportunity to write and record in their usual fashion, Soussan described their face-to-face collaborations as 'intense and very focussed.'

As usual, a basic drum, bass and guitar backbone was recorded for each song; however, each band member then worked in their home studios on their own parts, for example, performing and recording overdubs. Therefore, unlike the debut album where most of the songs were recorded collaboratively and live in the studio, this album was recorded in hybrid fashion.

Campbell claimed to have made a positive out of a difficult situation, since working from home gave him the time and opportunity to hone and improve his performances. The overall result, he maintained, was that the record represented the 'best of both worlds: the spirit of an energetic band performance, and the more reflective and nuanced qualities of our individual performances, too.'[628]

The band was active in other ways during the Covid pandemic. For example, they did a weekly online chat show called The Sickness, in which they shared news about their activities and answered fan queries. Mostly, however, band members used the programme to make each other laugh.

An acoustic version of 'Landslide' had been recorded for the Japanese release of *Last In Line II* and in late 2020 the band decided to shoot a performance video for it. On Last In Line's official YouTube channel the band explained how this came about: 'We decided to create a video as a tribute to memories of touring, to all the grounded artists, crews and venue staff and not in the least for our special fans and friends.'[629]

The mood of the song matched the sombre and reflective period in which it was released, and the video was shot in black and white to emphasise that emotional tone. New footage of Freeman and Soussan performing the song was recorded, and footage of Campbell and Appice was taken from backstage recordings and live performances.

Then in July 2022 came a surprise when the band released a digital version of The Beatles' track 'A Day In The Life,' together with a promotional video by artist Matt Mahurin. It had been recorded remotely early in the Covid crisis in Spring 2020.

At their record company's urging, in November 2022, the band released four tracks on a 12-inch EP, which was made available only as a coloured vinyl record, and then later as a download. (It is an EP rather than a mini-album as it was recorded to play at 45rpm rather than 33rpm.) It features 'Hurricane Orlagh,' a new track from the soon-to-be-released album entitled *Jericho*; two live tracks, 'Devil In Me' and 'Give Up The Ghost,' both of which were recorded at the 2017 Download Festival; and the band's cover of 'A Day In The Life.'

This cover version was unexpected: although the band are all Beatles' fans, with Soussan in particular being an admirer of Paul McCartney's bass playing, none had spoken about The Beatles in interviews about Last In Line, and the band's musical origins go back only so far as 1970s rock.

Campbell revealed: 'We were discussing what would be an appropriate and interesting cover for us to do. We didn't wanna do something from the genre, so it wasn't like we were gonna try and do an AC/DC song or something from the hard rock world. We decided we wanted to tackle something that would be a little left field.' Soussan suggested 'A Day In The Life' and everyone quickly came on board.[630] Last In Line's arrangement stays faithful to the original, although Campbell's muscular guitar work replaces much of the original instrumentation. The result is interesting and worthy, although hardly groundbreaking.

In September and November 2022, after all Covid restrictions had ended, the band put together a tour to support the EP, which consisted of 18 gigs across the US, scheduled as usual mainly around Friday, Saturday, Sunday dates in theatres, clubs and halls. The setlist from the gig at Jergel's Rhythm Grille in Pittsburgh consisted of seven Dio songs, four songs from *Last In Line II*, two songs from *Heavy Crown*, and two songs from the EP, 'Hurricane Orlagh' and 'A Day In The Life.'

The album was released in March 2023 and was dedicated to the memory of their manager Steve Strange, who died in 2021. The cover art by artist Matt Mahurin is a disturbing image that seems inspired by Dante's

Inferno. It features a Christ-like hobo figure being threatened by snakes, who is flanked on either side by images of Heaven and Hell. Similar imagery can be found in the CD booklet. The artwork is more disturbing than on either of the previous albums, but it's in keeping with the apocalyptic 'End of Days' atmosphere of the Covid era.

Appice revealed that Soussan came up with the album title after a few other suggestions, including *Last In Line III*, were rejected.[631] He revealed it doesn't have any deeper meaning beyond the idea of the destruction of a city, although some lyrics on the album suggest a wider battle of good and evil, as well as the idea of urban decay and societal breakdown. Soussan suggested that the album's overall concept is about 'breaking down the walls to get to a better place.'[632]

When Campbell was asked if it was lyrically a dark album, he responded: 'Aye, well, we live in anxious times. And without presuming to know exactly what Andy is singing about, he reflects that. I'm an eternal optimist, and if I were to offer to help out with lyrics, I'd probably annoy him. I'd bring too much fucking sunshine!'[633]

The opening track, 'Not Today Satan,' seems to confirm that the album will follow the good versus evil album artwork. It's a fast-paced rocker built around a busy Campbell guitar riff. The guitar solo is unusual in that Campbell plays a lengthy descending pattern then a shorter ascending pattern, which seems to be leading to an epic solo which never comes. The song title, as well as Freeman's opaque lyrics, hint at a personal decision between choosing good or evil, but the lyrics are too vague to allow for only one interpretation. Instead, Freeman seems to aim for a general feeling and tone rather than an unambiguous message.

'Ghost Town' has a 'swing' beat, with Campbell playing a descending riff with dyads (a chord made up of only two notes). Campbell stops playing the riff to allow space for Freeman's vocal verse, making this almost a call and response technique. Campbell's guitar solo uses a fast, repeating pattern that would not be out of place on a heavy metal album, and of course Last In Line sometimes shifts from hard rock to a heavy metal vibe depending on the requirements of the song. The track ends with a guitar, drum, and bass breakdown, and some eerie sounds that Campbell squeezes out of his Gibson. Freeman called the beat a 'stomp boogie Van Halen-type thing' mashed up against a 'trippy' Alice In Chains/Janes Addiction signature style.[634]

Freeman's lyrics mention God and demons, which aren't meant to be taken at face value. Rather, they are metaphors for war and conflict. Freeman revealed that most of his lyrics are abstract in that they might mean something personal to him, but he tries to give them a timeless quality by removing specific references to himself. For example, 'Ghost Town's lyrics are about Freeman's friendship with a buddy who died, but out of those feelings came a song about a cycle of problems that cause frustration and leaving all that behind.[635]

Freeman explained that 'Bastard Son' had been written around the time of 'A Day In The Life' in Spring 2020. Freeman and Soussan worked on it most, and due to its epic nature Freeman called it 'our Kashmir.'[636] They originally fooled around with what Soussan called 'joke lyrics,' but it quickly turned into an epic track, with a 'Kashmir'-style ending.[637]

The track is built around an eastern-style guitar riff that sounds similar to the recurring riff in the chorus of the Def Leppard track 'Now,' from that band's 2002 album, *X*. In its entirety, however, 'Bastard Son' seems heavily influenced by another Leppard track co-written by Campbell, 'Paper Sun' from the band's 1999 *Euphoria* album. Campbell's guitar solo is among the heaviest and fastest he has recorded with Last In Line.

Although it's unclear if 'Dark Days' had a main writer, its modern punk feel points mainly towards Soussan, who is a fan of that particular style. When Soussan was asked which track seemed like an obvious single release, he responded that 'Dark Days' seemed the most likely, but the others disagreed. Very generally, Soussan revealed, the track's lyrics are about a world divided.[638]

'Burning Bridges' begins with slow arpeggios from Campbell, which leads to some harder riffing during the pre-chorus, after which Campbell returns to arpeggiated chords for the main chorus. Campbell plays two solos, using huge bends and pick squeals to give each note character. For the outro solo Campbell deliberately overbends the first squealing note, imposing his physicality on the song as Gary Moore once did with his playing. This is probably the most harmonious track on the album, and was a prime candidate for a single release, but it was not to be.

According to Appice, 'Do The Work' began with a riff from Campbell. However, Freeman claimed it came from some stuff he wrote for a solo project which fell through during Covid. He didn't have any lyrics at that point, so wrote them for the Last In Line version of the song.

The recorded version begins with some clean picking from Campbell, before a distorted riff kicks the song into motion. Rather than repeat the same riff throughout, Campbell plays a variety of rhythmic patterns that keep the song fresh, thereby avoiding the monotony of much rock and heavy metal music where simplistic 'fist in the air' riffs can quickly grow stale.

Campbell's tuneful solo, comprised of an ascending scale and huge bends, leads into mellow arpeggiated guitar patterns once more, their clean undistorted sound a real contrast to the distorted riffs and solo that led up to this point. The song ends powerfully, with a repetition of the chorus and a guitar, drum and bass breakdown.

Freeman revealed that 'Hurricane Orlagh' originated during the *Last In Line II* writing sessions and didn't have any lyrics at that point.[639] Freeman and Soussan wanted the track to sound powerful and put a lot of work into the background vocals.[640]

While 'hurricane' is mentioned in the lyrics, 'Orlagh' is not. Given its Irish origins, and the Irish meteorological office's practice of naming storms with female Irish names, it's possible Campbell came up with the title. Blabbermouth called the song a 'giddy whirlwind of bluesy metal riffs and wild vocal histrionics, with Freeman on particularly blistering form.' Campbell was awarded 'extra points' for his 'vicious solo.'[641]

'Walls Of Jericho' is based around a totemic drum beat from Appice. It begins with a riff similar to the opening lines of Iron Maiden's 'Wrathchild,' from their self-titled 1980 album. Given that Campbell was in Sweet Savage at this time and was paying close attention to NWoBHM bands like Iron Maiden, it's not hard to see this as a tribute of sorts, or possibly some subconscious influence. In fact, replace Freeman with Bruce Dickinson and this could be a Maiden song from the 1980s. Campbell plays a lengthy melodic solo that is a little at odds with the songs frantic riffing. It begins with a huge bend and Campbell uses finger tremolo effects to add colour.

'Story Of My Life' is another track that utilises Biblical imagery set against a fast riff. Campbell uses his wah-wah pedal to good effect on the solos, the second of which is particularly epic. Kris Peters of *Heavy* magazine called 'Story of My Life,' 'another up-tempo and punishing track that gains traction on the back of the incredibly precise musical interplay between Campbell, Soussan and Appice.'[642]

'We Don't Run' is a song about defiance in the face of adversity. Freeman's lyrics include references to god, soul, evil and faith, spiritual imagery that appears to be metaphorical in nature, hence the lower case 'god' rather than 'God.' These are likely personal devils the narrator grapples with. The track begins with arpeggiated guitar chords before some Scorpions-like melodic riffs help drive the song along. For once though, Campbell's solo and fills are unremarkable.

The lyrics of 'Something Wicked' are those that come closest to Ronnie Dio's, with fantasy imagery of serpents and shadows, and medieval wordplay about 'pyres' (rather than 'fires'). However, the central lyrical theme is the sentence 'Something wicked this way comes,' which is used 12 times in the song. It's a well-known phrase that comes originally from Shakespeare's Macbeth, but with more contemporary usage as the title of Ray Bradbury's popular 1962 fiction novel which, in part, explores the themes of growing up and facing evil. The musical tone is somewhat broody and dark, driven along by Campbell's heavy riffs and wicked slides. When the two-part solo arrives, it is brighter than the song's tone and lyrics might earlier suggest.

'House Party At The End Of The World' was a song Soussan had written decades earlier but which never got recorded. Campbell heard Soussan playing it in the studio and insisted it was something they could develop into an album track.[643] It's another song that uses the fantasy imagery of kings, tyrants, giants and magic, as well as the Biblical imagery of a transcending soul, the end of the world, and Revelations. The song's engine is Appice's massive drum sound and Campbell's frenzied riffing. Campbell's first solo plays during a break, and the second over the main riff.

**Promotional Videos**

Five promotional videos were shot, two for the digital download single releases of 'Ghost Town' and 'Do The Work,' and the others mainly as promotional videos for the album and tour. 'Ghost Town' was released on January 20, the same day as the album announcement, and 'Do The Work' was made available from February 18. 'House Party At The End Of The World' was released mid-March, shortly before the album appeared. An official audio video exists, but it is simply an image over which the song plays. The video for 'Bastard Son' was released in May 2023, while 'Not Today Satan' appeared in September 2023 and was likely made just to publicise the live dates the band planned for that month.

'Ghost Town' has a monochromatic performance video with a large image of the album cover as its backdrop. The band's performance is interspersed with brief footage of city scenes. While the video focuses mostly on Freeman, Soussan is shown singing backing vocals, and there are close ups of the fingerboard while Campbell plays his solo.

The performance video of 'Do The Work' begins in monochrome but shifts to full colour when the main riff starts, a trick used since 1939's *The Wizard of Oz*. The band performs against a black background, with strong lighting behind Freeman and Soussan. Everyone except Appice wears dark sunglasses, while Appice is adorned with his trademark black beanie hat. Camera time is shared equally between band members as Soussan sings backing vocals and Campbell plays his signature model Gibson Les Paul Custom.

In contrast to previous promotional videos from the album, 'Not Today Satan' is in full colour throughout. It is another performance video set against a dark background but with more visual gimmickry than the other videos, including effects such as fast editing, extreme close ups, out-of-focus imagery, split screen and quad screen. All four band members are shown singing, and at times Freeman is shown singing while at the wheel of a motor vehicle. Campbell plays a different guitar in this video: this time it's a Les Paul Goldtop, perhaps to provide a visual connection between wealth (gold) and images in the video of Caesars Palace Casino with its illusionary promise of wealth.

Subliminal commands such as 'conform' and 'obey' can be seen on screen, on occasion appearing on Campbell and Freeman's dark glasses. The word 'sheep' also appears on screen. The band's performance is set against a story showing a woman staring at Caesars Palace Casino where a large screen superimposed on the building commands onlookers to 'obey.' Another scene shows the woman outside the Omnia nightclub at the casino looking at a sign saying 'consume.' Together, these techniques form a concept video warning about conformity and consumerism. The video ends on a hopeful note, however, when these conformist orders are replaced by commands to 'resist' and 'wake up.'

The video for 'Bastard Son' begins with atmospheric colour images of clouds, a weather system rolling in over a city, and a lightning storm. It then transforms into a monochromatic performance video interspersed with images of concrete, traffic, and urban decay. The unmistakable message is that the awesome power of nature overcomes human achievement. A 'Grim Reaper' figure is shown walking an empty road to suggest a kind of apocalyptic end for humanity if it continues on its present course. All four band members are dressed in black, and Campbell plays his beloved black Les Paul, 72987537.

**Album Reviews**

Most reviews came from online rock and metal webzines and most were positive, although some had reservations about Freeman's lyrics or the supposed absence of stand-out tracks. For example, Richard Henry of *Metal Planet Music* called *Jericho* 'an outstanding album, full of great songs, fantastic playing from all the guys and really just an absolutely solid rock album, very highly recommended.'[644]

Bryan Rolli of *Ultimate Classic Rock* wrote that *Jericho* 'kicks up a ferocious hard-rock storm… delivering a torrent of machine-gun riffs, wrecking-ball rhythms and razor-wire solos.' If the album has a weakness, Rolli argued, it was Freeman's lyrics which 'amount to little more than their cliche song titles.'[645] Andy Thorley of *Maximum Volume Music*, also spoke enthusiastically about the album, claiming: 'There are highlights wherever you look... this type of rock music might not be this good anywhere else in 2023.'[646]

While David Randall of *Let's Get Ready To Rock!* bemoaned what he considered as the album's 'paucity of really killer tracks,' he nevertheless thought of it as 'a particularly good and evocative example of the genre.'[647]

Kaitlin Breslin of *MNPR* magazine claimed that the album provided evidence that Last In Line had shown musical progression. Breslin wrote: 'the album's rock-solid brick work displays a natural evolution from the band's previous efforts... experimenting further in style, influence, and intricacy... If the masterful masonry behind *Jericho* is anything to go by, there's no telling where this band's unbridled ambition will take them next.' Breslin's overall impression was that *Jericho* delivered 'one heart-thumping, thought-provoking track after another.'[648]

*Classic Rock*'s Dom Lawson also saw progression in the album, noting, for example, that *Jericho* felt 'looser and grittier' than either of its predecessors, with Freeman in particular 'audibly upping his game.' He concluded, 'class runs through this like a stick of (unusually thunderous) rock.'[649]

In contrast, Bryan Rolli singled out Appice and Campbell as a key ingredient of the album's success, and that its 'unadulterated thrill' was in 'hearing Campbell and Appice rock with 40 years of chemistry under their fingers.'[650] In fact, if there is one theme running through these indicative reviews it is praise for Campbell. For instance, David Randall called the guitarist 'a bit of a chameleon'... in that he adapts easily to any environment be it Dio, the wonderful Shadow King, or more obviously Def Leppard. But, Randall argued, it was Last In Line that gives the guitarist his best opportunity to shine. 'We're not just talking tone here,' said Randall, 'but the ability to really enhance a song whether it is in the riffage or the little fills and touches which make up the appealing whole.'[651]

*Classic Rock* magazine paid Campbell a particularly insightful compliment, saying that the album 'sounds like it could come have from the mind of the eighteen-year-old Vivian Campbell, in the sense that it has the feel of classic metal albums.' Given that Campbell's stint with Thin Lizzy helped him recapture some of that aggressive, youthful approach, and that experience caused him to form Last In Line, Campbell was pleased to acknowledge the compliment. He responded: 'I'm happy you think that, because that's definitely what I'm looking for, that idea of going back to when I was sixteen/ seventeen, murdering my Les Paul. I'm sixty years old now, but I still play like I'm sixteen, in my head.'[652]


**Tour**
The band hoped to play three live shows in April 2023, before Campbell had to rejoin Def Leppard for their World Tour. The US part of that tour

ended in August, leaving open the opportunity for Campbell to schedule 12 more Last In Line US dates in September. Then it was back to Def Leppard again for two shows in Japan in November, then three more shows in Australia a little later in the month. Last In Line played three more gigs in December to close out the year.

The first Last In Line gig on April 1 was an album release party at the Hard Rock Café in Las Vegas, hosted by Eddie Trunk. Two further gigs followed on April 13 at the Rialto Theatre in Tucson and on the following day at the Medina Entertainment Centre in Minnesota. Before the tour, Appice said the four tracks he was most looking forward to playing live would be 'Hurricane Orlagh,' 'Do The Work,' 'Ghost Town' and 'House Party At The End Of The World.'

That turned out to be an accurate prediction as all four were on the setlist for the Hard Rock Café gig. That night the band played six Dio songs, three from *Heavy Crown*, two from *Last In Line II*, and four from *Jericho*. That setlist marked the first time Last In Line's original songs outnumbered Dio songs at a full length gig, and that ratio remained for the rest of the tour.

In September, the band played 12 US dates in 23 days, mostly in clubs, halls and theatres. It had become evident at this point that Last In Line was probably never going to grow large enough to headline bigger arenas. However, given the band's peripatetic development, and its modest ambitions, this was not a major stumbling block. One-off larger, more high-profile festival gigs were always a possibility.

For example, the first of the band's final trio of gigs in December 2023 was in Mexico City at the Life After Death Festival. The band was scheduled to play on the third day, and was fourth on the bill behind headliners WASP, Accept and Saxon, but above ten other acts including veterans Lizzy Borden and Armoured Saint.

In late December the band announced new gigs for 2024. Beginning on January 26, at The Showroom at the Golden Nugget in Las Vegas, and running through early May, the band would play a total of 13 gigs, including three nights in February on the Rock Legends Cruise, Miami. Presumably they were hoping that lightning would not strike twice and there would be no repeat of the tragic events that led to Jimmy Bain's passing. The setlist for those Rock Legends Cruise gigs was a little shorter than usual, with 13 songs instead of 15. It was comprised of six Dio songs, three from *Heavy Crown*, two from *Last In Line II* and three from *Jericho*.

Another notable festival date was on the itinerary for May 4 at the M3 Rock Festival in Columbia, Missouri. The band played a truncated setlist of nine songs, five of which were Last In Line originals. This demonstrates again that even at festival gigs with a shortened setlist, the band remained confident enough to play their own original music rather than load the set with crowd pleasing and familiar Dio songs.

Campbell is committed to Def Leppard's extensive US tour which runs from July through September, and at time of writing, only one further Last In Line gig has been scheduled for 2024, at the Arcada Theatre, St. Charles, Illinois on October 25. Past example suggests more gigs will be added as the opportunity arises.

It's difficult to provide an assessment of a band while they are still developing. Bands control the narrative and usually keep problems under wraps. There is always the possibility of a line-up change, especially if financial issues arise.

For example, it's unlikely Last In Line's profile will rise much further, nor is it likely given the style of music they play that they will ever have chart-topping singles or albums. In younger bands, those factors often lead to dissatisfaction, arguments, and line-up changes: in older bands, not so much. However, even seasoned artists need to secure their financial future. Might financial concerns affect the band's longevity? It's possible for example, that the underlying reason Schnell was let go was that the band wasn't generating enough profit to survive as a five piece.

Nevertheless, Campbell has made it clear that finances aren't an issue for him, and he laughs off the differences between touring with Def Leppard and touring with Last In Line, not least the quality and cost of each band's accommodation: Campbell revealed that when on tour Last In Line stays in the Holiday Inn Express, whereas it's The Savoy for Def Leppard.[653]

Campbell explained: 'It's one of my happy places in life to be on stage murdering a Les Paul guitar and even if I'm just in some little club with Last In Line playing for beer money it's one of my happy spots, it's very cathartic and makes me feel alive.'[654]

Campbell has also suggested that finances aren't an issue for other band members either. 'Last In Line is about fun and camaraderie,' he insisted: 'none of us are really doing this for a living. There's not that sort of remuneration in it — it's more for the craic, y'know?'[655]

The evidence suggests we should take Campbell at his word. For example, there was no need for him to form his side project band, Sir Sodoff & the Trainwrecks, or to invest the time and energy required to play small clubs in Los Angeles probably for no monetary profit. He did that as an outlet for his guitar playing and to keep active during long periods of Def Leppard inactivity. Last In Line is a bit different in that Campbell has been touring consecutively with both bands, meaning he doesn't get much of a break between his Def Leppard commitments. Of course, Last In Line transformed from a live band playing only Dio songs to a band with three albums of original material under their collective belts.

Yet there is another reason why Campbell takes Last In Line so seriously: although he has had a storied career in some of the biggest rocks bands of the era, it has left him not entirely content with his musical legacy: 'I feel like I've been a little bit on the fringes of different things,' he revealed. 'I've been involved in so many different bands and different projects over the years, but this has been a different experience for me... because I've been in and out of so many bands over the years I've never had the chance to fully make my imprint and I'm trying to do that as much as possible.'[656] Undoubtedly, his cancer diagnosis helped clarify his musical priorities, and clearly the perception that he has of being almost peripheral to the success of bands has been on his mind, even if it's unfair self-analysis.

Campbell therefore approaches Last In Line differently to any of his other musical side projects. While he is not necessarily the band leader, because, as his experiences with Ronnie Dio and David Coverdale illustrate, he doesn't like the idea of one person doing all the decision-making, he is central to the band's success. He was responsible for contacting Appice and Bain to reunite three quarters of the original Dio line-up. It was Campbell who then suggested setting up some live gigs to perform in front of an audience.

It's also mainly, but not solely, around Campbell's schedule that Last In Line activities take place. Campbell calls the band 'a very serious side project' and explained the implications of that for him: 'When I'm not working with Def Leppard I devote all of my time to Last In Line because I'm invested in it and want it to be taken seriously... It takes up all of my time and I have to forego a lot of my personal life; I don't take vacations and stuff like that, but it fulfils me, it makes me feel alive.'[657]

Appice also noticed the effect the band was having on Campbell compared to playing with Def Leppard, particularly how he responds to the demands and expectations of each band. Appice said: 'Everybody's shocked the way he plays in this band because… Leppard's a different band and has two guitars.'

In contrast, Appice maintained, in Last In Line Campbell is 'the guy doing all the heavy lifting — he's got to play the solos, he's got to play the song and just keep it going you know so he's got his hands full yeah, but people are like wow man! ripping yeah! He's a great guitar player.'[658]

# Epilogue

In my previous music books, there has always been a natural finishing point. For example, when I wrote *Woodstock and Altamont* (Wymer 2019), the end came after I discussed the impact of the two main documentaries of these events, *Woodstock* (1970) and *Gimme Shelter* (1970). Of course, their stories didn't end there, but it seemed like a good place to end the book since popular memory of those festivals and the events surrounding them has been shaped mainly by that footage.

When I wrote *The Rolling Stones in America 1964-1972* (Wymer 2022), I ended the book with the release of *Exile on Main St.* in 1972 because that was a particular highpoint for the band and also the end of one era in the Stones' long history.

And when I wrote *Back On The Streets: The Gary Moore Story* (Wymer 2024) it ended with the Belfast guitarist's tragic death in 2011. However, with Vivian Campbell there is no natural end point: he is still a member of two bands, Def Leppard and Last In Line — or three if including Riverdogs — so his story is ongoing. Def Leppard and Last In Line show no sign of slowing down, and future recordings and live performances seem likely.

What of Riverdogs, the melodic rock band that Campbell originally left after the release of the band's self-titled debut album in 1990? Campbell's subsequent reconnection with the band is a good example of not quite knowing where his story ends: in fact, Campbell went on to record two more albums of original material with them, *World Gone Mad* (2011) and *California* (2017). Both pick up where their debut album left off, with a variety of electric and acoustic rock songs, and with the latter featuring some harder rock tracks propelled by Campbell's aggressive style of playing.

The origin of *World Gone Mad* was some demos the band recorded in 2003 after they reformed in Los Angeles just to play a few gigs. However, nothing came of those recordings until the label Melodic Rock Records approached the band in 2010 to ask if they were interested in re-recording these tracks for a new Riverdogs album release. The band agreed. However, as there weren't enough tracks for an album, they decided at that point to record a handful of new songs.

Lamonthe had the original idea for album opener, 'World Gone Mad.' He created the lyrics out of newspaper headlines, which collectively drew a picture of a dystopian and dysfunctional society. Its foundation is a funky electric guitar riff and some great vocals. Campbell plays some restrained fills and uses a wah-wah pedal in the playout. The track that follows, entitled 'Big Steel Town,' has a laid-back vibe set against Lamothe's downbeat lyrics. It begins with a three-string arpeggio which continues throughout, with Campbell also adding some muscular riffs. As with the original *Riverdogs* album, however, Campbell's playing never overwhelms the song.

'Best Day Of My Life' begins with an Eastern-style riff from Lamothe. It gains steam when Campbell's adds some meaty riffs. The track features some harmonious backing vocals and develops into quite a powerful song. There isn't much for Campbell to do on this track, which doesn't have a solo. 'Just A Little Higher' is an uplifting acoustic ballad that showcases Lamothe's vocals. His voice sounds like Jon Bon Jovi's but with more soul. Campbell provides only a few guitar patterns which are low in the mix, until his tuneful, bluesy solo adds some sparkle.

'For You' features some down and dirty Campbell riffs punctuated by restrained wah-wah fills. Mellow vocals are soon overshadowed as guitar riffs build towards a funky playout. Lamothe's warm vocals are once more in the foreground in 'This Empty Room.' Campbell plays some electric arpeggios, some riffs during the chorus, and some quick, tuneful fills.

'Glitter Town' is a mid-tempo rocker, and the only song on the album where Campbell really lets go with a great solo played using his wah-wah pedal. The final song on the album is a live cover of Badfinger's 'No Matter What.' Presumably this was to fill out the album and provide more value for money since the disc only lasts around 25 minutes and is not really the length CD buyers expect.

*World Gone Mad* came as something of a disappointment to fans who were expecting the band to emulate their debut album. The tracks are pleasant enough, the musicians top notch and on their game, and the album was mixed competently and produced professionally. However, considering the potential market for this type of melodic rock, the songs lack killer hooks and memorable melodies. It's a radio-friendly album created at a time when radio playlists were beginning to lose relevance. Moreover, Campbell's playing is very restrained, and one wonders how the album might have fared if he had cut loose a little more.

Skip forward half a decade and Frontiers Records, who were also Last In Line's label at the time, proposed to Campbell that Riverdogs reform to write and record a new album, asking specifically if the band could recreate the sound of their debut album. Campbell literally removed old guitars, amplifiers and equipment from storage to make that happen.

*California* is, though, a more guitar-driven album than the band's debut. On that album most songs were written by Lamothe on acoustic guitar, and Campbell then added tasteful rhythm guitar, fills, and sizzling lead breaks. However, *California* was written from scratch with Campbell fully involved. Therefore, his lead guitar parts felt more like integral parts of the song instead of decoration or afterthought.

Campbell explained how the writing process unfolded: 'It was mostly just a jam kind of thing. They'd say to me "Viv, have you got a riff?" I'd start playing something, and we'd piece it together... Everything except 'American Dream' and 'The Revolution Starts Tonight' [which Lamothe co-wrote with his son] pretty much started from a guitar idea of mine. They were very, very collaborative; I'm not saying I came in with songs, but I would start the ball rolling with the guitar riff and we'd make it into a song within a couple of hours.'[659]

The album came together in two songwriting sessions in Los Angeles in the summer of 2016. In the first, the band wrote six songs over three days, then recorded the demos. A month later, they wrote another six songs over four days and recorded demos of those. Campbell then re-recorded his demo guitar parts over four days in September 2016 at Serenity West studio in Hollywood. As with most of the Riverdogs catalogue, Campbell sings backing vocals, which is something he never does for Last In Line, and on *California* those backing vocals were recorded live in the studio so there was little margin of error.

The album's opening track, 'American Dream,' is an immediate demonstration of what was missing from *World Gone Mad*. Its high energy approach, memorable hooks, singalong chorus, and killer guitar solo from Campbell make an instant impact. A promotional video was created, which was shot on a California hillside as the sun was starting to set. It is mainly a performance video with some attempt at a narrative on the theme of homecoming. Campbell's lengthy solo shows him performing alone on an imposing rock formation, wielding 72987537 like a force of nature. It's an effective way of highlighting the guitarist's solo spot.

'The Revolution Starts Tonight' begins with some clean finger picking from Campbell. He then uses his wah-wah pedal to supply some heavy riffs. The song is melodramatic, simmering with tension and angst. 'Something Inside' follows, opening with a slow bluesy groove. It then shifts to melodic rock during the choruses, complete with arpeggiated chords. Carefully constructed and artful fills lead to a tasty solo based in the blues scale. Campbell's playing and Lamothe's gritty vocals contribute to the sombre mood.

'Golden Glow' is a powerful ballad (but not a power ballad) that begins with melodic arpeggiated A5 and B chords. These patterns form the backbone of the song. The chorus is an uplifting celebration of the 'Golden State,' and Campbell adjusts the patterns later in the song to make them sound less elegiac and more uplifting. His slow solo is imbued with emotion. 'You're Too Rock And Roll' is carried along by a busy, brooding guitar riff and some colourful fills. However, it's Lamothe's vocals and a catchy chorus that lift it above average, until a Campbell solo takes it to an even higher level.

'The Heart Is A Mindless Bird' begins tunefully with clean arpeggiated chords which are repeated throughout the song. This classy track is a showcase for Campbell's slow blues solos and Lamothe's great vocal tone. Both men sound like they're channelling blues emotional currents. When Lamothe sings the line 'we become alive,' it is the trigger for some hard riffing, a heavy guitar solo, and some fast picking. The track ends abruptly with a fast power slide.

'Searching For A Signal' is a pop-punk track driven along by heavy riffs from Campbell, and interrupted only by an oddly-placed interval of tuneful feedback and vocals. Returning to the main body of the song, another devasting Campbell solo follows, during which he makes liberal use of pick squeals. 'Welcome To The New Disaster' is a schizophrenic track that alternates between soulful guitar patterns and soft melodious intervals. Campbell plays a brief passion-filled solo and tuneful fills.

'Ten Thousand Reasons' begins with some fussy picking patterns from Campbell before developing into a moody soft rocker with some tranquil intervals. A change in tone is the signal for a fast guitar solo that is possibly symbolic of the broken relationship mentioned in the lyrics. This could be considered a prog rock track, with tempo, tone and mood changes aplenty. 'Catalina' is the track that comes closest to a 1970s American rock vibe with some epic riffing, before Campbell transforms the mood with open string arpeggios. Another skilful solo introduces the melodic playout.

The album's final track is 'I Don't Know Anything,' a title which thankfully avoids using a double negative. It begins with some delicate picking from Campbell and masterful vocals from Lamothe. A singalong chorus follows, and then a short lead break from Campbell. Another verse-chorus leads into a second melodic guitar solo, followed by a repeat of the delicate picking of the intro. The track then features repetition of the chorus and a slow playout from Campbell. Some acoustic chords from Lamothe end both the track and the album.

*California* must have seemed like unfinished business for Campbell. Over the years, the debut *Riverdogs* album developed a cult following and, unlike *World Gone Mad, California* captured some of the spark of the debut. Campbell features a lot on the album, but this time he gave himself permission to express what he wanted to say through his guitar. He thought he overplayed on the debut album but made no such critique this time around. And nor should he because this is a masterclass in melody, tone, and passion from a guitarist rejuvenated by his love of playing angry guitar and a cancer diagnosis that left him determined to give the music of Riverdogs a second chance to shine.

It's been seven years since the *California* album and it seems unlikely that there will be a follow up. For Campbell, that particular itch seems well and truly scratched, and he devotes much of his time these days to creating new music for Last In Line.

Of course, he remains a member of Def Leppard and continues to make music with the band. Their latest release is the 2023 album *Drastic Symphonies*, which features 16 of the band's older songs remixed and rearranged for orchestral accompaniment. While only one song co-written by Campbell appears on the album, everyone was involved in the decision-making process. The fact that the album was recorded at Abbey Road Studios with the Royal Philharmonic Orchestra not only demonstrates the high-class nature of the project but is also evidence that Def Leppard remains ambitious and hungry in their sixth decade of making music. Despite rumours to the contrary, Campbell still enjoys playing guitar in Def Leppard although he maintains that he finds the vocals more challenging than the guitar parts. It's telling that when Phil Collen was asked what Campbell adds to Def Leppard, Collen pointed to Campbell's vocals rather than his guitar playing. 'The vocal blends are better,' he said. 'Before we were very much a studio band, but now we've actually got into this groove with a great vocal blend.'[660]

Nevertheless, Campbell still gets a thrill from playing guitar onstage and with a group of musicians he calls friends. In 2017 he told the Belfast *News Letter*: 'Playing with Leppard is a lot of fun and I still love it... None of us take ourselves too seriously but we take the music very seriously... I've played Def Leppard's biggest hits literally thousands of times since joining them over 25 years ago and it never gets old. The extra band member is the audience and when they are appreciative the whole thing is just electric. Anytime we play Pour Some Sugar On Me in front of an audience it's a unique experience — it's never the same as it was before. The audience makes the show. Even after all these years playing with Leppard is still a hoot.'[661]

Sadly, his health issues remain: Campbell missed Def Leppard's first concert of 2025 at Foro Mazda in León, Mexico on January 18. From the stage, Joe Elliott explained that John Zocco, Phil Collen's guitar technician, would be standing in for Campbell, who was currently recovering from cancer treatment. Soon after, Campbell explained more fully on social media, that he was recovering from a bone marrow transplant. The immunotherapy treatment he had been taking since 2015, and which had helped him with day-to-day management of Hodgkin lymphoma, had become less effective and, after taking medical advice, he had recently undergone a bone marrow transplant. Happily, Campbell announced that the treatment was successful and that he was currently in a 100-day primary recovery period.

Although the immediate future is, then, a little uncertain, Campbell has the full support of his band mates, and no doubt will rejoin the band as soon as his health allows. After all, with over 40 years in the music business behind him, he is still making music, still playing live, continues to give interviews, tell stories, and crack jokes. He still recites the serial number of his black Gibson Les Paul at any opportunity. And now that he has found a home in Def Leppard and Last In Line, his days of being an Irish rover, moving from one unsatisfying band to another, now seem well and truly at an end.

# Discography & Videography

## Sweet Savage (1979-1983)

'Take No Prisoners' c/w 'Killing Time' (Park Records, 1981)
7-inch vinyl single.

*Demo 81*
(featured *The Friday Rock Show* versions of 'Queen's Vengeance', 'Eye Of The Storm', 'Killing Time', and 'Into the Night').

Self-published cassette.

## Dio (1983-1986)

*Holy Diver* (1983)
*The Last In Line* (1984)
*Sacred Heart* (1985)
*Intermission* (live album, 1986)
*The Dio EP*
('Shame On The Night,' 'Egypt (The Chains Are On),' 'Hungry For Heaven' and 'Hide In The Rainbow')
*Dio Live In Concert* (VHS video cassette, 1983)
*A Special From The Spectrum* (VHS video cassette, 1984)
*At Donington UK: Live 1983 & 1987* (2010)

## Whitesnake (1986-87)

Campbell performed in the promotional videos for the *Whitesnake 1987* album, namely 'Still of the Night,' 'Here I Go Again '87,' 'Is This Love,' and 'Give Me All Your Love.'
Campbell recorded new studio guitar work for the single release 'Give Me All Your Love ('88 Mix)'
*Whitesnake 1987 30th Anniversary Super Deluxe Edition* (2017). The bonus CD entitled *Snakeskin Boots* features eleven previously unreleased tracks recorded during the band's 1987-88 tour.

## Riverdogs

*Riverdogs* (1990)
*World Gone Mad* (2011)
*California* (2017)

## Shadow King

*Shadow King* (1991)

## Def Leppard (1992-present)

Seven studio albums from 1995 to 2022, as well as numerous live releases, anthologies, greatest hits packages, and video appearances.

## Studio Albums

*Slang* (1996)
*Euphoria* (1999)
*X* (2002)
*Yeah*! (2006)
*Songs from The Sparkle Lounge* (2008)
*Def Leppard* (2015)
*Diamond Star Halos* (2022)

## Live Albums

*Mirror Ball – Live & More* (2011)
*Viva! Hysteria* (2013)
*And There Will Be a Next Time... Live from Detroit* (2017)
*London To Vegas* (2020)
*One Night Only: Live at the Leadmill* (2020)

## Clock

*Through Time* (2004)

## Solo album

*Two Sides Of If (2005)*

## Thin Lizzy

*Thin Lizzy – Live In London 2011 - 22.01.2011 Hammersmith Apollo*
(Label: Concert Live)
*Thin Lizzy – Live In London 2011 - 23.01.2011 Indigo2*
(Label: Concert Live)

## Notable Collaborations & Contributions

1986: Hear 'N Aid, 'Stars'
7 & 12-inch vinyl, cassette.

*Hear 'n Aid: The Sessions* video documentary.

1988: Appeared on Vixen's self-title debut album, performing on the track 'Desperate.'

1989: Appeared on Lou Gramm's solo album *Long Hard Look*, performing on the tracks 'Broken Dreams,' 'Day One.' and 'Hangin' On My Hip.'

1989: Appeared on Jack Bruce's album *A Question of Time*, performing on the track 'Obsession.'

1989: Appeared on the *Shocker* movie soundtrack, performing as The Dudes of Wrath on the tracks 'Shocker' and 'Shockdance.'

1991: Appeared on the Steve Plunkett album *My Attitude*, performing on the track 'Louie, Louie.'

1996: Performed 'Led Boots' for the Jeff Beck tribute album *Jeffology - A Guitar Chronicle*.

1997: Appeared on the album *Carmine Appice's Guitar Zeus II*, performing the track 'Doin' Fine.'

2007: Appeared on the compilation album *Butchering The Beatles: A Headbashing Tribute*, performing on the tracks 'Revolution' and 'I Saw Her Standing There.'

2013: Appeared on the Manny Charlton album *Hellacious*, performing on the tracks 'Stone Crazy and 'Bringing Me Down.'

2014: Appeared on the Steel Panther album *All You Can Eat*, performing on the track 'Gangbang At The Old Folks Home.'

# Notes

## Introduction

1 'Big family occasion for Def Leppard guitarist receiving top music prize,' *News Letter* (Belfast), November 7, 2017.

2,,Chapter 1 Born To Play Loud: Sweet Savage  Sean Kelly, *Don't Call It Hair Metal: Art in the Excess of '80s Rock* (ECW Press, 2023).

## Chapter 1

3 Emma Heatherington, 'Me And My Rock Star Cousin,' *Belfast Telegraph*, December 9, 2015, pp. 25-26.

4 Nick Bowcott, 'Gary Moore, the British Ace,'*Circus* 315, May 31, 1986, p. 71.

5 'Gary Moore Remembers Rory Gallagher,' *Hot Press* 1995. https://www.hotpress.com/music/gary-moore-remembers-rory-gallagher-14356584?fbclid=IwAR2pdanaNpPpMeZbRR_hAGYjqgj_VWozTQvfY8Of7HMCem48HDpvxXZdRpg

6 Sarah Henderson, 'Electric Dreams: Guitar Hero Poised For Local Honour,' *Sunday Life* (Northern Ireland), November 5, 2017, pp. 24-25.

7 'Soundtrack of my Life: Vivian Campbell,' *Guitar & Bass*, Vol. 27, No. 6, March 2016, p. 22.

8 'Soundtrack of my Life: Vivian Campbell,' *Guitar & Bass*, Vol. 27, No. 6, March 2016, p. 22.

9 Other albums Campbell pointed to as influential were Lynyrd Skynyrd's debut, *(Pronounced 'Lĕh-'nérd 'Skin-'nérd)* (1973), Thin Lizzy's *Live And Dangerous* (1978), Irish Celtic rock band Horslips' *The Táin* (1973), Deep Purple's *Come Taste The Band* (1975), and UFO's *Light's Out* (1977).

10 Sarah Henderson, 'Electric Dreams: Guitar Hero Poised For Local Honour,' *Sunday Life* (Northern Ireland), November 5, 2017, pp. 24-25.

11 *Irish News*, September 29, 2017, Section A3F4.

12 Gerry Kelly, BBC Radio Ulster, November 11, 2017. https://learningonscreen.ac.uk/ondemand/index.php/prog/100E2AC1?bcast=125509118

13 Ralph McLean, 'I Refuse To Let Cancer Beat Me,' *Sunday Life*, November 25, 2018.

14 Gerry Kelly, BBC Radio Ulster, November 11, 2017. https://learningonscreen.ac.uk/ondemand/index.php/prog/100E2AC1?bcast=125509118

15 Steve Hammonds, 'Holy Savage,' *Metal Forces* 2, Winter 83-84, p. 28.

16 Geoff Barton, 'If You Want Blood (and Flashbombs and Dry Ice and Confetti) You've Got It: The New Wave of British Heavy Metal,' *Sounds*, May 19, 1979.

17 Richard Bienstock, 'Vivian Campbell: My Career in Five Songs,' *Guitar Player*, September 29, 2021. Available online at: https://www.guitarplayer.com/players/vivian-campbell-my-career-in-five-songs

18 Sean Kelly, *Dont Call It Hair Metal: Art in the Excess of '80s Rock* (ECW Press, 2023).

19 Michael Hann, *Denim and Leather: the Rise and Fall of the New Wave of British Heavy Metal* (London: Little, Brown Book Group, 2022), Foreword.

20 *Irish News*, September 29, 2017, Section A3F4.

21 Richard Bienstock, 'Vivian Campbell: My Career in Five Songs,' *Guitar Player*, September 29, 2021. https://www.guitarplayer.com/players/vivian-campbell-my-career-in-five-songs

22 Robert Cavuoto, 'Vivian Campbell – Heavy Crown is the Noise Last in Line Makes!,' My Global Mind webzine, February 14, 2016. https://myglobalmind.com/2016/02/14/interview-with-vivian-campbell-guitars-last-in-line-def-leppard-former-dio/

23 Nick Bowcott, 'Vivian Campbell on his own,'*Circus* 317, July 31, 1986, p. 74.

24 Carlos Cavazo, 'Guitar Clinic: Vivian Campbell,' *Circus* 300, Feb 28, 1985, p. 122.

25 *Record Mirror*, Dec 13, 1980, p. 3

26 'ZZ Top : Cheap Sunglasses with Vivian Campbell of Def Leppard, Dio, and Last In Line,' Couch Riffs Podcast, Youtube channel, May 8, 2019. https://www.youtube.com/watch?v=XP6_GuUiE88

27 Peter Nielsen, Thin Lizzy Guide. https://www.thinlizzyguide.com/tours/year/1981.htm

28 David Ling, 'Leps Get Their Man,' *RAW* 96, April 29-May 12, 1992, pp. 10-11.

29 'Def Leppard Vivian Campbell/Phil Lynott March 2023. Def Leppard Tour History Youtube channel, April 1, 2023. https://youtu.be/DxZmxK1XZrk

30  Review of 'Straight Through The Heart' by Sweet Savage. *Kerrang!* 61, February 9-22, 1984, p. 40.

31  Steve Hammonds, 'Holy Savage,' *Metal Forces* 2, Winter 83-84, p. 28.

32  Review of 'Straight Through The Heart' by Sweet Savage. *Kerrang!* 61, February 9-22, 1984, p. 40.

33  Steve Hammonds, 'Holy Savage,' *Metal Forces* 2, Winter 83-84, p. 28.

34  Mick Wall, *Enter Night: Metallica The Biography* (London: Orion, 2012), pp. 59-60.

35  Ivan Little, 'Reunion was bittersweet; homecoming for top guitarist,' *Sunday Life,* March 20, 2011, p. 26.

36  Vivian Campbell interview with Maurice Jay on U105 radio, Belfast, November 10, 2017. https://www.youtube.com/watch?v=HElEb9Uviyw

37  Gerry Kelly, BBC Radio Ulster, November 11, 2017. https://learningonscreen.ac.uk/ondemand/index.php/prog/100E2AC1?bcast=125509118

38  Michael Smolen, 'Dio's Back On Top,' *Circus* 298, Dec 31, 1984, pp. 96-99.

## Chapter 2 Rainbows and Dragons: The Dio Years

39  Dante Bonutto, '(Un) Holy Diver,' *Kerrang* 44, June 17-30, 1983, pp. 18-20.

40  Michael Smolen, 'Dio's Back On Top,' *Circus* 298, Dec 31, 1984, pp. 96-99.

41  Vivian Campbell interview with Maurice Jay on U105 radio, Belfast, November 10, 2017. https://www.youtube.com/watch?v=HElEb9Uviyw

42  Mick Wall, 'Little Dio Man,' *Classic Rock* 185, July 2013, pp. 50-53, 122.

43  Vivian Campbell interview with Mark Jeeves of My Planet Rock. Backstage Pass Rock News Youtube channel, June 22, 2023. https://www.youtube.com/watch?v=jMk0GXBOZIk

44  Michael Smolen, 'Dio's Back On Top,' *Circus* 298, Dec 31, 1984, pp. 96-99.

45  Dante Bonutto, '(Un) Holy Diver,' *Kerrang!* 44, June 17-30, 1983, pp. 18-20.

46  Vivian Campbell talking about his time in Dio & Whitesnake on Igor's Deep Purple Universe Youtube channel, December 07, 2019.

https://www.youtube.com/watch?v=jNoth8OlLt4&t=15s

47  Malcolm Dome, 'Souper Trouper,' *Kerrang!* 46, July 14-27, 1983, pp. 40-41.

48  Vivian Campbell interview with Maurice Jay on U105 radio, Belfast, November 10, 2017. https://www.youtube.com/watch?v=HElEb9Uviyw

49  Vivian Campbell talking about his time in Dio & Whitesnake on Igor's Deep Purple Universe Youtube channel, December 07, 2019.

https://www.youtube.com/watch?v=jNoth8OlLt4&t=15s

50  Malcolm Dome, 'Souper Trouper,' *Kerrang* 46, July 14-27, 1983, pp. 40-41.

51  Vivian Campbell interview with Maurice Jay on U105 radio, Belfast, November 10, 2017. https://www.youtube.com/watch?v=HElEb9Uviyw

53  Dave Ling, 'The Death of a Rogue,' *Classic Rock* 221, April 2016, pp. 82-85.

54  Paul Elliott, 'High 'N' Dry,' *Kerrang!* 465, 1993, pp. 38-42.

55  Dave Ling, 'The Death of a Rogue,' *Classic Rock* 221, April 2016, pp. 82-85.

56  Mick Wall, 'Little Dio Man,' *Classic Rock* 185, July 2013, pp. 50-53, 122.

57  Robert Cavuoto, 'Vivian Campbell – Heavy Crown is the Noise Last in Line Makes!,' My Global Mind webzine, February 14, 2016. https://myglobalmind.com/2016/02/14/interview-with-vivian-campbell-guitars-last-in-line-def-leppard-former-dio/

58  Malcolm Dome, 'Souper Trouper,' *Kerrang!* 46, July 14-27, 1983, pp. 40-41.

59  Mick Wall, 'Dio,' *Classic Rock*, March 3, 2020.

60  Mick Wall, 'Little Dio Man,' *Classic Rock* 185, July 2013, pp. 50-53, 122.

62  Dave Dickson, Review of *Holy Diver, Kerrang!* 44, June 17-30, 1983, p. 46.

63  Steve Hammonds, 'Holy Savage,' *Metal Forces* 2, Winter 83-84, p. 28.

64  Charles C. DuBois, Rev. of *Holy Diver. Reading Eagle* (Pennsylvania), June 19, 1983, p. 20.

65  Richard Bienstock, 'Vivian Campbell: My Career in Five Songs,' *Guitar Player*, September 29, 2021. https://www.guitarplayer.com/players/vivian-campbell-my-career-in-five-songs

66  Mick Wall, 'Dio: the acrimonious story behind Holy Diver,' *Classic Rock*, July 10, 2016. https://www.louder-sound.com/features/dio-story-of-holy-diver

67 Malcolm Dome, 'Souper Trouper,' *Kerrang!* 46, July 14-27, 1983, pp. 40-41.

68 Dave Ling, 'The Death of a Rogue,' *Classic Rock* 221, April 2016, pp. 82-85.

69 Bob Ruggiero, 'Ronnie James Dio: Soaring on the Wings of a Demon,' *Houston Press*, August 14, 2003.

70 *Creem*, Review of *Holy Diver*. January 1984, p. 55.

71 Dennis Hunt, 'Dio In A Devilish Mood,' *Los Angeles Times*, November 11, 1984, p. W80.

72 Geoff Barton, 'Dutch Courage,' *Kerrang!* 71, June 28-July 11, 1984, pp. 18-21, 37.

73 Gary Graff, 'Dio plays heavy metal rock 'n' roll, but he's an advocate of the values of being a solid citizen,' *Evening Independent* (St. Petersburg), September 2, 1985, p. 5B.

74 Dave Dickson, Review of *Holy Diver*. *Kerrang!* 44, June 17-30, 1983, p. 46.

75 Dave Dickson, Review of *Holy Diver*. *Kerrang!* 44, June 17-30, 1983, p. 46.

76 Malcolm Dome, 'Souper Trouper,' *Kerrang!* 46, July 14-27, 1983, pp. 40-41.

77 David Ling, Review of *Holy Diver*. *Number One*, June 4, 1983, p.35.

78 Gary Karr, 'Dio Crash Bangs,' *Los Angeles Times*, Aug 28, 1983, p. S78.

79 Charles C. DuBois, Review of *Holy Diver*. *Reading Eagle* (Pennsylvania), June 19, 1983, p. 20.

80 Michael Lawson, 'The devil in metal designed as eye-grabber,' *The Leader-Post* (Regina, Saskatchewan) June 15, 1983, p. C13.

81 *Creem*, Rev. of *Holy Diver*. January 1984, p. 55. This is surely the Dio equivalent of Spinal Tap's infamous two-word *Shark Sandwich* review, 'Shit Sandwich.'

82 Malcolm Dome, 'Souper Trouper,' *Kerrang!* 46, July 14-27, 1983, pp. 40-41.

84 Malcolm Dome, 'Souper Trouper,' *Kerrang!* 46, July 14-27, 1983, pp. 40-41.

85 Malcolm Dome, *Kerrang!* 48, August 11-24, 1983, p. 8.

86 Steve Hammonds, 'Holy Savage,' *Metal Forces* 2, Winter 83-84, p. 28.

87 *Kerrang!* 54, November 3-16, 1983, p. 14.

88 Tony Jasper, Review of 'Rainbow in the Dark.' *Music Week*, October 29, 1983, p. 28.

89 'Shoot Us!,' *Classic Rock*, March 3, 2020.

90 Malcolm Dome, *Kerrang* 48 August 11-24, 1983, p. 8.

91 Dave Ling, 'The Death of a Rogue,' *Classic Rock* 221, April 2016, pp. 82-85.

92 Mick Wall, 'Dio: the acrimonious story behind Holy Diver,' *Classic Rock*, July 10, 2016. https://www.louder-sound.com/features/dio-story-of-holy-diver

93 Geoff Barton, 'Dutch Courage,' *Kerrang!* 71, June 28-July 11, 1984, pp. 18-21, 37.

94 Steve Hammonds, 'Holy Savage,' *Metal Forces* 2, Winter 83-84, p. 28.

95 Steve Hammonds, 'Holy Savage,' *Metal Forces* 2, Winter 83-84, p. 28.

96 Howard Johnson, 'Monsters of Rock,' *Kerrang!* 48 August 11-24, 1983, p. 2.

97 Steve Hammonds, 'Holy Savage,' *Metal Forces* 2, Winter 83-84, p. 28.

98 Dave Dickson & Howard Johnson, 'Monsters of Rock Festival, Castle Donington,' *Kerrang!* 50, September 8-21, 1983, p. 32.

99 Wayne Parry (Associated Press), Audio Review of Dio *At Donington UK: Live 1983 & 1987*. *Telegraph Herald* (Dubuque, Iowa) November 14, 2012, p. E2.

100 Paul Elliott, 'Hammer of the Gob,' *Sounds*, August 3, 1985, pp. 46-47.

101 See 'Dio: Holy Diver Tour Dates.' http://www.dio.net/tour/holy_diver.html

102 Dot Willig, Review of Dio at the Hammersmith Odeon. *Electronics & Music Maker*, December 1983, p. 52.

103 Review of *Dio Live in Concert*. *Music Week* July 14, 1984, p. 26.

104 Paul Roland, Review of *Dio: Live in Concert*. *Kerrang!* 71, June 28-July 11, 1984, p. 21.

105 *Kerrang!* 59, January 12-25, 1984, pp. 22-23.

106 Malcolm Dome, 'Vivian Campbell,' *Kerrang!* 65, April 05-18, 1984, p. 32.

107 *Kerrang!* 61, February 9-22, 1984, p.3.

108 Pierre Perrone, 'Ronnie James Dio; Singer who worked with Ritchie Blackmore in Rainbow and replaced Ozzie Osbourne in Black Sabbath,' *Independent Extra*, May 18, 2010.

109 Roy Trakin, 'Oy Solo Dio,' *Creem*, December 1984, pp. 55.

110 Mark Putterford, Review of *The Last in Line*. *Kerrang!* 72, July 12-25, 1984, p. 9.

111 Geoff Barton, 'Dutch Courage,' *Kerrang!* 71, June 28-July 11, 1984, pp. 18-21, 37.

112 Geoff Barton, 'Dutch Courage,' *Kerrang!* 71, June 28-July 11, 1984, pp. 18-21, 37.

113 Deborah Frost, 'Heavy Metal Rears Its Ugly Head Again,' *Rolling Stone*, 27 September 1984; and Mark Putterford, Review of *The Last in Line. Kerrang!* 72, July 12-25, 1984, p. 9.

114 Michael Lawson, Review of *The Last in Line. Star-Phoenix* (Saskatoon), August 9, 1984, P. C1.

115 Mark Putterford, Review of *The Last in Line. Kerrang!* 72, July 12-25, 1984, p. 9.

116 Roy Trakin, 'Oy Solo Dio,' *Creem*, December 1984, pp. 55; Mark Putterford, Review of *The Last in Line. Kerrang!* 72, July 12-25, 1984, p. 9.

117 Mark Putterford, Review of *The Last in Line. Kerrang!* 72, July 12-25, 1984, p. 9.

118 Deborah Frost, 'Heavy Metal Rears Its Ugly Head Again,' *Rolling Stone*, 27 September 1984.

119 Mark Putterford, Review of *The Last in Line. Kerrang!* 72, July 12-25, 1984, p. 9.

120 Rick Evans, 'Dio: The Evil Eye,' *Hit Parader* 245, February 1985, pp. 16-17; Andy Secher, 'Swords and Sorcery,' *Hit Parader* 254, November 1985, pp. 4-6.

121 Tommy Vance, FM Broadcast: https://www.youtube.com/watch?v=VfyEeIjWQPA

122 Roy Trakin, 'Oy Solo Dio,' *Creem*, December 1984, pp. 55; Deborah Frost, 'Heavy Metal Rears Its Ugly Head Again,' *Rolling Stone*, 27 September 1984.

123 Edward W. Said, *Orientalism* (USA: Pantheon, 1978).

124 The Visual Art of Heavy Metal. Barry Jackson, *The last in Line* (1984). https://thevisualartofmetal.tumblr.com/post/156248267051/artwork-by-barry-jackson-dio-the-last-in-line

125 Michael Lawson, Review of *The Last in Line. Star-Phoenix* (Saskatoon), August 9, 1984, P. C1.

126 Geoff Barton, 'Dutch Courage,' *Kerrang!* 71, June 28-July 11, 1984, pp. 18-21, 37.

127 Robert Cavuoto, 'Vivian Campbell – Heavy Crown is the Noise Last in Line Makes!,' My Global Mind webzine, February 14, 2016. https://myglobalmind.com/2016/02/14/interview-with-vivian-campbell-guitars-last-in-line-def-leppard-former-dio/

128 Michael Smolen, 'Dio is last in line,' *Circus* 296, October 31, 1984, p. 34.

129 Michael Smolen, 'Dio's Back on Top,' *Circus* 298, December 31, 1984, pp. 96-99.

130 Mark Putterford, Review of *The Last in Line. Kerrang!* 72, July 12-25, 1984, p. 9.

131 Deborah Frost, 'Heavy Metal Rears Its Ugly Head Again,' *Rolling Stone*, 27 September 1984.

132 Roy Trakin, 'Oy Solo Dio,' *Creem*, December 1984, pp. 55.

133 Howard Johnson, Review of 'The Last in Line.' *Kerrang!* 73, 1984, p. 39.

134 Ethlie Ann Vare, 'Sacred Heart Tour Features Elaborate Special Effects,' *Billboard* Vol. 97, No. 34, August 24, 1985, pp. 40 & 42.

135 Mick Wall, Review of 'We Rock.' *Kerrang!* 75, August 23- September 5, 1984, p. 22.

136 Steve Gett, 'Dio sports a rainbow's colors at Nassau Coliseum,' *Circus* 297, November 30, 1984, pp. 26-28.

137 Geoff Barton, 'Dutch Courage,' *Kerrang!* 71, June 28-July 11, 1984, pp. 18-21, 37.

138 Paul Gallotta, 'A new Dio, but it's the same old fireworks,' *Circus* 319, September 30, 1986, pp. 38-40.

139 The full set was 'Stand Up and Shout,' 'Straight Through the Heart,' 'One Night in the City,' 'We Rock,' 'Holy Diver,' 'Stargazer,' 'Heaven and Hell ,' 'Rainbow in the Dark,' 'Man on the Silver Mountain,' and the encore 'Don't Talk to Strangers.'

140 Geoff Barton, 'Dutch Courage,' *Kerrang!* 71, June 28-July 11, 1984, pp. 18-21, 37.

141 Steve Gett, 'Dio sports a rainbow's colors at Nassau Coliseum,' *Circus* 297, November 30, 1984, pp. 26-28.

142 M.D. Review of *A Special at the Spectrum. Creem*, October 1986, p. 65.

143 Steve Gett, 'Dio sports a rainbow's colors at Nassau Coliseum,' *Circus* 297, November 30, 1984, pp. 26-28.

144 Malcolm Dome, 'Vivian Campbell,' *Kerrang!* 65, April 5-18, 1984, p. 32.

146 Dave Fanning, 'Dio at the SFX,' *Irish Times*, September 10, 1984, p. 10.

147 Paul Suter, *Kerrang!* 75, August 23-September 5, 1984, p. 48.

148 Carlo Wolff, 'Ronnie Dio Delivers Heavy Metal Heaven,' *Schenectady Gazette*, November 5, 1984, p. 52.

149 Geoff Barton, 'Dutch Courage,' *Kerrang!* 71, June 28-July 11, 1984, pp. 18-21, 37.

150 Robert Cavuoto, 'Vivian Campbell – Heavy Crown is the Noise Last in Line Makes!,' My Global Mind webzine, February 14, 2016. https://myglobalmind.com/2016/02/14/interview-with-vivian-campbell-guitars-last-in-line-def-leppard-former-dio/

151 Bruce Taylor, 'Dio, Whitesnake pour on the power, punishment,' *Spokesman-Review* (Spokane, Washington), July 25, 1984, p. 13.

152 February 14, 2016. https://myglobalmind.com/2016/02/14/interview-with-vivian-campbell-guitars-last-in-line-def-leppard-former-dio/ To complicate matters, Dio told Dante Bunotto in a 1985 interview that he wasn't happy with 'Hungry For Heaven' appearing on the *Sacred Heart* album (1985) because it was too commercial. See Dante Bonutto, 'Little Dreamer,' Part 1, *Kerrang!* 100, Aug 8-21, 1985, pp. 12-14 & 16.

153 'Craig Goldy Says Vivian Campbell Must Have Done Something Pretty Insulting To Get Himself Fired From Dio,' Blabbermouth.Net, May 2, 2022. https://blabbermouth.net/news/craig-goldy-says-vivian-campbell-must-have-done-something-pretty-insulting-to-get-himself-fired-from-dio

154 Steffan Chirazi, 'Dio: No Sleep Till Donington!,' *Kerrang!* 152, August 6-19, 1987, pp. 30-32.

155 Mark Putterford, 'Back on the War Path,' *RAW* No. 10, January 11-24, 1989, pp. 34-6.

156 Valerie Potter, 'Soldier of Fortune,' *Metal Hammer* Vol. 2, No. 2, February 6, 1989, pp. 10-13.

157 Michael Lawson, 'Rush Recording A Chancy Project,' *Leader-Post* (Regina, Saskatchewn), September 22, 1982, p. C15.

158 *Billboard* Vol. 95, No. 3, January 22, 1983, p. C15.

159 Paul Elliott, 'Hammer of the Gob,' *Sounds*, August 3, 1985, pp. 46-47.

160 Robert Cavuoto, 'Vivian Campbell – Heavy Crown is the Noise Last in Line Makes!,' My Global Mind webzine, February 14, 2016. https://myglobalmind.com/2016/02/14/interview-with-vivian-campbell-guitars-last-in-line-def-leppard-former-dio/

161 Dante Bonutto, 'Little Dreamer,' Part 1, *Kerrang!* 100, Aug 8-21, 1985, pp. 12-14 & 16.

162 Andy Secher, 'Dio: the king of rock and roll,' *Hit Parader Annual*, Fall 1986, pp. 34-36.

163 Dante Bonutto, 'Little Dreamer,' Part 1, *Kerrang!* 100, Aug 8-21, 1985, pp. 12-14 & 16.

164 Paul Elliott, 'Hammer of the Gob,' *Sounds*, August 3, 1985, pp. 46-47.

165 The Art of Robert Florczak. http://robertflorczak.com/about-artist.html

166 Robert Florczak, *Sacred Heart*: http://robertflorczak.com/art/sacred-heart.html

167 Ralph Kisiel, Review of *Sacred Heart. Toledo Blade*, September 14, 1985, p. G3.

168 Dante Bonutto, 'Little Dreamer,' Part 1, *Kerrang!* 100, Aug 8-21, 1985, pp. 12-14 & 16.

169 Andy Secher, 'Dio: the king of rock and roll,' *Hit Parader Annual*, Fall 1986, pp. 34-36.

170 Andy Secher, 'Swords and Sorcery' *Hit Parader* 254, November 1985, pp. 4-6.

171 Dante Bonutto, 'Little Dreamer,' Part 1, *Kerrang!* 100, Aug 8-21, 1985, pp. 12-14 & 16.

172 *Kerrang!* 89, March 7-20, 1985, p. 3; Dante Bonutto, 'Little Dreamer,' Part 1, *Kerrang!* 100, Aug 8-21, 1985, pp. 12-14 & 16.

173 Bruce Taylor, 'Heavy metal with a difference,' *Spokesman-Review*, July 20, 1984, p. 8.

174 Dante Bonutto, 'Little Dreamer,' Part 1, *Kerrang!* 100, Aug 8-21, 1985, pp. 12-14 & 16.

175 Dante Bonutto, 'Little Dreamer,' Part 1, *Kerrang!* 100, Aug 8-21, 1985, pp. 12-14 & 16.

176 Gary Graff, 'Dio plays heavy metal rock 'n' roll, but he's an advocate of the values of being a solid citizen,' *Evening Independent* (St. Petersburg), September 2, 1985, p. 5B.

177 'Rock Superstars Speak Out!,' *Circus*, October 31, 1987, p. 76.

178 Steffan Chirazi, 'Dio: No Sleep Till Donington!,' *Kerrang!* 152, August 6-19, 1987, pp. 30-32.

179 Paul Gallotta, 'Taking Video to the Stage,' *Circus* 308, October 31, 1985, pp. 32 & 34.

180 Review of *Sacred Heart. RPM* Vol. 43, No. 1, September 14, 1985, p. 10.

181 Andy Secher, 'Swords and Sorcery,' *Hit Parader* 254, November, 1985, pp. 4-6.

182 Review of *Sacred Heart. Billboard* Vol. 97, No. 34, August 24, 1985, p. 62.

183 Gary Graff, 'Dio plays heavy metal rock 'n' roll, but he's an advocate of the values of being a solid citizen,' *Evening Independent* (St. Petersburg), September 2, 1985, p. 5B.

184 Ralph Kisiel, Review of *Sacred Heart. Toledo Blade*, September 14, 1985, p. G3.

185 Dave Dickson, Review of *Sacred Heart. Kerrang!* 101, Aug 22-Sept 4, 1985, p. 10.

186 Dante Bonutto, 'Little Dreamer,' Part 1, *Kerrang!* 100, Aug 8-21, 1985, pp. 12-14 & 16.

187 Paul Elliott, 'Hammer of the Gob,' *Sounds*, August 3, 1985 p. 46-47.

188 Ethlie Ann Vare, 'Sacred Heart Tour Features Elaborate Special Effects,' *Billboard* Vol. 97, No. 34, August 24, 1985, pp. 40 & 42.

189 Ethlie Ann Vare, 'Sacred Heart Tour Features Elaborate Special Effects,' *Billboard* Vol. 97, No. 34, August 24, 1985, pp. 40 & 42.

190 Paul Gallotta, 'Vivian Campbell won't be upstaged,' *Circus* 311, January 31, 1986, p. 69. *Circus* 306, August 31, 1985, pp. 102-103.

191 ert,' *Hit Parader* 258, March 1986, pp. 9-10.

192 *Circus* 306, August 31, 1985, pp. 102-103.

194 Dan Daley, 'Dio and the Sacred Heart tour: an unforgettable knight,' *Circus* 312, February 28, 1986, pp. 19-20.

195 Martin Morrow, 'Dio delivers savage shine,' *Calgary Herald*, January 5, 1986, p. E2.

196 Paul Elliott, 'Hammer of the Gob,' *Sounds*, August 3, 1985, pp. 46-47.

197 Andy Secher, 'Dio: the king of rock and roll,' *Hit Parader Annual*, Fall 1986, pp. 34-36.

198 Dan Daley, 'Dio and the Sacred Heart tour: an unforgettable knight,' *Circus* 312, February 28, 1986, pp. 19-20.

199 Pete Bishop, 'Spectacular stage show underscores Dio's melodic heavy metal,' *Pittsburgh Press*, September 23, 1985, p. C3.

200 Ralph Kisiel, 'Special effects included in concert by Ronnie Dio,' *Toledo Blade*, October 24, 1985, p. 2; Ethlie Ann Vark, *Billboard* Vol. 97, Issue 51, December 21, 1985, p. 47.

201 Clay Hutto, 'Dio conjures cacophonous castle for crowd,' *Spokesman-Review* (Spokane), December 31, 1985, p. B5.

202 Andy Secher, 'Dio: Caught in the Act,' *Hit Parader* 258, March 1986, p. 48.

203 Christina O'Neill, 'Vivian Campbell: Dio needed proper manager, not wife Wendy,' Classic Rock, November 11, 2016. https://www.loudersound.com/news/vivian-campbell-dio-needed-proper-manager-not-wife-wendy

204 Dave Dickson, 'Little Big Man,' *Kerrang!* 119, May 1-14, 1986, pp. 34, 36 & 39.

205 'Hear 'N Aid Launched, Campbell out of Dio,' *Kerrang!* 117, April 3-16, 1986, p. 4; Dante Bonutto, 'Campbell in the Soup?,' *Kerrang!* 118, April 17-30, 1986, pp. 8-9.

207 Sal Treppedi, 'Metal News,' *The Hard Report*, August 21, 1987, p. 25.

208 Dante Bonutto, 'Campbell in the Soup?,' *Kerrang!* 118, April 17-30, 1986, pp. 8-9.

209 Steve Hammonds, 'Holy Savage,' *Metal Forces* 2, Winter 83-84, p. 28.

210 'Wendy Dio Says Vivian Campbell Wanted To Take Dio In A More Commercial Direction,' Blabbermouth.Net, September 22, 2022. https://blabbermouth.net/news/wendy-dio-says-vivian-campbell-wanted-to-take-dio-in-a-more-commercial-direction

211 Paul Elliott, 'Hammer of the Gob,' *Sounds*, August 3, 1985, pp. 46-47.

212 Paul Elliott, 'Hammer of the Gob,' *Sounds*, August 3, 1985, pp. 46-47.

213 Paul Elliott, 'Hammer of the Gob,' *Sounds*, August 3, 1985, pp. 46-47.

214 Dave Dickson, 'Little Big Man,' *Kerrang!* 119, May 1-14, 1986, pp. 34, 36 & 39.

215 Dave Dickson, 'Little Big Man,' *Kerrang!* 119, May 1-14, 1986, pp. 34, 36 & 39.

216 Rob Andrews, 'The Metal Terminators,' *Hit Parader* 280, January 1988, p. 54.

218 Andy Secher, 'Dio: the king of rock and roll,' *Hit Parader Annual*, Fall 1986, pp. 34-36.

219 Tony Reed, 'Dio Wanna Rock,' *International Musician & Recording World*, June 1986, pp. 68 & 71.

220 'Vinny Appice Says He Was 'Bummed' When Vivian Campbell Was Fired From Dio: It's "Not True" That Everybody Is Replaceable,' Blabbermouth.net, February 13, 2023. https://blabbermouth.net/news/vinny-appice-says-he-was-bummed-when-vivian-campbell-was-fired-from-dio-its-not-true-that-everybody-is-replaceable

221 Jimmy Kay and Alan Dixon, Interview with Claude Schnell on Canada's *The Metal Voice*, August 20, 2018, excerpts of which are transcribed at: https://www.hairbandheaven.rocks/single-post/2018/08/20/Ex-Dio-Claude-Schnell-Vivian-Campbell-was-basically-set-up-to-get-him-kicked-out-of-Dio

222 'Craig Goldy Says Vivian Campbell Must Have Done Something Pretty Insulting To Get Himself Fired From Dio,' Blabbermouth.Net, May 2, 2022. https://blabbermouth.net/news/craig-goldy-says-vivian-campbell-must-have-done-something-pretty-insulting-to-get-himself-fired-from-dio

223 Mick Wall, 'Little Dio Man,' *Classic Rock* 185, July 2013, pp. 50-53, 122. Quote at p. 53.

224 Ian Winwood, '"He was for the downtrodden": remembering Ronnie James Dio, the most decent man in rock,' *The Telegraph*, September 30, 2022.

225 'Wendy Dio Says Vivian Campbell Wanted To Take Dio In A More Commercial Direction,' Blabbermouth.Net, September 22, 2022. https://blabbermouth.net/news/wendy-dio-says-vivian-campbell-wanted-to-take-dio-in-a-more-commercial-direction

226 'Why Wasn't Vivian Campbell Interviewed For Ronnie James Dio Documentary? Co-Director Explains,' October 1, 2022. https://blabbermouth.net/news/why-wasnt-vivian-campbell-interviewed-for-ronnie-james-dio-documentary-co-director-explains

227 Jimmy Kay and Alan Dixon, Interview with Claude Schnell on Canada's *The Metal Voice*, August 20, 2018, excerpts of which are transcribed at: https://www.hairbandheaven.rocks/single-post/2018/08/20/Ex-Dio-Claude-Schnell-Vivian-Campbell-was-basically-set-up-to-get-him-kicked-out-of-Dio

228  Jimmy Kay and Alan Dixon, Interview with Claude Schnell on Canada's *The Metal Voice*, August 20, 2018, excerpts of which are transcribed at: https://www.hairbandheaven.rocks/single-post/2018/08/20/Ex-Dio-Claude-Schnell-Vivian-Campbell-was-basically-set-up-to-get-him-kicked-out-of-Dio

229  All these events were subject to legal claims, some of which were judged in favour of the Osbournes and others in favour of artists involved. There isn't space or need here to discuss these issues in depth and it's suffice to say that such a management approach is both canny and ruthless, legally defensible for the most part, but morally dubious at best.

230  Mick Wall, 'Little Dio Man,' *Classic Rock* 185, July 2013, pp. 50-53, 122.

231  Christina O'Neill, 'Vivian Campbell: Dio needed proper manager, not wife Wendy,' Classic Rock,  November 11, 2016. https://www.loudersound.com/news/vivian-campbell-dio-needed-proper-manager-not-wife-wendy

232  'Craig Goldy Says Vivian Campbell Must Have Done Something Pretty Insulting To Get Himself Fired From Dio,' Blabbermouth.Net, May 2, 2022. https://blabbermouth.net/news/craig-goldy-says-vivian-campbell-must-have-done-something-pretty-insulting-to-get-himself-fired-from-dio

233  Dante Bonutto, 'Sacred Secrets,' Part 2, *Kerrang!* 101, Aug 22-Sept 4, 1985, pp. 30 & 33.

234  Paul Gallotta, 'A new Dio, but it's the same old fireworks,' *Circus* 319, September 30, 1986, pp. 38-40.

235  Steffan Chirazi, 'Dio: No Sleep Till Donington!,' *Kerrang!* 152, August 6-19, 1987, pp. 30-32.

236  Don Mueller, 'Dio: The Metal Magician,' *Hit Parader* 276, September 1987, p. 56.

237  Rob Andrews, 'The Metal Terminators,' *Hit P*arader 280, January 1988, p. 54.

238  Rob Andrews, 'The Metal Terminators,' *Hit P*arader 280, January 1988, p. 54.

239  David Ling, 'Leps Get Their Man,' *RAW* 96, April 29-May 12, 1992, pp. 10-11.

240  Oliver Klemm, 'Dio: I Will Never Call You Craig!,' *Metal Hammer* Vol. 4, No. 16, August 21, 1989, pp. 20-23.

241  Edgar Klusener, 'Dio: Rock 'n' Roll is Just a Game,' *Metal Hammer* Vol. 4, No. 3, 1989, pp. 10-14.

242  Oliver Klemm, 'Dio: I Will Never Call You Craig!,' *Metal Hammer* Vol. 4, No. 16, August 21, 1989, pp. 20-23.

244  A summary and Campbell's quote can be found here: 'Vivian Campbell: Dio Is 'One Of The Vilest People In The Music Industry,' Blabbermouth.Net, October 29, 2003. https://blabbermouth.net/news/vivian-campbell-dio-is-one-of-the-vilest-people-in-the-music-industry

245  'Ronnie James Dio Slams Vivian Campbell as he signs autograph,' Celebrity Signing, Youtube October 2, 2007. https://youtu.be/zOwZBo8FQvo?si=S-h5Ihvz3OsSD9Vk /

246  Gary Graff, 'Vivian Campbell Moves Between Last in Line and Def Leppard Without Missing a Step,' *Guitar Player*, May 31, 2023. Available online at: https://www.guitarplayer.com/news/vivian-campbell-last-in-line-jericho

247  Vivian Campbell interview with Maurice Jay on U105 radio, Belfast, November 10, 2017. Available online at: https://www.youtube.com/watch?v=HElEb9Uviyw

248  Dante Bonutto, 'Campbell in the Soup?,' *Kerrang!* 118, April 17-30, 1986, pp. 8-9.

249  Richard Hogan and Ben Liemer, 'Mötley Tops Readers' Poll,' *Circus* 312, Feb 28, 1986, p. 31.

250  *Metal Hammer* Vol. 5, No. 5, March 20, 1989, p. 20.

251  Dante Bonutto, 'Campbell in the Soup?,' *Kerrang!* 118, April 17-30, 1986, pp. 8-9.

252  Review of 'The Dio EP.' *Kerrang!* 121, May 29-June 11, 1986, p. 35.

253  Paul Elliott, 'Hammer of the Gob,' *Sounds*, August 3, 1985, pp. 46-47.

254  Steffan Chirazi, 'Dio: No Sleep Till Donington!,' *Kerrang!* 152, August 6-19, 1987, pp. 30-32.

255  *Kerrang!* 121, May 29-June 11, 1986, p. 3.

256  Review of *Intermission. HiFI Stereo Review*, November 1986, p.126.

257  Dave Dickson, Review of *Intermission. Kerrang!* 124, July 10-23, 1986, p. 19.

258  Dave Dickson, Review of *Intermission. Kerrang!* 124, July 10-23, 1986, p. 19.

259  Dennis McDougal, 'Heavy Metal Rockers To Give Aid Too,' *Los Angeles Times*, April 11, 1985, p. 16.

260  Dante Bonutto, 'Sacred Secrets,' Part 2, *Kerrang!* 101, Aug 22-Sept 4, 1985, pp. 30 & 33.

261  Jeff Tamarkin, 'Metal Stars Form Hear 'N Aid To Stop Hunger,' *Circus* 305, July 31, 1985, p. 94.

262  Ethlie Ann Vare 'Heavy Metal Artists Join For Another Charity Single,' *Billboard* April 20, 1985, p. 6.

263  Richard Hogan, 'Beyond star fears with Ronnie James Dio,'*Circus* 310, December 31, 1985, pp. 80-83 & 85-86.

264  'Heavy Metal Artists Relieve Famine With Hear 'N Aid,' *Back Stage* Vol. 26, Iss. 39, September 27, 1985, pp. 28B-29B.

265  'Heavy Metal Artists Relieve Famine With Hear 'N Aid,' *Back Stage* Vol. 26, Iss. 39, September 27, 1985, pp. 28B-29B.

266 Paul Gallotta, Vivian Campbell's Hear 'n' Aide report,' *Circus* 310, December 31, 1985, p. 22.

267 John Horn, 'Stars Is Rock's Answer To World,' *Los Angeles Times*, May 24, 1985, p. J2.

268 'Hear 'N Aid Controversy,' *Cash Box*, April 19, 1986, p. 33.

269 'View from the Bar!,' *Kerrang!* 119, May 1-14, 1986, p. 30.

271 Drew Murray, *FMQB*, April 11, 1986, p. 36.

272 Mark Madden, 'Heavy-Metal Star Has A Soft Side, Too,' *Pittsburgh Post-Gazette*, June 13, 1986, p. 16.

274 Ethlie Ann Vare, 'Heavy Metal Releases Aid Famine Relief,' *Billboard* Vol. 98, Issue 18, May 3, 1986, p. 24; Wendy Dio's commentary in *Dio: Dreamers Never Die*. Dir. Don Argott and Demian Fenton. 9.14 Pictures, 2022.

276 'Hear 'N Aid Projects To Be Released,' *Cash Box*, April 26, 1986, p. 7.

## Chapter 3 Snakes, Dogs, and Kings

277 Nick Bowcott, 'Vivian Campbell on his own,'*Circus* 317, July 31, 1986, p. 74.

278 Dante Bonutto, 'Campbell in the Soup?,' *Kerrang!* 118, April 17-30, 1986, pp. 8-9.

279 Paul Gallotta, 'Vivian Campbell: Good Things Come In Threes,' *Circus* 327, May 31, 1987, p. 24.

280 Paul Gallotta, 'Vivian Campbell: Good Things Come In Threes,' *Circus* 327, May 31, 1987, p. 24.

281 Paul Gallotta, 'Vivian Campbell: Good Things Come In Threes,' *Circus* 327, May 31, 1987, p. 24.

282 Dave Dickson, 'Rudy Sarzo: Rhythm Machine,' *Metal Hammer* Vol. 3, No. 4, February 15, 1988, pp. 60-61.

283 *Circus*, Special Issue: The Year in Rock, December 31, 1987, pp. 38-39, 42-44.

284 Paul Gallotta, 'Vivian Campbell: Whitesnake Is A Band,' *Circus*, September 30, 1987, p. 22.

285 Vivian Campbell interview with Maurice Jay on U105 radio, Belfast, November 10, 2017. Available online at: https://www.youtube.com/watch?v=HElEb9Uviyw

286 Mark Madden, 'Whitesnake,' *Pittsburgh Post-Gazette*, July 31, 1987, weekend section p. 3.

287 Dante Bonutto, 'Snake Charmer,' *Kerrang!* 30, December 2-15, 1982, pp. 22-26, 37.

288 Malcolm Dome, 'John Sykes,' *Kerrang!* 61, February 9-22, 1984, p. 48.

289 Dante Bonutto, 'Snake Charmer,' *Kerrang!* 30, December 2-15, 1982, pp. 22-26, 37.

290 Mark Madden, 'Whitesnake,' *Pittsburgh Post-Gazette*, July 31, 1987, weekend section p. 3.

291 *Cash Box*, December 5, 1987, p. 5.

292 Ant Heeks, 'Vandenberg's Moonkings,' *Fireworks* 81, Jan-Mar 2018, pp. 24-25.

293 Andy Secher, 'Whitesnake: Overcoming Adversity[, *Hit Parader* 276, September 1987, p. 10.

294 *Circus*, Special Issue: The Year in Rock, December 31, 1987, pp. 38-39, 42-44.

295 Mark Madden, 'Whitesnake,' *Pittsburgh Post-Gazette*, July 31, 1987, weekend section p. 3.

296 Mick Wall, 'The Year Of The Snake,' *Kerrang!* 168, December 26, 1987, p. 30, 35 & 37.

297 Ant Heeks, 'Vandenberg's Moonkings,' *Fireworks* 81, Jan-Mar 2018, pp. 24-25.

298 Ant Heeks, 'Vandenberg's Moonkings,' *Fireworks* 81, Jan-Mar 2018, pp. 24-25.

299 Peter B. King, 'Whitesnake spoils music with sour note on taste,' *Pittsburgh Press*, February 4, 1988, p. B3.

300 Martin Kielty, 'How Viv Campbell made up with Coverdale,' *Louder*, December 25, 2015. https://www.louder-sound.com/news/whitesnake-viv-campbell-made-up-david-coverdale-def-leppard

301 Peter B. King, 'Whitesnake spoils music with sour note on taste,' *Pittsburgh Press*, February 4, 1988, p. B3.

302 Elianne Halbersberg, 'Sweet Taste Of Success,' *Hit Parader* 281, February 1988, pp. 34-35.

303 Moira McCormick, 'Whitesnake's veterans: happy at last,' *Circus*, June 30, 1988, pp. 40-43.

304 Mark Madden, 'Whitesnake,' *Pittsburgh Post-Gazette*, July 31, 1987, weekend section p. 3.

305 Moira McCormick, 'Whitesnake's veterans: happy at last,' *Circus*, June 30, 1988, pp. 40-43.

306 Mick Wall, 'The Year Of The Snake,' *Kerrang!* 168, December 26, 1987, p. 30, 35 & 37.

307 *Metal Hammer* Vol. 3, No. 12, June 20, 1988, p. 5.

308 Matt Peiken, 'On the record: crowd cool to Mötley Crüe,' *Union Democrat* (Sonora), Oct 16, 1987, p. 19.

309 Bruce Haring, *Billboard*, February 13, 1988, p. 22.

310 Peter B. King, 'Whitesnake spoils music with sour note on taste,' *Pittsburgh Press*, February 4, 1988, p. B3.

311 Mark Madden, 'Snakes hit Arena right between the eyes,' *Pittsburgh Post-Gazette*, February 4, 1988, p. 19.

312 Eric Snider, 'Whitesnake show lacks excitement,' *St. Petersburg Times* (Florida), February 21, 1988, p. 6B.

313  Gary Starr, *Cash Box*, April 23, 1988, pp. 6-7.

314  Craig MacInnis, 'Heavy metal forged anew and cagey old rock pro David Coverdale's still stoking the fire,' *Toronto Star*, July 12, 1988, p. H1.

315  Elianne Halbersberg, 'Sweet Taste Of Success,' *Hit Parader* 281, February 1988, pp. 34-35.

316  Elianne Halbersberg, 'Sweet Taste Of Success,' *Hit Parader* 281, February 1988, pp. 34-35.

317  Mick Wall, 'The Year Of The Snake,' *Kerrang!* 168, December 26, 1987, p. 30, 35 & 37.

318  John Baker, 'Never Surrender,' *Hit Parader* 283, April 1988, pp. 40-41.

319  Dave Dickson, 'Rudy Sarzo: Rhythm Machine,' *Metal Hammer* Vol. 3, No. 4, February 15, 1988, pp. 60-61.

320  Moira McCormick, 'Whitesnake's veterans: happy at last,' *Circus*, June 30, 1988, pp. 40-43.

321  Ant Heeks, 'Vandenberg's Moonkings,' *Fireworks* 81, Jan-Mar 2018, pp. 24-25.

322  Mick Wall, 'The Year Of The Snake,' *Kerrang!* 168, December 26, 1987, p. 30, 35 & 37.

323  Mick Wall, 'The Year Of The Snake,' *Kerrang!* 168, December 26, 1987, p. 30, 35 & 37.

324  Dan Hedges, 'At Road's End,' *Hit Parader* 290, November 1988, p. 42.

325  Vivian Campbell interview with Maurice Jay on U105 radio, Belfast, November 10, 2017. Available online at: https://www.youtube.com/watch?v=HElEb9Uviyw

326  Moira McCormick, 'Whitesnake's veterans: happy at last,' *Circus*, June 30, 1988, pp. 40-43.

327  'Adrian Vandenberg on Why David Coverdale Fired Vivian Campbell After 1987 Album/Tour,' Full In Bloom Plus youtube channel, May 20, 2021. https://www.youtube.com/watch?v=oo0TJ7CynLo

328  *Herald-Journal* (Spartanberg, S Carolina) December 17, 1988, p. A2.

329  Moira McCormick, 'Whitesnake's veterans: happy at last,' *Circus*, June 30, 1988, pp. 40-43. In fact, Campbell's partner was called Julie Devoney and they had been married since February 1987. *Circus* either got it wrong or Campbell provided false details to maintain his family's privacy.

330  Dave Dickson, *Metal Hammer* Vol. 3, No. 2, January 28, 1988, p. 15.

331  Mick Burgess, 'Def Leppard guitarist Vivian Campbell talks about their Whitesnake and Black Star Riders tour,' *Newcastle Chronicle*, December 4, 2015.

https://www.chroniclelive.co.uk/whats-on/music-nightlife-news/def-leppard-guitarist-vivian-campbell-10547543

332  'Adrian Vandenberg Sets Story Straight About Vivian Campbell,' Real Music With Gary Stuckey youtube channel, September 19, 2023. https://www.youtube.com/watch?v=uzp4Nvm6ur4

333  *Metal Hammer* Vol. 5, No. 5, March 20, 1989, p. 20.

334  Gary Graff, 'Whitesnake's Coverdale seeks stability for his fame, fortune,' *Boca Raton News*, March 23, 1990. p. 18W.

335  Mick Burgess, 'Def Leppard guitarist Vivian Campbell talks about their Whitesnake and Black Star Riders tour,' *Newcastle Chronicle*, December 4, 2015.

https://www.chroniclelive.co.uk/whats-on/music-nightlife-news/def-leppard-guitarist-vivian-campbell-10547543

336  Martin Kielty, 'How Viv Campbell made up with Coverdale,' *Louder*, December 25, 2015. https://www.louder-sound.com/news/whitesnake-viv-campbell-made-up-david-coverdale-def-leppard

337  Mick Burgess, 'Def Leppard guitarist Vivian Campbell talks about their Whitesnake and Black Star Riders tour,' *Newcastle Chronicle*, December 4, 2015.

https://www.chroniclelive.co.uk/whats-on/music-nightlife-news/def-leppard-guitarist-vivian-campbell-10547543

338  Lou O' Neill Jr., 'Lou Gramm out from the Shadows,' *Circus*, January 31, 1992, p. 98.

339  Brian Brandes Brinkerhoff, Lou Gramm Universal Ampitheatre, Los Angeles, *Kerrang!* 304, August 25, 1990, p. 50.

340  Lou Gramm and Vivian Campbell, Shadow King interview. Classic Vinyl youtube channel.

https://www.youtube.com/watch?v=ULnhZgLn-Uk

341  Lou Gramm and Vivian Campbell, Shadow King interview. Classic Vinyl youtube channel.

https://www.youtube.com/watch?v=ULnhZgLn-Uk

342  Blair S. Watson, 'U.S. rock star touring his new country,' *Calgary Herald* (Alberta, Canada), July 17, 1999.

343  *On Air*, CBS/Epic, 1990.

344  Lou Gramm and Vivian Campbell, Shadow King interview. Classic Vinyl youtube channel.

https://www.youtube.com/watch?v=ULnhZgLn-Uk

345  Advertisement in *Radio & Records*, August 10, 1990, p. 57.

346  Thomas K. Arnold, 'Pop Music,' *Los Angeles Times*, September 26, 1990, p. SDF2.

347  *CMJ: New Music Report*, June 8, 1990, p. 43.

348  Craig Rosen, 'Networks and Syndication: Music Specials,' *Billboard*, June 23, 1990, p. 16.

349  Blair S. Watson, 'U.S. rock star touring his new country,' *Calgary Herald* (Alberta, Canada), July 17, 1999.

350  'Campbell On The Move,' *Metal Hammer*, Vol 6, No. 3, February 4-17, 1991, p. 8.

351  *Hard Report*, February 14, 1992, p. 57.

352  'Vivian Campbell & Marc Danzeisen interview Riverdogs 2017 California album,' Jason McNamara - JasonVideoMusicTokyo Youtube channel, Jun 23, 2017.

 https://www.youtube.com/watch?v=eQcB8dOqSlE&t=12s

353  Paul Elliott, 'Shadow Boxing,' *Kerrang!* 371, December 14, 1991, pp. 42-43.

354  Lou Gramm with Scott Pitoniak, *Juke Box Hero: My Five Decades in Rock 'N' Roll,'* Chicago: Triumph Books, 2013, p. ?

355  Paul Elliott, 'Shadow Boxing,' *Kerrang!* 371, December 14, 1991, pp. 42-43.

356  Lou Gramm and Vivian Campbell, Shadow King interview. Youtube channel *Classic Vinyl*.

https://www.youtube.com/watch?v=ULnhZgLn-Uk

357  *Hard Report*, 'Radio Comments,' December 6, 1991, p. 54.

358  *Hard Report*, 'Radio Comments,' February 14, 1992, p 65.

359  Lou Gramm and Vivian Campbell, Shadow King interview. Classic Vinyl youtube channel.

https://www.youtube.com/watch?v=ULnhZgLn-Uk

360  Kent Zimmerman, Review of 'I Want You.' *The Gavin Report*, September 20, 1991, p. 46.

361  Lou Gramm and Vivian Campbell, Shadow King interview. Classic Vinyl youtube channel.

https://www.youtube.com/watch?v=ULnhZgLn-Uk

362  Paul Elliott, *Kerrang!* 384, March 21, 1992, p. 4.

363  Review of *Shadow King. Billboard*, Vol. 103, Issue 40, October 5, 1991, p. 92.

364  Review of *Shadow King. New Sunday Times*, December 11, 1991, p. 28.

365  Paul Elliott, Rev. of *Shadow King. Kerrang!* 360, September 28, 1991, p. 17.

366  Paul Elliott, 'Shadow Boxing,' *Kerrang!* 371, December 14, 1991, pp. 42-43.

367  Lou Gramm and Vivian Campbell, Shadow King interview. Classic Vinyl youtube channel.

https://www.youtube.com/watch?v=ULnhZgLn-Uk

368  Lou O' Neill Jr., 'Lou Gramm out from the Shadows,' *Circus*, January 31, 1992, p. 98.

369  James Gaden, Review of *Shadow King. Fireworks* 82, April-June, 2018, pp. 121-122.

370  Sheila Rene, Hear And There,' *The Gavin Report*, October 4, 1991, p. 39.

371  *Hard Report*, 'Radio Comments,' February 21, 1992, p. 60.

372  Paul Elliott, Review of *Shadow King. Kerrang!* 360, September 28, 1991, p. 17.

373  Paul Elliott, 'Shadow Boxing,' *Kerrang!* 371, December 14, 1991, pp. 42-43.

374  Neil Jeffries, 'Made in the shade,' *Kerrang!* 372, December 21-28, 1991, p. 68.

375  Dave Ling, 'Foreign Fairy Tales For The Def!,' *RAW* 93, March 18-31, 1992, p. 7.

376  Lou Gramm and Vivian Campbell, Shadow King interview. Classic Vinyl youtube channel.

https://www.youtube.com/watch?v=ULnhZgLn-Uk

377  Lou Gramm and Vivian Campbell, Shadow King interview. Classic Vinyl youtube channel.

https://www.youtube.com/watch?v=ULnhZgLn-Uk

378  Display Advert. *Los Angeles Times*, February 16, 1992, p. F62.

379  Dave Ling, 'Foreign Fairy Tales For The Def!,' *RAW* 93, March 18-31, 1992, p. 7.

380  Paul Elliott, *Kerrang!* 384, March 21, 1992, p. 4.

381  John Bowden interview with Lou Gramm, 'What Lou Gramm Thinks of Current Foreigner Singer Kelly Hansen & His Mick Jones Relationship,' Rock History Music youtube channel. https://www.youtube.com/watch?v=OFxfkH-dGFvg

382  Ed Masley, 'Life and Def,' *Pittsburgh Post-Gazette*, September 3, 1993. Weekend section, p. 2.

383  Eric Walden, 'Q&A with Def Leppard's Vivian Campbell,' *Salt Lake Tribune*, September 24, 2015.

## Chapter 4 'All I ever wanted to do was play guitar in a Rock band': Def Leppard

384  Will Byers, 'Grunge committed a crime against music — it killed the guitar solo,' *The Guardian*, July 30, 2008. https://www.theguardian.com/music/musicblog/2008/jul/30/schoolofrockguitarsolos

385  'Campbell Lands Leppard Job,' *Kerrang!* 389, April 25, 1992, pp. 4-5.

386  John Mackie, 'Guitar-for-hire finds home as super-metal hero,' *Vancouver Sun* (British Columbia), September 30, 1992, p. C5.

387  Brenda Herrmann, 'InDEFinitely: The secret to staying Leps and bounds ahead,' *Chicago Tribune*, August 23, 1992, p. M12.

388  Dave Ling, 'Cat Scratch Fever!!,' *RAW* 93, March 18-31, 1992, pp. 22-26; 'Def Leppard Pumped & Ready,' *Hit Parader*, July 1992, pp. 46-49.

389  Dave Ling, 'Cat Scratch Fever!!,' *RAW* 93, March 18-31, 1992, pp. 22-26.

390  Eddie Fitzmaurice, 'Why We Hit The Rocks; Ulster-born guitarist on Whitesnake split,' *Sunday Life*, July 13, 2008, p. 18.

391  Steve Newton, 'Def Leppard's Vivian Campbell never wanted to be Joe Guitar Hero,' *Georgia Straight* (Vancouver), September 24, 1992. https://earofnewt.com/2014/04/26/def-leppards-vivian-campbell-never-wanted-to-be-joe-guitar-hero/

392  Brenda Herrmann, 'InDEFinitely: The secret to staying Leps and bounds ahead,' *Chicago Tribune*, August 23, 1992, p. M12.

393  Dennis Hunt, 'Def Leppard: Famously Faceless,' *Los Angeles Times*, May 17, 1992, p. F55.

394  Richard Paton, 'Sound Assault,' *Toledo Blade*, August 16, 1992, pp. 1-2.

395  John Mackie, 'Guitar-for-hire finds home as super-metal hero,' *Vancouver Sun* (British Columbia), September 30, 1992, p. C5.

396  'Campbell Lands Leppard Job,' *Kerrang!* 389, April 25, 1992, pp. 4-5.

397  Paul Elliott, 'Def Leppard: the making of Diamond Star Halos and the return of the electric warriors,' *Classic Rock*, July 01, 2022. https://www.loudersound.com/features/def-leppard-the-making-of-diamond-star-halos-and-the-return-of-the-electric-warriors

398  George Simpson, 'Steve Clark tragically died almost thirty years ago and now Joe Elliott has opened up on Def Leppard's "Brian Jones" and why the band didn't split,' *Daily Express*, June 19, 2020.

399  Brenda Herrmann, 'InDEFinitely: The secret to staying Leps and bounds ahead,' *Chicago Tribune*, August 23, 1992, p. M12.

400  Kiri L. Billik, 'Shadows of death, alcohol follow band,' *Victoria Advocate*, September 13, 1992, p. 1E & 12E.

401  Brenda Herrmann, 'InDEFinitely: The secret to staying Leps and bounds ahead,' *Chicago Tribune*, August 23, 1992, p. M12.

402  Jodi Summers, 'Five Alive,' *Hit Parader* 338, November 1992, pp. 30-31.

403  A press release the day before the Dublin club gig was the first official confirmation that Campbell had joined the band. Def Leppard Tour History: http://www.deflepparduk.com/2019newsapr82.html

404  Rob Andrews, 'Return of the Fab Five,' *Hit Parader* 337, October 1992, pp. 60-63.

405  James Muretich, 'Critics' disdain doesn't bother Def Leppard,' *The Record* (Kitchener-Waterloo, Ontario), October 15, 1992, p. C6.

406  John Mackie, 'Guitar-for-hire finds home as super-metal hero,' *Vancouver Sun* (British Columbia), September 30, 1992, p. C5.

407  Dennis Hunt, 'Def Leppard: Famously Faceless,' *Los Angeles Times*, May 17, 1992, p. F55.

409  J.D. Considine, 'Def Leppard: Life On The Road,' *St. Louis Post-Dispatch* (Missouri), December 13, 1992, p. 4E.

410  Ed Masley, 'Life and Def,' *Pittsburgh Post-Gazette*, September 3, 1993. Weekend section, p. 2.

411  Vivian Campbell and Friends, live at the Guitar Institute Of Technology, Hollywood, California 1991. Rock Goes To Underground youtube channel: https://www.youtube.com/watch?v=0azQ0uh90Qo&t=383s

412  Richard Paton, 'Sound Assault,' *Toledo Blade*, August 16, 1992, pp. 1-2.

413  John Street, 'Solid riffs in the round,' *The Times* July 1, 1992.

414  David Howell, Def Leppard Puts Fun Back In Show,' *Calgary Herald* (Alberta, Canada), June 30, 1993, p. E2.

415  Andy Martin, 'Big In Des Moines,' *MF* (Metal Forces) 2, February 1993, pp. 66-67.

416  See, for example, a review of the November 11 Dane County Coliseum gig in Madison, Wisconsin entitled 'Def Leppard Offering Is Slick, Predictable,' *Wisconsin State Journal* (Madison, WI), November 12, 1992; and Alison Joy's review of Def Leppard at Brown County Arena, Green Bay, Wisconsin, Tuesday, December 8, in *Kerrang!* 425, January 9, 1993, pp. 50-51.

417  Dave Reynolds, 'Sheffield Steel,' *Kerrang!* 445, May 29, 1993, pp. 54-59.

418  John Street, 'Solid riffs in the round,' *The Times* July 1, 1992.

419  *Gavin Report*, August 21, 1992, p. 4.

420  Melinda Newman, 'Def Leppard: The Spectrum, Philadelphia,' *Billboard* Vol. 104, No. 34, August 29, 1992, p. 18.

421  Louise King, 'Def Leppard Energizes Arena's Capacity Crowd,' *St. Louis Post-Dispatch* (Missouri), December 18, 1992, p. 14G.

422  Kiri L. Billik, 'Shadows of death, alcohol follow band,' *Victoria Advocate*, September 13, 1992, p. 1E & 12E.

423  Daina Darzin, 'Def Leppard: Brendan Byrne Arena Tuesday, Oct. 27,' Hollywood Reporter, October 29, 1992.

424  Scott Iwasaki, 'Tuneful passion rise from the Def after tragedy,' *Deseret News*, September 14, 1992, p. C6.

425  John McCarthy, 'Great green lasers, but I might as well have been Def,' *Lewiston Tribune*, October 2, 1992, p. 9A.

426  Dennis Huspeni, 'Def Leppard Rocks Palouse Fans,' *Moscow-Pullman Daily News*, October 1, 1992, p. 1.

427  Valerie Buck, 'Def Leppard plays old hits on new tour,' *Spokesman-Review*, October 2, 1992, p. D3.

428  Louise King, 'Def Leppard Energizes Arena's Capacity Crowd,' *St. Louis Post-Dispatch* (Missouri), December 18, 1992, p. 14G.

429  Jim Hutchinson, 'Pouncing on the fans: Def Leppard cranks up volume to mighty roar,' *The Record* (Kitchener-Waterloo, Ontario), October 22, 1992, p. C5.

430  Jim Hutchinson, 'Pouncing on the fans: Def Leppard cranks up volume to mighty roar,' *The Record* (Kitchener-Waterloo, Ontario), October 22, 1992, p. C5.

431  Michael Hochanadel, 'Def Leppard Sounds Resourceful,' *Daily Gazette* (Albany), October 29, 1992, p, D4.

432  Edna Gundersen, 'MTV's riotous awards,' *USA Today*, September 9, 1992, p. 1D.

433  'Joe Elliott's tour diary part 1,' *Kerrang!* 413 October 10, 1992, pp. 24-26.

434  John Mackie, 'Def Leppard is rock escapism at its best,' *Vancouver Sun* (British Columbia), October 5, 1992, p. C3.

435  James Muretich, 'Def Leppard brings circus,' *Calgary Herald* (Alberta, Canada), October 6, 1992, p. D1.

436  Daina Darzin, 'Def Leppard: Brendan Byrne Arena Tuesday, Oct. 27,' *Hollywood Reporter*, October 29, 1992.

437  Jason Arnopp, 'Everyday People,' *Kerrang!* 449, June 26, 1993, pp. 38-41.

438  'Def To Danzig!,' *Kerrang!* 455, August 7, 1993, p. 14.

439  Dave Reynolds, 'Don Valley Done Great!,' *Kerrang!* 447, June 12, 1993, pp. 20-21.

440  Joe Elliott's tour diary part 2, *Kerrang!* 421, December 5, 1992, pp. 38-40. See also *Kerrang!* 425 & 427.

441  'Joe Elliott's tour diary part 1,' *Kerrang!* 413 October 10, 1992, pp. 24-26.

442  Paul Elliott, 'High 'N' Dry,' *Kerrang!* 465, 1993, pp. 38-42.

443  Paul Elliott, 'High 'N' Dry Part Two,' *Kerrang!* 466, October 23, 1993, pp. 16-18.

444  Alison Joy, Review of Def Leppard, Brown County Arena, Green Bay, Wisconsin. Tuesday, December 8. *Kerrang!* 425, January 9, 1993, pp. 50-51.

445  Paul Elliott. Review Monterrey, Mexico, Saturday, September 25. *Kerrang!* 467, October 30, 1993, p. 18.

446  Paul Elliott. Review Monterrey, Mexico, Saturday, September 25. Kerrang! 467, October 30, 1993, p. 18.

447  Paul Elliott, 'High and Dry,' *Kerrang!* 465, October 16, 1993, pp. 38-42.

448  'Def Leppard Offering Is Slick, Predictable,' *Wisconsin State Journal* (Madison, WI), November 12, 1992.

449  Ed Masley, 'Life and Def,' *Pittsburgh Post-Gazette*, September 3, 1993. Weekend section, p. 2.

450  Andy Martin, 'Big In Des Moines,' *MF* (Metal Forces) 2, February 1993, pp. 66-67.

451  Brian Brandes Brinkerhoff, 'Def Leppard The Forum, Los Angeles,' *MF* (Metal Forces) 2, February 1993, p. 71.

452  Richard Paton, 'Sound Assault,' *Toledo Blade*, August 16, 1992, pp. 1-2; Paul Elliott, 'High 'N' Dry,' *Kerrang!* 465, 1993, pp. 38-42.

453  Paul Elliott, 'High and Dry,' *Kerrang!* 465, October 16, 1993, pp. 38-42.

454  Paul Elliott, 'High and Dry,' *Kerrang!* 465, October 16, 1993, pp. 38-42.

455  Alison Joy, 'We're the least offensive band around!' *Kerrang!* 427, January 23, 1993, pp. 38-41.

456  Melinda Newman, 'Leapin' Leppards! Chart Giants Skip Usual Recording Gap For Retro Active Collection,' *Billboard* Vol. 105, Iss. 45, November 6, 1993, p. 18.

457  Troy J. Agusto, Rev. of 'Two Steps Behind.' *Cash Box*, August 21, 1993, p. 11.

458 Paul Elliott. Review Monterrey, Mexico, Saturday, September 25. *Kerrang!* 467, October 30, 1993, p. 18.

459 Steve Beebee, 'Last Action Hero,' *Kerrang!* 476, January 8, 1994, pp. 24-27.

460 Dale McGarrigle, 'Def Leppard to Adrenalize Portland,' *Bangor Daily News*, March 31, 1993, pp. 17-18.

461 'Talking 'Bout Resolutions: Joe Elliott,' *Kerrang!* 475, January 1, 1994, p. 20.

462 Steve Beebee, 'Last Action Hero,' *Kerrang!* 476, January 8, 1994, pp. 24-27.

463 Paul Rees, 'Let's Get Rocked!,' *Kerrang!* 489, April 9, 1994 pp. 14-15.

464 Paul Rees, 'Let's Get Rocked!,' *Kerrang!* 489, April 9, 1994 pp. 14-15.

465 Steve Beebee, 'Last Action Hero,' *Kerrang!* 476, January 8, 1994, pp. 24-27.

466 Joe Jackson, 'Def But Not Dumb,' *Irish Times*, October 27, 1995, p. 12.

467 Dale Martin, 'Metal's Def Leppard finds a new sound on Slang CD,' *Victoria Advocate* (Texas), June 2, 1996, p. 3D.

468 Jon Matsumoto, 'Happy To Be Faces In The Crowd,' *Los Angeles Times*, August 28, 1996, p. OCF2.

469 Dean Golemis, 'Def Leppard lingers in the sounds of its past,' *Chicago Tribune*, July 7, 1996, p. SW A7; David Quantick, Review of *Slang. Q*, June, 1996.

470 Paul Elliott, 'Lep The Good Times Roll,' *Kerrang!* 596, May 11, 1996, p. 42.

471 Amy Kelly, 'Vivian Campbell: Def Leppard Guitarist Calls Songwriting "A Painful Process",' Ultimate-guitar.com, 2009. https://www.ultimate-guitar.com/news/interviews/vivian_campbell_def_leppard_guitarist_calls_song-writing_a_painful_process.html

472 Kira L. Billik, Associated Press International, June 8, 1996.

473 Rashmi Vaish, '15 going on 16,' *Times of India*, November 29, 1998, p. A3.

474 Tom Harrison, 'Def jam,' *Vancouver Province* (British Columbia), January 11, 2000, p. B1.

475 Alan Sculley, 'Tuesday's concert kicks off comeback,' *Bismarck Tribune* (North Dakota), January 3, 2000; Dean Goodman, 'Def Leppard still on the prowl,' *The Record* (Kitchener-Waterloo, Ontario), June 14, 1999, p. A11.

476 Arlene Watson, 'Def Leppard concert sold out at Multiplex,' *Prince George Citizen* (British Columbia), January 7, 2000, Communitz section, p. 13.

477 Gerald Martinez, Rev. of *Euphoria. New Straits Times*, July 18, 1999, p. 30.

478 Dean Goodman, 'Def Leppard still on the prowl,' *The Record* (Kitchener-Waterloo, Ontario), June 14, 1999, p. A11.

479 Tim Tresslar, 'Recordings On Review: Def Leppard,' *Dayton Daily News* (Ohio), June 25, 1999, Go! section.

480 Brian Logan, 'Pop Rockers of ages Def Leppard Wembley Arena,' *Guardian*, October 16, 1999, p. 19; Tim Tresslar, 'Recordings On Review: Def Leppard,' *Dayton Daily News* (Ohio), June 25, 1999, Go! section.

481 Philip Maramba, 'Rock of ages: Guitarist talks Britney, kids & at 40, rockin' till they drop,' *Charleston Daily Mail* (West Virginia), July 24, 2003, Section: Life, p. P1D.

482 Sandy MacDonald, 'Def Leppard tries different chord with X: Superstar rockers still going strong after 25 years,' *Halifax Daily News* (Nova Scotia), August 4, 2002, p. 23.

483 Sandy MacDonald, 'Def Leppard tries different chord with X: Superstar rockers still going strong after 25 years,' *Halifax Daily News* (Nova Scotia), August 4, 2002, p. 23.

484 Carol Simmons, 'Def Leppard ready to 'Rock Rock,' *Cox News Service: Entertainment, Television and Culture*, March 21, 2003.

485 Michael Paoletta, Rev. of *X. Billboard*, August 17, 2002, p. 22.

486 Neil McKay, 'Enormously good fun,' *Belfast Telegraph*, February 14, 2003.

487 Michael Paoletta, Rev. of *X. Billboard*, August 17, 2002, p. 22.

488 John McGurk, 'Music Life: Now's the time,' *Sunday Life*, August 11, 2002; Alan Sculley, 'Collaborations on *X* breathes new life into Def Leppard,' *Boca Raton News*, April 25, 2003, pp. 8e & 10e.

489 Adrian Roberts, 'Living with their cliche,' *Morning Star*, November 08, 2003, p. 11.

490 John McGurk, 'Music Life: Now's the time,' *Sunday Life*, August 11, 2002.

491 Associated Press. 'Def Leppard's stuck in the '80s, and that's not good,' *Wilmington Morning Star*, August 2, 2002, p. 11.

492 John McGurk, 'Music Life: Now's the time,' *Sunday Life*, August 11, 2002.

493 Michael Paoletta, Rev. of *X. Billboard*, August 17, 2002, p. 22.

494 Associated Press. 'Def Leppard's stuck in the '80s, and that's not good,' *Wilmington Morning Star*, August 2, 2002, p. 11.

495  Melissa Ruggieri, 'Still Much More Than Hair,' *Richmond Times Dispatch* (Virginia), July 31, 2003, Section: WEEKEND, p. D11; Adrian Roberts, 'Living with their cliche,' *Morning Star*, November 08, 2003, p. 11.

496  Carlton Fletcher, 'Rockers Def Leppard battle dreaded nostalgia act tag,' *Albany Herald*, May 2, 2003, pp. 1B & 3B.

497  Carlton Fletcher, 'Rockers Def Leppard battle dreaded nostalgia act tag,' *Albany Herald*, May 2, 2003, pp. 1B & 3B.

498  Carlton Fletcher, 'Rockers Def Leppard battle dreaded nostalgia act tag,' *Albany Herald*, May 2, 2003, pp. 1B & 3B.

499  'Def Leppard,' *Hollywood Reporter*, December 13, 2002.

500  Lynn Saxberg, 'Rock Steady; After 30 years, fist-pumping rockers Def Leppard still work hard to create a monster buzz,' *Ottawa Citizen*, April 10, 2008, p. E1.

501  Amy Kelly, 'Vivian Campbell: Def Leppard Guitarist Calls Songwriting "A Painful Process",' Ultimate-guitar.com, 2009. https://www.ultimate-guitar.com/news/interviews/vivian_campbell_def_leppard_guitarist_calls_song-writing_a_painful_process.html

502  Lynn Saxberg, 'Rock Steady; After 30 years, fist-pumping rockers Def Leppard still work hard to create a monster buzz,' *Ottawa Citizen*, April 10, 2008, p. E1.

503  Thomas Ki, Rev. of *Songs From the Sparkle Lounge. Lodi News-Sentinel* (California), May 17, 2008, p. 24.

504  Nathalie Baret, 'Def Leppard still packing the stadiums,' *Albuquerque Journal*, August 28, 2009; Wayne Parry, 'Def Leppard CD Sparkles,' *Albany Herald*, May 9, 2008, p. 10B.

505  'Def No More Full Albums,' *The Mirror* (Eire), June 9, 2011, p. 25.

506  'Def Leppard will play its multiplatinum 1987 album Hysteria in its entirety for Viva Hysteria!,' *USA Today*. https://eu.usatoday.com/story/life/music/2012/11/12/def-leppard-hysteria-las-vegas/1696779/

507  Martin Kielty, Vivian Campbell Says It's 'Important' to Make New Def Leppard Album,' *Ultimate Classic Rock*, May 7, 2018. https://ultimateclassicrock.com/def-leppard-2019-album/?utm_source=tsmclip&utm_medium=referral

508  'Def Leppard plan new album and UK tour,' *Bang Music*, June 10, 2014.

509  John Carucci, 'Rocking on; Def Leppard isn't foolin' around when it comes to rock,' *Leader-Post* (Regina, Saskatchewan), April 23, 2015, Section: Arts &; Life, p. B1.

510  'Def Leppard come to Vancouver with "best album we've made in 23 years" in their arsenal,' *Postmedia Breaking News*, April 14, 2015.

511  'Interview – Vivian Campbell Of Last In Line & Def Leppard,' Cryptic Rock, April 21, 2016. https://crypti-crock.com/interview-vivian-campbell-of-last-in-line-def-leppard/

512  Maurice Krais, 'Cancer robbed me of long hair but gave me a fresh focus, says rocker Vivian,' *Belfast Tele-graph*, April 28, 2014, p. 19.

514  John McGurk, 'Never mind the cancer b******s' I'm with a great girl and I want to marry her,' *Sunday Life*, March 9, 2014, pp. 24-25.

515  Adrian Gomez, 'Rock of Ages: Def Leppard is making new music, and playing '80s favorites,' *Albuquerque Journal*, September 25, 2015; 'Def Leppard's Joe Elliott Explains Decision To Make New Album Self-Titled Affair,' Blabbermouth, August 27, 2015.

516  John Anson, 'Def Leppard back on road and bang on form,' *Lancashire Telegraph*, December 9, 2015.

517  Mick Burgess, 'Def Leppard guitarist Vivian Campbell talks about their Whitesnake and Black Star Riders tour,' chroniclelive.co.uk (Newcastle), December 4, 2015.

519  Rev. of *Def Leppard. Total Guitar*, October 23, 2015.

520  Elysa Gardner, 'Def Leppard doesn't get old, just more defiantly Def,' *Chicago Sun-Times*, October 30, 2015.

521  'Def Leppard back with rocking self-titled studio album,' *Digital Journal*, December 25, 2015.

522  Richard Bienstock, 'Def Leppard's Joe Elliott on New Music and Not Being a Critical Favorite,' Billboard, November 2, 2015. https://www.billboard.com/music/features/def-leppards-joe-elliott-interview-new-album-6746329/

523  Dave Donnelly, 'talks to Joe Elliott,' *The Sun* (England), December 4, 2015, Section: Something For The Weekend; Features, pp. 4-5.

524  Rick Koster, 'Not Changing Their Spots: Def Leppard Continues To Rock As They Always Have,' *The Day* (Connecticut), May 15, 2016.

525  'Interview – Vivian Campbell Of Last In Line & Def Leppard,' *Cryptic Rock*, April 21, 2016. https://crypti-crock.com/interview-vivian-campbell-of-last-in-line-def-leppard/

526  'Def Leppard's Joe Elliott Explains Decision To Make New Album Self-Titled Affair,' Blabbermouth, August 27, 2015. https://blabbermouth.net/news/def-leppards-joe-elliott-explains-decision-to-make-new-album-self-titled-affair

527  Dave Donnelly, 'talks to Joe Elliott,' *The Sun* (England), December 4, 2015, Section: Something For The Weekend; Features, pp. 4-5.

528  Gary Graff, 'Def Leppard Members Talk Health Issues & Treatment Ahead of Upcoming Tour,' Billboard, February 17, 2016. https://www.billboard.com/music/music-news/def-leppard-spring-tour-2016-interview-6882038/

529  'Def Leppard's Rock Of Ages Reigns Supreme With The First Of Four Planned Career-Spanning Box Sets,' PR Newswire, March 26, 2018.

530  Joe Lynch, 'Def Leppard Shares Video for Cover of Depeche Mode's Personal Jesus,' billboard, November 27, 2018. https://www.billboard.com/music/rock/def-leppard-depeche-mode-personal-jesus-8486782/#!

531  Matt Olson, 'Cue the hysteria; 40 years on, Def Leppard still brings the bombast and big music to every performance,' *Leader-Post* (Regina, Saskatchewan), July 20, 2019, Section: 'YOU,' p. B2.

532  Melissa Ruggieri, 'Def Leppard recruits Alison Krauss for upcoming 12th album,' *Columbus Dispatch*, March 24, 2022.

533  Melissa Ruggieri, 'Def Leppard recruits Alison Krauss for upcoming 12th album,' *Columbus Dispatch*, March 24, 2022.

534  Lauryn Schaffner, 'Why Vivian Campbell Didn't Write Any Songs on New Def Leppard Album,' *Loudwire*, May 26, 2022. https://loudwire.com/why-vivian-campbell-didnt-write-songs-new-def-leppard-album/

535  Dave Gil de Rubio, 'Def Leppard finds freedom to get riffing,' *Atlanta Journal-Constitution*, June 15, 2022.

536  Paul Jeeves, 'From heavy metal to heavy parenting duties: Def Leppard singer Joe Elliott on the great rock revival, meeting the Queen… and the upside of home-schooling,' *Daily Express*, June 2, 2022.

537  Joe Bosso, 'Phil Collen & Vivian Campbell break down their new album,' *Guitar World*, June 14, 2022.

538  Mark McStea, 'Def Leppard,' *Guitar Player*, May 31, 2022.

539  Neil Jeffries, Review of *Diamond Star Halos. Classic Rock*, April 29, 2022; Joe Bosso, 'Phil Collen & Vivian Campbell break down their new album,' *Guitar World*, June 14, 2022.

540  Joe Bosso, 'Phil Collen & Vivian Campbell break down their new album,' *Guitar World*, June 14, 2022; John Meagher, Joe Elliott: "We'll Never Make A Record The Old Way Again",' *Irish Independent*, May 21, 2022, pp. 14-15.

541  Dave Gil de Rubio, 'Def Leppard finds freedom to get riffing,' *Atlanta Journal-Constitution*, June 15, 2022.

542  Review of *Diamond Star Halos. Guitarist*, April 1, 2022.

543  Jenna Scaramanga, 'Guitarists Phil Collen and Vivian Campbell on the art of the stadium rock banger,' *Total Guitar*, May 6, 2022.

## Chapter 5 Clock, Two Sides Of If, Thin Lizzy, and Last In Line

544  *LIFE: Def Leppard*, New York: Dotdash Meredith Publishing, 2022, p. 74.

545  'Def Leppard Stars Give Drummer's Wife A Boost,' WENN Entertainment News Wire Service, January 6, 2009.

546  Mitch Lafon, 'Vivian Campbell - Two-Sided,' BraveWords, December 8, 2005. https://bravewords.com/features/vivian-campbell-two-sided

547  Clock's *Through Time* album features the following tracks: 'Just Like You,' 'Underdog,' 'Fine Mess,' 'To Be Alive,' 'No Matter,' 'Infamy,' 'Don't Waste My Time,' 'Lifeless,' 'What's Wrong With You,' 'Forget,' and 'Tough Luck.'

548  Mitch Lafon, 'Vivian Campbell - Two-Sided,' BraveWords, December 8, 2005. https://bravewords.com/features/vivian-campbell-two-sided

549  Jerry Ewing, 'The Adrenaline Flows,' *Metal Forces* 70, March 1992, pp. 16-19; Alison Joy, 'Talkin' 'bout Revolutions,' *Kerrang!* 441, May 1, 1993, p. 62.

550  Eric Walden, 'Q&A with Def Leppard's Vivian Campbell,' *Salt Lake Tribune*, September 24, 2015.

551  John McGurk, 'Axe man plays his cards; Ulster rocker includes TWO Rory Gallagher covers in solo album,' *Sunday Life*, October 30, 2005.

552  William G. Moseley, 'Blues Beyond Belfast,' *Guitar Player*, January 2006. https://www.vintageguitar.com/2999/vivian-campbell/

553  Amy Kelly, 'Vivian Campbell: Def Leppard Guitarist Calls Songwriting "A Painful Process",' Ultimate-guitar.com, 2009. https://www.ultimate-guitar.com/news/interviews/vivian_campbell_def_leppard_guitarist_calls_songwriting_a_painful_process.html

554  Mitch Lafon, 'Vivian Campbell - Two-Sided,' BraveWords, December 8, 2005. https://bravewords.com/features/vivian-campbell-two-sided

555  Amy Kelly, 'Vivian Campbell: Def Leppard Guitarist Calls Songwriting "A Painful Process",' Ultimate-guitar.com, 2009. https://www.ultimate-guitar.com/news/interviews/vivian_campbell_def_leppard_guitarist_calls_songwriting_a_painful_process.html

556  Harry Shapiro, 'How Gary Moore reignited the British blues scene with the help of a famous guitar,' *Classic Rock*, August 12, 2014. https://www.loudersound.com/features/gary-moore-the-story-of-still-got-the-blues

557  Mitch Lafon, 'Vivian Campbell - Two-Sided,' BraveWords, December 8, 2005. https://bravewords.com/features/vivian-campbell-two-sided

558  'Vivian Campbell - Willin' For Satisfaction - 2005-09-28 - album release show at the Mint in LA.' Bigdigs26 youtube channel. https://www.youtube.com/watch?v=KUx1ipoLO7U&t=7s

559  The band consisted of Campbell on vocals and lead guitar, Kara Grainger on rhythm and lead guitar, backing vocals, Michael Fell on harmonica, Lou Castro on bass and vocals, and Glen Sobel from Alice Cooper's band on drums.

560  Neil McKay, CD Reviews. *Sunday Life*, November 20, 2005.

561  William G. Moseley, 'Blues Beyond Belfast,' *Guitar Player*, January 2006. https://www.vintageguitar.com/2999/vivian-campbell/

562  Mick Burgess, 'Black Star Riders tour; Def Leppard have equal billing with Whitesnake and Black Star Riders at the Metro Radio Arena on December 9,' *Newcastle Chronicle* (chroniclelive.co.uk), December 4, 2015.

563  Lisa Sharken, 'Thin Lizzy's Scott Gorham and Vivian Campbell Live and Still Dangerous!,' *Vintage Guitar*, July, 2011. https://www.vintageguitar.com/10865/thin-lizzys-scott-gorham-and-vivian-campbell/

564  Lisa Sharken, 'Thin Lizzy's Scott Gorham and Vivian Campbell Live and Still Dangerous!,' *Vintage Guitar*, July, 2011. https://www.vintageguitar.com/10865/thin-lizzys-scott-gorham-and-vivian-campbell/

565  Rob Laing, 'Vivian Campbell on Gary Moore,' *Music Radar*, April 6, 2022. https://www.musicradar.com/news/gary-moore-vivian-campbell-thin-lizzy

566  Lisa Sharken, 'Thin Lizzy's Scott Gorham and Vivian Campbell Live and Still Dangerous!,' *Vintage Guitar*, July, 2011. https://www.vintageguitar.com/10865/thin-lizzys-scott-gorham-and-vivian-campbell/

567  Simon Rushworth, 'Lynott's legacy lives as Thin Lizzy hits the road again,' *The Journal* (Newcastle), January 5, 2011, Section A, p. 38..

568  David Sinclair, 'It's difficult to live up to triumphs of the 1970s,' *The Times* (London), Section T2; Features; p. 17.

569  Fiona Shepherd, *The Scotsman*, January 10, 2011.

570  Will Stones, 'Supergroup-of-sorts no thin Lizzies,' *Morning Star*, January 31, 2011.

571  Simon Rushworth, 'Thin Lizzy at Newcastle City Hall,' *The Journal* (Newcastle), January 11, 2011.

572  Dave Craig, 'Thin Lizzy,' *Edition 1* (Scotland), January 9, 2011, p. 5.

573  Music DVD/CD Reviews. Blogcritics.org Music, Newstex Web Blogs, September 28, 2011.

574  'Music Interview: Thin Lizzy,' *Yorkshire Evening Post*, December 23, 2010.

575  'Thin Lizzy's Vivian Campbell Pays Homage to the Late Gary Moore,' AOL Music, Newstex Web Blogs, April 6, 2011.

576  Ivan Little, 'One Moore Gig; Thin Lizzy Bandmates Pay Tribute To Guitar Ace Gary,' *The Mirror* (Ulster Edition), February 10, 2011, p. 11.

577  Ivan Little, 'Reunion was bittersweet; Homecoming For Top Guitarist,' *Sunday Life*, March 20, 2011, p. 26.

578  Mick Burgess, 'Black Star Riders tour; Def Leppard have equal billing with Whitesnake and Black Star Riders at the Metro Radio Arena on December 9,' *Newcastle Chronicle* (chroniclelive.co.uk), December 4, 2015.

579  Martin Popoff, *The Sun Goes Down: Thin Lizzy's Final Years* (Bedford: Wymer, 2012), p. 89.

580  Rob Laing, 'Vivian Campbell on Gary Moore,' *Music Radar*, April 6, 2022. https://www.musicradar.com/news/gary-moore-vivian-campbell-thin-lizzy

581  'Vinny Appice Says Last In Line And Dio Disciples Are Two Different Things,' Blabbermouth.net, January 19, 2019. https://blabbermouth.net/news/vinny-appice-says-last-in-line-and-dio-disciples-are-two-different-things

582  Vivian Campbell interview with Maurice Jay on U105 radio, Belfast, November 10, 2017. https://www.youtube.com/watch?v=HElEb9Uviyw

583  'Vivian Campbell (Last In Line) interview with Matt Mason @Bloodstock-Open-Air 2013,' Total Rock Youtube channel, August 16, 2013. https://www.youtube.com/watch?v=BXGHEZ1psYg.

584  Andrew Johnston, 'Legends of rock prove their metal at debut gig,' *Belfast Telegraph*, August 9, 2013.

585  Vivian Campbell interview with Maurice Jay on U105 radio, Belfast, November 10, 2017. https://www.youtube.com/watch?v=HElEb9Uviyw

586  John J. Moser, Def Leppard Hopes For Renewed Hysteria: Rockers hitting Arena ahead of new album's release,' *Spokesman Review* (Spokane, WA), September 25, 2015, Section C, p. 4.

587  Visage Star Steve Strange Taking Control Of New Rock Supergroup,' WENN Entertainment News Wire Service, March 19, 2014.

588  Mike Bell, 'Cancer shifts Def Leppard guitarist's outlook,' *Calgary Herald*, April 21, 2015.

589  Eric Walden, 'Q&A with Def Leppard's Vivian Campbell,' *Salt Lake Tribune* (Utah), September 24, 2015.

590  llboard, February 18, 2016. https://www.billboard.com/music/music-news/vivian-campbell-last-in-line-debut-album-jimmy-bain-6882409/

591  'Claude Schnell Says His 2015 Dismissal From Last In Line Was A Little Too Spinal Tap-Like For His Taste,' Blabbermouth.net, May 20, 2020. https://blabbermouth.net/news/claude-schnell-says-his-2015-dismissal-from-last-in-line-was-a-little-too-spinal-tap-like-for-his-taste

592  'Heavy Crown (Band Album Commentary),' Last In Line Youtube Channel. https://www.youtube.com/watch?v=ZYyX5i5c10g&t=10s

593  'Andrew Freeman - Last In Line - Jericho - MTTV Episode 68,' Metal Talk Youtube Channel, March 27, 2023. https://www.youtube.com/watch?v=ftHO7tuimsA

594  Mónica Castedo-López, 'Last In Line,' *Fireworks* 74 (Spring), April-June, 2016, pp. 4-6.

595  Mónica Castedo-López, 'Last In Line,' *Fireworks* 74 (Spring), April-June, 2016, pp. 4-6.

596  Steve Swift, Rev. of Heavy Crown. *Fireworks* 74, Apr-June, 2016, p. 88.

597  'Review: Dio bandmates line up to carry on singer's legacy,' *Columbia Chronicle*, Columbia College, Chicago IL., Feb 23, 2016.

598  Rob Laing, Rev. of *Heavy Crown*. *Total Guitar*, February 12, 2016.

599  Simon Rushworth, 'Inglorious lay down the gauntlet to headliners Last In Line with a strident set which sets the tone for a memorable Newcastle gig,' *Newcastle Chronicle* (chroniclelive.co.uk), December 2, 2016.

600  Edward Roberts, 'Former Rainbow and Dio bassist Jimmy Bain dies aged 68; The musician's sad passing was confirmed by Def Leppard guitarist Vivian Campbell on Facebook,' *Daily Mirror* (mirror.co.uk), January 25, 2016.

602  Gary Graff, 'Vivian Campbell Ponders Future of Last In Line After Bassist Dies Before Debut Album Drops,' billboard, February 18, 2016. https://www.billboard.com/music/music-news/vivian-campbell-last-in-line-debut-al-bum-jimmy-bain-6882409/

603  Keith Caulfield, 'Billboard 200 Chart Moves,' billboard.com, March 4, 2016.

604  David Roy, Untitled interview with Vivian Campbell, *Irish News*, September 29, 2017, Section: A3F4.

605  News item. *Classic Rock*, January 8, 2019.

606  Last In Line *II* Album Insight & Band Commentary. Last In Line Youtube Channel, February 21, 2019. https://www.youtube.com/watch?v=S69w0mWTQJs

607  Last In Line *II* Album Insight & Band Commentary. Last In Line Youtube Channel, February 21, 2019. https://www.youtube.com/watch?v=S69w0mWTQJs

608  Fraser Lewry, 'Last In Line: the band's track-by-track guide to new album *II*,' *Classic Rock*, February 22, 2019. https://www.loudersound.com/features/last-in-line-the-bands-track-by-track-guide-to-new-album-ii

609  Last In Line *II* Album Insight & Band Commentary. Last In Line Youtube Channel, February 21, 2019. https://www.youtube.com/watch?v=S69w0mWTQJs

610  Ian Johnson, 'Last In Line II,' *Fireworks* 86, April-June 2019, p. 89.

611  Fraser Lewry, 'Last In Line: the band's track-by-track guide to new album *II*,' *Classic Rock*, February 22, 2019. https://www.loudersound.com/features/last-in-line-the-bands-track-by-track-guide-to-new-album-ii

612  Fraser Lewry, 'Last In Line: the band's track-by-track guide to new album *II*,' *Classic Rock*, February 22, 2019. https://www.loudersound.com/features/last-in-line-the-bands-track-by-track-guide-to-new-album-ii

613  Fraser Lewry, 'Last In Line: the band's track-by-track guide to new album *II*,' *Classic Rock*, February 22, 2019. https://www.loudersound.com/features/last-in-line-the-bands-track-by-track-guide-to-new-album-ii

614  Fraser Lewry, 'Last In Line: the band's track-by-track guide to new album *II*,' *Classic Rock*, February 22, 2019. https://www.loudersound.com/features/last-in-line-the-bands-track-by-track-guide-to-new-album-ii

615  Jake Doetkott, 'Album Review: Last in Line II,' College Media Network, University Wire, July 23, 2019, Section: Music, p. 1.

616  Fraser Lewry, 'Last In Line: the band's track-by-track guide to new album *II*,' *Classic Rock*, February 22, 2019. https://www.loudersound.com/features/last-in-line-the-bands-track-by-track-guide-to-new-album-ii

617  Ian Johnson, 'Last In Line II,' *Fireworks* 86, April-June 2019, p. 89.

618  Fraser Lewry, 'Last In Line: the band's track-by-track guide to new album *II*,' *Classic Rock*, February 22, 2019. https://www.loudersound.com/features/last-in-line-the-bands-track-by-track-guide-to-new-album-ii

619  Fraser Lewry, 'Last In Line: the band's track-by-track guide to new album *II*,' *Classic Rock*, February 22, 2019. https://www.loudersound.com/features/last-in-line-the-bands-track-by-track-guide-to-new-album-ii

620  Malcolm Dome, 'Last In line II: Ex Dio-ites find their own style,' *Classic Rock*, March 5, 2019.

# Notes

621  Ian Johnson, 'Last In Line II,' *Fireworks* 86, April-June 2019, p. 89.

622  Paul Davies, Rev. of Last In Line *II*, *Daily Express* (Express Online), February 26, 2019.

623  Jake Doetkott, 'Album Review: Last in Line II,' College Media Network, University Wire, July 23, 2019, Section: Music, p. 1.

624  Rachel Gorman, 'Rock fans revel in Download mud,' *Nottingham Post*, June 17, 2019, pp. 6-7.

625  Def Leppard Tour History 2019. http://www.deflepparduk.com/2019newsnov20.html

626  Last In Line *II* Album Insight & Band Commentary. Last In Line Youtube Channel, February 21, 2019. https://www.youtube.com/watch?v=S69w0mWTQJs

627  Mónica Castedo-López, Last In Line: Interview With Vivian Campbell,' *Fireworks* 86, April-June 2019, pp.58-59.

628  'Last In Line: *Jericho*,' earMusic. https://www.ear-music.net/last-in-line/

629  Last In Line - 'Landslide - Acoustic.' Last In Line Youtube Channel. https://www.youtube.com/watch?v=dslx-T7kXXeg

630  Last In Line Feat. Vivian Campbell, Vinny Appice: Fall 2022 U.S. Tour Announced,' Blabbermouth.net, August 27, 2022. https://blabbermouth.net/news/last-in-line-feat-vivian-campbell-vinny-appice-fall-2022-u-s-tour-announced

631  'Vinny Appice On Last In Line New Album Jericho,' Sonic Perspectives Youtube channel, February 25, 2023. https://www.youtube.com/watch?v=EJbXmWOjUac

632  'Last In Line interview - Phil Soussan,' FaceCulture Youtube channel, Apr 3, 2023. https://www.youtube.com/watch?v=mWzcyzGYD_A

633  'Vivian Campbell reboots his side band – "but it's a serious side band for me" – with album number three,' *Classic Rock* 313, April 4, 2023, p. 16.

634  'Andrew Freeman - Last In Line - Jericho - MTTV Episode 68,' Metal Talk Youtube Channel, March 27, 2023. https://www.youtube.com/watch?v=ftHO7tuimsA

635  'Andrew Freeman - Last In Line - Jericho - MTTV Episode 68,' Metal Talk Youtube Channel, March 27, 2023. https://www.youtube.com/watch?v=ftHO7tuimsA

636  'Andrew Freeman - Last In Line - Jericho - MTTV Episode 68,' Metal Talk Youtube Channel, March 27, 2023. https://www.youtube.com/watch?v=ftHO7tuimsA

637  'Last In Line interview - Phil Soussan,' FaceCulture Youtube channel, Apr 3, 2023. https://www.youtube.com/watch?v=mWzcyzGYD_A

638  'Last In Line interview - Phil Soussan,' FaceCulture Youtube channel, Apr 3, 2023. https://www.youtube.com/watch?v=mWzcyzGYD_A

639  'Andrew Freeman - Last In Line - Jericho - MTTV Episode 68,' Metal Talk Youtube Channel, March 27, 2023. https://www.youtube.com/watch?v=ftHO7tuimsA

640  'Last In Line interview - Phil Soussan,' FaceCulture Youtube channel, Apr 3, 2023. https://www.youtube.com/watch?v=mWzcyzGYD_A

641  Dom Lawson, Rev. of 'A Day In The Life,' Blabbermouth.net, undated. https://blabbermouth.net/reviews/a-day-in-the-life

642  Kris Peters, 'LAST IN LINE: 'Jericho',' *Heavy* magazine, March 31, 2023. https://heavymag.com.au/last-in-line-jericho/

643  'Last In Line interview - Phil Soussan,' FaceCulture Youtube channel, Apr 3, 2023. https://www.youtube.com/watch?v=mWzcyzGYD_A

644  Richard Henry, 'Album Review : Last In Line – Jericho,' Metal Planet Music, March 23, 2023. https://metalplanetmusic.com/2023/03/album-review-last-in-line-jericho/

645  Bryan Rolli, 'Last in Line, 'Jericho' Album Review,' UCR: Ultimate Classic Rock & Culture, March 29, 2023. https://ultimateclassicrock.com/last-in-line-jericho-album-review/

646  Andy Thorley, 'REVIEW: LAST IN LINE – JERICHO (2023),' Maximum Volume Music, April 10, 2023. https://maximumvolumemusic.com/review-last-in-line-jericho-2023/

647  David Randall, 'Album review: LAST IN LINE – Jericho,' Get Ready To Rock!, April 15, 2023. https://getreadytorock.me.uk/blog/2023/04/album-review-last-in-line-jericho/

648  Kaitlin Breslin, 'Album Review: Last In Line: *Jericho*,' *MNPR Magazine* (UK), March 23, 2023. https://www.mnprmagazine.com/album-reviews/album-review-last-in-line-jericho/

649  Dom Lawson, 'Last In Line looser and grittier than before on the classy Jericho,' *Classic Rock*, April 3, 2023. https://www.loudersound.com/reviews/last-in-line-jericho-album-review

650  Bryan Rolli, 'Last in Line, 'Jericho' Album Review,' UCR: Ultimate Classic Rock & Culture, March 29, 2023. https://ultimateclassicrock.com/last-in-line-jericho-album-review/

651 readytorock.me.uk/blog/2023/04/album-review-last-in-line-jericho/

652 'Vivian Campbell reboots his side band – "but it's a serious side band for me" – with album number three,' *Classic Rock* 313, April 4, 2023, p. 16.

653 Jonathan Graham, 'Vivian Campbell Talks Def Leppard, Last in Line, Dio and More,' Guitar Interactive Youtube channel, Sep 20, 2023. https://www.youtube.com/watch?v=QjFgDgc-_2I

654 David O'Dornan, 'Def Leppard's Vivian Campbell: My new drug is not curing my lymphoma, but it's certainly not getting any worse, so I can go on and live my life,' *Belfast Telegraph*, November 29, 2019.

655 David Roy, Interview With Vivian Campbell, *Irish News*, September 29, 2017, Section: A3F4.

656 David O'Dornan, 'Def Leppard's Vivian Campbell: My new drug is not curing my lymphoma, but it's certainly not getting any worse, so I can go on and live my life,' *Belfast Telegraph*, November 29, 2019.

657 Mónica Castedo-López, Last In Line: Interview With Vivian Campbell,' *Fireworks* 86, April-June 2019, pp.58-59.

658 'Vinny Appice On Last In Line New Album Jericho,' Sonic Perspectives (Robert Cavuoto) Youtube channel, February 25, 2023. https://www.youtube.com/watch?v=EJbXmWOjUac

## Afterword

659 Anthony Morgan, 'Riverdogs – The American Dream,' *Metal Forces Magazine*, July 2017. https://www.metal-forcesmagazine.com/site/feature-riverdogs-07-17/

660 Scott Tady, What? Def Leppard's Back? We've Never Actually Gone Away,' *Beaver Country Times* (Pennsylvania), March 20, 2003, p.12.

661 'The guitar is my passion and my life's work,' *News Letter* (Belfast), September 22, 2017.